PERSUASION:

Reception and Responsibility
Third Edition

Charles U. Larson

Northern Illinois University

Wadsworth Publishing Company
Belmont, California
A Division of Wadsworth, Inc.

To Mary, Martha, and Ingrid:
You still light up my life.

Communications Editor: Kristine Clerkin
Production: Del Mar Associates
Designer: John Odam
Manuscript Editor: Lillian R. Rodberg
Photographer: Stewart W. Blakley

Printed in the United States of America
4 5 6 7 8 9 10—87 86 85

ISBN 0-534-01329-5

Library of Congress Cataloging in Publication Data

Larson, Charles U.
   Persuasion: reception and responsibility.

   Includes index.
   1. Persuasion (Psychology) 2. Listening. 3. Mass
media. I. Title.
BF637.P4L36 1983   302.2'4   82-16069
ISBN 0-534-01329-5

Contents

Preface

When the first edition of this book was being written, our country was seething with internal self-hate engendered by the tragic and hopeless war in Southeast Asia. That hatred spawned scores of talented and often unscrupulous persuaders on both sides of the issue. Thousands of young people of college age were affected by those persuaders in good ways and bad. I felt the need then, in 1972, for a book that dealt with persuasion as a process but emphasized the role of the persuadee in critically consuming persuasive messages. That approach was unique in the Speech/Communication field, as witnessed by the many adoptions of the book and by subsequent articles, books, and manuals that picked up the consumer approach. Teachers who gave advice for the second edition wanted this approach continued and even strengthened. They wanted more coverage of the effects that modern media can have on the persuasive message; they wanted more emphasis on the influence of language and style in persuasion. Some wanted a chapter dealing with the process of becoming a persuader. Those changes have been made in response to their advice. The second edition was published at a time when the public was beginning to see larger and larger areas of individual life becoming depersonalized. Persuasion was grouping masses together for the purpose of appealing to them through what the National Council of Teachers of English called "doublespeak," or intentional miscommunication and deception.

This third edition has also been designed as much as possible on the basis of the advice and requests of its consumers. Because so many teachers requested more emphasis on language and style—a second chapter on this subject has been added. Some users asked for specific emphasis on contemporary propaganda because they used the text in courses in propaganda analysis. I specifically requested that one of the three readers of the first draft of the manuscript be a teacher who used the book in such a course. The result was the addition of a chapter on contemporary propaganda techniques that was carefully constructed and revised with the insightful advice of that reader. All the reviewers stressed their desire that the book's unique approach be continued, and it has been. You, the consumer of persuasion, are still at the center of *Persuasion: Reception and*

Responsibility. In fact, if you are reading this foreword as it should be read—before beginning the book itself—you will hear this message time and again: As a persuadee, you must train yourself to be a careful, cautious processor of persuasive messages, sifting and evaluating, using the tools that this book and this course can offer you. Training yourself to detect doublespeak and the misleading pitch—whether from an advertiser; an "image" politician, an unethical religious fanatic, or any of hundreds of other persuaders who want you to follow their advice—will be to your advantage as you face a persuasion world.

Books such as this are never the product of a single person, although a single individual's name is often listed as the author. The "others" who have helped make this edition possible deserve our collective thanks. So on behalf of myself and you who will use the third edition, thanks should go to Jackson Huntley, University of Minnesota at Duluth; Norman Heap, Trenton State College; and Dennis Alexander, University of Nevada, who read and commented on the first draft of this edition. They kept me on track and wisely helped me spot parts that were overly difficult, inappropriate, or awkwardly worded. Without their help and advice, reading this book would be much more difficult than you will now find it.

People who help with the mechanical side of producing a book deserve our thanks too. Typists like Beverly Overmeyer, Julie Swatzell, and Joan Kubasiak lightened the task of getting the manuscript(s) into acceptable condition. Thanks to them for their understanding and patience with me.

Thanks to colleagues like Herb Hess, Mary Larson, Charles Tucker, and Dick Johannesen and to students who have used the book before you; much of what you will learn from this book has been taught me by them. Thanks to Lillian Rodberg, manuscript editor, for technical editing and helpful suggestion on content, and to Nancy Sjoberg, of Del Mar Associates, who handled production. Finally, no book would ever be possible without the steady guiding hand of an editor. So to Kevin Howat, who worked most closely with this edition, and to Becky Hayden, who worked with the first two editions and advised both Kevin and myself on this one, thank you for the privilege of sharing my ideas with the students of the 1980s.

Sycamore, Illinois
Charles U. Larson

1
Persuasion
in Today's World

We live in a world of persuasion. The old ways of getting people to do what we want them to are useless. Children no longer take their parents' word as law, so parents must persuade them to do well in school, to look at drug abuse realistically, to help save energy. Religious bodies can no longer control their congregations through fear and so must persuade them to give more money, to attend services, or to use or not to use birth control or abortion. Our government, without the draft to keep the armed services up to strength, must persuade young people that joining will bring them skills, education, security, and travel. Politicians, without political machines to get them elected or even nominated, must persuade slate-makers and voters that they are best qualified for a nomination or an office.

In marketing, sellers cannot count on brand loyalty or on price alone to sell a product. Instead, they have to persuade consumers of a product's quality and its ability to satisfy their needs. They may even have to persuade consumers that they *have* a particular need (success, security, sex appeal).

Persuasion has become a factor in education, too. The days of rote learning or of pounding lessons into the heads of students are gone. Teachers need to persuade students that the class material is relevant and will be useful in years to come. They may even need to persuade students that their mode of teaching is valid.

We could go on and on. Clearly, persuasion pervades our world. Clearly, too, in such a world we need training in persuasion: not only in how to persuade others but in how—and how not—to be persuaded.

Of course, you might decide you'll simply reject all the persuasion directed at you. But. . . . If you reject all persuasion by politicians, how will you know whom to vote for? If you reject all advertising, how will you compare brands or learn about new products? If you reject the persuasion of your teachers, how will you know what courses to focus on or which area to major in? Perhaps you could personally investigate the record of every politician on the ballot or personally test every detergent or motor oil or ski wax on the market. Maybe you could even take one of every kind of course and evaluate its career possibilities. But if you do, you'll have little time for anything else!

The world around us tells us that we need to be persuaded, if only to reduce our alternatives before making choices. At the same time, we need to be prepared for the many potent and perhaps mistaken—even negative—things our persuasion world can do to us. In a *U.S. News and World Report* interview, noted communications expert Neil Postman called attention to just one aspect of persuasion and its potency in shaping our values: the television commercial. According to Postman, by the time you're twenty, you're likely to have seen about a *million* commercials.[1] That averages out to a thousand a week. That figure may seem too high—and it does conflict with some other reports—but it averages out to 180 commercials a day, or twenty to twenty-five for each of the seven to eight hours the average American spends with the TV set.

Imagine what we would think if a propaganda artist in the Big Brother mode were pumping persuasion down our throats that often every week. Some would call us robots. What impressions do we get from these commercials? Here is Postman's analysis:

> This makes the TV commercial the most voluminous information source in the education of youth.... A commercial teaches a child three interesting things. The first is that all problems are resolvable. The second is that all problems are resolvable fast. And the third is that all problems are resolvable fast through the agency of some technology. It may be a drug. It may be a detergent. It may be an airplane or some piece of machinery....
>
> The essential message is that the problems that beset people—whether it is lack of self-confidence or boredom or even money problems—are entirely solvable if only we will allow ourselves to be ministered to by a technology.[2]

How often have you or I been affected by this very simple little belief or value? How often have we bought that bottle of Old Spice or Ban, or those Hanes stockings because we subconsciously believe that they will make us more attractive to the opposite sex and give us a successful love-life? Or help us land a job or impress a teacher? How many of us believe that the atmosphere will be saved by technology or that some little old scientist in Lake Wobegon, Minnesota, will invent a tablet that will convert water to gasoline, thus saving us from the energy shortage? At one time or another, every one of us has fallen for a pitch like this.

One of the purposes of this book is to make us at least aware of what is happening to us in this persuasion world. The title of this book, *Persuasion: Reception and Responsibility*, suggests the direction we will take. Our focus is on the training of *persuadees*—those on the receiving end of all the persuasion. We need to learn to be critical, to observe and judge the persuasion coming at us.

---

1. Neil Postman, Interview, *U.S News and World Report*, January 19, 1981, p. 43. (David Burmeister, who is cited in Chapter 9, reports the number is being around 350,000.)

2. *Op. cit.,* p. 43.

Doublespeak in a Persuasion World

Even in a persuasion-riddled world like ours, you would not need persuasion training if all persuaders stayed out in the open, and if all of them talked straight. Too many persuaders speak in **doublespeak.** Doublespeak is the opposite of language: it tries to *not communicate*; it tries to conceal the truth and to confuse. For instance, in doublespeak, unprovoked mass bombings could be—and were—called "anticipatory protective reaction strikes." During the Vietnam War, would that bit of U.S. government doublespeak have persuaded you that bombings were justified? The Vietnam War is over, but doublespeak goes on.

Nor is government the only offender. We always have promotion specialists trying to blind us to the defects in their products, candidates, and ideas. It has been estimated that today's average 18-year-old has seen more than 20,000 hours of television,[3] including almost 1000 commercials per week. Of course, not all commercials are doublespeak, but enough of them are so that we can scarcely ignore the problem. Moreover, doublespeak is spreading, and we are becoming more and more numbed by it. Advertisers can tell us the obvious—"V.O. is V.O."—and get results. They can ask us a confusing (and ungrammatical) question—"If You Can't Trust Prestone, Who Can You Trust?"—and expect that our confusion will bring them increased sales. They can ballyhoo a candidate for office by promising "Together a New Beginning" and can expect to influence voters. And now we are seeing more and more of a deadly kind of communication that is coercive if not persuasive—terrorism: Individuals or groups blow up pubs in Northern Ireland, sabotage airliners in France, take hostages in Iran, or lace the water supply of an Idaho town with poison.

And if, as critics from right to left are complaining, the news industry itself is just one more persuasive device to fool and manipulate us, how can we make ourselves better at detecting doublespeak? By providing ourselves with analytical tools to help us take apart the many sales pitches that confront us. Let us begin by looking at what persuasion is—how it has been defined at various times by various people.

Definitions of Persuasion: A Potpourri

In ancient Greece, persuasion was the main means of achieving power and of winning in the courts of law. The study of persuasion, or *rhetoric*, was central in the education of all Greeks. The Greek philosopher Aristotle, who was one of the first to study rhetoric in depth, called it "the faculty of observing in a given case the available means of persuasion." Persuasion, according to Aristotle, could be

---

3. David Burmeister, "The Language of Deceit" in *Language and Public Policy*, ed. by Hugh Rank (Urbana, Ill.: National Council of Teachers of English, 1974), p. 40.

based on a reputation for credibility, or *ethos*. It could use logical argument (*logos*), and emotion-stirring appeals, or *pathos*.[4]

Roman students of persuasion added specific advice on what a persuasive speech ought to include. The Roman orator Cicero identified five elements of persuasive speaking: inventing or discovering evidence and arguments, organizing them, styling them artistically, memorizing them, and finally delivering them skillfully. Another Roman theorist, Quintilian, added that a persuader had to be a "good man" as well as a good speaker.

Those early definitions clearly focus on the sources of messages and on persuaders' skill and art in building a speech. Later students of persuasion reflected the changes that have come with a mass-media world. In *Persuasion, a Means of Social Change* (1952), Winston Brembeck and William Howell, two communication professors, described persuasion as "the conscious attempt to modify thought and action by manipulating the motives of men toward predetermined ends."[5] In their definition we can see a notable shift from the use of logic toward the internal motives of the audience. By the time Brembeck and Howell wrote their second edition in the early 1970s, they had changed their definition of persuasion. Now, they called it "communication intended to influence choice."[6] In the mid-1960s, Wallace Fotheringham, another communication professor, defined persuasion as "that body of effects in receivers"[7] that had been caused by a persuader's message. Here the focus is almost entirely on the receiver, who actually determines whether persuasion has occurred. By this standard, even unintended messages such as gossip overheard on a bus could be persuasion if they caused changes in their receiver's attitude, belief, or action. Kenneth Burke, literary critic and theorist, defines persuasion as the artful use of the "resources of ambiguity."[8] Here persuasion involves avoiding the specific and creating "identification" (Burke's term) through appeals so ambiguous that no one could object to them.

In the first edition of this textbook, persuasion was defined as "a process" that changes attitudes, beliefs, opinions, or behaviors.[9] In that definition, the *process* of persuasion gets the attention. Persuasion occurs only through cooperation between source and receiver. Following Burke's lead, persuasion is defined here as *the co-creation of a state of identification or alignment between a source and a receiver that results from the use of symbols*. Once you identify with the kind of

---

4. Aristotle, *The Rhetoric*, translated by R. Robert, in *The Works of Aristotle* (Oxford: Clarendon Press, 1924), p. 1355b.

5. Winston L. Brembeck and William S. Howell, *Persuasion: A Means of Social Change* (Englewood Cliffs, New Jersey: Prentice-Hall, 1952), p. 24.

6. Brembeck and Howell (2d ed., 1976), p. 19.

7. Wallace C. Fotheringham, *Perspectives on Persuasion* (Boston: Allyn and Bacon, 1966), p. 7.

8. Kenneth Burke, *A Grammar of Motives* (Berkeley: University of California Press, 1970). Introduction.

9. Charles U. Larson, *Persuasion: Reception and Responsibility* (Belmont, Calif.: Wadsworth Publishing Co., 1973), p. 10.

world a huckster wants you to like—say Marlboro Country—persuasion has occurred. You may never smoke, but you have been changed. The world of Marlboro Country has become attractive to you. Maybe you'll buy a cowboy hat—or maybe you'll just swagger a little. Perhaps you'll venture into the "great outdoors" and get a little weathered and tan. You now want to be like the folks in Marlboro Country. Your attitudes, opinions, and behavior have been changed by symbols: "Come to Where the Flavor Is—Marlboro Country." In other words, the pictures and slogan in the Marlboro ads symbolized an image you wanted for yourself and caused your shift in alignment.

The focus of persuasion is not on the source, the message, or the receiver. It is on *all* of them equally. They all *cooperate* to make a persuasive process. The idea of **co-creation** means that what is inside the receiver is just as important as the source's intent or the content of the message. In one sense, *all persuasion is* **self-persuasion**—we are rarely persuaded unless we *participate* in the process. This is what the ancients meant when they referred to finding "common ground." I will be persuasive to the extent that you see me as having common ground— shared values, goals, interests, and experiences—with you.

The words co-created and self-persuasion are central. Persuasion is the result of the combined efforts of source and receiver. Furthermore, we agree to be persuaded from choice, not coercion. Even techniques for altering behavior like hypnosis or brainwashing require a willing receiver at some point in the process. For example, even the brainwashed kidnapee who is forced to commit crimes cooperated at some point in being persuaded. The person who is hypnotized into avoiding sweets has to relax enough to let the hypnotist work.

Since the receiver is central to persuasion, it's a good idea for each of us to study the process of persuasion from that point of view. We need to watch ourselves being persuaded, trying to see why and how it happens so that we can be more conscious of our changes. Our knowledge will allow us to be more critical and therefore more effective in rejecting persuasive messages when appropriate— and in accepting others when it seems wise to do so.

Getting Ready for a World of Persuasion

Young children are often persuaded by TV spots that promote toys—Hot Wheels racetracks, Barbie dolls, monster masks, and so forth. Suppose you want to teach a child to be more critical of those TV spots. How do you make the child a better doublespeak detector? Well, you might point out that the spot is not really designed to help children; it is made to sell something. Here, you are teaching the child to be wary of the *source's* motives, the first of which is profit. The child may now be able to say, "That's just advertising—they just want you to buy." Next, you might try asking the child what the TV people really mean by "You can have loads more fun with a Barbie Beach Bus." Now you are focusing on the *message* itself and not on the motives of the source. You would be questioning some *tactics* of persuading. Then you might try to get the child to think about why the toy is wanted. Does the child want the toy for the friends it will attract, or is it the "in"

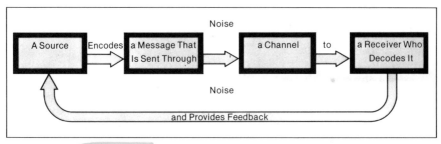

Figure 1.1. The SMCR model.

toy this year? You might warn the child that camera tricks are making the race-track look much larger than it actually is and that the sound effects heard when the toy is shown are not part of the package. The race cars won't screech and roar as they do on TV, and the Barbie Beach Bus won't have all that music with it. Now you would be teaching the child to be critical of the *channel* or *medium* that is used for the persuasive message.

Just as you might try to alert a child to the various pitches made on Saturday-morning commercials, you can also alert yourself to the kinds of pitches being made to you in the media, by your fellow students, on the job, and even by our society as a whole. A good way to begin is to look at several models of the communication/persuasion process to see if it is useful to be aware of the various parts and stages in being persuaded.

The simplest model of communication, and the one most widely referred to, is the SMCR model (Figure 1.1) suggested by Claude Shannon and Warren Weaver in 1949 and modified since that time by others such as David Berlo.[10] The model contains four essential elements:

A **Source** (S), who or which is the encoder of the message. The code may be verbal, nonverbal, visual, musical, or some other modality.

A **Message** (M), which is meant to convey the source's meaning through any of the codes.

A **Channel** (C), which carries the message and which may have distracting noise.

A **Receiver** (R), who decodes the message, trying to sift out channel noise and adding his own interpretation.

These elements are also part of the persuasive process that is the focus of our definition of persuasion. Being prepared for persuasion involves being critical of all four elements. We must be alert to the motives of the source, whether they are obvious or disguised. We must pay attention to the message—its symbols and its

10. Claude E. Shannon and Warren Weaver, *The Mathematical Theory of Communication* (Urbana: University of Illinois Press, 1949). See also David K. Berlo, *The Process of Communication* (New York: Holt, Rinehart and Winston, 1960).

meaning. It is a good idea to think about the channel or medium being used to send the message—what kinds of effects does it have? Finally, we need to be aware of our own role in persuasion—what are we adding?

One of our goals is to explore various tools that we can use to try to determine a **source's motives.** Language choice, for example, can tip us off to source intent. The ideas the source thinks will be persuasive to the audience are often expressed in the words the source chooses, the metaphors the source uses, and even the kinds of sentences in the message. Are they questions? Exclamations? Short and punchy? Long and soothing?

For example, the Schick razor company recently came out with a "cosmetic" razor called "Personal Touch." What do the words "cosmetic," "personal," and "touch" tell you about the Schick company's view of its potential customers? Are they aiming at a "macho man"? A business tycoon? A sports enthusiast? Or are they aiming at women who feel they deserve special attention and haven't been getting it lately? Analyzing the source has two benefits. First, it alerts us to the persuasion being aimed at us. Second, it tells us things about the source that can help us when the source becomes our persuadee. In a way, sources tip us off to their *own* persuasive weaknesses. If you hear a friend trying to persuade you by using statistics, for instance, you can pretty safely bet that statistics will be a big help when you are trying to persuade that person of something. Of course, we may misinterpret or read too much into a source's words. But at least, if we stay alert, we won't be dumbly led around by the nose.

Another of our goals is to explore tools that allow us to analyze the **message** and what it is intended to say. We will look at the organization of the message, its style, and the appeals that it makes. You will learn to look at the evidence contained in the message and at how it relates to the persuasive goal. You may want to look at the nonverbal as well as the verbal elements in the message to see which of these codes has what kinds of effects. Consider this example: The president of Brazil told reporters, "I intend to open this country to democracy, and anyone who is against that I will jail, I will crush!"[11] He certainly deserved the Doublespeak prize of the National Council of Teachers of English for 1980. Most messages aren't as obviously revealing; nonetheless, looking at messages analytically can help us get ready to accept or reject persuasion.

A third goal is to train ourselves to be alert to the kinds of effects that various **channels** have on persuasion. Does the impact of television, for example, make a message more or less effective? Has TV made us more vulnerable to certain message types? What are the effects of other kinds of media, such as radio and billboards? Are certain kinds of ballyhoo more useful or persuasive than others? Why do some media use certain techniques and other media use different ones?

Finally, you will need to explore ways of looking into yourself, the **receiver,** to discover why you are more or less likely to respond to some messages. For instance, I was always a sucker for games of chance at carnivals and fairs. Once I took a look at what seems to motivate me, I understood that I thought winning would be easy for someone as quick and clever as I. Later, I discovered that I had overestimated my skills. Games of chance lost their appeal.

---

11. "Welcome to the Land of Doublespeak," *Ford's Insider,* 1981. p. 5.

Identifying doublespeak depends on understanding the four elements in communication: source motives, message characteristics, channel effects, and receiver input.

Rank's Model of Persuasion

As part of the National Council of Teachers of English (NCTE) Project on Doublespeak, several persons were asked to suggest ways of teaching people to be critical receivers of persuasion. In 1976, Hugh Rank, a researcher on the project, put the challenge this way:

> These kids are growing up in a propaganda blitz unparalleled in human history. . . . Will the advertisers and political persuaders of 1980 or 1984 be less sophisticated, less informed, less funded than they are today? . . . Schools should shift their emphasis in order to train the larger segment of our population in a new kind of literacy so that more citizens can recognize the more sophisticated techniques and patterns of persuasion.[12]

Rank outlined a model of persuasion that could help teach people to be critical receivers. He called it the **intensify/downplay schema** and tried to keep it as simple as possible. It can serve as a good overall model for you.

The basic idea behind Rank's model is that persuaders usually use two major tactics to achieve their goals. They either **intensify** certain aspects of their product, candidate, or ideology, or they **downplay** certain aspects of their cause. Often they do both. Like a magician, they want to draw attention away from some things and toward others in order to pull off the illusion. Rank depicted his model and the major ways of intensifying or downplaying as shown in Figure 1.2.

According to this model, the persuader has four ways to go and six major tactics to use. Let us apply Rank's system to a simple persuasive slogan: "At Avis, We Try Harder." The original campaign stressed the idea that Avis's second-place status among car-rental companies was actually an advantage. The Avis strategy was to intensify the good points of Avis and the bad points of the competition, while downplaying its own bad points and the competition's good points. It suggests, indirectly, that the competition gives poor service. The slogan is repeated in one form or another in all Avis's TV, radio, billboard, and print advertisements (if we hear or see something enough times, it sticks).

Now, there may be disadvantages to going with a second-best company. You might get a car so continually used that it had not been properly maintained. There might be a limited choice of colors or body styles. There might be fewer places to pick up or drop off a car. How does Avis keep these disadvantages from entering the consumer's mind? It uses the tactic of diversion to draw our attention from all the bad things that could go along with "second place" and to focus it on the false issue of effort.

---

12. Hugh Rank, "Teaching about Public Persuasion" in *Teaching about Doublespeak*, ed. Daniel Dieterich (Urbana, Illinois: National Council of Teachers of English, 1976), Chapter 1. The discussion of the intensify/downplay model in this chapter is based on this study.

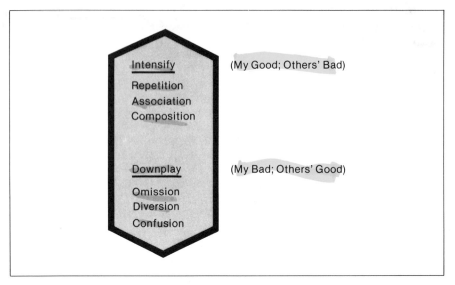

Figure 1.2. The intensify/downplay schema. (Hugh Rank, "Teaching about Public Persuasion," in *Teaching about Doublespeak*, ed. Daniel Dieterich. Copyright © 1976 by the National Council of Teachers of English. Reprinted by permission of the publisher and the author.)

Let us consider a test case. I've taken my car to a mechanic to get my engine to stop missing and to get better mileage. He is a bad mechanic, but I got involved with him for the repair work before I knew that. Now I'm stuck with him because of my initial investment. He doesn't charge me double just because I keep bringing the car back; in fact, I've only had the first charge. Although he tries harder and harder every time I return the car, he keeps making it worse and worse. So, where is the advantage in trying harder?

Another point the Avis slogan avoids is that the third-, fourth-, and fifth-place firms may also be trying harder. So even if trying harder is an advantage, Avis doesn't have a corner on it. Despite all these obvious flaws, the campaign, "At Avis, We Try Harder" has succeeded. The ad campaign is famous and the slogan has entered national slang. Why? Because we persuadees too seldom take time to explore promotional claims very carefully.

Let's look in more depth at the six major tactics Rank outlined in his model. You can try them out on various forms of persuasion you meet each day. Perhaps your class will want to do a team project analyzing an issue on campus and how advocates of one side or the other use the tactics discussed below.

Intensification

As we noted earlier, we can intensify our own good points or our competition's bad points. Candidates can talk about their stands on the issues and on their opponents' stands on the same issues. Touters of one kind of aspirin can talk about how fast it works without upsetting the stomach and thus can imply that other aspirins are slow and cause stomach upset. The evangelist claims that his way of believing is the only one. They all engage in the *strategy* of intensification.

What are the *tactics* of intensification? Basically, there are three: repetition, association, and composition.

Repetition Good or bad points about a product, a candidate, or an idea can be intensified by **repetition.** We all find ourselves humming jingles. Hit radio stations repeat the same "top forty" all day. As Joseph Goebbels, the propaganda minister of the Nazi Party, noted, if you tell a lie often enough, people will begin to believe it, no matter how big a lie it is. The repetition can be used to intensify the good in one's own cause or the bad in the opponent's position.

Association Rank cites three steps used by persuaders in creating what he called **association.**

1. A cause, product, candidate is linked

2. to something already loved or hated by

3. the audience.

Persuaders engage in careful audience analysis to identify the fears, wants, and biases of their target audience. They then mesh their goals with this set of alignments. For example, politicians, knowing that we have fears about nuclear power, tie these fears to their own cause by stating that they would put a freeze on all building of new nuclear power plants if elected. An advertiser might associate a product—say British Sterling aftershave lotion—with a certain lifestyle. The man who wears British Sterling has a tweedy look, lives in a stately old mansion, sips on a glass of Scotch, and has several gorgeous-looking women catering to his every whim. The persuadee is supposed to identify (align) with the lifestyle and rush out to buy a gallon or two of the lotion. Association can be accomplished by verbally linking two ideas or persons or by nonverbally depicting two persons, ideas, or things together, as is done in many ads. For example, Bruce Jenner, the Olympic decathlon winner, is seen eating a breakfast featuring Wheaties.

Favorable and unfavorable beliefs are also culturally embedded in various societies. For example, one of the central values in our culture is the idea of Progress. We bring out new models of cars, outboard motors, refrigerators, stoves, toys, and clothing each year knowing that they will soon be out of style or obsolete. However, we persuade ourselves that this is good because it is "progress." If critics object to a certain policy or to a certain change, we can attack their credibility by charging that they are against "progress." What we really have done is to use association. We associate built-in obsolescence with the idea of "progress." We associate objection to change with being against "progress." What might have been a legitimate—even wise—objection becomes an example of stubbornness, reactionary thinking, and keeping your head in the sand.

Composition We can intensify goodness or badness by contrasting it with something else. For example, the letters U.S.A. have a meaning. If we print the letters this way—U.$.A.—a new meaning emerges; a persuasive statement is made by the visual **composition** of the letters. To some, this intensifies a "bad-ness" (i.e., the profit motive) about our country. On the other hand a persuader trying to lure immigrants to America might have used the same composition to intensify the concept of "streets paved with gold." In the late 1960s, those who thought this country was fascistic spelled America Germanic style—AmeriKa, stressing the *K* to associate the United States with Nazism as well as the Ku Klux Klan. During the 1980s, a group of persons calling themselves the Moral Majority tried to elect certain politicians and to defeat others. The group was religiously oriented and associated right-minded voting with godliness. They wrote the word vote this way in their literature

$$-V \quad O \qquad E-$$

thereby emphasizing that voting was the "Christian" thing to do. In the field of advertising we see the use of composition even more clearly. Ban deodorant placed the word BAN inside the traditional octagonal, red-and-white configuration of a stop sign. Presumably, the idea is to warn us of "wetness" and odor while implying that Ban stops these "offenses." Composition is also used by persuaders who create comparison and contrast in the media. McLuhan called this technique the ". . . brushing of information against information."[13] One bit of information about a candidate for political office is pictured in a certain scene—say the U.S. Capitol—and then a sound-track highlights some point we want to make about the candidate. If we play the National Anthem and have a deep voice read the Gettysburg Address over the music, we create one meaning. If we play sinister-sounding music and have a voice-over saying "Senator Loghead *says* he favors the free enterprise system that made this country great. He *says* he wants to limit welfare. But what does he *do* about these things?" we will achieve another effect. Both effects use association as a tactic for intensifying their own good or another's bad.

Downplaying

Sometimes persuaders do not want to intensify or call attention to something (their own shortcomings, for example) because this would defeat their persuasive purpose. Likewise, it would not be useful to advertise the strong points of your competition. What the persuader does is to **downplay** his own bad and/or the competitor's good points. If you are selling Chrysler K-cars, and they do not have the same frame strength as the GM J-cars, it is best not to mention the frame at all. If you are running against candidate X, you will not dwell on your opponent's honesty and integrity—you will focus on your own. If you have been caught by the IRS on an income-tax audit, you probably won't mention that, either.

What are some of the *tactics* that can be used to downplay either one's own shortcomings or the strengths of one's competition? Where do we see these in the real world that we see, feel, hear, smell, taste, and touch every day? The three basic tactics of downplaying are: omission, diversion, and confusion.

---

13. Marshall McLuhan, *Understanding Media: The Extensions of Man* (New York: Signet Books, 1964).

Omission Sometimes persuaders downplay their own shortcomings or their competition's advantages by the simple **omission** of information. You can't tell the whole story in a 30- or 60-second TV spot, after all. A billboard should try to promote only a single idea and then in only a few words.

Another way to omit key information is to be silent—to avoid giving information that might harm the persuader's cause. A politician accused of under-the-table dealing might refuse to respond to the charges.

Euphemism is another way to omit information or to conceal it. This technique uses words to avoid talking about the issue directly. It is very popular in politics. Rank uses the example of the word bomb being concealed through the words nuclear device. As a consultant to the women's apparel industry, I have discovered the need for a euphemism for the word fat. There is a great deal of money to be made in selling "half-sizes" or "women's" clothes designed for over-weight persons, but you can't even politely say "overweight," or you will offend your potential customers. Some euphemisms that have been tried in the past: "big beautiful women," "queen sizes," and "beautiful and bountiful." One shop-owner took the size tags off clothing and replaced them with colored tabs. When an overweight customer came into the shop, the salesperson could simply say, "Step over there to the purples, violets, and blues, dear, and I'll be right with you."

Real estate advertisements are fertile fields for downplaying—usually by omission or euphemism. Some houses are advertised as "handyman specials," which is a euphemism for run-down or dilapidated. Others are listed as being "cozy," or "a doll house." What does that mean? Chances are, "cozy" means small and a "doll house" is miniscule. The employment ads also abound with examples. "Need 20 sharp people for part-time sales work" translates to telephone salespersons. What does "convenient student hours" mean? Late nights at the Pizza Hut? Sunday afternoons? There are even examples of euphemism in college course descriptions. Take, for example: "Individualized and open instructional format." This means there is no structure and the instructor rarely shows up.

Diversion Persuaders can downplay by **diversion** of attention from key issues or key points. For example, politicians might try to sidetrack attention from their deficiencies by pointing to sham issues. One might divert attention from the welfare program by challenging the voters to think about property-tax rates. Politicians often divert attention from their failings by pointing out those of their opponents, intensifying the badness in the diversion.

Advertisers have long diverted attention from the negative health aspects of sugar-coated breakfast cereals by loudly announcing that there is a "FREE PLAS-TIC MODEL INSIDE!" The Federal Trade Commission has tried to combat misleading ads by compelling the offenders to publish apologies. The tactic of diversion is a favorite in such "apologies." Wonder Bread advertisers softly admit that the bread doesn't "build bodies in twelve ways" as they had claimed. They then shout that its new formula guarantees week-long freshness.

Humor is sometimes used to divert attention from key issues. Franklin Roosevelt was once charged with sending a warship to pick up his dog, which had been left behind at a conference in a distant port. He countered the accusations by making sport of the Republicans, accusing them of carrying dirty politics to the point of attacking "my little dog, Fala." The humor diverted attention from whether the incident occurred at all and made those who pursued the matter seem like dog-haters.

Other tactics for diverting attention cited by Rank include setting up a "straw man" to draw fire; focusing on a false issue, or "red herring"; using emotional appeals based on the opponent's personality; and hairsplitting or nitpicking. Each tactic downplays a persuader's weak points or faults.

Confusion A final tactic for downplaying one's own weak points or the competition's strengths is to create **confusion** by introducing jargon, overdetailed information, contradictory information, and so on. An insurance salesperson recently suckered me into listening to his pitch for an evening by promising a computer analysis of my protection status that would cover estate protection, too. The pitch claimed that insurance was needed even after children were grown and independent because of estate taxes that might follow the death of both my wife and myself. Such pitches always focus on the large amount of money the beneficiaries will collect. The fact that the purchaser has to die before anyone collects is a point insurance salespeople are trained never to mention.

Consider the advertisement for a Canon A-1 camera shown in Figure 1.3. Note that the headline confuses through the use of jargon. What in blazes is "hexa-photo-cybernetic technology"? By looking more closely you see that the Canon A-1 has six supposed advantages. That explains *hexa* (as in hexagon). Then we see that it has several automatic devices to match shutter speed with lens opening, which is usually called automatic exposure. This involves some mathematical programming of the apparatus, and moreover, the settings are digitally displayed. So the word cybernetic can be honestly used. And photo relates to camera. Nevertheless, "hexa-photo-cybernetic" is pseudoscientific ad lingo intended to impress if not to confuse. The ad omits mentioning that many cameras in the same price range have very similar features, and Canon is not alone among cameras having some kind of automatic exposure sensors.

Another device for downplaying one's own weaknesses or the competition's strengths through confusion is the use of **faulty logic**. "She's Beautiful! She's Engaged! She uses Earth Balsam Hand Creme!" would be an example. The supposed logical flow is that because "she" uses the hand cream, she is beautiful, and because she is beautiful she met and won the man of her dreams and is now engaged. Not even fairly naive consumers are likely to buy this whole "package," but the idea that the hand cream will make the user more attractive to men is fairly likely to stick.

Rank cites a number of other ways to confuse, including *being inconsistent, contradicting,* and *talking in circles*—"V.O. is V.O." or "So Advanced, It's Simple."

Self-protection: A Method

In his discussion of doublespeak, Rank goes on to offer some general advice on how to detect the flaws of persuaders who use various tactics to intensify or downplay. "When they intensify, downplay," says Rank. That is, when we recog-

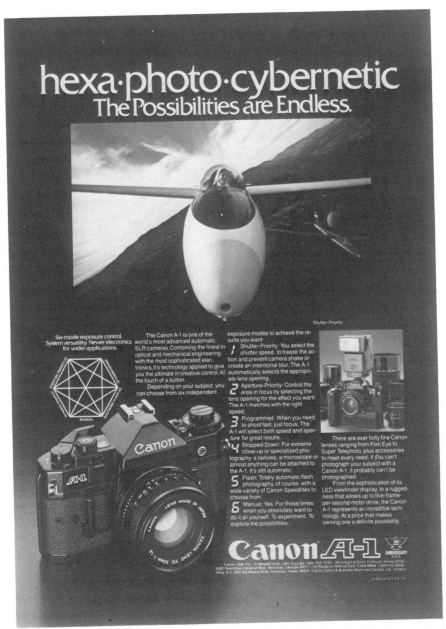

Figure 1.3. How is Rank's *confusion* used here? (Used by permission of Canon U.S.A., Inc.)

nize a propaganda blitz, we should be cool, detached, and skeptically alert not only to the inflated puffery of advertising with its dreams and promises, but also to intensified attack propaganda, the threats and exploitation of fears by a demagogue or government agent, elected or appointed. Rank also says, "When they downplay, intensify." A way to do this systematically is to divide a sheet of paper

Intensify Own Good	Intensify Others' Bad
1.	1.
2.	2.
Downplay Own Bad	Downplay Others' Good
1.	1.
2.	2.
3.	3.

Figure 1.4. Intensify/downplay scorecard. (Hugh Rank, "Teaching about Public Persuasion," in *Teaching about Doublespeak,* ed. Daniel Dieterich. Copyright © 1976 by the National Council of Teachers of English. Reprinted by permission of the publisher and the author.)

in quarters as shown in Figure 1.4, then to cite the kinds of downplaying and intensifying that are being done. Simply by seeing those, the persuadee can become more alert to the kind of manipulation that is going on.

Let's try this technique with a brief example. Consider the ad for Smirnoff vodka shown in Figure 1.5. First let's look at the intensification used in the ad. Remember that the persuader may intensify by repeating, by association, and by shifting the composition of the message.

Notice the *repetition* of the product name in the ad. (This is also *intensification* of the product's own good, since consumer folklore includes the belief that the only true or authentic vodka must be Russian—and the name Smirnoff does seem Russian.) Then, the ad uses *association* in its copy. Smirnoff vodka is associated with "Europe's elite," with "proper food," with a "delicious evening," with being "impeccable," with being "memorable," and with fine crystal. So association is used to intensify the own-good aspect of the message. *Composition* is used to intensify in several ways. Look at how the picture is organized. The wine glasses are untouched, while the highball glasses are in people's hands and clearly have been sampled. *Word choice* is used to intensify—another example of composition. The ad also intensifies the opposition's bad points: "The wine just sat there. Wine can ruin your palate." Again, word choice intensifies the "badness" of wine. Wine is made to seem disreputable because it "plays with your palate," because it is "forceful."

Now, does the persuader *downplay* anything? Vodka can be potent, especially if you drink it like water during a dinner party. That fact is omitted. Instead we are told that it "Leaves You Breathless"—no one can smell that you've been drinking. There is some faulty logic here as well. Why is it amusing that while the Smirnoff flowed, the wine "only sat there"? Why is that "not surprising"? With all these allusions, the ad *confuses* the reader. But by identifying the many tactics at work, persuadees can become alert and critical to the persuasive messages that come their way.

We will discuss a number of other tools of analysis as we proceed, but Rank's intensify/downplay tool is a good general one to use at first. You will want to try it with a variety of persuasive messages that you encounter. In future chapters we will discuss the role of language as it is used to persuade. We will also look at how

Figure 1.5. Intensification and downplaying in a persuasive message. (Courtesy Ste. Pierre Smirnoff, a division of Heublein.)

the internal motives and drives in each of us can be used by those who wish to persuade us. Our preferences for certain kinds of logic can be used by the persuader who designs the message. Cultural premises that are trained into us from birth are the basis for many persuasive appeals. Finally, we are also affected by the way we respond to the different media used in persuasion.

A Review and Conclusion

If you are now more alert to the possible ways you are being manipulated, you are well on your way to becoming a critical receiver. You are ready to arm yourself with some of the tools of analysis that make wise consumers, and there is a bonus for learning. In learning how you are persuaded and in exploring the tactics that other persuaders use, you can become a more skillful persuader yourself. Seeing what works, in what circumstances, with what kinds of people, will be useful as you prepare to become a persuader. Skillful consumers of messages learn to be more effective producers of messages. As we move ahead, it will be useful to apply the tools of persuasion on your own or through using the study questions and exercises outlined at the end of each chapter.

Questions for Further Thought

1. Describe the context in which persuasion has occurred in your past. Who persuaded you? Where? When? (Discuss briefly in a paragraph or two.)

2. Define how you are generally persuaded. Compare that definition with the one offered in this chapter. What differences are there?

3. Beginning with the definition of persuasion offered by this text, attempt to create a model that reflects all of the important elements of the definition. (Note: You might begin with a model such as that offered by David K. Berlo in *The Process of Communication* and elaborate on it or make appropriate adaptations.)

4. Identify three different types of persuasion you have received recently (advertisements, speeches, persuasive appeals in discussions with others, or some other type), and analyze each of them according to the definition offered in this chapter. (What are the symbols? What is the persuader's intent? What does the persuasion "say" about the persuadee's probable frame of reference?)

5. What are the tactics of intensification? How do they work? Give examples of their use on television, in print, on radio, by politicians, and by advertisers.

6. What are the tactics of downplay? How do they work? Give examples of their use on television, in print, on radio, by politicians, and by advertisers.

7. What is a "propaganda blitz"? Identify one that is presently going on in media or in regard to some political issue. Give an example of one that has been used on your campus or that is being used on campus now (for example, fraternity or sorority rush or a series of investigative news articles focused on some topic like increased student fees).

Experiences in Persuasion

1. Write to an advertiser and ask the company to substantiate some of its claims (for example, ask why the product is faster, safer, or better). Compare the answers with the original claims. If your entire class does this, compare your findings with those of your classmates.

2. After having identified the claims of some ad, do an analysis of them, using Rank's intensification/downplay system. See how your analysis matches up with the analyses of others in your class.

3. Keep a communication logbook for one day. Count the number of hours you spend reacting to media like television and radio. How many commercials are aired in each hour of television or radio time? Compare your totals with those of others in your class.

4. Listen to politicians. Identify how they downplay and intensify in talking about themselves and their opponents.

2
People:
Makers and Users of Symbols

Across the history of humanity's time on this planet, the major advances made by our species have been related to our ability to make symbols. Before humans developed speech, our culture was no more complex than that of the beasts—and sometimes less complex. The average human of the prespeech era probably lived and hunted alone, mating only when the physiological need arose. Homemaking and care of the young fell to women for reasons of anatomy and relative strength, not because of symbolic notions like "duty" or "responsibility." With the development of speech, however, humans could begin to live in less limited ways than the beasts. Not only could these early men and women court and woo one another with words and gestures, but families could band together and form tribes. Tasks could be assigned, with specialists in hunting, farming, weaving, tool-making, and weapon-making emerging across the centuries.

Underlying the human ability to speak was a prior power to *create symbols*. Before the development of speech, communication was probably mimetic—if you wanted to communicate something about thunder, you had to mimic or imitate it, perhaps "saying" or "sounding" something like "bummmmbummbu." Some language theorists believe that these early mimetic soundings were the roots for many of our contemporary words. The word thunder has a slight resemblance to the sound of thunder and to the "bummmmbummbu" sound. The communications were what we call signs or signals. They did not stand for thunder; they signaled it or imitated it. When the word thunder or its predecessor emerged and was finally used without loud rumbling sounds in the imitation of the clouds crashing, you had a true **symbol**. It did not signal or imitate thunder; it stood for thunder and permitted its user to "carry" thunder around, chatting about it here and there as in "Boy, oh, boy! the thunder was loud last night, huh?"

Whenever and however persuasion occurs, symbols are the basic carrier of the message. Imagine a television advertisement for Michelob beer. Now, try to identify some of the verbal symbols (that is, those that employ spoken or written language). First there are the song lyrics—"Weekends were made for Michelob." They call up a mental picture of a time of companionship and enjoyment. The lyrics also associate the product with a kind of free and exciting lifestyle that the truly "in" people are supposed to have. Superimposed on these aural symbols might be written verbal symbols such as the word Michelob or the written slogan—"Weekends were made for Michelob"—which reinforces the images presented aurally (and, of course, in pictures). In addition, the entire message (for example, the colorful sunsets, the clothing worn by the actors, and the musical score) can symbolically build and reinforce the brewer's persuasive message.

You can study persuasion from a receiver's perspective more effectively once you appreciate the symbolic process. It is useful to know why an advertiser or politician chooses certain words and disregards or avoids others. How does what is said affect receivers? What might the symbols persuaders choose tell us about their motivation and intent? All people use words, and we select particular words because they please us. Our choices reveal our tastes and our intentions. As receivers, we can train ourselves to have a critical "feel" for persuasive symbols by doing the following:

1. Understanding the symbol-making process. Symbol-making is an artistic act; it is selective. So it can also be a motive-revealing act. Artists and persuaders always reveal something of themselves in their creations, especially words and visual images.

2. Investigating ways to listen more efficiently and systematically, developing tools for analyzing a persuader's style.

3. Finally, learning how our tools can reveal a persuader's motives and goals.

Thinking about Language and Its Roots

The word persuasion may suggest loaded language or the emotional words that have persuaded us to vote or to purchase. Jimmy Carter's 1976 campaign slogan is a good example—"Leadership for a Change." The words "for a change" have a dual meaning. First, they suggest that there has been no leadership recently (that is, to have some would be "a change."). Voters who felt that there was a leadership vacuum may have voted to fill that vacuum. The words carried a different meaning for those who wanted a change in the political climate and national direction. These people voted for the concept of change, not for the idea of leadership. Four years later the voters again opted for a change—Ronald Reagan. This time they voted to try "Together—A New Beginning." These words may have conveyed the idea of change in yet a different way.

Persuasion also brings to mind moments of great eloquence and lofty ideals, on occasions when artists of words were able to turn the tide with their writing or speaking. History records many such persuaders—Jesus, Tom Paine, Harriet Beecher Stowe, Abraham Lincoln, Julia Ward Howe, Susan B. Anthony, Winston Churchill, Martin Luther King Jr., and many more. When language is used with artistry and force, the persuader and the audience respond to the beauty of the word symbols.

Eloquent persuasion is unique and fresh. It strikes us as having caught the moment; it may even prophesy the future. The speech made by Martin Luther King Jr. the night before he was killed had elements of prophecy. He said that God had allowed him "to go up to the mountain," that he had "seen the promised land," and that he doubted that he would get there with his followers. He concluded, "And I am happy tonight! I'm not fearing any man! Mine eyes have seen the glory of the coming of the Lord!" Though the words were drawn from the Old Testament and Julia Ward Howe's *Battle Hymn of the Republic,* King's use of them was unique in the context of the movement he was leading. After his assassination, they seemed prophetic.

When we think about persuasion, then, we are inevitably faced with the artistic process of making word symbols. There are symbolic *acts*—like the assassination of a president or Pope, which mean to express rejection of authority, outrage at capitalism or Catholicism, or some other objection—but these are not the usual stuff of persuasion. Language is.

Where did language come from? How did humans discover that they could speak and why did the ability progress from simple to complex symbols? Some think that the development of human speech parallels the progression from the babbling of infancy to the use of words and then sentences.[1] Others explain the development of language by tracing it to certain stages in the development of the brain and its many cells. By the time a child reaches age two, the brain is ready to learn language. The two-year-old talks almost nonstop, sometimes making mistakes, sometimes being cute, and sometimes adding new and different words.

A useful view is offered by philosopher Susanne K. Langer in her book *Philosophy in a New Key.*[2] Langer argues that it is neither use of tools nor language that makes humans unique among the beasts. Chimpanzees use "tools" on occasion, and the honeybee communicates through a "dance" signaling the location of flowers, their type and their distance. The story is told of a researcher who made an electric bee that could do the honey dance. The problem was that the bees in the hive answered the electric bee with a dance of their own—something like "Okay, we're on the way." The electric bee, however, didn't receive messages. Like so many people, the bee just sent them. So the little machine continued the message of "lots of roses, a hundred yards northwest of the hive," over and over. The real bees were angered and attacked the electric bee, finally ruining it. Communication, even in bees, is two-way and fairly complex. We could probably learn something from the bee about how to handle compulsive talkers.

Langer suggests that one aspect of behavior that only humans display is the ability to make symbols.[3]

Even the earliest cave dwellings show this impulse. Long before we had a

---

1. Roger Brown, *Words and Things* (New York: Free Press, 1958).

2. Susanne K. Langer, *Philosophy in a New Key* (New York: New American Library, 1951).

3. *Ibid.* The notion that use of symbols is uniquely characteristic of human beings is also seen in *A Grammar of Motives* by Kenneth Burke (Berkeley: University of California Press, 1970) and *A Rhetoric of Motives* by Kenneth Burke (Berkeley: University of California Press, 1969) and in several other works, such as *The Presence of the Word* by Walter S. Ong, S. J. (New Haven, Connecticut: Yale University Press, 1967). Susanne Langer refers to it throughout her book.

spoken language, we humans painted on cave walls and made charms to ward off evil or to bring luck. Symbols were also associated with magic and rituals. They were used to signify adulthood and to cast evil spells on enemies. Today, we also use symbols to control others. We use them to create works of art like poetry. We use symbols to reject, to cajole, to seduce, to comfort, and to anger others. Sociologist Hugh Duncan links every society to its symbols. They provide the clearest image of a culture, as the title of his book suggests—*Symbols and Society*.[4]

Susanne Langer says that the need to make symbols is akin to a biological drive—it is instinctive. Even when people have crippling handicaps, the urge to create symbols remains strong. Renoir demanded that paintbrushes be taped to his arthritic hands in his old age; he had to paint. There are paralyzed people who paint with their mouths—even with their feet. Mentally retarded children often spend hours painting, drawing, and humming. The process of making symbols drives us.

An example of the power of symbol-making was reported by Helen Keller in her autobiography. Blind and deaf from age two, Keller had been deprived of an outlet for her symbolic drives. Then Anne Sullivan, her private tutor, began to teach her sign language through the sense of touch. Keller could not speak but could now ask for simple things. The scene in which Keller discovers that a word can stand for a thing (be a symbol) is most dramatic:

> As the cool stream gushed over my hand she spelled into the other the word water, first slowly, then rapidly. I stood still, my whole attention fixed upon the motion of her fingers. Suddenly I felt a misty consciousness as of something forgotten—a thrill of returning thought; and somehow the mystery of language was revealed to me. I knew then that w-a-t-e-r meant the wonderful cool something that was flowing over my hand. . . . I left the well-house eager to learn. Everything had a name and each name gave birth to a new thought.[5]

We have all felt the same thrill of learning the power of word symbols as children.

Language Use as an Art Form

Most of us cannot be artists, but we all can make symbols—and through our use of language, we do. Since the process is selective, like the act of artistic creation, we can expect that our words will reveal various things about ourselves. Seneca put it this way—"As a man speaks, so is he." Receivers can learn a lot about a persuader's motives by listening to the words the persuader chooses. They reveal his or her intentions and attitudes toward the audience. You and I listen to our companions and acquaintances and decide whether or not to continue the relationship or to deepen the acquaintance on the basis of the language we hear. If

4. Hugh Duncan. *Symbols and Society* (New York: Oxford University Press, 1968).

5. Helen Keller. *The Story of My Life* (New York: Doubleday, Doran & Co., 1936). pp. 23–24.

a person uses unnecessarily complex language, we may label that person "stuffy." Another uses "in" language, so we label that one a "trend-setter."

The receiver of persuasive messages can learn a lot about a persuader's motives by paying careful attention, not only to the whole message, but to its particular words. Consider the language used by Hitler and other German Nazis of the 1930s in referring to the Jews: vermin, sludge, garbage, lice, sewage, insects, and bloodsuckers. Those words were red flags signaling Hitler's road toward an "ultimate solution"—concentration camps and gas chambers. If more Europeans of Jewish heritage had listened carefully to Hitler's *words*, they might have fled in time to avoid the fate of six million Jews who were treated like vermin or lice—by extermination. Isn't that what we're supposed to do with rats? Hitler's words helped the S.S. Corps to feel they were doing their duty when they methodically rounded up and killed the Jews, wove their hair into rug pads, pried out their gold teeth, then efficiently killed them and rendered their bodies into soap.

Even in less dramatic, less obvious situations, persuaders reveal their motives and beliefs in their choice of words. Advocates of women's liberation object to sexist language use. Take lady doctor, for example. Does the term reveal sexist motives or attitudes? Isn't it something like gentleman farmer? How seriously should we take his interest in farming? Will he be a financial success in agriculture? Probably not. So why should a lady doctor be taken seriously?

Product names often reveal their producers' attitudes toward their customers, or even toward the public in general. Oster Corporation has a "food crafter" instead of a "food chopper." The choice of words tells us Oster is taking a gourmet approach. (Chopping sounds like work. Crafting? Now, that's art.) In the status-conscious 1950s and 1960s cigarettes had "classy" names like Viceroy, Pall Mall, Marlboro, and Benson and Hedges. If you were status-minded, those were brands for you. Quite a different attitude is suggested by the names of brands more recently introduced—Fact, True, Merit, Vantage, and More. These suggest a more honest, open, and "up-front" audience. Virginia Slims, on the other hand, made a fortune from women's lib. How "nonsexist" do you think their approach is?

Similar plays to perceived public attitudes are shown in the names given to cars. Before the emphasis on the energy shortage and conservation, automakers used names like Roadmaster, Continental, Charger, Impala, Delta 88, or Thunderbird to symbolize speed, luxury, and especially—power. Now cars get names like Rabbit, Aries, Horizon, or Omni to suggest quick starts and light weight (Rabbit), long range (Horizon), or space-age engineering (Aries, Omni). Yet, the Horizon and the Omni are identical except for trim. What might be a hypothetical name for a new model of auto? You wouldn't be likely to use Turtle, or Snail. You might use names like Hawk, Condor, or even Wren—all of which suggest swiftness, compactness, and grace.

Knowing about the artistic aspect of language symbols enables persuadees to look beyond the surface and to delve deeper into the meaning of the message and motives of the source. Persuaders, on the other hand, can analyze receivers and artistically craft their words and phrases to appeal to them. They can "listen" to their audience for clues to what receivers need and want to hear.

For example, the term self-starter is persuasive to business people. Job-seekers who want to persuade prospective employers that they are eager and qualified for a job might use words like self-starter. By proclaiming "Have It Your Way!" Burger King hooks into audience feelings of insecurity, or helplessness. The advertisers saw consumers of hamburgers as being tired of assembly-line treatment. The promotion experts were listening to their audience.

How can *we* learn to listen in this critical way? One way is to investigate how language scholars view the power and use of words. An early but useful approach to language use is that of the general semanticists.

The Semantic Approach to Language Use

Beginning in 1933 with a landmark work—*Science and Sanity*, by Alfred Korzypski[6]—scholars who called themselves **general semanticists** began a semi-scientific, systematic study of the use and meaning of language. Their purpose was to improve understanding of problems and to teach themselves and others to be very careful about using language. The general semanticists were highly aware of the dangers involved in stereotyping, especially in view of the electronic communication devices coming into general use in the 1930s: radio, public-address systems, and motion pictures. By making skillful use of the new techniques to popularize ethnic stereotypes and emotional appeals, men like Hitler, Franco, and Mussolini had risen swiftly to prominence and had gained enough early public support to institute dangerous regimes. The general semanticists believed that one good way to prevent such dictatorships would be to teach people to be aware that the appeals of demagogues reflected "the map [inner perception] and not the territory [reality]."

Everything changes, the semanticists reasoned. Even when based on the observed traits of an individual, stereotypes are unreliable, simply because no member of a class or group is exactly like any other member. An exercise I like to use with my classes is to write on the chalkboard a few stereotyped terms that have been used in the past or are presently in vogue. Then I offer my students the chance to add to the list while I write down the terms. I begin in a rather low key way with names like Dumb Swede (which I can say with a clear conscience, being a Swede myself), Mick, Limey, and Ivan. Then I sort of "up the ante" with words like Dago, Spic, and Hun. We discover that nationality isn't the only basis on which to stereotype.

Affiliation with certain groups or religions can be used—Frat-Rats are well known, as are Sorority Queens. Then, there are Minnow-Munchers, and Preppies, Kikes, Sheenies, and Bible-Thumpers. Sexual preference is another basis of stereotypes. Of course, race is an old standby for lumping people together. And then my students tell me that body type is a criterion for stereotyping—you have Blimps and Beached Whales on the one hand and Flamingos and Beanpoles on the other. And the list could go on and on. In fact, inside of ten minutes we cover every inch of all the chalkboards in my classroom with stereotypes.

That exercise is intended to demonstrate the very thing that the semanticists want people to be aware of. As Korzypski suggested, *the map is not the territory.*

---

6. Alfred Korzypski, *Science and Sanity* (Lakeville, Connecticut: The Non-Aristotelean Library, 1947).

In other words, the internal perceptions or conceptions of persons, groups, things, and ideas we carry around in our heads are most likely very different from the real persons, groups, things, and ideas. Our faulty concepts are usually expressed through language: We create and use words to convey them. Then we often react to the words as if they were the real person, group, thing, or idea.

The Signal Response

Reacting to a word as though it were real is what the semanticists called a **signal response.** Remember the distinction we drew earlier between a *sign(al)* and a *symbol.* The sign announces or accompanies the thing, as thunder announces or signals lightning and rain. The word thunder is a symbol for the thing and *stands in its place rather than announcing or accompanying it.* As a symbol, the word can stand for many kinds of thunder—the rip-crashing kind in my old home state of Minnesota or the prairie kind of thunder in my new home state of Illinois, where the thunder starts way off to the west in Iowa somewhere. You can hear it traveling all the way across the state in a kind of low-rumbling, rolling fashion. The word or symbol for thunder is so flexible that it can stand for other events and characteristics that do not actually involve rain and lightning. Two of Christ's disciples were called Sons of Thunder, and a good performance brings on thunderous applause.

The signal response is the reverse of symbolism. The semanticists explain it as the common human trait of reacting to symbols *as if they were signals.* Someone calls you a Dumb Swede or a Mick or a Queer or a Kike or a Frat-Rat and you are likely to punch that person out. You are responding to the symbol *as if it were a signal;* or to put it another way, you respond *as if the words made you* a dumb Swede and as if all Swedes were by nature dumb oafs.

More commonly, we see this happen with symbols that have a high emotional charge, such as the Flag or some religious symbol. For example, during the Vietnam War years, demonstrators often burned the U.S. flag or flew it upside down— the national signal for distress. Persons opposing the demonstrators frequently beat or arrested or even killed them because they were defacing the symbol of our country. When questioned about the fights, those opposing the demonstrators often said something like "Them long-haired Hippie freaks was burnin' my Country; it got me POed so I smashed 'em!" Again it is the signal response to language or symbols. No one was burning an entire country but people responded to the symbol for the country *as if it were* the country itself. They responded to the map *as if it were* the territory.

Extensional Devices for Avoiding the Signal Response. The semanticists approach language study by teaching people to be continually alert to the difference between signals and symbols. They isolate meaning in very concrete terms. For example, suppose I say to you that "Germans are highly authoritarian." Now, in itself, the word Germans isn't particularly negative. But it sounds as though I were saying that *all* Germans, each and every one, all the time, is highly authoritarian. If you happened to be of Germanic descent, you might punch me in the nose—a signal response for sure. I would communicate better with you, the semanticists would say, if I as a persuader used one or more of what they called **extensional**

devices.[7] These devices were suggested by Korzypski as a way to be more specific and concrete in order to avoid prompting signal responses.

For example, one extensional device is to modify my language concerning Germans by **dating**. Since all things change, the Germans I met yesterday are not the same today, and the ones I met in 1975 have probably changed even more. Including a reference to the dates on which my idea of Germans is based may help me to avoid misunderstanding and may make me a more effective communicator or persuader. Suppose I had said, "During World War II, Germans were highly authoritarian." Even if you were of Germanic descent, this very probably would bother you less than my original "Germans are highly authoritarian."

Another extensional device suggested by the semanticists is to **index** the cases on which a conception is based. Since no single case of any group is exactly like any other single case, it is helpful to mention the particular case or cases being referred to. If I were to use both indexing and dating in my sentence, it would come out something like this: "During World War II, Germans who were officials of the Nazi government and the armed forces were highly authoritarian." Given your hypothetical Germanic bloodlines, do you think that this sentence would prompt a punch in the nose? Probably not.

Another of Korzypski's extensional devices is the use of **quotation marks** to indicate that you are using words in a special way. This special way usually happens when we use the words that are abstract—words like power, democracy, morale, and truth. If I put quotation marks around such words, I indicate to the reader that I'm using them in a special way—my way. I am now talking about *my idea* of power, democracy, or morale. Let's see what this does to the sentence on Germans. "During World War II, Germans who were officials of the Nazi government or the armed forces were 'highly authoritarian.' " Now instead of being punched in the nose, I am likely to be asked what I mean by "highly authoritarian." If you are writing your communication/persuasion, so far, so good—but what if you are speaking it? The semanticists reply that you can signal the quotation marks by marking them in the air with the index and middle fingers of each hand or by giving the words some other sort of special indication through vocal tone, volume, or stress.

A final extensional device is the use of **etc.**, which Korzypski felt would be useful to remind us that we haven't said all there is to be said on the subject. More can be added by us or others. In other words, our views or descriptions are not the whole story. Let's return to the Germanic example again, using all four extensional devices this time to see whether we can focus more exactly on what is really meant. The sentence now reads, "During World War II, Germans who were officials in the Nazi government or the armed forces were 'highly authoritarian', among other things." From the semanticist point of view, that is a darned good sentence, it avoids lots of potential misunderstanding. It makes the map or sentence conform more closely to the territory than its initial version did. Another way to put it is that the revised sentence is much more *extensional* or *reality-based* and much less *intentional* or *perceptually based.*

For the persuader, then, it is probably wise to be careful, to be specific, and to

---

7. Robert Potter, *Making Sense* (New York: Globe Book Co., 1974).

be extensional in designing one's messages. For receivers, on the other hand, it is essential to listen to the words being aimed at them with the map/territory analogy in mind.

Advertising as a Map

Advertising, for example, is only a map of the product; it is not the product itself. In fact, it is often a pretty inaccurate map. Is wearing Sex Appeal by Jovan going to make the opposite sex crawl all over you? The smell of it may even repel some people. Not all users of Johnnie Walker Red become top executives, and drinking Chivas Regal is unlikely to make you rich. Eating Dannon yogurt won't make you a marathoner if you never get out of your chair, and drinking Pepsi Light won't slenderize you by itself.

There are other maps in our world, as well. A politician's campaign promises are a kind of map. This map depicts the territory that the politician envisions. This is why even sincere politicians often can't live up to their promises—the real territory isn't conducive to the kinds of alterations suggested by their maps. Our visions of disc jockeys are another example. We create internal pictures of them on the basis of their voices. Sometimes it is disconcerting to meet or see them in person. Likewise we invent voices for faces we see in print. Wouldn't it be a surprise if the Coppertone girl's voice were ultrabossy? Or what if the newest pro-football running back talked like a Munchkin?

What are some of the maps that you encounter every day? What kinds of maps are in your head, and how right or wrong are they? These are questions the receiver of persuasion ought to keep in mind.

The Psycholinguistic Approach to Language Use

As its name implies, the **psycholinguistic approach** to language combines two ways of studying human behavior. First, there is the *psychological approach*, whereby we try to discover or sense human motivation. Then there is the *linguistic approach*, whereby we try to discover patterns in language use. Hopefully, these will lead us to a pattern or a set of rules to explain why people talk or write in certain ways.

The combination of these two approaches came about only rather recently, following the rise of the behavioral and social sciences in the 1950s. An interesting example of how such research and study is done is the work of Charles Osgood, a noted language researcher.[8] Osgood wanted to find out if there were any differences in the linguistic style used in two kinds of suicide notes—those written by people who were asked to construct such a note from their imaginations and those written by people who actually had attempted suicide. He found that although most of the pretend suicide notes had similarities to the real suicide notes, certain language or stylistic features in the real notes were different. These included the proportion of certain parts of speech (nouns and adjectives were used more fre-

---

8. Charles Osgood, "Some Effects of Encoding upon Style of Encoding." In *Style in Language*, T. A. Sebeok, ed. (Cambridge, Massachusetts: M.I.T. Press, 1960.)

quently in the real notes compared to verbs and adverbs, for example) and the organization or disorganization of the words. The sentences in the authentic suicide notes were shorter, and the notes contained more errors and explosive segments. The point is that the writers' psychological state was reflected in their verbal style. This offers support for the basic premise of psycholinguistics: *Our underlying or subconscious motives, fears, or intentions can be reflected outwardly in our use of words.* If you happen to be a certain kind of psychologist, you call these reflections "Freudian slips" and make much of them.

Another kind of theorist looks carefully at the kind of sentence structure people use, or the phrases they repeat. Most of us do this kind of language analysis almost unconsciously. That is why comedians who imitate actors, politicians, and other public figures can make audiences believe in their impressions. They combine language patterns with nonverbal gestures and facial expressions that typify the person they are imitating. Richard Nixon, for example, over-used the phrase "Let me be perfectly clear," and that became a standard signal to audiences watching someone like Rich Little imitate Nixon.

Below you will find a curious letter that was actually sent to the chairperson of my department several years ago. I have removed the name of its author and other identifying information. Read it and then, for practice, try to determine what the writer was like. For example, on the basis of language and style used, see whether you think the person was a male or female. Did he or she come from an urban or a rural background? Would this person be likely to pledge a fraternity or sorority? How bright is the author? What kinds of entertainment might be marketed to this person? What kinds of books? What kinds of clothing? What political beliefs?

Though you won't be approaching style with the same scientific precision that Osgood did as he analyzed the real and bogus suicide notes, you will be training yourself to pick up hints of motives, attitudes, and intentions that are scattered through a persuader's style. The writer of the letter wishes to be exempted from taking the basic speech fundamentals course.

Dear Professor Jones,

I am interested in directives as to how one may proficiency out of the speech requirement. Having been advised to seek counsel from you "specifically"—I sincerely hope you will not be displeased with my enthusiasm by asking this indulgence. There is a basis for my pursuing this inquisition as I am an adept speaker with substantiating merits. I will be overburdened with more difficult courses this fall—at least they will be concomitant with my educational objectives in the fields of Fine Arts and Languages. It would be a ludicrous exercise in futility to be mired in an unfecund speech course when I have already distinguished myself in that arena. I maintained an "A" average in an elite "advanced" speech course in High School. I am quite noted for my bursts of oratory and my verbal dexterity in the public "reality"—quite a different platform than the pseudo realism of the college environs. There is a small matter of age—I shall be twenty-two this fall. I am four years older than the average college freshman. I am afraid that I would dissipate with boredom, if confined with a bunch of teenagers. Surely you can advise something that would be a more palatable alternative?

Yours sincerely,

P.S. Please do not misconstrue this "inquiry" as the enterprise of an arrogant student, but one who will be *so* immersed in serious intellectual pursuits that the "speech" requirement will be *too* nonsensical and burdensome.

If ever a student needed to know about communication, it was this person.[9] But what does the language usage here tell you about the writer of the letter? She uses $64 words—perhaps a clue to insecurity—but she seems unsure about the words she has chosen: several times she puts words into quotation marks. She says that she is pursuing an inquisition, when she means an inquiry. (An inquisition is a tribunal for suppressing religious heresy.) She says she has substantiating merits when she probably means that she has substantial reasons for being excused from the course.

Now, whether your analysis was accurate or not, it is clear that you and I make judgments about others on the basis of their use of language—especially their stylistic choices. A problem with doing so, however, is that we can make mistakes like those you probably made in regard to that student's letter. It's easy to misassess others, because we seldom go about our analysis very systematically, and we may be poorly equipped with analytical tools. In Chapter 3 you will find several tools that can help you assess a persuader's motives, attitudes, and intentions on the basis of the persuader's word choice, sentence construction, and use of metaphor. In other chapters you may find additional tools to help you determine a persuader's intentions. In your own encounters with persuasion, you may choose to use one or two of these tools—or many. The important thing is that you do analyze on a variety of bases. Your judgment may differ from mine, but all of us need to be able to analyze a persuader's style systematically—or at least to just listen more critically to the persuasive appeals that bombard us every day.

A Review and Conclusion

In conclusion, we can see that language use in persuasion is very important not only to the persuader but to the receiver as well. Just as persuaders must be attuned to their audiences' language preferences so they can tailor the persuasive message to fit, responsible receivers must listen carefully to the persuaders' language choices to analyze the patterns they observe. We live in an era of "option overload." Modern society offers us a multitude of alternatives and modern communications make us more aware of them than ever before. To make our decisions wisely we must systematically examine the symbols others use for clues to future behavior, underlying motivation, and persuasive potential. Whether we choose to look at the art of language from the stance of the semanticists or of the psycholinguist, the very least we can do is to train our eyes and ears to be critical receivers—and ourselves to be critical consumers of persuasion.

As we move on to the tools for becoming informed critics of language that

---

9. To determine how right or wrong you might be about the student who wrote this letter, here is what we do know about *her*. Yes—the writer was female. She lived on a farm, as the letter gave a rural-route box number in a nearby farming community. And the student never came to N.I.U.

future chapters present, put the tools to work in your everyday life. Ferret out the underlying meanings in speeches, advertisements, posters, and conversations.

Questions for Further Thought

1. What are three aspects of language that we have examined in Chapter 2? Give examples of each.

2. In what way does Susanne Langer think language makes humans unique? How is language use an art form? What good does it do for receivers to think of language as an art?

3. Whose persuasive language have you studied recently? Do you think you can figure out what people are like from their language use? Give examples.

4. What did the semanticists consider the major purpose in studying semantics?

5. What are the four extensional devices the semanticists recommend? Give an example of each.

6. What is the meaning of: "The map is not the territory"? What are some of your maps? How is advertising a map?

7. What are the two principal approaches used by the psycholinguists? Give examples of psycholinguistic analyses.

Experiences in Persuasion

1. Make a scrapbook of various magazine advertisements you come across this term. Identify the language usage in them. Try to show map and territory distinctions in them. Try to analyze some of the psychology of the advertisements: How do they view the product? the audience? Write a brief paragraph about each ad and its use of language.

2. In all likelihood, a Presidential speech or news conference will be broadcast over television and radio at least once during this term. Listen to it and try to analyze the language being used. The full text of Presidential speeches is usually published in the newspapers the day after the broadcast. Comparing your reactions to the live and the print versions may be useful. Do both give the same impressions? Try to identify patterns in the speech. If they might reveal something about the President, discuss this with your class.

3. Construct two "Letters to the Editor" that concern the same subject and make the same arguments. Write one of them in a formal style, using lots of the extensional devices of the semanticists. Write the other with a very informal style using few or none of these devices. Send them off to your local paper and see which one(s) get published. Several of you in the class or even the whole class might enjoy doing this.

3
Tools for Analyzing and Developing Persuasive Language

$\mathbf{I}$n Chapter 2, you had the chance to explore language and its use in persuasion from several perspectives. This chapter introduces you to some tools of analysis that may help you to explore particular uses of language in advertisements, political appeals, and other attempts at persuasion that you will certainly encounter in the days, weeks, and years ahead. It is important to observe that even if your analysis of a particular persuader is not perfectly accurate and on target, doing some kind of analysis is better than doing none and responding by reflex to the persuasion aimed at you. We can never be 100-percent certain about what a persuader means or intends. That is why we deal in probabilities.

Symbolic Expression and Persuasive Language

Let's begin this introduction to some of the tools of analysis by looking at several dimensions of language. In Figure 3.1, language is represented as a globe that contains all the various qualities that words and sentences can carry and elicit from the listener. Running through the globe are several axes along which certain types of meaning could be charted. On one axis may be the possible meanings that a word or a series of words can have. This might be called the **semantic axis.** Along another axis might be the purposes the words serve in the sentence. Certain words name things. Others connect ideas. Some words activate. Others are used by speakers or writers to reduce the value of their opponents. This axis could be called the **functional axis.** Along the third axis are thematic combinations that can result from word choice. These combinations give us the texture or the feel of words or combinations of words. For example, most people derive a soft, slithery, smooth association from these slogans—"Feel Black Velvet" or "Isn't Black Velvet Smooth." Advertisers especially try to persuade you through the use of words along the **thematic axis** that have great textural appeal. And, of course, there could be many other axes cutting across the globe of language—the OKness axis, the Freudian axis, and so on. Let us begin with these three dimensions of language—the *semantic,* the *functional,* and the *thematic* aspects of language. As you train yourself as a receiver, you can add others.

36

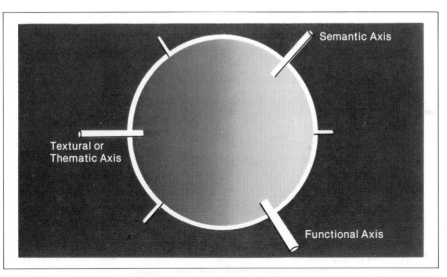

Figure 3.1. This figure is based on a description of a model for meaning suggested by Charles E. Osgood, George J. Suci, and Percy H. Tannenbaum in *The Measurement of Meaning* (Urbana: University of Illinois Press, 1957.) They suggest that semantic meaning for any word or concept can be located by charting it in "semantic space" using the Semantic Differential, a tool whereby receivers respond to a word, phrase, or concept along several polar scales. Each end of the scale represents an adjectival description (for example, good/bad or heavy/light). The globe here expands such charting to include two other attributes/functions and "feel," or motif, of words. An investigator could add other axes to chart the sexual, aggressive, dialectical, or other qualities of a particular symbol.

Consider this line of copy from a magazine advertisement: "Sudden Tan from Coppertone tans on touch for a tan that lasts for days."[1] On the *functional* axis the words Sudden Tan name a product. *Semantically*, however, much more is involved. The word sudden indicates that the tan is almost instantaneous, and indeed this is a major advantage of the product—it dyes your skin on contact to look tanned. The headline on the ad is reinforced by the semantic meaning of the word sudden, as is the photo over which the words are printed. The headline is "Got a minute? Get a tan." The photo shows before-and-after pictures of an attractive blonde who has been dyed tan by the product.

On a *textural* or *thematic* level, the words that name the product do even more. The word sudden sounds or feels like the word sun, so the product name sounds like the word suntan. The sounds *s* and *t* are also repeated in the line of copy. The repetition reinforces the notion of suntan. Try to describe how the message would make you feel if the meanings of the words disappeared and only their sound remained.

Here are some more examples of the thematic or textural qualities that language can have: The Presto Corporation names its new corn popper The Big Poppa! in hope that our minds will establish a thematic link with the sounds of popping corn while we chuckle at the takeoff on the familiar "Big Daddy" cliché and the popper/poppa play on words. A well-established cleaning product suggests that it

---

1. *House and Garden*, June 1977, p. 31.

will save you work—Lestoil is its name. A new product associated with the energy shortage is the Kero-Sun heater, which burns kerosene and warms your house like the sun. You can have a Soup-erb Supper with a package of Hamburger Helper's beef-vegetable soup. And then there is the product that will make every woman Smooth, Soft, and Sexy.

The Functional Axis: What Do the Words Do?

Words have jobs. We have traditionally grouped these jobs into grammatical classes—nouns, verbs, adjectives, adverbs, prepositions, conjunctions, interjections, and so on. We have all memorized some of the definitions of these—for example, "a noun is the name of a person, place, thing, or idea." It would be impossible for us to diagram all the sentences we hear. Diagraming might show a preferred pattern of sentence structure or a tendency to use certain words or word classes more frequently than others. Such preferred patterns are normal for most speakers and really would tell us little about the source. We need a way to answer the question "What are the words doing *in this message?*" On this level, we are interested in the form of the message, not the content. Consider the following example:

"Some Leaders Are Born Women." The sentence does a surprise syntactical (functional) reversal on the old chestnut "Some Men Are Born Leaders." Then it adds extra emphasis to the Women's Movement by substituting the word women for the word men. The functional aspects of the message are in reverse order. The substitution of words is a semantic shift that also catches our attention. In this example, then, we are looking at what words can *do (functional meaning)* and what *connotations* or *denotations* words have *(semantic meaning)*.

Persuaders want their message to perform at least three jobs:

1. Identify, or locate, an issue or topic.

2. Assign a cause or a cure for a problem associated with the issue.

3. Motivate the audience to take action.

These three functions—location, identification of cause, and motivation—are served by language, or words. Look at them as you are being persuaded. Where is the persuader taking you? How is the issue located? What words assign cause? What is the motivational technique used?

The Semantic Axis: What Do the Words Mean?

The semantic axis tries to answer the question "What do the words mean *in this message?*" This second axis focuses attention on why certain words are used instead of others. Take, for example, the slogan of the Kennedy Administration— "The New Frontier." Why is the word frontier used? The words vista or future might have been chosen as well. Most would agree that the word suggests challenge, effort, adventure, and discovery. Those synonyms are different from the synonyms for a word like future. Listing synonyms is a useful way to determine what words mean. Comparing the chosen word with the possible alternatives can tip us off as to a persuader's intent.

What, for instance, might be the word choice you would make for naming an antiacne lotion? A new high-mileage, four-wheel-drive subcompact? A low-calorie pop-wine? One can think of several possibilities. How about Stopzit or NoBlem or Sanitize for the lotion? Each has different potential connotations. How about the Go-Four or The Otter or the Bit-O-Power for the four-wheel-drive subcompact? Again, several possible shades of meaning emerge from each. Consider the possibilities for the pop-wine that you yourself might choose.

A good way to train one's "receiver" for the nuances of meaning in persuasion is to consider the alternatives that a persuader could have chosen for real products, slogans, and so on. Look around you and try renaming the Eagle from AMC, the K- or X-cars, or Schlitz Lite. Try restating the political slogans that bloom during every election season.

The Thematic Axis: How Do the Words Feel?

A third kind of question we can ask: "What unites the words used *in this message?*" "What underlying theme is suggested by them?" Answers to these questions depend on the textural qualities of language—the flavors or "feel" of the words used. This characteristic of language analysis relies on intuition or feeling. We probably would find only minimal agreement among observers on the "texture" of language, but that is not crucial. The problem facing persuadees in our information age is not how to make the *best* choice, but how to make a choice at all.

Take, for example, these passages from Ronald Reagan on his apparent 1981–1983 tax-cut victory. He referred to it as "the beginning of a new Renaissance in America" and said that it would bring ". . . a new era of prosperity." He closed his nationwide TV speech seeking citizen support with a request that viewers contact their congressional representatives and added, "We have done so much and come so far, let us not stop now." The theme of a new dawn hooked up with his campaign slogan, "Together—A New Beginning." Note the resonance of the "new Renaissance" and the "new era" here as well as the "journey" reference and the plea to "not stop now." They all fit with the theme of the future and the image of dawn. As you read these pages other politicians will be building similar sets of thematic clusters to harmonize with one another. This resonance has a kind of textural quality to it and gives us a feel of how the politician will act in the future.

Richard Weaver, in *The Ethics of Rhetoric,*[2] noted that style is a process of accumulation. We really discover a persuader's style only after listening to it over time. A single word, sentence, or paragraph is not enough to give us the full story. Winston Churchill was one of the best-known persuaders of the first half of the twentieth century. One of the thematic devices of Churchill's persuasion was to cast light/dark images,[3] or pictures related to day and night. The Nazis were always pictured as thugs or "gangsters" engaging in monstrous acts in dark places; on the other hand, the English were bright, sturdy, and capable of overcoming this "darkness" with the "light of their resolve." Churchill's light/dark metaphors were a trademark.

---

2. Richard Weaver, *The Ethics of Rhetoric* (Chicago: Henry Regnery Co., 1953).

3. Michael Osborne, "Archetypal Metaphors in Rhetoric: The Light-Dark Family," *Quarterly Journal of Speech,* April 1967, pp. 115–126.

As we consider messages of persuaders across the dec 'es, the trends of their word choices indicate some universal patterns. Consider the ⸱ ⸱mantic, functional, and thematic or textural qualities of some words in the fo̶l̶owing portion of a speech delivered by Jimmy Carter during the 1976 campaign when he was trying to capture the Democratic nomination.

> I have been accused of being an outsider. I plead guilty. Unfortunately, the vast majority of Americans are outsiders. We are not going to get changes by simply shifting around the same group of insiders, the same old tired rhetoric, the same unkept promises, and the same divisive appeals to one party, one faction, one section of the country, one race or religion or interest group. The insiders have had their chances, and they have not delivered. Their time has run out.[4]

Some of the words have done a semantic reversal. It is usually bad to be an outsider—generally, we don't like to be considered outsiders. As Carter used the word, he set a different frame of reference. It became good to be an outsider; in fact, most of us became outsiders. The same thing occurs with the word "insider," which usually refers to someone in the know who has savvy. In the Carter context, the word implied "political hack." Functionally, the word "outsider" creates identification between Carter and his audience; the word "insider" debunks. Another word tied to insiders is the word "same." Notice how many times it is used in just a few lines. Through repetition, Carter recalled the feeling we get with a line like "the same old thing, day in and day out." This feeling colors our whole image of those insiders—they are boring, plastic, and disgusting. Interestingly, the outsider image boomeranged when Carter got into office. Shortly before announcing his primary campaign against the incumbent President Carter, Senator Ted Kennedy told political analyst Theodore H. White:

> We wanted the same things ... [but] this ... this *outsider* can't solve our problems. ... Even on issues we agree on, he doesn't know how to do it.[5]

These examples should have alerted you to one of the abilities you already have, an ability based on your years as a language user. Because you are a regular language user—sending and receiving—you have had to learn to be a somewhat critical listener. All we really need to do to improve your abilities is to provide you with some tools in order to make your various analyses more systematic. Consider the language used in each of the following presidential campaign slogans or catch-phrases:

1960: The New Frontier (John F. Kennedy)

1964: A Great Society (Lyndon B. Johnson)

1968: Bring Us Together *and* Nixon's the One (Richard M. Nixon)

---

4. "Jimmy Carter: Not Just Peanuts," *Time*, March 8, 1976, p. 16.

5. Theodore H. White, *America in Search of Itself: The Making of the President 1956–1980* (New York: Harper & Row, 1982), pp. 274–275.

1972: Re-Elect the President (Richard M. Nixon)

1976: Leadership—For a Change (Jimmy Carter)
      I'm Feeling Good about America (Gerald Ford)

1980: Together—A New Beginning (Ronald Reagan)

How would you go about interpreting each of these slogans, considering what they seem to mean? Would you look at who was the ghostwriter for them? Would you look at the situations that gave rise to them? Or would you look at both? The problem is to choose a method of analysis that allows you to proceed objectively. Many methods can be used to psych out the style of a persuader. You should experiment with several of the methods discussed in Chapter 2 and then work out your own. Your goal is to take apart the persuasion directed at you and to look behind the words for some indication of what the persuader is like, how messages affect you, and why you should be alert and interested in what is said.

Return to the presidential slogans. Offhand, what can we say about any of them? Well, we can first describe their structure and form—the *functional axis.* Kennedy used a three-word descriptive phrase: a definite article (the word "the"), an adjective (the word "new"), and a noun (the word "frontier"). Johnson also has a three-word descriptive phrase with an article, adjective, and noun. It differs from the Kennedy slogan in that its article is indefinite (the word "a" denotes one of several, whereas the word "the" refers to the only one). One 1968 Nixon slogan has self-centered qualities—"Nixon's the One." The other 1968 Nixon phrase is not descriptive—it is imperative (it gives an order for action, not a description of a situation). It begins with a verb, "bring," followed by a pronoun, "us," and ends with an adverb, "together." This pattern was again followed by Nixon in 1972. Again the word order is imperative—"Re-elect the President." This imperative too shows an obsession with the self. This time there is no collective pronoun, and the order has shifted direction. In 1968, it was an order from the people to the candidate.

By 1972, the order is from the candidate to the people. The 1972 slogan provides a tip-off as to the persuader's attitude and motivation: He *is* the President and the people are beneath him, subject to his commands. Moreover, there is no longer a candidate to be elected or defeated; instead, there is an office to be verified. The candidate has become the office and has ceased to have an individual personality.[6] The Ford slogan is the longest. It describes a personal feeling. The winning slogan for that year (Carter's) was "Leadership—for a Change."

The 1980 slogan rings of John Kennedy's New Frontier in many ways. It suggests a futuristic outlook and a kind of redawning as we have already noted. It also suggests a basic faith in power of people when they are united. Reagan appealed to that power many times, using his office as a platform from which to muster support. A kind of "togetherness" was usually evoked by taking the issues to the public and asking them to write or phone their congressional representatives.

---

6. Dan F. Hahn and Ruth M. Gonchar, "The Rhetorical Predictability of Richard M. Nixon," *Today's Speech*, vol. 19 (Fall 1971), pp. 3–14. Hahn and Bonchar did a frequency count on the usage of various parts of speech and grammatical patterns in Nixon's major addresses and news conferences and compared them with average frequencies of the same items in the speeches of other presidents.

Reagan's slogan is also similar in basic structure to the 1976 Carter/Mondale slogan "Leadership—For a Change." Both slogans operate from a cause/effect perspective. The cause is first stated—either Leadership or Together. This word stands as a complete thought in itself as indicated by the use of the dash. Then the effects this cause will have are described, again in a kind of single thought. With Carter, the cause (Leadership) will bring about a true change. However, it is possible to read another meaning into the words if one assumes that voters felt the incumbent President Ford was no leader.

In the Reagan slogan, the cause (Togetherness) will produce "A New Beginning," which carries several possible meanings. Alone, "A New Beginning" implies that there was once a beginning of a new way of government, perhaps way back in 1789 when the Constitution was framed, or even in 1776. The beginning has been botched, however, and now we need to have a "New" and rededicated "Beginning." In some ways, the phrase suggests going back to square one and getting the engine of state back on the track.

Of course, we are only speculating and can offer little in the way of objective proof that these meanings are what was intended by the framers of the slogans. But looking at them with some care forces us to ask the question "What if the author of the slogans means ___?___ by it?" This is a useful forewarning for consumers of political persuasion to have.

We can do more than look at word order and grammar. On the *semantic* dimension, we can speculate about the meaning of some of the words. For example, take the adjectives in the Kennedy and Johnson word strings. What does "new" suggest? What kind of word is it? Could other words have been used? Which ones? Initially, I would say that the word new suggests innovation, progress, and an orientation to the future. Very few words could have been substituted for it without a loss of flavor. "The Innovative Frontier" would not have worked well. For one thing, it's too clumsy. The slogan also has links with the "New Deal" of Franklin D. Roosevelt and the "New Freedom" of Woodrow Wilson; in addition to its thrust toward the future, it has historical roots. It is an exciting word when we look at it in this context.

What about the word great in Johnson's slogan? It seems oriented more to the present than to the future; it describes a state of affairs at hand. It too could not easily be replaced. Grand might have been used, or proud, with less loss than a replacement for new, but neither of these words works well. Grand sounds pompous, and proud has an egotistical smack to it. It sounds like bragging.

What about the nouns in the slogans? Kennedy's word frontier could be replaced with vista or horizon with little loss of meaning or texture. But frontier, while it is future oriented and dramatic, also connotes the legends of our past— think of the challenges of the old frontier, the tests of ability, the discoveries, the heroes. Johnson's word society seems less exciting and less flexible than a frontier. He might have used country or culture or some other word, but again it would not have worked well. The words offer little challenge; they do not stir the imagination as frontier does. Neither do they call attention to the future. (You can see a frontier and can imagine it, but a society seems less concrete.) Let us draw these word characteristics together:

Kennedy: Definite, future-oriented, flexible noun; inflexible adjective, rooted in the past, dramatic.

Johnson: Indefinite, somewhat inflexible in both adjective and noun, present- or status quo-oriented, static, perhaps egotistical.

Using Symbolic Expression

In the case of campaign slogans we have admittedly been doing amateur psychoanalysis—reading the candidates' minds on the basis of their words. However, given the power of persuasion in our times (remember that if you're eighteen, you've spent years of your life watching TV), it is better to be overly skeptical about the persuasion we encounter than to painfully discover too late that candidates meant all their slogans implied. Given the power of symbols to motivate peoples and cultures, it is wise to look for the motives the symbols carry.

It's been learned, for example, that the kinds of symbols that people use and respond to can affect their health. People who use expressions like "I can't stomach it" or "I'm fed up" or "It's been eating away at me now for a year" have more stomach ulcers than others. The symbols (stomach words) become reality (ulcers) for these people.[7] Symbolic days like birthdays can also have dramatic effects. In nursing homes, more persons die during the two months after their birthdays than die during the two months before. Thomas Jefferson and John Adams both died in 1826, precisely on the Fourth of July,[8] a date of tremendous significance for both of them. Jefferson is even reported to have awakened from a deathlike coma on July third to ask his doctor if it was the Fourth yet.

The human body responds in highly symbolic ways to events like death. Some postmenopausal widows begin the menstrual cycle again after the death of their spouses. Some people die soon after the death of a loved one—and from the same disease. In other words, symbolic sympathy pains can be real. In the mid-1970s, Dr. Arnold Mandel, a psychiatrist, reported on an in-depth study of a pro-football team. Hired to try to find out why the team was losing, he found instead that the various players symbolically acted out their on-the-field roles while they were off the field. Wide receivers were narcissistic and always groomed themselves carefully, whereas defensive linemen and linebackers—the destroy boys—had the most run-ins with the law for barroom brawling and unpaid parking tickets. Quarterbacks saw themselves as saviors of the team on the field and were most likely to hold strong religious beliefs.[9]

Not only do symbols deeply affect individuals, but they also serve as a kind of psychological cement for holding a society or culture together. The central symbol for the Oglala Sioux Indians was a sacred hoop representing the four seasons of

---

7. "Fed Up? It May Lead to an Ulcer." *Chicago Daily News*, November 24, 1972, p. 30. For a more detailed discussion, see Howard Lewis and Martha Lewis, *Psychosomatics: How Your Emotions Can Damage Your Health* (New York: Viking Press, 1972).

8. Peter Koenig, "Death Doth Defer." *Psychology Today*, November 1972, p. 83.

9. This study has been reported in several places: CBS's *60 Minutes*, January 5, 1975, which featured an interview with Dr. Arnold Mandel; "Psychiatric Study of Pro-Football," *Saturday Review/World*, October 5, 1974, pp. 12–16; and "A Psychiatrist Looks at Pro-Football," *Reader's Digest*, January 1975, pp. 89–92.

the earth and the four directions from which weather might come. In the center of the hoop were crossed thongs that symbolized the sacred tree of life and the crossroads of life. Shortly after the hoop was broken during the massacre of the battle of Wounded Knee in 1890, the tribe disintegrated. An Oglala wise man named Black Elk explained the symbolic power of the circle for his tribe:

> You have noticed that everything an Indian does is in a circle, and that is because the Power of the World always works in circles, and everything tries to be round. In the old days when we were a strong and happy people, all our power came to us from the sacred hoop of the nation and so long as the hoop was unbroken the people flourished.... Everything the Power of the World does is done in a circle. The Sky is round and I have heard that the earth is round like a ball and so are all the stars. The Wind, in its greatest power, whirls. Birds make their nests in circles, for theirs is the same religion as ours. The sun comes forth and goes down again in a circle. The moon does the same, and both are round.
>
> Even the seasons form a great circle in their changing and always come back again to where they were. The life of a man is a circle from childhood to childhood and so it is in everything where power moves. Our tipis were round like the nests of birds and these were always set in a circle, the nation's hoop, a nest of many nests where the Great Spirit meant for us to hatch our children.[10]

Black Elk felt that the Sioux had lost all of their power or medicine when the whites forced the Indians out of their traditional round teepees and into the square houses on the reservation.

What are the central symbols of *our* society and how are they used by persuaders who are marketing their products or ideas to *us?* Certainly success in its many symbolic forms is the basis of appeals like the name of Sears, Roebuck's inexpensive mattress—it is called the "Sears-O-Pedic Imperial Elite." Another message that is sent to the members of our culture in a number of ways is that we are extraordinary in the world; so we hear that the United States is a superpower and we invented Superman and a department store offers a "super big, super thick, super thirsty, super soft, super plus towel" at "super sales prices." The importance of the law is noteworthy in American culture. The symbols that we print on our money refer to our legal system and laws; the courthouse or city hall is the symbolic center of many towns and cities; and in reaction to many perceived problems Americans tend to say, "There ought to be a law."

The power of symbols is enormous; they not only can reveal motive but also can affect our health, our self-image, and our national character.[11] Let us turn now to consideration of some of the tools that are available to persuadees for analysis

10. Black Elk, *Touch the Earth*, edited by T. C. McLuhan (New York: Outerbridge and Dienstfrey, 1971), p. 42.

11. Those who wish to explore the relation between symbols and human expression should consult Hugh D. Duncan, *Communication and Social Order* (London: Oxford University Press, 1963); Kenneth Burke, *A Grammar of Motives* (Berkeley: University of California Press, 1970); or Mircea Eliade, *The Myth of the Eternal Return; or Cosmos and History* (Princeton, New Jersey: Princeton University Press, 1971).

of the functional, semantic, and thematic axes of language. Remember that these tools can overlap from axis to axis. In developing listening skills, the important thing is to apply them when and where you can.

Tools for the Functional Axis

We shall consider three functional tools: (1) the "rhetorical aspects of grammatical categories" suggested by philosopher Richard Weaver, (2) the ways in which word arrangement or syntax affects persuasion, and (3) how ambiguity helps in persuasion.

Grammatical Categories

Weaver said that the grammatical form used by persuaders may indicate their intentions. He argues that sentence structure, for example, may reflect a person's method of using information and of coming to conclusions. The person who uses simple sentences does not see a complex world. As Weaver puts it, such a person "sees the world as a conglomerate of things ... [and] seeks to present certain things as eminent against a background of matter uniform or flat."[12] The simple sentence sets the subject off from the verb and object; it sees *causes* that *act* to have *effects* upon objects. When a persuader uses this form, the persuadee ought to look at what is being highlighted, at what affects what, and at how action occurs.

The complex sentence features a more complex world—several causes and several effects at the same time. Weaver says that it "is the utterance of a reflective mind,"[13] which tries "to express some sort of hierarchy."[14] Persuaders who use this kind of sentence express basic principles and relationships, with the independent clauses more important than the dependent clauses. For example, consider the following paragraphs from an advertisement run by the Mobil Oil Company in its campaign to get the public to influence Congress to grant more offshore oil leases to the major producers:

Economic obstacles: It defies all logic to raise the price of already-discovered oil through taxes, while denying the oil companies a share of the resulting revenues. The producers will be forced to sell oil from existing wells at far below its replacement cost. Ignored is the fact that today's petroleum exploration and development is growing ever more costly because of the need to explore in remote frontier areas like Alaska or in deep water offshore, and to resort to expensive recovery methods to squeeze more oil from reservoirs.

12. Richard M. Weaver, *Op. Cit,* p. 120. For a discussion of the Platonic idealism and political conservatism underlying Weaver's conception of rhetoric, see Richard L. Johannesen, Rennard Strickland, and Ralph T. Eubanks, "Richard M. Weaver on the Nature of Rhetoric," in Johannesen, ed., *Contemporary Theories of Rhetoric* (New York: Harper & Row, 1971). pp. 180–195.

13. Weaver, p. 121

14. Ibid.

How long could any businessman stay in business if he must sell his inventory at prices substantially lower than he will have to pay to restock?

What America has, in short, is a "Catch 22" policy toward developing its oil and gas resources. The President indicates we need to develop more domestic energy. The U.S. Geological Survey says the oil and gas is probably there. The oil companies want to look for it. But the government not only is making it harder and harder to explore the most promising offshore locations but insists on keeping price controls which deny the industry the needed capital. And then along come those who tell us the oil companies can't do the job of increasing domestic supply. How's that for a self-fulfilling prophecy?

We urge that the national energy debate focus on the paramount issue: development vs. non-development of U.S. energy supplies. We believe that the social and economic consequences of development are being grossly overestimated by many in Washington and that, as subsequent messages in this series will point out, the social and economic consequences of non-development are being grossly underestimated.[15]

Examine each complex sentence. Look at the first sentence. The clause stating the principle is independent—it can stand alone. The dependent clause (". . . while denying . . .") states the minor message elements. The independent material is higher on the source's ladder of values than the dependent material. It is probably more important to Mobil corporate management that people realize the undesirability of imposing taxes to raise prices on oil already discovered than that profits be questioned. Most people realize that Mobil has a vested interest in getting a share of profits from high-priced oil. Identify some of the other complex sentences in the excerpt and see if Weaver's prediction doesn't hold true. The major premise being sold in a complex sentence is usually the one stated in the independent clause; the minor premise is usually stated in the dependent clause.

Remember what Weaver said about the use of the simple sentence to depict "the world as a conglomerate" in which certain facts were to be highlighted against a rather flat background? Note what Mobil does in the second paragraph. With one exception, all the sentences of that paragraph are simple. The tactic is to rattle off a series of assertions as if they were absolute truths. This rat-tat-tat style is convincing.

Weaver says that the compound sentence sets things either in balance (for example, "He ran, and he ran fast") or in opposition (for example, "He ran, and she walked"). It expresses some kind of tension—whether resolved or unresolved. Weaver says it "conveys that completeness and symmetry which the world ought to have, and which we manage to get, in some measure, into our most satisfactory explanations of it."[16] Persuaders who use this sentence type see the world divided into polar opposites or similarities—totally against one another or in concert with one another. The union leader, for example, says, "You are either against us, or you are with us!" and thus oversimplifies a complex world by using the compound sentence.

---

15. *1977 Mobil Current Energy Series #3* (New York: Mobil Oil Corporation, 1977) reprinted in *The Chicago Tribune*, July 28, 1977, Section 1, p. 8.

16. Weaver, p. 127.

For example, consider the following sentences from a *New York Times* story about the revitalized Ku Klux Klan. Notice the difference in sentence structure between the paragraphs written by the reporter, Wendall Rawls, and the sentence that is quoted from an FBI agent.

> Cullman Ala., Sept. 26. Hidden in the hills of Northern Alabama, a small contingent of Ku Klux Klansmen, and a woman, are training to become commandos prepared to provide security at Klan rallies and to kill black people in "the race war that's coming," their leader says.... FBI officials in Birmingham acknowledge that they are watching the activities of this Klan group. "Of all the Klan groups, this is the most unpredictable," an agent said, "and I guess that would make them potentially the most dangerous."[17]

The reporter used the complex sentence and thus set up a hierarchy of importance to be attached to the various parts of his sentence. The independent elements contain the heart of the story—that KKK members are training to kill blacks. The less important parts are dependent and rank lower on the hierarchy of importance—that the training is being done in hiding or that the group has one woman member, for example. The FBI agent, using the compound sentence, simplifies the world and sets things in balance by linking the problem of unpredictability to the idea of possibly dangerous actions that the group could take. Unpredictability also makes the group difficult to defend against. This is a part of the problem that the agent's compound sentence focuses on. Later in the story a Mr. Hadley, who is the Imperial Klaliff or vice-president of the Klan group, is also quoted. Note that he uses the simple sentence.

> The 35 year old sheet metal worker said he is not active in the unit because he is recovering from back surgery and is receiving a disability pension. "I have a lot of time to think and plan for the white race," he said.[18]

The world is indeed simple to Mr. Hadley, and he sees himself and his group as the cause of many future actions that he believes will benefit his race. So in this example we can see all three kinds of sentences operating, and we can speculate about the kind of person who frames these sentences.

Weaver also had some observations about types of words. For example, nouns, since they are thought of as words for things and as labels for naming, are often reacted to as *if they were the things they name*. They "express things whose being is completed, not whose being is in process, or whose being depends upon some other being."[19] Thus when someone calls a policeman a pig, he makes the policeman into an object—a thing. It is easy to spit on a pig. The pig is an object; the policeman is a person with a family and feelings. One of the functions of a noun is to label something as we want it to be. Looking at persuaders' nouns may

---

17. Wendell Rawls Jr., "Klan Group in Alabama Training for 'Race War'," *The New York Times*, September 28, 1980.

18. *Ibid.*

19. Weaver, p. 128.

clue us as to their perception of things. They may reveal what the persuader intends to do about those things. When persuaders reduce persons to things or objects, they do it for a reason. They indicate that the persuader wishes to deal with them as things and not as people (see Chapter 2).

The function of an adjective is to add to the noun, to make it special. To Weaver, adjectives are second-class citizens. He called them "question-begging" and said that they showed an uncertain persuader. If you have to modify a noun, Weaver would say you are not certain about the noun. In Weaver's opinion, the only adjectives that are not uncertain are *dialectical* (good and bad, hot and cold, light and dark). Examination of adjectives used by persuaders may reveal what they are uncertain about, and what they see in opposition to what.

The adverb, to Weaver, is "a word of judgment."[20] Unlike the adjective, it represents a community judgment—one with which others can agree and which reflects what the persuader thinks the audience believes. For example, adverbs like surely, certainly, or probably suggest agreement. When persuaders say, "Surely we all know and believe that thus-and-such is so," they suggest that the audience agrees with them.

An advertisement for the 1981 Ford Escort (a newly introduced model), promised that it had Sure-Footed Handling and a Smooth Comfortable Ride. Why did the advertiser choose these question-begging adjectives? Could the choice be related to customer fears about the effects of the front-wheel drive, an innovation for Ford in 1981? In any case, the adjectives suggest some uncertainty about how customers will evaluate the Escort's ride and maneuverability.

An interesting footnote on word choice comes from research done by the Family Television Research Program at Yale University. The researchers there found that heavy TV watchers (defined as watching three hours of TV per day or more) among children were affected in four ways in their language use:

1. They used fewer adjectives.
2. They used shorter sentences.
3. They used fewer adverbs.
4. They used simpler sentences.

Light TV users (defined as one hour per day or less) used more advanced vocabularies and spoke in more complete sentences than did the heavy TV watchers.[21]

Syntax as an Analytical Tool

Another functional characteristic of language is revealed in the way words are ordered in a sentence. The persuadee can take note of persuaders' syntax and be alert to the way in which they order their thoughts.

20. Weaver, pp. 129–130.

21. Marilyn Preston, "On TV," *The Chicago Tribune*, May 14, 1981, Sec. 1, p. 15. The researchers did frequency counts of the usage in the normal everyday speech of various children and correlated this with hours of television watched per day.

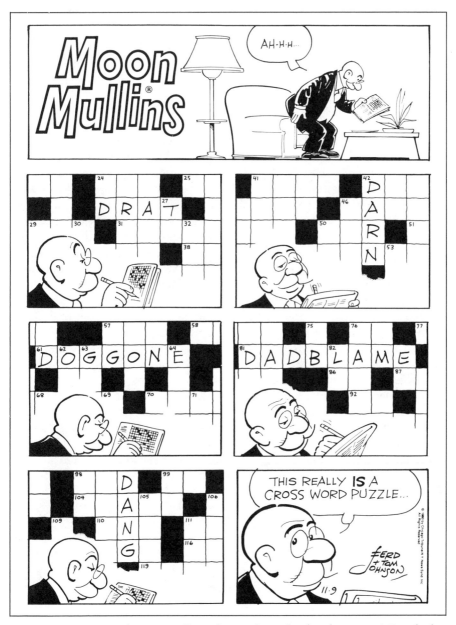

Figure 3.2. How might Moon Mullins' adjectives be used to beg the question? How do they indicate uncertainty? (Reprinted by permission of Tribune Company Syndicate, Inc.)

For example, suppose a persuader said, "There is no greater hypocrite than the dedicated environmentalist who preaches clean air and drives home in a 350-horsepower gas guzzler!" The word order of the sentence alerts us to the theme: hypocrisy. However, we are left wondering until the last phrase why hypocrisy is involved; then the large car is revealed. The persuader could as easily have said,

"Environmentalists who own 350-horsepower gas guzzlers while they preach clean air are the kind of hypocrites we don't need to have around!" The second version lacks the drama of the first. It does not get the listener involved with the task of trying to discover the cause of the hypocrisy. It has a preachy quality about it—as if the persuader knows he is right. It may reveal a certain closed-mindedness or dogmatism about the persuader.

Consider the following sentence from an editorial by Robert Shrum of *New Times* magazine. Shrum was lamenting the swing to conservatism that seemed to be occurring in the late 1980s. "The House has approved the neutron bomb, the ultimate weapon of a dehumanized capitalism; it will kill people but leave the real property standing."[22] The word order here also signifies something about its author. His first clause stands as an indictment of the House of Representatives. His second phrase elaborates upon the indictment, expanding on it in highly accusatory terms. His last clause explains his indictment. It gives us his reasoning for making the judgment. The order of the argument reveals a deductive thinker waiting until the conclusion to offer his specific pieces of evidence. He tends to move from the general to the specific. That persuasive syntax is quite different from the following copy from an advertisement for a Rita Coolidge album: "Her clear voice, perfect pitch, and instinctive emotional delivery takes the greats and makes them greater. Because Rita was born to sing." The persuader could have reversed the order here, beginning with the general conclusion that Rita was "born to sing" and then giving us the reasons with something like "and you will know it when you hear her clear voice, her . . ." but this style is inductive and assumes that the reader wants to think the same way.

A number of questions can be asked about a persuasive message if the receiver takes a few minutes to examine the syntax of the proposition. Why didn't the persuader do it differently? Does the word order suggest anything about a view of the world? of the audience? Does it indicate a certainty about judgments? Is the audience lured into the sentence? Does the source let receivers do a search for meaning and relationships? These questions and others can tell us how the message is working—that is, what its functions are.

Suppose you are talking to someone on the telephone. The person says to you "I know you're busy, so I'll make just one more point before I let you go. You see, in regard to. . . ." What function is served by beginning the sentence with the acknowledgment of how busy you supposedly are? Is it meant as a description of the person's consideration for your busy schedule or is it just the opposite—the person being concerned about his or her own busy schedule? What else might it mean?

Ambiguity as a Functional Device of Style

Another element in style is the degree to which the words are specific or ambiguous. At first thought, the most effective persuasion ought to be that which is simplest. Yet if you think about it a little longer, and especially if you think about the fact that no two people will ever see the world in exactly the same way,

---

22. Robert Shrum, "Party Lines," *New Times*, July 22, 1977, p. 4.

the simple might not be best. Let us suppose that I were trying to persuade you to buy a certain kind of automobile. If I told you the reason why *I* thought you should buy the car, I might antagonize you. I would never be able to really touch the key strings of motivation that might cause you to actually make the purchase. For example, suppose I said that the car was dependable and sturdy in construction. If the key motivation for you is sex appeal—how the car symbolizes potent sexuality, for example—I would lose the sale. Dependability and sturdiness seem more tied to vehicles like tractors, Jeeps, or family station wagons than to sexy sports models or hatchbacks. A better strategy for me would be to be less specific. The strategy should let you sell yourself on the sexy body style, color, or interior design. In other words, by being ambiguous I allow you to enter into the persuasive process. I let you define the terms (and a good salesperson listens carefully to customers and reinforces their statements). Furthermore, the same strategy will work with diverse sets of people if the message is ambiguous enough. Most politicians are judged by media reporters as being fuzzy on the issues at one time or another. Perhaps they are just being ambiguous in hope of persuading as many of their constituents as possible and alienating as few as possible. Although this may not result in the most intelligent votes or in the best person being elected, it probably does result in more winning and less losing for the skillful politician—which gives us another reason for being responsible persuadees.

Tools for the Semantic Axis

There are several ways in which persuaders can create persuasive messages. One way is *semantically*. Here the persuader carefully chooses words that can be interpreted in many ways, often in contradictory ways, depending on the receivers. For example, a politician favors "responsibility in taxation and the education of our youngsters." Those who think teachers have been underpaid and need substantial raises could hear this as a call for *spending* tax dollars. Those of a reverse view could as easily interpret the statement as saying that educational spending needs to be *cut*. There are other possible interpretations. The key word that increases the ambiguity is "responsibility." It sets up the rest of the sentence. Thus, not only can ambiguity operate on the functional level. It can also operate semantically, as we shall see.

Take the words fiscal responsibility, which were in vogue during the budget-cutting 1980s. Many politicians claimed that they were for "fiscal responsibility"—but what did that mean? To some politicians responsibility meant cutting taxes on corporations to allow for capital investments in machinery to modernize industry. They felt that American industry was becoming old-fashioned and was being outpaced by the Japanese. To them, it would be irresponsible not to encourage corporate tax cuts. To others, fiscal responsibility meant that the government would have to run in the black—no more deficit spending. Still others felt that fiscal responsibility meant controlling the growth of the money supply. Probably, some politicians embraced all these definitions. Besides, which of them would dare take a position *opposing* "responsibility"? The words fiscal responsibility derived their persuasive power not from their specificity but from their ambiguity, which allowed many interpretations. In this sense the words were rich with meaning.

The term black power, which emerged in the late 1960s as part of the Civil Rights Movement, relied on semantic ambiguity. The key word there was power—what kind of power? Economic? Political? Social? There could be many interpretations. In its time, the term was striking in its use of the word black, a term that the National Association for the Advancement of Colored People (NAACP) had been fighting for years. The group hated "black." Given that context, use of the term by the black militants rejected the leadership of existing groups. The term black power was unsettling and thus attracted attention.

Another way that persuaders can create ambiguity semantically is by paradox or by altering such things as syntax or sentence/phrase/clause structure to startle the receiver. Take the term moral decay. It refers to the decay of morals, but by using the word moral as the first word in the pair, meaning grows. We respond to "moral decay" in the same way we respond to tooth decay. We recall the ads showing microscopic views of bacteria squirming around on teeth, the social rejection when we forget to brush, and so forth. The term also gains meaning because a positively loaded word—moral—is paired with a negatively loaded word—decay. This plus/minus conflict is tension-producing and thus involves the persuadee emotionally. The words child pornography operate in a similar way. The plus of the first word strikes the minus of the second word and creates tension, meaning, and ambiguity. Is it pornography involving children or aimed at children or what?

The number of syllables in the words in a phrase can create a kind of rhythm that also affects our responses to the term. For example, they could have named Virginia Slims the Sue Thins or the Betty Slims, but the 4:1 syllable ratio of the words gives a kind of image to the product name that the 1:1 or 2:1 options do not. Furthermore, the state of Virginia is a prime growing place for tobacco. Rebecca Slims would have come closer. Hildegarde Slims would have flopped—structural and semantic dimensions interact with one another.

In addition to these dimensions of the semantic axis, other approaches are being suggested. General semanticists (Chapter 2) try to develop tactics for increasing semantic meaning by asking people to add more descriptive qualities to their language. For example, the semanticists recommend that instead of saying "car" you ought to say "station wagon" or better yet "blue Ford station wagon" or even better "1980 blue Ford Country Squire station wagon with a dent in the left front fender." Thus, the semanticists argue, you can sanitize language by reducing ambiguity. If ambiguity persuades, however, this tactic may not have persuasive impact.

Kenneth Burke, in his book *A Grammar of Motives*, suggests a better tool.[23] The title of his book gives a clue to his purpose: He wants to present a set of terms or a grammar for identifying motives. Burke should be helpful to us. He calls his

---

23. Kenneth Burke, *A Grammar of Motives* (Cleveland: Meridian Books, 1962). See the introduction especially, pp. xvii–xxv.

device the **dramatic pentad.** It is a device for analyzing language usage and also for developing persuasive language strategy on the semantic level. Burke believes that when we communicate/persuade we choose words because of their dramatic potential. Different individuals find different elements in the drama more potent than others. Some may believe that great people affect the outcome of events; when persuading, such persons will mention examples of individual effort winning the day. Burke says their persuasion is based in the *agent* or actor. For other persons, the setting or *scene* may be the motivating element. They will choose scenic words and phrases to persuade. Let us look at Burke's pentad in more detail.

The Dramatic Pentad

The basic premise put forth by Burke is that human beings see the world in terms of drama. Each person focuses on one of these terms as most important or as most essential to him or her. This focus is seen in how each of us talks about the world. We can infer the world view of persuaders from the focus they take. There are five elements of drama that Burke says are comprehensive and include all the possible parts of dramatic action:

Scene—or place where action occurs (perhaps the persuasive situation). Persons who focus on the scene are *materialists.* They believe that changing the scene or environment will change people. They would support urban renewal, for example.

Act—or the action that occurs. Persons who focus on the act are *realists.* They process and record information and believe that a mixture of causes directs human affairs.

Agent—or the actor who acts out the action or plot. Persons who focus on the agent are *idealists.* They believe that people control their own destiny. Persuaders who focus on the agent would support self-help programs.

Agency—or the tool the actor uses to accomplish his ends. Persons who focus on the agency are *pragmatists.* They search for the most speedy and most immediately practical solutions. They might support gas rationing, for example.

Purpose—or the reason why people do what they do. Persons who focus on purpose are *mystics,* according to Burke. They believe a power or focus beyond them directs human destiny.

Consider the following description of a dramatic situation:

A young man and a young woman are standing in front of an altar rail in a church. They are dressed for the sacrament of marriage (he in tuxedo, she in a white dress). A young and handsome minister is preparing to conduct the "Repeat after me . . ." portion of the service, when he suddenly turns from the altar rail, walks swiftly back to the altar itself, takes down a massive brass candlestick, and bludgeons the bride to death as the groom smiles.

Which element of this drama is most intriguing to you? The tension between the act of murder and the setting of a church? The character of the young minister? The use of a holy object to kill? The reason why the groom does nothing to stop the murder and even smiles about it? Burke would argue that your interest in one particular element over others may reflect how you see the world operating— what you think prompts action and gives meaning. Further, Burke would predict that you would choose to talk about the world according to what struck you as most important; your words would reflect your preference. If you thought that people control their own destiny, you would focus on the agent. If you felt that circumstances compelled action, you would focus on the scene. If you felt that high principles and ideals carried even weak people through trying times, you would focus on the purpose.

Persuaders tend to center their topic on one of the elements of the pentad. They choose their evidence in relation to this concept, and they devise metaphors drawn from it. Persuadees can use this tendency to predict what persuaders are likely to say and do. Further, knowing people's *key terms* helps us analyze their weak spots if we want to persuade them. Of course, persuaders may draw on the other elements, but they emphasize only one—that is Burke's proposition. Thus, if you are interested in the agent you react differently from someone whose focus is on the act, and you will each choose different language to discuss the same problem.

Consider the following:

> Over the past few years the image of politics that has taken shape for me is that of an immense journey—the panorama of an endless wagon train, an enormous trek, a multitudinous processing of people larger and more confused than any of the primitive folk migrations.
>
> There—ahead—lies the crest of the ridge, and beyond it perhaps the plateau or the sunlit valley—or danger. The procession stretches out for endless miles, making its way up the tangled slopes through strange new country. . . .
>
> Up there, at the head of the advance column, the leaders quarrel bitterly among themselves, as do the people behind. From their heights they have a wider view of the horizon.[24]

The scenic quality of the quotation is clear. The author has a vision of a setting and a background. What is important is the panorama—the view from the ridge—the scene. The author sees the setting as powerful, drawing people and leaders on, forcing them onward, even in ignorance of what lies ahead.

Other persons may see the world as being motivated in a different way. For example, consider the words of the following letter I recently received from an organization called the Wilderness Society:

---

24. Theodore H. White, *The Making of the President: 1964* (New York: Atheneum, 1966), p. v.

Dear Friend,

"Like putting a fox in charge of a henhouse."

That's how John Oakes of *The New York Times* referred to President Reagan's nomination of James Watt as Secretary of Interior.

We couldn't agree more.

And that is why we at *The Wilderness Society* have felt compelled to establish a special task force—called WILDERNESS WATCH—to monitor every policy, every critical decision, every speech and appearance before Congress, every important action made by Secretary Watt to duly determine just how those actions will affect the public lands, wilderness and wildlife we all cherish. . . . Though he has been in office only about 100 days, Mr. Watt has already:

—Announced plans to push ahead with oil and gas exploration and hard-rock mining in units of the National Wilderness System, stating, "No federal area is sacred, and all acreage will be considered for possible development of its natural resources";

—Reported his intention to search for oil in National Wildlife Refuges;

—Encouraged private concessioners to take over operations of campgrounds and entrance stations in Yosemite National Park, work traditionally handled by Park Service employees;

—Enunciated plans to promote mineral exploration in statutory wilderness areas; and

—Suggested in the face of ever-rising travel costs, that the National Park Service should divest itself of such important urban parks as Gateway National Recreation Area in New York and New Jersey, San Francisco's Golden Gate Park, and the Santa Monica National Recreation Area near Los Angeles.[25]

The letter then went on to describe Secretary Watts's career as a legal advisor to business groups and mining and oil interests and concluded by announcing the addition of Gaylord Nelson as its new chairman:

The Wilderness Society is also excited about the addition to its staff of Gaylord Nelson, the former governor of Wisconsin and for the past 18 years a distinguished Senator from Wisconsin. Gaylord will serve as full-time Chairman of the Society. His record of environmental accomplishments is legend. He founded Earth Day in 1970. He introduced the first legislation to control strip-mining. He was the Senate's principal co-author of the Wild and Scenic Rivers Act. He helped lead the long, bittersweet fight for the Alaska Lands Bill through Congress. The Society is fortunate to have a man of Gaylord's ability and stature.

Gaylord Nelson, Joe Fisher, and the Society's staff stand ready to blow the whistle if James Watt moves to turn back the clock on conservation.[26]

They made their final pitch for donations:

Won't you please consider joining us in our important work?

---

25. Correspondence from The Wilderness Society, 1901 Pennsylvania Avenue, Washington, D.C., September 1981.

26. *Ibid.*

Your $20 membership fee is tax deductible, and it will bring you *The Living Wilderness*, our handsome quarterly magazine. Through its beautiful color photography you will explore our nation's wilderness areas and public lands in all their diversity. You'll be kept up-to-date on our Economic Policy Department's findings, and you will help ensure that our country's needs are not ill-served by a Secretary of the Interior who says his only quarrel is with environmental extremists—which he defines as anyone who would "deny economic development on public lands.[27]

"Scenic pressures" and "demands" do not move the world that the Wilderness Society perceives. "Powerful agents" do, and only if individuals (other agents or counteragents) work together, can the environmental exploitation be stopped. Look at the letter carefully. Notice how much credit for the problems is attributed to one man. Anyone who has ever worked in government will tell you that although high-ranking political figures have great power, no agent can act very effectively alone. He or she will need the help of staff, support of the person who appointed him or her, party support, and even the compliance of many members of the opposition. But in this case, the Wilderness Society wants to prompt individual donations. What better way to persuade than to suggest that a single individual is doing many questionable things, and hence the world is motivated by agent. If single individuals can cause problems, single individuals can solve them by joining.

Did the direct mail pitch work? Well, I sent them the twenty bucks, even though I was initially set against it, if only because of the envelope, which pictures Secretary Watt (Figure 3.3) with a headline that announces "This Man Must Be Watched!"

The same sort of analysis can be done with the act and the agency as keys. A persuader who was convinced that means were more important than ends might be an agency-oriented persuader. Phone company persuaders often focus on the means (long distance) over scenes (home). For example, they advertise that "Long Distance Is the Next Best Thing to Being There." Or they urge you to "Reach Out and Touch Someone," combining the idea of transcending distance with the appeal of touching a loved one. An act-oriented persuader would probably describe an action that has taken place and then imply that another action can remedy or improve the situation. Take, for instance, this ad copy: "Overdone by the sun? When the sun burns you up and makes you sizzle, when you're overdone by the sun, stop sunburn pain fast with Solarcaine. . . ."

The dramatic pentad of Kenneth Burke can be used in these ways—to discover the persuasive focus and hence the underlying beliefs or key elements of an advocate. It can also be used to discover and to label a persuader's characteristic symbols and rituals. When we look at what persuaders say and at how they use language (what kinds of words they use frequently), their view of the world and their view of human motivation become clear. Burke described such analysis, when done with literature, as the use of *associational clusters*. The word or symbol clusters serve as benchmarks to the persuader's own beliefs and agendas

---

27. *Ibid.*

Figure 3.3. What responses does this photograph arouse in you? Would you contribute to the appeal inside the envelope? (Courtesy The Wilderness Society)

for following through on those beliefs. As receivers, we need to isolate such clusters whenever possible before responding to the persuasive appeals that surround them. If we agree with the persuader's clusters or *key terms* (another of Burke's names for symbolic preferences) and see the world as the persuader does, we can follow his or her advice. If we find that the view of the persuader doesn't match up to our own, we can reject, or question, or investigate it further, depending on circumstances.

Tools for the Thematic Axis

The thematic axis of language refers to a quality that is really neither functional nor semantic. It is not concerned with word order or emotional responses to particular words or to the referent for particular words. Rather, it refers to the *texture* of the language. A classic example is shown when we try to rewrite Lincoln's Gettysburg Address—"Eighty-seven years ago the signers of the Declaration of Independence started a new country designed to have liberty and equality for everyone. . . ." We find a semantic correspondence between this set of words and Lincoln's version, but there are obvious thematic differences.

Sometimes thematic differences come from a repeated sound. (Burke argues, for example, that his childhood prayer: "God love me/Guard me in sleep/Guide me to Thee" relies on a G—d or "God" form.) Sound repetition is one of the textural qualities of language. *Onomatopoeia* (or phonetic sounds that resemble their referents—for example, "swish" or "rustle") is another example. We will now look at three thematic or textural tools in some detail: (1) the use of motifs and metaphors, (2) the development of God and Devil terms, and (3) the pragmatic versus the unifying style. Beyond these, there are other tools you may want to explore.

Motifs and Metaphors

Persuaders can establish a great deal of their message by setting the mood for the persuadees. They can depict a setting appropriate for the message by repeatedly using certain sounds and images. Michael Osborn has made a study of the use of archetypal metaphors (or universal and primal images consistent within and even across cultures), in particular the light/dark comparison. He maintains that, traditionally, we identify light with the sun, warmth, growth, comfort, and so on; while we see dark associated with mystery, night, cold, and other uncomfortable and troubling things. Osborn points out that persuaders often use repeated reference to this dichotomy.[28] John F. Kennedy, in his Inaugural Address, used this archetypal metaphor when he talked about passing a torch from one generation to another and predicting that the light from this symbolic torch could illuminate the world for freedom—the light was viewed as good, warm, friendly, and virtuous. Elsewhere the world was filled with darkness and poverty.

There are other archetypal metaphors. For example, the power of the sea and the life-giving power of water may explain the holy or magical powers that are given to water (for example, the fountain of youth or baptism). Mircea Eliade is convinced that there is an archetypal metaphor of "the center." We repeatedly look for a central point—a symbolic navel for our world. For some groups it is a specific place (Mecca for Moslems, Munich for Nazism, Jerusalem for Jews and Christians).[29] For some students, a certain place on campus may be the symbolic center—their dorm room, the student center, or a fraternity house. During the 1960s and 1970s many campuses had "free speech areas" where speeches protesting the draft, the Vietnam War, racism, and so on could be made. These served as symbolic centers for some students. The White House is a sacred center for some persons. There can be defiled centers as well. For example, to antiwar activist Abbie Hoffman, the Pentagon was such a defiled center. Consider his trial testimony in regard to his arrest for trying to exorcize the Pentagon:[30]

ABBIE: I said that the Pentagon was a five-sided evil symbol in most religions and that it might be possible to approach this from a religious perspective. If we got large numbers of people to surround the Pentagon, we could exorcize it of its evil spirits.

MR. WEINGLASS: (Hoffman's attorney): Prior to the date of the demonstration which is October, did you go to the Pentagon?

ABBIE: Yes. I went about a week or two before with one of my close brothers, Martin Carey, a poster maker, and we measured the Pentagon, the two of us, to see how many people would fit around it. We only had

---

28. Michael Osborn, "Archetypal Metaphor in Rhetoric: The Light-Dark Family," *Quarterly Journal of Speech*, Vol. 53 (April 1967), pp. 115–126.

29. Mircea Eliade, *The Myth of the Eternal Return* (Princeton, New Jersey. Princeton University Press, 1971).

30. Chicago Seven trial testimony as reported in *Counterculture and Revolution*, ed. David Horowitz et al. (New York: Random House, 1972), p. 34.

to do one side because it is just multiplied by five. We got arrested. It's illegal to measure the Pentagon. I didn't know it up to that point. When we were arrested they asked us what we were doing. We said it was to measure the Pentagon and we wanted a permit to raise it 300 feet in the air, and they said, "How about 10?" So we said "O.K." . . . We also introduced a drug called *lace* which, when you squirted it at the policemen made them take their clothes off and make love—a very potent drug.

Most archetypal metaphors, like those described above, relate to life experiences that all people—primitive as well as modern—can relate to. The light/dark metaphor probably emerged eons ago from a fear of the unseen things that lurked in the darkness of night and the lessening of fears that came with light. The power of the water metaphor probably relates to water's cleansing abilities as well as its life-giving and life-sustaining powers. What might be some other universal experiences that humans share from culture to culture and from age to age? When you discover them, you will see that they are often used in advertising and political persuasion, and that perhaps even you may use them in your interpersonal encounters as you try to persuade others.

God and Devil Terms

Another thematic or textural characteristic of style—often used in persuasion—is the development of families of terms. Persuaders, like the rest of us, like to see the world as divided into neat categories. They also use these categories to try to persuade others and are often successful. One of these category sets is the creation of God terms and Devil terms, as noted by Richard Weaver.[31] Weaver said that terms or labels are really only parts of propositions. However, they are often linked with other terms or labels to shape a message or a persuasive sense. He defines "God term" as an expression "about which all other expressions are ranked as subordinate and serving dominations and powers. Its force imparts to the others their lesser degree of force. . . ."[32] Weaver sees a God term as an unchallenged term that demands sacrifice or obedience in its name. He uses three terms as examples of God terms: progress, fact, and science. Though these were God terms for the 1950s when Weaver wrote, their force has changed. We do not now attach high positive values to "progress"—counterterms have identified it with waste, war, pollution, and a series of other ills. Science has lost some of its credibility, for science has produced, along with constructive marvels, nuclear weapons and technology that may destroy the earth through pollution.

During the 1970s a "counterculture," triggered by the Vietnam War, developed across the country. This movement had its God and Devil terms, also. It was good to be an "individual," to "do your own thing," and to have "an alternative lifestyle."

---

31. Weaver, *op. cit.*, pp. 211, 212, and 214.

32. Weaver, p. 211.

How frustration affects productivity in your business.

Ever get that sinking feeling? It's a feeling any conscientious executive might experience, when he or she seems overwhelmed by a sea of paperwork.

Over a million tons of paper pass through American offices every day. That much paperwork can actually *hinder* the timely flow of vital business information.

Frustrating, to say the least. And, at A.B.Dick, we know that simple, human frustration can be a real deterrent to office productivity.

So we serve customers throughout the world with a broad line of automated office products and systems—to help *stem* the tide of paperwork. *Before* it can affect productivity.

A.B.Dick believes *all* your office systems should work like this, to help you rise *above* frustration.

In fact, that's the philosophy behind every piece of equipment we make at A.B.Dick.

Word processors. Record-processing systems. Ink-jet printing systems. Plain-paper copiers. Off-set printing equipment. Stencil and spirit duplicators. Plus accessories, supplies and paper.

We feel machines are here to serve people. Not the other way around.

So we design office products and systems that put human factors first.

From keyboards to displays, we make sure every part, every piece of A.B.Dick equipment is in tune with the skills and sensibilities of the people who will use it.

How far should an operator's hands have to reach? Where should the display be positioned for the most accurate reading? What type of screen is easiest on the eyes?

We're careful to build in time- and cost-saving benefits. But always on a human scale.

And we back them up with A.B.Dick's highly responsive customer service and training staff, worldwide.

At A.B.Dick, we won't let frustration get you in over your head.

For your free copy of our new report, "Frustration in the Workplace: Its Effect on Productivity," prepared by Towers, Perrin, Forster & Crosby (available in English, French, German and Spanish versions), write: A.B.Dick Company, Dept. 325-COR, 5700 West Touhy Avenue, Chicago, IL 60648.

AB DICK.

We're putting frustration out of business.

Figure 3.4. The A. B. Dick Company uses the idea of the whirlwind, which may be a universal or archetypical metaphor, to persuade firms to buy its products. The experience of being overwhelmed by responsibilities and details is also common and adds to the appeal. (Used courtesy A.B. Dick Company, Chicago, Illinois.)

On the other hand, it was highly negative to be associated with the "Establishment," which was run by the "military/industrial complex" which "ripped off" common people and "exploited" natural resources and people's lives as well. Though some of these God and Devil terms persist, many have faded, and some have disappeared altogether. The Human Potential Movement of the 1970s was an elite subculture of people who went to various seminars and "growth centers" and studied and practiced various kinds of "therapies." They also developed their set of God and Devil terms—"acceptance," "letting go," "owning your feelings," "going with the flow," and being "open" became some of the God terms. People who had "agendas" or who were "closed" or who were "manipulative" were bad. Interestingly, in the opening of the 1980s it seemed to be perfectly all right and maybe even commendable to have "agendas" or to be "closed" in order to "manipulate" things to one's own advantage. What are the God and Devil terms of your or other subcultures? Explore the possibilities, for they will alert you to potential persuasive appeals that you might use in your own persuasion. More important, they are most likely being used on you day in and day out.

Weaver points out that sometimes certain negative terms can be reversed in connotation and can become neutral or even positive.[33] Take, for example, the expression "wasted" or "getting wasted," which in the early 1980s often referred to getting drunk or smoked up. Its use during the 1970s referred to killing Viet Cong or others perceived to be the enemy during the Vietnam War. Thus a Marine sergeant might report how he had "wasted" an entire "gook village." Are there any such terms in vogue today? Search the language used in the worlds of advertising and politics. In all likelihood you will find several reversed connotations.

Weaver described other kinds of terms that he called the charismatic terms. He described them as "... terms of considerable potency whose referents it is virtually impossible to discover.... Their meaning seems inexplicable unless we accept the hypothesis that their content proceeds out of a popular will that they *shall* mean something.[34] His example is the word freedom, which has no apparent concrete referent but which seems, even thirty-five years after Weaver used it, to have considerable potency for many people. For example, in the early 1980s, a broad-based union movement in Communist Poland emerged, calling itself the "Solidarity Movement." It drew tens of millions of members and attracted worldwide attention and admiration. The word "solidarity" was soon picked up and used in other countries because of its charisma. Even when martial law was declared, and Solidarity's leaders were jailed, and the movement was outlawed, it continued to flourish in Poland and the word retained its charismatic quality there and elsewhere in the world. In fact, it became a kind of universal name for the drive to speak up and be free. In the United States, the old union organizers' song *Solidarity Forever* began to be sung and the word Solidarity was seen on posters even at nonunion activities. In Chicago, where so many Poles emigrated, local radio and television stations had the word printed on buttons so people could show their support for the movement. The word Solidarity certainly had charismatic power. "Vigor" was another such charismatic term during the years of the Kennedy Administration. It was probably related to the penchant the Kennedy brothers had for physical activities like touch football, skiing, and sailing. "Power"

---

33. Weaver, pp. 224–226.

34. Weaver, p. 230.

was such a charismatic term in the 1970s, and we saw Black Power, Student Power, Gay Power, Red Power, Chicano Power, and even Gray Power for the retired people.

The development of sets of words with high positive or negative value-loadings for their user—God and Devil terms—is one of the tactics used by persuaders to lend texture or a thematic quality to their discourse. Things seem to be consistent and to "go" with one another. As a persuadee you can learn much from identifying persuaders' sets of positive and negative terms, for they signal the kinds of relationships they see operating in the world—what they see in opposition to what.

Pragmatic versus Unifying Style

A final characteristic that builds a thematic wholeness or gives a kind of texture to persuasion is the reliance of a persuader on one of two kinds of styles—the **pragmatic style** or the **unifying style**.[35] These styles can be thought of as signifying two separate strategies; and persuaders can use the tactics of either strategy, or they can combine the two extremes.

Pragmatic persuaders usually find it necessary to convince listeners who do not necessarily support their position. As a result, they must try to change minds, as opposed to reinforcing beliefs, and must choose appropriate tactics. The unifying persuaders are faced with a much more comfortable position. They talk to people who, in large measure, already believe what is going to be said. They do not need to change minds; they only need to reinforce beliefs—to whip up enthusiasm and dedication or to give encouragement. These two styles demonstrate two opposing situations, and they describe the problems facing the persuader in these situations. The problems for pragmatic persuaders are very practical—they must change opinion before they can expect action. Unifying persuaders can be much more idealistic—they can usually afford to be more bombastic without offending the audience. These persuaders can be more emotional and less objective than the persuader faced with a questioning audience. What are the stylistic devices of these extremes?

The unifying persuader can afford to be idealistic and will focus on the then-and-there—on the past or on the future, when things were ideal or when they can become ideal. The position of these persuaders is that things look better in the future, particularly if we compare them with the present. Since the audience will fill in the blanks, language choice can be abstract. It is usually poetic and filled with imagery; these attributes (imagery and abstractness) excite the imagination of the audience. Though there may be little that is intellectually stimulating (or that requires careful logical examination) about what unifying persuaders say, there is much that is emotionally stimulating to the audience. The words and images offered by such persuaders are precisely the words listeners believe they would have said if they were talking. The unifying persuader is thus the mouthpiece or sounding board for the entire group, providing them with the cues, but

---

35. For examples of speeches illustrating these styles, see Wil Linkugel, Ron R. Allen, and Richard L. Johannesen, eds., *Contemporary American Speeches* (Prospect Heights, Illinois: Waveland Press, 1981).

not the details, of the message. The audience can participate with the persuaders in the creation of the message; in fact, audiences sometimes participate actively by yelling encouragement to unifying persuaders or by repeating shibboleths to underscore their words—"Right on" or "Amen, Brother" or "Tell it like it is."

Pragmatic persuaders, because they must win an audience, cannot afford to take the risk of appealing to abstract ideals. They must be concrete, focusing on facts instead of images, emphasizing that which cannot be disputed or interpreted so easily. They will not try to depict an ideal situation in subjective there-and-then terms. Instead they will have to focus on real aspects of immediate problems familiar to the audience—problems of the here-and-now, which are realistic, not idealistic. Their orientation is toward the present instead of the future. Since pragmatic persuaders are forced into a position where they must be concrete and realistic, their language is concrete and prosaic. Lofty thoughts are of little value, especially if they are expressed in equally lofty words. The persuader tends to focus on facts and statistics instead of imagery.

Clearly, these two extremes are not an either/or proposition—persuaders may, on occasion, utilize the tactics of both perspectives. When they do this they are probably responding to their audience's level of doubt or overly favorable initial position. Let us examine a few examples of these two differing styles.

In the following editorial by Meg Greenfield of *Newsweek* magazine, notice the down-to-earth language, the references to specifics, the use of statistics, and the generally common-sense approach. She is neither pro- nor anti-administration in the editorial, but she is critical. The readers of *Newsweek* are generally middle of the road, politically independent, and upper middle class, so she can expect an audience that is not unified for or against the Reagan administration. She must be a pragmatic persuader in this case.

Reagan came to office with a pretty clear and well-known view of this over-all situation. Except in military matters, he seemed to favor a let-nature-take-its-course approach, the exact opposite of the leave-nothing-to-chance school of social planning that had created the worse along with the better government programs in the first place. His response to the "do everything" theory of government appeared to be "do nothing." At least that was the message at the outset when we heard how a wide variety of Federal interventions were going to be stopped once and for all. Better to dismantle the overkill machine, to call off the sortie altogether, than to conduct so wasteful and inefficient and troublemaking an operation. People could live their lives healthily and fairly and productively without all that burden and claptrap. . . . Can the U.S. Government, acting as a kind of symbol of, and surrogate for, the society as a whole, concoct sensible, humane and relatively efficient answers to at least a respectable proportion of the problems we face? Will the Reagan government have the guts to move into that truly difficult area where you do neither everything nor nothing—but something that has risks proportionate to the prospective gain? While everyone is waiting for the economic plan's impact to be felt one way or, God help us, the other, there will be plenty of other case studies to observe in the Administration's evolution toward a style and philosophy of governing. Civil-rights legislation, most particularly renewal of the Voting Rights Act, is one case. The really hot case of the moment, however, is that of the good old MX missile and basing system.

The full-fledged, 200-missile/4,600-shelter, now-you-see-it-now-you-don't, moving-van MX system has always struck me as almost a parody of the overdone, oversize government contrivance that purports to be a solution— and which everyone knows, somehow, just isn't going to happen and won't work if it does. If the Pentagon hadn't thought it up, Mel Brooks would have. To his credit, Reagan and his aides seem to have begun trimming it down, not just for money reasons, but for program reasons as well. I think in fact that the way the President disposes of the broad array of military questions now before him will provide plenty of clues as to whether he can really do something about the huge and semi-senseless government reaction-machine he has complained of. For inspiration and guidance he should, whenever possible, contemplate the lowly fruit fly.[36]

Contrast that example of the pragmatic style with this example of the unifying style. In the following editorial by Tom Paugh of *Sports Afield*, there are no statistics. He uses the historical references to establish a then-and-there perspective, and the language and examples are likely to stir the emotions of Paugh's audience—those who hunt and/or fish. Because the audience is already polarized around Paugh's position there is no need to convince them that his position is right. He merely needs to excite them and perhaps to activate them.

You have to wonder what brought these people to the conclusion that hunting is such a dishonorable pastime. The hunter, once sole provider of meat for his family, is now considered by some as little better than a murderer. The modern-day providers of table meat—cattle and sheep ranchers, chicken and turkey farmers, slaughter house owners and workers, butchers and your local A&P and MacDonald's outlets—are not to my knowledge being harassed for their part in the process of killing "helpless animals."

Wildlife managers who develop habitat conducive to deer herds or other huntable wildlife are also under fire from the antis. But ranchers who set aside millions of acres for a single species with the bottomline purpose of turning these animals into steaks and chops, go unscathed. Perhaps they're next on the antis' list.

In this country's short history we have come very quickly from total dependence on wildlife for our meat to the simplistic notion that steaks are produced in factories and that their natural habitat is inside plastic wrappers. Actually, hamburger, any way you grind it, was once a walking-around cow. Somebody had to raise it, clean it, chop it up and sell it. And the person who

---

36. Meg Greenfield, "The Overkill Machine," *Newsweek*, September 7, 1981, p. 88. (Used by permission of *Newsweek*.)

cooks it and/or eats it is just as much a part of that process as all the others. If there is guilt involved, all must share equally.

But, why should we feel guilty? We did not create ourselves. Man is a carnivore. Fish eat fish, animals eat animals, and man eats both. This has nothing to do with intellect, morality or religion. It is a biological fact. Those of us who hunt understand these things in ways others are not able to grasp. We have the knowledge and ability to remain an integral part of the food-gathering process. We do not deny that killing is a part of this process nor do we revel in that fact. All things live and die and along the way should serve some useful end. Deer meat on the table is a useful end as long as the species survives. And the species is thriving.

The world is experiencing difficult times. Inflation, war and acts of international terror abound. In our own country, as in others, pollution of land, water and air threaten our survival. All these problems menace man as a species as well as threaten other life forms. The hunter represents no threat to society. He has always hunted, and his quarry has always been hunted. This is the cycle of life, and energies expended to change these facts are wasted.

Hunters are not only providers, they are survivors. The sick and the perverted are those who pay to have their killing done for them and then attack the ancient and honorable skill of hunting to cover up their own perverted feelings of guilt.[37]

Both Greenfield and Paugh have probably used unifying as well as pragmatic styles, depending on the audiences they face from time to time. Paugh, for example, has probably had to debate the ethics of hunting and gun ownership on the speaking circuit. When he defends these before a group of National Rifle Association members, his style will be much different than when he faces an audience that is not always united around his positions, such as a PTA or some other civic group. These two styles are functions of the audience and not of the speaker. We can learn something about persuaders by observing which style they choose for which kinds of audiences. Often, persuaders make mistakes that destroy the persuasiveness of the message. Persuadees can also gain insight into how they are being seen by the persuader by identifying the pragmatic or unifying styles used in messages.

Tuning One's Ear for Cues

Persuadees—to be aware and critical—ought to tune their ears for the various clues to style and motives already discussed. What are some ways in which you can tune your ear? Trying to use some of these tools is one way. If you have thought about these tools, if the theory about self-revelation through symbols has sparked your imagination, or if you have tried to apply these tools to the persua-

---

37. Tom Paugh, "Who's Really Sick?" *Sports Afield*, March 1981, p. 8. Copyright © 1981 The Hearst Corporation. All rights reserved.

sion around you, you have already started the tuning process. Applying the study questions at the end of this and other chapters is another good way to continue the process. There are at least three other things you might do to make yourself more critical of style and to "read" or "psych out" persuaders:

1. **Role-play the persuader.** Assume that you are the persuader or a member of a group with a persuasive cause. How would you have shaped the persuasion you hear? For example, if you were favoring high salaries for ballplayers, how would you go about framing a pragmatic message for half-hearted believers, those who are neutral, or others who are only moderately opposed? You would mention things like the shortness of most players' careers (hence a low over-all salary across a lifetime in spite of high yearly salaries). You might compare ballplayers to entertainers who make several million dollars per year for relatively little actual work time. You might cite over-all profits made by ballclubs and the rather meager retirement programs in pro sports. If your audience were the annual meeting of Association of Professional Baseball Players, you could afford to bypass the numbers and use highly emotional and abstract language to motivate the audience. You might create images of club owners as filthy-rich bloodsuckers who mindlessly use up the best years of a man's physical life as the strip-miners ravage the landscape. Your language would probably be there-and-then—referring to new goals of the group or talking about past abuses. So the style would show your view of the audience.

2. **Restate a persuasive message numerous times.** Instead of pretending that you are the ghostwriter for the persuader, just try to restate what has been said in several different ways. Ask yourself what the options were (as we did sketchily with the seven presidential slogans earlier in this chapter). Then try to determine how these options would have changed the intent of the message and its final effects. This process should lead you to draw some conclusions about the persuader's intent. You might want to determine what the persuader's pentadic emphasis was and then try to restate the persuasion from the viewpoint of the other four elements of the dramatic pentad.

    For example, take the following slogan for Grand Marnier Liqueur: "There Are Still Places on Earth Where Grand Marnier Isn't Offered after Dinner." The slogan is printed on a photo of a deserted island. The appeal is scenic. An agent-oriented version of this slogan might be "People with a Taste for the Good Things of Life Offer Grand Marnier." A purpose-oriented version might read something like: "When You Want to Finish the Conference, Offer Grand Marnier." An agency-oriented version might say, "From a Secret Triple Orange Recipe," stressing the method of production. The act might be used by saying "Do the Right Thing Now, Offer Grand Marnier." Of course, these slogans should be used with appropriately matched visuals.

3. **Attend to language features in discourse.** Don't allow yourself passively to buy into any persuasive advice that is being hawked. Instead, get into the habit of looking at the style of messages. Analyze messages on billboards and

in TV spot commercials, the language used by your parents in discussions with you, the wording on packages you purchase or in discussions between you and friends, enemies, or salespersons. In other words, start listening not only to *ideas*—the thrust of the messages aimed at you—but to *words* or the packaging of those ideas. Try it on me. What kind of words do I use? Why? What do you think I'm like? How does my style differ from Richard Johannesen's (see Chapter 11)? From other persuasion textbook writers? From the way you would have said it? Focusing on these features in as many situations as possible will give you an intriguing pastime in which you operate as a kind of amateur psychoanalyst. Further, you will develop an ear for stylistic tip-offs, a skill that will prove valuable in your interpersonal relations—it allows you to predict and respond to the communication of others.

A Review and Conclusion

There are, then, several ways to become a responsible receiver of persuasion. They relate to the language a particular persuader chooses. We can gain a general insight by looking at the semantic connotations of the words chosen. We can look at word order or syntax. We can look at the degree to which various parts of speech are chosen. The degree of ambiguity used by the persuader is often revealing, as can be the case with a dramatistic analysis such as that suggested by Burke. The motifs and metaphors chosen by a persuader are often motive revealing also. Finally, persuadees can "psych out" the persuader by looking at the families of God and Devil terms that are used, as well as the choice of *pragmatic* versus *unifying* style.

All these critical devices are, of course, enhanced in their potential by role-playing, restating, and developing awareness of the words and style as well as the ideas in a persuasive message, be it a speech, a TV documentary, a film, a political slogan, a social movement, a package designed to sell a product, or a friend's request.

Questions for Further Thought

1. Transcribe the lyrics of a popular song. Now analyze them according to the functional tools presented here. Is there a preference for a certain word type? A certain sentence structure? Is the message ambiguous or concrete? Explain.

2. What are the semantic tools suggested here? What do you think is the pentadic perspective of the author of this book? Why? Give examples. What do you think is the pentadic favorite of your instructor?

3. What are the tools for a thematic or textural analysis of language? Use some of these to analyze the persuasion occurring in a recent political campaign. What do these analyses tell you about the candidate? Explain.

4. What are the God terms held in esteem by your parents? What are their Devil terms? Shape a request for something from your parents, expressed in terms similar to God terms. Now do the same thing with Devil terms. Try them both out as an experiment.

5. How does a unifying persuader differ from a pragmatic one? Find examples of each type of persuader in your class, in persuasive attempts of the past, or in some persuasive issue being discussed on campus or in your community. Are there other differences between these two types? What are they?

6. What are three ways to tune your ear to the symbolic and ego-revealing aspects of language use? Give an example of where you have done this. Make a prediction about a persuader, based on your analysis of him or her, using the tools of this chapter and the three suggestions offered at the end of the chapter. Present the reasons for your prediction in an essay or speech.

Experiences in Persuasion

1. Attend a film with a persuasive message (that is, one that does more than merely tell a story). Analyze the words of one or more of its characters, using the tools of this chapter. Do you think the tools work in other symbolic media like film? Why or why not? Why is the film persuasive to you? Analyze your own reasons for saying that it is or is not persuasive. What in the film made you react that way? Was that thing a scenic phenomenon, or did it focus on actions, agents, principles, or methods (for example, someone might say that Hitler's propaganda film *Triumph of the Will* was persuasive because of the spectacle it presented—tens of thousands of people, huge flags, and the like—all scenic items, while someone else may have found *E.T.* persuasive because of the sensitivity of Elliot.)

2. Analyze the persuasive impact of a particular show on TV—it may be a talk show or a dramatic show. Does its persuasiveness come from a particular part of the pentad? Which one? Give examples. Now look at each of the participants in the episode. Explain how each of them tried to persuade others. Refer to the kinds of words they use, their sentence structure, and so on; use the tools of this chapter.

3. Catalog the uses of obscenity you find in popular literature or reported as being used by persuaders for certain causes. What word classes are they (see the discussion by Weaver)? Which element of the pentad do they represent? Why are they called profane? Who gets bothered by these words? What is being responded to in the words? Refer to the tools of this chapter.

4. Make a poster showing various uses of functional, semantic, and thematic meaning in popular advertisements. Discuss these language uses with your class.

4
Process Premises:
Tools of Motivation

Everyone who has ever been persuaded or who has tried to persuade someone else knows instinctively that if you can skillfully tap into someone's emotional state, you can persuade that person quite easily. The most powerful speakers and speeches in history utilize the emotional appeal. In Shakespeare's *Julius Caesar*, Mark Antony's funeral oration played so skillfully upon the emotions of the audience that they reversed their opinions of Caesar. From hating him as a villain they shifted to grieving for him as a martyred hero. Further, they were so riled up by Antony that they tore up paving stones and used them to kill Caesar's assassin. Lincoln, in the depths of the Civil War, used emotional appeals in the Second Inaugural to set the tone for his reconstruction plans for the South. In the worst days of the Great Depression of the 1930s, Franklin Roosevelt used emotional appeals to calm people's fears and promised them that he would "throw the moneychangers out of the Temple."

During World War II, Winston Churchill's emotional appeals were unique in their ability to inspire the English to fight on after the fall of France and the disastrous retreat at Dunkirk. While London was being bombed to rubble he vowed to fight the Germans in the streets and hills or if necessary from the countries of the Empire. The phrases he used are classics of the art of persuasion.

> We shall not flag or fail. We shall go on to the end. We shall fight in France, we shall fight on the seas and oceans, we shall fight with growing confidence and growing strength in the air, we shall defend our island, whatever the cost may be, we shall fight on the beaches, we shall fight on the landing grounds, we shall fight in the fields and in the streets, we shall fight in the hills; we shall never surrender.[1]

We know from Churchill's diaries that he himself doubted that what he called for was possible. Nonetheless, his emotional speeches braced up English resolve to endure until America entered the war.

---

1. Winston S. Churchill, Speech on Dunkirk, House of Commons, June 4, 1940.

Using emotional appeals to the U.S. Congress, Lyndon Johnson persuaded them to send the Army, Air Force, and Navy to Vietnam to retaliate for what later turned out to be a minor attack on a U.S. vessel—an attack that may have been staged in the first place. And we have heard recent presidents use emotional appeals to urge us to conserve energy, to fight terrorism, to cut taxes, and to reduce Social Security benefits. Undoubtedly we will hear future presidents using emotional appeals. And we are repeatedly targets of such appeals in the thousands of advertisements that tell us we will be gigantic flops in the social world if we don't use such-and-such deodorant or mouthwash. They tell us that we will never reach the top unless we drink Dewar's Scotch. They tell America's youth to buy a pair of Calvin Klein jeans so that they can look as attractive as Brooke Shields. Any logical consideration of these appeals would make them a laughingstock, but we aren't responding to them with logic. Instead we respond to them because of psychological or emotional needs to be loved or to succeed. In this chapter we will look at some of these needs and at how they motivate us.

The Classical View on Emotional Appeals

As we have already noted, the study of persuasion in any kind of systematic way really began with the Greeks and Romans. They categorized emotional or nonlogical appeals into several types. One kind of emotional appeal was the use of figures of speech, highly charged words, and other elements of style to appeal to "the passions or the will." Many of the examples cited above (e.g., Mark Antony, Churchill, and so on) demonstrate just such language usage. Another kind of nonlogical appeal relied on pseudologic or fallacious reasoning to circumvent the rational side of human beings. One such fallacy, for example, was the *ad vera cundium* fallacy or the argument from authority or tradition. This argument says because someone who is authoritative does something, or because it has always been done that way, you should do it also. Van Heusen shirts ran an advertisement right after the election of Ronald Reagan to the Presidency. It depicted a young Reagan in the Fifties buttoning up a Van Heusen shirt. The caption on the ad read, "Sooner or Later Everyone's Dream Comes True." The implication was that the shirt helped the dream to come true. We know that this is just plain false. Many dreams never come true. But the ad implies that because Reagan's dream came true and because he wore Van Heusen shirts in the past, we should buy some also to guarantee that our dreams will come true. Of course, anyone who has tried to change some long-standing method of doing something on a job, for instance, has experienced the argument from tradition—"It's always been done that way!"

Finally, the ancients believed that the technique of delivering a message could emotionally charge up the audience. Being outraged or bombastic in one's delivery, for instance, could stir up the audience. Weeping or crying out during the speech might also awaken the audience's emotions. Speaking very softly might force audience attention and might hint of inside knowledge that the speaker would share with the audience. One look at the headlines of the *National Enquirer* will show you a selection of these classic approaches to emotional appeals, and the *Enquirer* has the largest newspaper circulation in the United States.

Contemporary Views on Emotional or Psychological Appeals

Since the early Greek and Roman theorists wrote about persuasion, many others have added to the storehouse of theory and evidence about persuasive appeals. Important work has been done in the twentieth century, particularly in the last thirty or forty years. The field of psychology has offered us several theories of human motivation. Sociology has added both theory and evidence on why groups of people are motivated in certain ways. Even the hucksters of the world of advertising have increased our knowledge of human motivation. In terms of persuasion as we are looking at it here, these theories allow us to identify premises that persuaders can use, rely on, or build upon. These premises are usually based on some kind of psychological **process** that can be assumed to operate in all or almost all people. By appealing to those processes, persuaders can urge the audience to action or belief. In this way, the **process premises** that we will be discussing serve as the major premises in what the classical writers called *enthymemes*—syllogisms in which one premise was assumed to be already believed by the audience. As you can see, contemporary views are integrally related to classical ones.

The Behavioristic Theories

One set of theories could be associated with the tradition of the behavioral sciences. These theories of how people are persuaded grew out of fields of study like psychology (e.g., attitude change theories, dissonance theory, balance theory) or sociology (e.g., peer pressure theories, social field theories). Typically, these approaches to human behavior and persuasion rely on experimental proof. Their goal is to predict and ultimately to control behavior through such methods as conditioning.

The name most identified with the word "behaviorism" is of course B. F. Skinner, and while this book is not a psychology textbook and this course is not a psychology course, much of what Skinner offers us is applicable to the study of persuasion. For example, Skinner identified what he called **schedules of reinforcement.** This concept referred to how frequently and for what kind of behavior positive or negative stimuli (or what most of us call rewards or punishments) were presented. If a positive stimulus was presented for every instance of the specified behavior, the schedule was a *continuous* one. We all behave in conformity with such schedules in our everyday lives. Vending machines are good examples of continuous reinforcement, unless of course they are not functioning properly. (We have all heard stories in which someone shoots or smashes a vending machine that won't return a product for the coins that are inserted.)

Another kind of schedule was the *ratio* schedule. This meant that the stimulus was presented only after the required behavior had occurred a specified number of times. Again, we all have behaved in accordance with ratio schedules at various times in our everyday lives. Piecework is an example. Practicing a musical instrument is another. Doing math homework problems is another. For each of these examples, the required behavior is elicited a certain number of times and a reinforcement occurs—pay, praise, or a grade. Recently, soda-pop companies have run contests in which the customer is required to peel off the seals under the bottletop. Beneath the seal is a symbol, a word, or a number identifying the value of that particular lid. Initially, the companies distribute many tops worth small monetary prizes—10¢, 25¢, and 50¢. In a sense, these early bottletops are examples of continuous reinforcers. The customer always gets something—either money or tops that help to spell out the words in the $1000 slogan—Pepsi Over Coke, for example. Later, though, the buyer peels the seal and gets letters that he or she already has. It may be that the buyer has to go through a whole eight-pack before getting a lid that has monetary value or a needed letter. But the customer is "hooked" by the early continuous reinforcement and so goes on peeling seals even when the system has shifted to a ratio schedule.

Another kind of schedule is called an *interval* schedule. This means that reinforcement (or reward) is given only after the recipient has been behaving in the desired way for a specified period of time. Payday is an example of an interval schedule; final grades are another; graduation is another. In terms of persuasion, this kind of schedule has certain disadvantages. One of them is that we all have a tendency to drag our heels at the start and slack off in the middle of the interval. You all know how that is at the beginning of the semester or term. Only when the end of the interval approaches does behavior pick up. Then papers get written; workers show up on time; projects get finished. At many industrial plants, absenteeism is highest on Mondays and lowest on Fridays or paydays (which usually coincide).

The most powerful kind of reinforcement is called *random intermittent*. Here there is no way to predict how long it will take or how many times required behavior must be completed before reinforcement will occur. This is how parents train children to behave, to be polite, to use the toilet, and so on. It is also the way many jobs operate. You may get praise from the boss today and next week and then not until six weeks have passed. Most advertisements are based on random intermittent reinforcement. Gentlemen don't *always* prefer the woman in the Hanes pantyhose. In fact, the woman can't really determine analytically when or after how many repeated wearings of Hanes stockings a man will give her the eye.

Now, none of this is very complicated when you think of it. You and I knew these things before we ever read about B. F. Skinner and his theories. He merely systematized and labeled the process of reinforcement. But his work was extremely important because it helped people in a wide variety of contexts to determine analytically if they were appropriately reinforcing others—children, workers, voters, customers, and so on. In a recent example, Skinner worked with the Emery Air Freight company to increase employee productivity and accuracy. Giving verbal rewards to the employees for answering the phone within two rings, for routing deliveries efficiently, and for packaging items efficiently, Skinner was able to get extremely significant improvements in a short time. We could say that he used praise to "persuade" the workers to improve.

One task for persuaders, then, is to analyze the audience to determine what patterns of reinforcement will work best with the target audience. Let's look to the world of advertising for some examples of how schedules of reinforcement are used or appealed to in order to persuade. Consider the ad for Chivas Regal scotch in Figure 4.1. The six panels depict a repeated gesture—the giving and receiving of Chivas on special occasions. The advertisers have even custom-wrapped the Chivas and surrounded it with appropriate symbols. The wrapping for the bon voyage party includes ship-side streamers and the "new home" Chivas is wrapped in a blueprint. The ad is intended not for the person getting the Chivas but for the person who gives it. Everyone knows the good feelings one gets for bringing the perfect gift, and the reward of being considered thoughtful and clever by others. That is the positive reinforcer.

In the world of politics, the persuader's task is to determine the pattern of reinforcement which exists in the voter's mind and experience. In the late 1970s, Jane Byrne of Chicago used one pattern of reinforcement very effectively to upset the incumbent mayor, Mike Bilandic—a bland fellow who had been hand-picked by the Chicago machine. Political disaster struck Bilandic in the form of Chicago's worst winter ever. The city had nearly nine feet of snow that winter. Three feet of it came within three days, bringing the city to a halt. Commuter trains were stalled or were jammed by snowbound suburbanites, making it impossible for city-dwellers to get on. Streets were impassable and clogged with cars stuck in the drifts and snowbanks. City workers used freshly plowed parking lots to dump snow cleared from streets. One worker even went berserk and drove his snow-plow around town ramming cars, finally killing a motorist. Byrne tied vivid memories of these negative reinforcers, plus his lackluster image, to the incumbent mayor in the primary campaign and defeated him handily—to the surprise of the machine. Once in office, Byrne received constant publicity for firing patronage workers, moving into all-black housing projects to investigate and experience the high-crime slums, and so on. She used negative reinforcement to defeat the incumbent and then began establishing a pattern of positive reinforcers tied to herself to build voter approval for reelection.

Persuadees, on the other hand, need to study their own patterns of reinforcement to find out their vulnerable spots. Some people are suckers for the "free gift" that is sometimes linked to an expensive product or a long-winded sales pitch. Others are vulnerable to the promise of attention from members of the opposite sex. And others are open to appeals promising love from the family if you serve them Hamburger Helper. Persuadees also need to identify what acts as a generalized or secondary reinforcer for them—social prestige, status, flirtation.

Skinner is probably the most objective of the behaviorists. He refused to accept what he called "black box" constructs: explanations for behavior based on a motive which is inside people's minds—the "black box." These would include instincts, drives, guilt, attitudes, and so on. For Skinner, motivation was simply the number of hours that the subject—rat or human—had been deprived of whatever was being used as a reinforcer, whether it was a food pellet, praise, or a successful seal-peel. Other behaviorists are not so single-minded and are willing to consider "black box" constructs. We will be looking at some of these in depth.

Why wait for Christmas?

12 YEARS OLD WORLDWIDE · BLENDED SCOTCH WHISKY · 86 PROOF · GENERAL WINE & SPIRITS CO. NEW YORK, N.Y.

Figure 4.1. What is the purpose of the different types of gift wrappings in this ad? (Used courtesy General Wine and Spirits Corp.)

In some cases, persuasion is accomplished by changing people's attitudes—by altering their perspectives on issues or changing their environment in some way. Other theorists believe that persuasion occurs because of psychological discomfort or "dissonance." Sometimes, the social field and peer pressure are linked to persuasion. In all these cases some aspect of the environment—the speech, the peer pressure, or the group identification—serves as the intervening cause for the choice. The foundation for any of these explanations, however, is *operant conditioning:* We learn our attitudes through reinforcing experiences, and we use our attitudes, in statement form, to create identification with others that is also reinforcing. Peer pressure is a reinforcer that we have learned to encourage or avoid. And we do things that will maintain our ties with those groups with whom we identify. So, Skinner's reinforcement theory remains at the root of most behavioristic explanations of motivation.

The Symbolistic Theories

A somewhat different approach to explaining why people behave as they do is sometimes referred to as the **symbolistic** or **humanistic** approach. Unlike the behavioristic view, which holds that people behave in certain ways to get specific rewards like praise, pay, food, or pleasure, the symbolistic or humanistic approach believes that most of what humans do is for symbolic reward. In other words, people don't buy a Cadillac for its ride, its looks, or its durability. They buy a Cadillac because it symbolizes something to them—most likely status or prestige. Most of the pitches we see as we thumb through magazines or watch television offer such symbolic rewards or punishments. We buy Binaca and use it even if it doesn't work or even if we don't need it. We buy and use it to avoid the symbolic punishment of offending that "special someone." And everyone loves to hate J. R. Ewing of *Dallas* because he is symbolic of various parts of real people we have met and known and disliked—all rolled into one. Much of what is referred to as "motivation research" in the field of advertising relies on this symbolic approach as the research staffs of ad agencies delve into the minds and motives of potential customers.

Needs: The First Process Premise

Human beings, like other organisms, have needs—some weak, some strong—that must be met from time to time. The problem is to identify these needs, for they often serve as the first premise in persuasive argument. For example, a person dying of thirst can easily be persuaded to take drastic action in order to get to water to fulfill the need for liquid. The need for H_2O is an important premise in persuading that dehydrated person. These needs are *process premises* because most operate in some kind of psychic sequence or process. For example, the need to feel loved is partially met by pets, parents, siblings, friends, spouses, children, lovers, fraternal groups, and so forth. The key is the word "partially" because we probably all feel the need to be loved more than we are, in spite of all those sources of love. Our needs make us vulnerable to persuasion, and effective persuaders are those who successfully determine our needs. If they analyze our needs incorrectly, persuasion can boomerang. For example, a well-known luggage manufacturer once spent thousands of dollars to produce a very impressive and clever TV ad. The spot opened with luggage being handled roughly as it was loaded into the cargo bay of a huge airliner. The central piece of luggage was made by the sponsor. The plane was next seen in flight. We were shown a slight problem—someone had failed to latch the cargo bay door. As the plane banked, our star piece of luggage fell out of the now-open bay door. The camera followed the suitcase as it fell through 30,000 feet of space and landed with a huge thud on some rocks. Then the case was opened to reveal the undamaged contents. Now, that ought to be pretty convincing as to which kind of luggage to buy. However, airing of the commercial was followed by a tremendous drop in sales. Why? Using in-depth interviews, researchers found that most people, even regular airline travelers, have some fear that the plane may crash. They resented the implication that their luggage would survive them in event of a crash and so rejected that brand.

In the late 1950s, some of the motivation research done on behalf of the advertisers was chronicled by author and critic Vance Packard in a book entitled *The Hidden Persuaders.* It was promoted with sentences like these:

> In this book you'll discover a world of psychology professors turned merchandisers. You'll learn how they operate, what they know about you and your neighbors, and how they are using that knowledge to sell you cake mixes, cigarettes, cars, soaps and even ideas.

In his book Packard reported that a majority of the hundred largest ad firms in the country had been using a psychoanalytic approach. He noted that other professional persuaders—public relations execs, fund-raisers, politicians, and others— were turning to psychological theorists to discover the motives of customers. They then tied their products, candidates, and causes to these motives. Packard quotes one ad executive as saying:

> Motivation research . . . seeks to learn what motivates people in making choices. It employs techniques designed to reach the subconscious mind because preferences generally are determined by factors of which the individual is not conscious. . . . Actually in the buying situation the consumer acts emotionally and compulsively, unconsciously reacting to images and designs which in the sub-conscious are associated with the product.[2]

Another advertiser gave some examples of how the research was used:

> The cosmetic manufacturers are not selling lanolin; they are selling hope. . . . We no longer buy oranges, we buy vitality. We do not buy just an auto; we buy prestige.[3]

It was clear that psychology had entered the field of advertising. According to Packard, market researchers operating from this perspective had three assumptions about people. First, they assumed that people don't always know what they want when they make a purchase. Second, they assumed that you cannot rely on what people say about what they like and dislike. Finally, they assumed that people do not act logically or rationally. Packard gave several examples of how

---

2. Packard, p. 5.

3. Packard, p. 5.

these assumptions operate. For instance, motivation researchers wondered what it was that made housewives buy laundry detergent. The housewives *said* they bought it because of its cleaning power. A sample group of housewives were given three boxes of detergent. They were asked to test the three types and report back. Actually the three boxes contained the same detergent—only the color of the boxes was different. The housewives reported that the detergent in the yellow box was too harsh. The one in the blue box was too weak; it left clothes gray after washing. But the stuff in the yellow-and-blue box was great.

The psychoanalytic approach to marketing most closely reflects the symbolistic tradition of psychology. Indeed, much of the in-depth research that Packard describes is almost like psychoanalysis. The researchers used in-depth interviews that encouraged customers to describe the fears, pleasures, nightmares, fantasies, and lusts they associated with the product or the ad for it. Other researchers used complex psychological tests like the Minnesota Multiphasic Personality Inventory (MMPI) or Thematic Apperception Test (TAT). Still others used projective tests in which people completed sentences about the product or described the "real meaning" behind cartoon vignettes related to the product. The trend continues and operates today, nearly thirty years after Packard first described it.

In his research, Packard found eight "compelling needs" that were frequently used in selling products via the motivation research approach.[4] We will see that the marketing folks still use them today, although probably with more sophistication.

Packard's Eight Hidden Needs

The hidden needs that Packard described were discovered using methods like the depth interview or the projective test. Once the needs were determined to be "compelling," merchandisers designed their ads to promise some degree of symbolic fulfillment of the needs. You can almost imagine Freud himself heading one of the motivation think-tanks. Here are the eight emotional needs Packard describes.

The Need for Emotional Security We live in an insecure world. War seems imminent. The streets and subways are dangerous places. The economy seems always to be on the edge of going bust. Assassinations are occurring more frequently. Prices are unpredictable. The world seemed more secure in the Fifties when Packard did his work, but even then he found that people were insecure and that they bought products that symbolized or promised security. Home freezers, for instance, allowed people to think that they might survive a nuclear attack or another Depression. Air conditioners allowed people to feel that their homes were secure because windows could be kept locked.

Today, deodorants promise us social security—we won't offend our boss or our sweetheart with B.O. Smoke alarms, fire extinguishers, and home insurance make us feel safe from fires. *A Prairie Home Companion*, a nationally syndicated entertainment show on public radio stations, spoofs ads that appeal to this hidden

---

4. Packard, pp. 61–70.

Figure 4.2. The symbolistic approach to marketing involves delving into hidden needs consumers have and then offering a symbolic answer in the product. (©1981 NEA, Inc. Used by permission.)

need for security. The Peabody Award-winning show is supposedly sponsored by the "Fear Mongers' Shop" and "Home Defense Hardware" in the mythical town of Lake Wobegon, Minnesota. The Fear Mongers play on people's insecurity by drumming up obscure fears and then promoting a phony protection: snake-proof toilet seats, lead mattress covers to ward off lightning, and so forth. Such satire is probably a good indicator that the need for emotional security noted by Packard still operates in the 1980s; it is still being appealed to by advertisers, politicians, and idea promoters. See if you can find such an appeal in your world.

The Need for Reassurance of Worth   We live in a highly competitive and impersonal society in which we feel like mere cogs in a machine. Packard noted that people need to feel valued for what they do. This need was particularly important for many housewives of the 1950s and 1960s who saw themselves as mere drudges doing the dirty work of the family for no real payoff. Product advertisers who could promise that their brands would lead to appreciation were usually successful in gaining new adherents. Sta-Pruf starch promised that hubby would succeed on the job with a crisp white shirt and would kiss wifey when he came home with the raise she helped him get. Today, as in the Fifties, politicians often promise to return us to our earlier national greatness. Many social service agencies promise that volunteers can do something "worthwhile in the world" if they give several hours of time per week. So the need to be valued serves as a powerful persuasive premise.

Need for Ego Gratification   One step from worth needs are needs to stroke one's own ego: "Not only am I worth something, I am really pretty special." Packard refers to a heavy road-equipment manufacturer who increased sales by featuring the drivers of the machines in magazine ads instead of the machines themselves. Operators have major say-so in purchase decisions. Persuaders often identify a group whose members feel they have been put down for some time— teachers, police, or social workers, for instance. It is easy to sell products, ideas, or candidates by hooking into the out-group's ego needs. In the late 1970s, one candidate promised a "pro-family" emphasis. For years, the family idea had been out of vogue in favor of living together, communes, gay marriage, and rising divorce rates. The appeal worked. Factory safety campaigns often have a scoreboard to record the number of accident-free days achieved by workers, thus gratifying their egos.

Need for Creative Outlets In our age, few products can be identified with a single craftsman. Many of the earlier outlets for creativity have been bypassed. For instance, take the increased popularity of prepared foods, microwave ovens, and eating out instead of creatively cooking a meal from scratch. Yet people still seem to need to demonstrate their own handicraft skills. Given this need, macramé, gourmet-cooking classes, bonsai gardens, home improvement tools, and other hobby-type activities are bound to succeed. Even with prepared foods, from which the art of cooking has been almost totally removed, manufacturers are finding that creativity still sells. Hamburger Helper leaves room for you, the cook, to add your own touch. Noodles Romanoff makes you a chef worthy of the Czar. Even Old El Paso taco dinner reminds you of all the creative toppings you can put on a taco shell. In our town, a high-status thing for young mothers is to be the Picture Lady at the grade school. Picture Ladies bring works of art to one of the grades and give question/answer type lessons about them. You can cite many situations in which persuaders are using the need for creative outlets to get you to buy their product or idea.

Need for Love Objects People whose children have grown up—the empty-nest syndrome—need to replace the child love object. For some the replacement is a pet; for others it is a child met through the organization Foster Grandparents. It may be childlike entertainment personalities such as Donny and Marie Osmond. Perhaps people who are not yet in the childless years are motivated by the need for another kind of love object to replace the parents whom they left or the lover who has never appeared on the scene. This could account for the recurring emergence of stars with great sex appeal—for example, Robert Redford or Jacqueline Bisset. The major audience for pro wrestling is elderly women; the wrestlers may serve as love objects to these women.

Need for a Sense of Power If you have ever driven a motorcycle on the open road, you know what it feels like to have this need. We Americans, more than members of any other culture, seem to be programmed to buy potency and power and also to gratify this need symbolically. The bigger the engine, the better. Snowmobiles and their counterparts for summer fun are marketed by the sense of power they give. Almost any automotive product will feature the phrase heavy-duty to convince you that you are getting a powerful replacement part. Although some of our politicians are short or have slight builds, the big powerful types seem to win more frequently.

Need for Roots The increasing interest in genealogical research intensified by Alex Haley's novel *Roots* and the TV show based upon it testifies to the continuing importance of this need. Perhaps the fact that most people move several times during their lives accounts for this lack of roots and the natural need to find some substitute for roots. You, as college students, are especially vulnerable to appeals to your need for roots. You may enjoy living in a dorm room or an apartment because Mom isn't there to nag you, but if you are like the typical college graduate, you are just beginning a very transient life. College graduates move on the average of ten times in the first decade after graduation. Several moves will be across county lines and at least one will be to another state. Perhaps many of you have already experienced this rootless life if your parents are mobile and are in jobs where transfers are frequent. The need for roots will be appealed to many times and in many ways.

Ronald Reagan's 1980 campaign slogan promised a kind of substitute for roots. The nation would become our home as we worked "Together" for "A New Beginning." Pepperidge Farm ads promise "home-baked" flavor, feature an old-fashioned delivery man with a Maine accent, and tell you "Pepperidge Farm remembers." Heartland cereal appeals to this need, as does Ma Bell in the "Reach Out and Touch Someone" ads, which focus on reuniting the long-distance family and friends. A glance through almost any magazine today will reveal a score of such appeals. The need for roots, like the need for emotional security, is as powerful in the 1980s as it was when Packard first identified it—if not more powerful.

Need for Immortality None of us believe in our own mortality. We like to think that life will go on and on in much the same way as at present. Packard suggests that the fear of dying and the need to believe in an ongoing influence on the lives of others underlies many insurance appeals. The breadwinner is made to feel that in buying insurance, he or she buys "life after death" in the form of financial control over the family. The buyer can help the kids go to college even if he or she isn't there.

Other products make similar appeals to the fear of death. Dannon yogurt ran a series of ads featuring people from the Ukraine who have lived well past 100 years, supposedly because they ate yogurt. Many cosmetics ads picture mother and daughter side by side and ask the reader to guess which is which. The mother looks so young that it would be easy to make a mistake—after all, she uses Wrinkle-Gone face cream. As the ad executive noted in an earlier quote, we aren't buying lanolin (or Polly Bergen's secret turtle oil); we are buying hope—hope for a chunk of immortality and youth.

As critical consumers of persuasion, it behooves you to make yourself more aware of the pitches you will encounter. Let's look at another way to identify the needs that are appealed to by clever persuaders.

Maslow's Pyramid

Abraham Maslow, a well-known psychologist, offered us a starting point for examining gross need levels.[5] He noted that people have various kinds of needs that emerge, subside, and emerge again as they are or are not met. For example, the need for food or water emerges and then recedes as we eat or drink. Maslow argued that these needs have a *prepotency*—that is, they are tied together in such a way that weaker needs, like self-respect, emerge only after stronger needs, like

---

5. Abraham H. Maslow, *Motivation and Personality* (New York: Harper & Row, 1954).

*"Have you ever considered what would become
of your mate if a dinosaur were to eat you?"*

Figure 4.3. Insurance companies have long used the fear of death to sell their product. (©1982. Reprinted courtesy *Parade Magazine* and Bill Hoest.)

the need for food, have been filled. We probably could not persuade our dehydrated desert wanderer to clean up a little before going to the well. We had better fulfill the need for H_2O first. Our need to slake thirst is prepotent; until it is fulfilled, it is literally impossible for us to consider other ideas.

Maslow arranged the various needs in a clear and understandable model. He said that needs are arranged in pyramid fashion, with lower levels having the stronger needs and higher levels having the weaker needs (Figure 4.4). Remember that the pyramid is only a model and that the lines between needs are not as distinct as the picture suggests. It should also be noted that higher needs are not superior to lower ones. They are just different and, in all likelihood, weaker and less likely to emerge until stronger needs are met.

Basic Needs On the bottom level are the strongest needs we have—basic needs. These are the physiological needs of each human being. We need regular fulfillment of our needs for air, food, water, sex, sleep, and elimination of wastes. Until these are met, we cannot concern ourselves with other, higher needs. The basic needs are too strong to be forgotten in favor of other needs.

Security Needs The second level of Maslow's pyramid contains our needs connected with security. There are several ways one might look at our need for security. We may want to feel secure in our ability to get basic needs. If we feel that our job may end shortly, we have a strong need to get income security. We may want to get another more secure job. Or we might want to save money for hard times. This is one kind of security. At the same time, we might look at this need level in another light. Let us suppose that we have job security—our boss assures us that we will be the last to be let go. We may still feel insecure because of the rising crime rates in our neighborhood. We might take drastic action to ward off thieves. We might install a burglar alarm system, or we may sleep with a

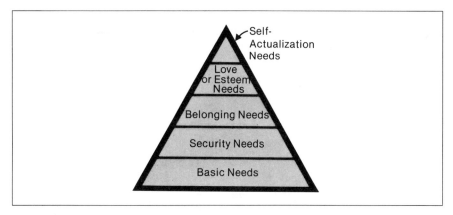

Figure 4.4. The Maslow pyramid of needs.

loaded pistol under the pillow. Even when we feel secure about home, we may still feel insecure about world politics. We may feel that our country needs more missiles or antimissile missiles. A person may have social insecurity and as a result spend money on self-improvement classes, deodorant, hair transplants, and mouthwash. In other words, this need for security emerges and reemerges as various threats to our security become evident and must be met. Once the need is met, it redefines itself and thus is always present to some degree.

Belonging Needs Once we feel that security needs are met at least in part (we know we will have a job in the future and that thugs will have problems robbing us), we become aware of other needs on the third level. These are belonging needs. Persons who feel fairly secure, like the horse who looks at the field of clover across the road, look to other things that they now feel are needed. A number of options are open to us in meeting the need for association. We may choose to fulfill these needs in our immediate family. We all know of people who relate to no group other than at the job and in the family. This way of meeting belonging needs is the exception rather than the rule, however. Usually the individual seeks groups with which to fill this need. Suburbia is filled with persons who seem to have a strong need for belonging—they are the joiners of our society. They become members of dozens of groups like the PTA, bowling leagues, churches, golf clubs, or service groups. Usually we keep the number of groups we join small, and though we may be members of several, we are active members in only a few. Regardless of how many groups we join or of how active we are in any of them, we only partially meet our belonging needs. We will continue to join groups throughout our lives, for this need is also a reemerging one.

Love or Esteem Needs Once we satisfy belonging needs, we will feel the emergence of other needs. This is level four of Maslow's model, the need for love or esteem. Once we are part of a group, we want to feel that the group—be it family, lodge, or bowling team—values us as a member. As human beings we want to feel wanted and valued. We are happy when our families understand and admire the things we do. The esteem need is also a reemerging need. That is, if we find that we are needed and esteemed and loved by our family, the need for esteem does not fade away. Instead, its focus shifts. We want now to feel needed and loved by our co-workers and our boss or by our friends. Once we get this kind of esteem, the need becomes less compelling. However, it is never fully satisfied, and we try to seek other circumstances in which we can achieve status and rank that will help meet our need for love and esteem by others. Many product appeals offer a kind of symbolic substitute for esteem. You will be held high in your fellow workers' eyes if you read the *Wall Street Journal.* Your spouse will adore you if you make him that Betty Crocker cake. Your kids will love you if you take them to Disney World—all great Dads do that. And the examples could go on and on.

Self-Actualization Needs Although Maslow initially put self-actualization at the top of his pyramid, thereby implying that it would rarely emerge, he later came to believe that in a way the need to self-actualize or to live up to one's potential is an integral part of everyone's life. At first, Maslow believed that individuals could live up to their own potential only when all four of the lower needs were fulfilled. Once you had become President of the United States and had thus received the greatest possible esteem from your fellow citizens, *then* you could begin to self-actualize. Once you were promoted to president of the bank, *then* you could begin to live up to your own potential.

In many ways those initial ideas of Maslow are accurate. It is hard for a young person on the way up to think about self-actualizing, just as it is hard to achieve love or esteem if you do not belong to some group that can give you love or esteem—a family, a fraternity, a church. Yet Maslow's later thinking about all these needs and their prepotency is valid, too. He came to see self-actualization as occurring through what he called "peak experiences"—events in which people could enjoy themselves, learn about themselves, or experience something they had only dreamed of before. Thus the person who went out into the Boundary Waters Canoe Area wilderness and learned to be self-reliant and not to fear isolation had enjoyed a peak or self-actualizing experience. The same might apply to people who learned something about themselves when they took their first job after high school or college and discovered that they had abilities that were of value to a company or to fellow workers.

Many of the persuasive appeals made to us are aimed at our need for peak experiences. You are asked to "Be All That You Can Be" by joining the Army. You are invited to "Experience the Bahamas" or to build America back to its former greatness.

Maslow's pyramid can be used in many everyday persuasive opportunities. When we want to persuade a teacher that a certain grade or method of evaluation is unfair, we must analyze what kinds of needs the professor has. Is he or she likely to feel insecure? Is he or she in need of esteem? Is he or she trying to self-actualize? Or suppose you were trying to persuade your roommate to take a trip to Florida with you instead of working over the break period. You want to know what kinds of needs were being fulfilled by the potential trip or by the plan for work during the vacation. Many marital quarrels are rooted in differing motivations—a wife may want to take a trip to San Francisco for the vacation, while a husband is interested in going to fishing country, with each trying to fulfill different needs. Ultimately, one side or the other will agree to give up his or her plans.

What kinds of needs might the professor, the roommate, or the potential purchaser of insurance be exhibiting if we used Packard's listing? How might particular appeals be restated, in terms of several of Packard's needs? For instance, the appeal to status that lies behind many ads for luxury cars could be restated in ways that would make the ads appeal to potency or the need for ego gratification. Try restating such persuasive appeals from several perspectives.

Some Uses and Conclusions

In conclusion, people seem to be motivated by the desire to be similar to others and by their need states. This first process premise operates on the belief that people have drives that need to be reduced by meeting them. The drives probably reemerge from time to time and thus motivate us throughout our lives and probably throughout the life of our nation. Persuaders can take advantage of this by directing their messages toward audience needs, promising or perhaps only hinting that by following their advice, the need can be filled or reduced. As persuadees, we can take advantage of our knowledge of this first process premise by being alert to the goal of persuasion aimed at us and by restating messages that aim at our needs. This will make the persuader's strategy clearer and will also alert the persuadee to the hidden reasons for choosing to buy a certain toothpaste, to vote for Senator Fogbound, or to join the "No Nukes" protest group.

Thus, at the process level, the need state is one given. Persuaders may capitalize on need levels if they know that the audience has certain needs or drives that must be fulfilled. Relying on this process, the persuader shapes messages directed at particular needs. The idea of a need state is like a premise in an argument; the argument runs like this: "Since you have within you a need for X, I will show you how to get X. You will get X by following my advice." Success in persuasion largely depends upon the ability to assess need states accurately.

We may wish to relabel our needs in terms other than those of Maslow or Packard, but their categories serve as good general descriptions of human needs. We ought to consider the requests persuaders make of us from the perspective of our own need states. For example, if a persuader asks us to use a new brand of soap because it pollutes less, we ought to ask if our security is really threatened to the degree that we ought to change brands of soap at extra cost and with little hope of reducing pollution.

As persuaders, we ought to examine the current needs of those we wish to influence. If we do that, not only are we more likely to succeed, but we are also more likely to do our audience a service by giving them a means to satisfy their needs.

A good way to train yourself to evaluate appeals from this critical perspective—as persuadee or persuader—is to try to restate existing pieces of persuasion, such as TV commercials, while considering the five need levels of Maslow's hierarchy or Packard's list of eight needs.

Attitudes: The Second Process Premise

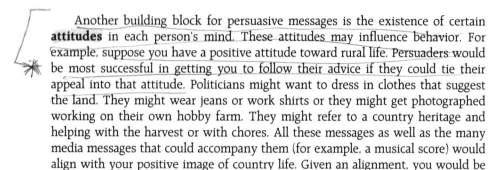

Another building block for persuasive messages is the existence of certain **attitudes** in each person's mind. These attitudes may influence behavior. For example, suppose you have a positive attitude toward rural life. Persuaders would be most successful in getting you to follow their advice if they could tie their appeal into that attitude. Politicians might want to dress in clothes that suggest the land. They might wear jeans or work shirts or they might get photographed working on their own hobby farm. They might refer to a country heritage and helping with the harvest or with chores. All these messages as well as the many media messages that could accompany them (for example, a musical score) would align with your positive image of country life. Given an alignment, you would be likely to vote for the candidate—at least that is what most attitude theories predict.

Really, attitudes are only part of a kind of family of influences on behavior. Probably the most easily changed factor of human behavior is **opinion.** We have opinions about the competence of Presidents based on what was said during the campaign and on what they have done since entering office. These opinions can change, however, especially if a President makes a few key errors—a foolish statement, fighting the Congress on a particular issue, or choosing to support a friend who turns out to·be corrupt. The Gallup and Harris polls record such shifts of opinion on a regular basis. It should be remembered, however, that opinions may not influence the behavior of persons who hold them. Take the examples just discussed. Though our opinions about a President may slip toward negative across a few months, we may still vote for that person in the next election. This is not to say that opinions are not related at all to behavior—only that they exert very weak influence.

Given a large enough change in opinion we may not support a President in the next campaign; or, given enough small shifts in our opinions, we may change our over-all **attitude** toward that President. Thus attitudes become the second level of internal pressure on behavior. We have an *attitude* toward smoking composed of many *opinions*: that it is costly; that it is unhealthy; that it is dirty; that it bothers others; that it destroys the body's supply of vitamin C, and so on. Opinions are verbal statements of part of the attitude. Philip Zimbardo, a prominent sociologist, puts it this way when he notes that attitudes are "either mental readiness or implicit predispositions that exert some general and consistent influence on a fairly large class of evaluative responses."[6]

Notice that Zimbardo stresses the enduring quality of attitude shifts. There is

---

6. Philip G. Zimbardo, Ebbe E. Ebbesen, and Christina Maslach, *Influencing Attitudes and Changing Behavior* (Reading, Massachusetts: Addison-Wesley Publishing Co., 1976). p. 20.

even a school of advertising research that goes under the acronym DAGMAR. The philosophy is that ad agencies ought to Design Advertising Goals so they can be Measured by Attitudinal Response. In other words, the goal of advertising is attitudinal change toward the company or product and not purchase behavior. It is hoped that if we have an improved image for a product—say Rice Chex—there will be an increase in purchase of the product. Unfortunately, this attitude/behavior linking has been very difficult to demonstrate, perhaps because of the many intervening variables that might also cause purchase of a product. Simple awareness of a product's name, packaging, display location in the store, or the kind of background music being played may cause purchase. Other factors like time of day or sex of purchaser may be the key. Even in carefully controlled experiments with many of these causes filtered out, the attitude and behavior do not consistently link up. Researchers blame this on poor design in research studies or a weak measuring instrument.

Thus what we know about attitudes is not how or whether they determine actions; instead, we know about how they change and which of them are most likely to change. In his early studies, psychologist Carl Hovland found that attitudes that changed were usually not ego-involving, were not central, or were based on previous experience or commitment of the people studied. Hovland studied these factors, because otherwise his research team would "run the risk of no measurable effects, particularly with small scale experiments."[7] Later research did use socially significant and ego-involved topics. Until recently, most researchers measured attitude shift as Hovland did—using short, one-time messages, and measuring the shift by pencil-and-paper tests. Remember that, as Zimbardo pointed out, a verbalized attitude is really an opinion statement. Opinions are the most easily changed and most fickle of the family of internal factors on which we base our actions. It was no surprise that such research found that attitudes were easy to change, and debate raged as to which theory could best explain the changes.

One of the more recent advances in the study of this second process premise is the work done by Martin Fishbein.[8] He substituted the term "behavioral intention" for the concept of attitude. He then measured what people say they intend to do and not how they feel about a particular product, candidate, or idea. More recent research has thus moved from looking at a general feeling toward a topic to the more concrete—what people think they will do about that topic, object, or person. This makes sense, for given any attitude toward or image of a politician, for example, there are several things that a voter might do—vote for the candidate, stay home from the polls, donate money to the campaign, work for the opponent, and so on. To discover over-all attitude toward the politician does not tell us much about the probability of any of these behaviors.

Probably attitudes and opinions are social tools as well as internal states.

---

7. Zimbardo, et al, p. 92.

8. Martin Fishbein and Icek Ajzen, *Belief, Attitude, Intention and Behavior: An Introduction to Theory and Research* (Reading, Massachusetts: Addison-Wesley Publishing Co., 1975).

They help us to get along in various social situations. We can sound slightly conservative when talking about gun control with good old Uncle Harry who is the president of the local National Rifle Association. In other circumstances, we can use our opinion statements to sound outraged that the local discount store is selling the deadly AR-15, which can easily be converted to a machine gun, or takedown rifles, which can be packed neatly into a briefcase or umbrella. Uncle Harry would rage against our complaints, but when he is not on the social scene, we can use such data to align ourselves with persons we believe are like us.

What does all this mean to the persuadee who is in the business of listening critically in a world of doublespeak? In other words, what can we do to uncover the persuader's intentions and beliefs about the audience? One of the advantages of at least being aware of attitudes is that we can second-guess about our image in the eyes of the persuader. For example, what kind of attitude is the customer presumed to have in the ad for a grandfather clock shown in Figure 4.5? The persuader obviously believes that members of the target market have high status needs. They have strong attitudes about the importance of financial success. They are somewhat snobbish, and they cultivate taste. Are these the people who read *House and Garden*, the magazine in which the ad appeared? If you read the ad would you be persuaded to go in and look at the clock? How would the company advertise in another kind of magazine—say *Playboy* or *Outdoor Life?* By seeking out the attitude that persuaders assume we have, we can become more critical receivers. Philip Zimbardo explains that attitudes have a consistency to them; a given attitude will operate the same way in similar situations, for our acts are seldom inconsistent with our attitudes (as opposed to our opinions).

Beliefs are similar to attitudes but are probably harder to change. This is because we have had some real-world experience that has confirmed our belief. For instance, most people believe that success is better than failure. As a result, they act in certain ways—they go to school to get an education so they can succeed. They get jobs and try to improve their job slots. They try to show their success through the display of some signs of success—a trophy, a house, well-behaved children, an attractive spouse, and so on. We might change their attitudes about playing the stock market as one road to success, but it would be difficult to change their core belief about the value of success. They might drop stocks in favor of real estate, but their goal would still be financial success. Our experience in the world from earliest childhood has verified the value of success over failure—in the classroom, in sports, with friends, in child-rearing, in careers, and elsewhere. Thus the belief tends to endure even longer than the attitude.

Unfortunately, much of the research done on attitudes as predictors of behavior has dealt with attitudes as though they were beliefs. Beliefs do seem to have a potent, long-lived influence over what we think and do. Attitudes are much more fickle. They change and shift as we encounter new situations. Our attitudes toward the idea of usury (the charging of excessive interest rates) shifted rapidly in the 1980s as worldwide inflation, unemployment, and bank failures occurred. Soon, the average citizen was charging the U.S. government over 17 percent to

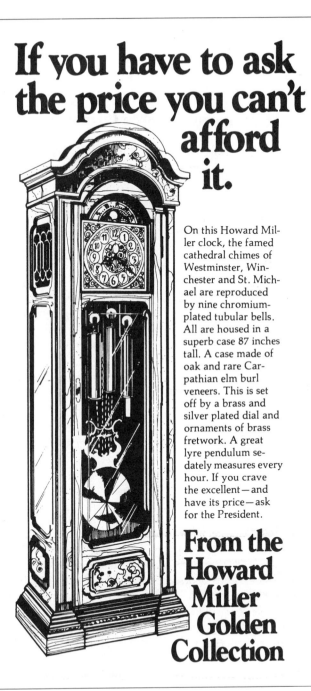

If you have to ask the price you can't afford it.

On this Howard Miller clock, the famed cathedral chimes of Westminster, Winchester and St. Michael are reproduced by nine chromium-plated tubular bells. All are housed in a superb case 87 inches tall. A case made of oak and rare Carpathian elm burl veneers. This is set off by a brass and silver plated dial and ornaments of brass fretwork. A great lyre pendulum sedately measures every hour. If you crave the excellent—and have its price—ask for the President.

From the Howard Miller Golden Collection

Figure 4.5. The company (persuader) reveals its attitudes toward potential customers (persuadees) as well as assumptions about their attitudes toward such things as spending, status, and quality. (Courtesy Howard Miller Clock Company. All rights reserved.)

borrow his or her money, banks were charging 20 percent, and most people looked back with nostalgia to home mortgages at 11 percent. The situation had changed and attitudes followed, instead of preceding, changes in lending and borrowing habits.

Balance and Consistency: The Third Process Premise

A large part of human existence revolves around successfully adapting to the world. For example, take new college freshmen. They are not aware of all that is going on in the confusion of registration, grades, book buying, using the library, finding buildings on campus, and other activities that will affect their lifestyle. How do they respond to this unknown world? As a general rule, they observe and search for patterns that will help them to adapt. Among many things, they learn that you can study at the library without interruption. They find that dorm food is fattening and that parking is available before but not after 10:00 A.M.

Much the same holds true for teachers, who cope with their classes and students through predictions. Unless the lectures they prepare lead to discussion or feedback, they will abandon their notes and shift to something else. Unless the students relate to the class in meaningful ways (that is, absorbing and applying the concepts instead of sleeping through class), the instructor will be forced to change the class or leave it.

These examples show the basis for the third kind of premise that humans respond to—the *need for predictability*. This premise relates to the good feeling we have when our predictions about the world are on target. Humans want a resolution of psychological conflict. We cannot tolerate confusion in our world. This desire for resolution provides a potent process premise to which persuaders appeal.

Two ways of looking at this problem of resolution of incongruity are found in Fritz Heider's balance theory and Leon Festinger's theory of cognitive dissonance.

Heider's Model: Balance/Imbalance

Heider's theory is relatively simple.[9] It reduces incongruity to its most elementary instance—one person talking to another person about a single topic or idea. Attitudes between the two persons (we could call one the persuader and the other the persuadee) can be represented by positive (+) signs or by negative (−) signs. Thus, the two persons could like (+) or dislike (−) one another; they could agree that the idea they are dealing with has bad (−) or good (+) values. They might disagree with one another so that one felt good (+) toward the topic while the other felt bad (−) toward it. Notice in Figure 4.6 that both the receiver and the source have good feelings about one another. Since they agree on the topic and

---

9. Fritz Heider, "Attitudes and Cognitive Organization," *Journal of Psychology*, Vol. 21 (January 1946), pp. 107–112.

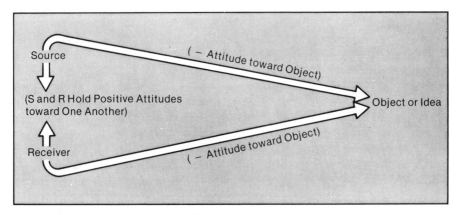

Figure 4.6. Heider's model: balance.

relate positively toward each other, there is a feeling of comfort—in Heider's word, balance.

There are three ways in which a person can feel this balance.

1. The source and receiver can have a negative attitude toward the object or idea and a positive attitudinal set toward one another, as in Figure 4.6.

2. The source and receiver can both have a positive attitude toward the object or idea and can have good feelings toward one another. (You and I can like the same idea or object and like one another, thus experiencing comfort and balance.)

3. The source and receiver can disagree about the idea or object and can dislike one another. (Since you and I are not alike and since we dislike one another, it is comforting to know that we disagree about the values of certain things or ideas.)

It is nice to know that those we respect and like have the same values and ideas as we do. It is also nice to know that those fools whom we dislike don't agree with us.

The persuader who tries to strengthen preexisting beliefs in an audience can do so by creating a *balanced* or comfortable situation for the receiver. As persuadees, we need to be aware of this strategy. When a persuader deals with you on a face-to-face basis and tells you what you already know or believe (for example, that living in a suburb is bad, that the price of food is skyrocketing, that you are a wise person), you ought to realize that creating balance is the strategy.

Suppose that the persuader wants to *change* beliefs and attitudes. It will be foolish to try to create balance for the persuadees. Instead, the persuader will try to throw their view of the world out of whack by creating imbalance in which their beliefs are shaken. Consider Figure 4.7. In this situation, someone whom I do

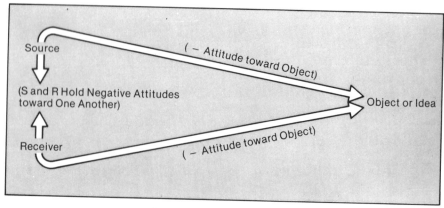

Figure 4.7. Heider's model: imbalance.

not respect dislikes the same things that I dislike. I am bound to feel uncomfortable or in a state of imbalance in such a case. How can I agree with such an idiot?

Suppose you want to persuade your parents to let you go to Europe this summer and to help finance your trip. You might already know that they oppose the trip. They are afraid you will be "led astray." They may also feel that they cannot afford to pay your way. They will feel the pinch of your not earning your own keep for the summer. Obviously, you will not get far telling them that you are grown up enough to handle yourself. Instead, you need to create imbalance in their beliefs. You might say getting involved with drugs is more likely at home when people are bored than while getting college credit on a European art tour. Or you might point out that you have done well in the past when given some freedom. Or you might remind them that there will be no cost for food while you are gone. All these tactics aim at creating imbalance in order to change minds.

There are probably only two ways in which to create imbalance in persuasive situations:

1. If the source and receiver favor one another but disagree about an object or idea, imbalance will be experienced.

2. If the source and receiver disfavor one another but agree on attitudes toward an object or idea, imbalance will be experienced.

Again, a principle we already know is operating. We want the world to live up to our expectations of it. If it does not, we experience imbalance; if it does, we experience balance.

Persuaders who want to get receivers to change their minds about an idea or object can create feelings of psychological imbalance or discomfort. When persuaders destroy your beliefs (for example, they prove that joining a fraternity or some other group will detract from your social life, not add to it), you ought to realize that they create imbalance for you. They want to change your opinion by relying on your need for psychological balance or comfort.

Festinger's Model: Consonance/Dissonance

Heider's theory is, of course, fairly limited. Not often do people hold beliefs that are simply positive or negative. Beliefs have magnitude as well as direction. We can have strong positive opinions toward a topic or relatively weak positive feelings. The theory proposed by Leon Festinger in his book *A Theory of Cognitive Dissonance* attempts to deal with some of the shortcomings in Heider's theory.[10] Festinger calls imbalance **dissonance,** which he defines as a feeling resulting from the existence of two nonfitting pieces of knowledge about the world: ". . . considering the two alone, the obverse of one element would follow from the other." **Consonance,** Festinger's pair term for balance, exists when "considering a pair of elements either one does follow from the other." The degree to which one of these elements may or may not follow from one another can vary, which is not true in balance theory. Though I may greatly dislike door-to-door sales representatives as a group, my weak positive feelings toward a certain salesman may create only slight feelings of dissonance or imbalance.

As in balance theory, there are times when things fit or "go together." This is *consonance,* or, in Latin derivation, "sound at the same time, harmonize, agree." Festinger says that any two beliefs could be shown as two parallel lines (see Figure 4.8). The solid line shows belief A, and the X on the line marks an attitude toward that belief. The broken line represents other information about A. The Y on this line represents our position on the new information, which we might call belief B. The distance between these two points—X and Y—is the amount of *dissonance* we feel when the two beliefs are not congruent. We feel psychic discomfort—the world is not acting as it should. The feeling comes from the dissonant cognitions. The dissonance must be reduced. This is the basis for many actions. Some persons change their beliefs by moving them closer to one another. Others rationalize the problem away; one way is to discredit the source of the cognitions. Others escape from feelings of dissonance by the processes of selective perception, selective retention, or selective exposure; in other words, they choose to forget or not to receive/perceive or not to be exposed to the information.

Let's look at a real case. Suppose that you smoke cigarettes—assume, for the sake of argument, a pack or more a day. Now assume that you hear that the odds of lung cancer are seventy times higher for smokers. Under Festinger's theory, you will be uncomfortable because of these two sets of information or beliefs (your smoking habits and the information relating to the danger of these habits). You may try to reduce this discomfort. You might cut down to fifteen cigarettes a day; you might quit; you might ignore the information and switch to some other more comfortable message; or you might rationalize (for example, hope for a cancer cure soon; discredit the source of the message).

---

10. Leon Festinger, *A Theory of Cognitive Dissonance* (Stanford, California: Stanford University Press, 1962). See also Shel Feldman (ed.), *Cognitive Consistency* (New York: Academic Press, 1966).

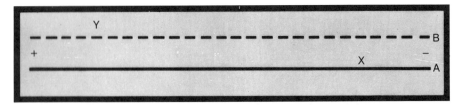

Figure 4.8. Festinger's model: dissonance.

Psychological discomfort is caused by inconsistency between our beliefs and information inputs. The tension created must be relieved in some way. Festinger suggested several ways by which people try to relieve tension:

1. They devalue initial beliefs.

2. They devalue the information by labeling it as biased, unproven, or untrue.

3. They perceive the input as a hatchet job. Researchers call this selective perception—seeing what we want to see.

4. They may try to forget about the new information. This is called selective retention or selective remembering and forgetting. (Parents are good at this one sometimes.)

5. They may rationalize by saying something like "Oh, well, things are like that all over."

In some cases, people may use more than one of these ways at the same time. They may change their attitude about a topic in general while devaluing the information and rationalizing. This combination is familiar among smokers who, after hearing of the dangers of smoking and its links to fatal diseases, devalue the research and rationalize that you have to die of something anyway. At any rate, this experience with dissonance is common, and persuaders often try to create it to get the persuadees to feel psychologically uncomfortable and thus to nudge them to change.

Though Festinger does not deal very deeply in his book with the notion of consonance, it seems clear that most seek it. We listen to the candidate of our choice, and more often than not avoid listening to the person we will not vote for. A good deal of research shows that we seek information that fits with our beliefs and avoid data that conflict with our beliefs. Conservative people read conservative newspapers; liberal people read liberal newspapers. It's another way of saying "birds of a feather flock together." This is probably why people try so hard to avoid political or religious arguments. You really can't persuade anyone on matters like these, it seems, so you just change the topic to something more neutral.

For example, let's suppose that you have decided to major in computer sciences, even though you have never been very good in mathematics. You find that not only are your classes tough and time-consuming, but they are boring to boot. You now go to the computer lab center and hear fellow students around the vending machines complaining about how hard their classes are. They talk about how much time they spend debugging programs and so on. You will probably think something like "Whew! Then it's not just me." You add some conversation to the effect that "Yeah, and some of it isn't the most interesting stuff in the world either." You are seeking that final bit of consonant information. Much to your delight, those gathered there come back with sentences like "You said it!" or "That's the understatement of the year, but at least we'll make big bucks when we graduate." You experience consonance, especially since it was the attractive job opportunities that lured you into the field anyway. With such confirmation there is no need to resolve any inconsistency or psychic discomfort.

Experiences like this are common; we find information confirming our position, and that makes our belief stronger. There are many actions we can take as a result of feelings of consonance:

1. We can revalue our initial beliefs, making them stronger in all likelihood—it really was a good idea to major in computer sciences.

2. We can revalue the source of the information input. "Boy! those other students majoring in C.S. are really sharp and on the ball. They'll go far in this world."

3. We may perceive the information as stronger than it actually is and focus on the strongest parts of it.

4. We may remember the most positive parts of the information and choose to highlight those that best support our belief—the high salaries, maybe.

5. We may seek more supporting information by going over to the placement office, for instance, and copying down the salaries that the computer science people are going out at.

6. We may do more than one of the above.

The tactic of creating consonance, then, is used to create stronger attitudes, to undergird existing cognitions, and to increase one's source of credibility. Consonance negates the old saying that "flattery gets you nowhere" and turns it around to "flattery gets you everywhere." People enjoy exposure to consonant information—it proves that they are right.

A Review and Conclusion

Among the premises to which persuaders appeal are those that arise out of psychological processes that occur in all of us. One is the presence of certain need states. There are many ways of labeling need states; but, for the receiver, the set of labels is not so important as is the process of identifying the need states to which persuaders are appealing in their messages. So it does not matter if you realize that a persuader is trying to appeal to your belonging needs or to your reassurance-of-worth need. The important thing is that as a receiver you do not fall blindly for a message that plays on your weakness. The same principle holds true as we examine attitudes. Knowing that a persuader is trying to appeal to attitudes that we hold or values that we have helps to reveal the persuader's purposes. This can aid us in making the choices presented to us by various persuaders. Finally, looking at our states of balance/imbalance or dissonance/consonance can identify our vulnerabilities. Knowing where we are weak can help alert us to persuasive appeals to those weaknesses.

Questions for Further Thought

1. What other needs (aside from those listed in Maslow's hierarchy or in Packard's list of needs) do humans experience? Which of them could be translated into Maslow's terms? How? Give examples.

2. What is the difference between a *process premise* and a *language premise?* Cite several examples where these have operated in your life recently.

3. If a person favored more lenient marijuana laws and then heard that a favorite politician opposed such a change, would the person experience consonance or dissonance?

4. What about a person who opposed more lenient marijuana laws?

5. Describe a consonant situation and a dissonant situation for person X who has an initial attitude favoring energy conservation.

6. Cite examples of the following methods of reducing dissonance:

   a. Devalue the source of inputs or information causing the dissonance.

   b. Selectively expose oneself to nondissonance-producing information.

   c. Selectively forget information that causes dissonance.

   d. Selectively remember information that reduces dissonance.

   e. Change attitudes or beliefs.

   f. Selectively perceive the world in order to reduce dissonance.

   You may wish to follow a single case through these methods of reducing dissonance (for example, your parents facing a dissonance-producing problem, such as letting their "baby" have an apartment off campus), or you may cite several different examples.

7. Cite examples of the following methods of increasing the feelings of psychological comfort experienced in consonance; follow the directions given for question 6:

   a. Revaluing the source of the consonance-producing source.

   b. Selectively exposing oneself to consonance-producing information.

   c. Selectively remembering consonance-producing information.

d. Selectively perceiving things that are consonance producing.

e. Changing one's attitudes or beliefs.

f. Selectively forgetting things that do not lend themselves to feelings of consonance.

Experiences in Persuasion

1. Select newspaper and magazine advertisements for a certain product or type of product (deodorant, for example). When you have a good selection (ten to twenty), analyze them according to the needs on Maslow's hierarchy to which they appeal. The ads may be doing several things at once and may appeal to more than one level. Discuss this concomitance of appeal. Argue for the effectiveness or ineffectiveness of one of the ads in particular.

2. Write a letter to the editor of your campus paper or your local paper, couching it so that it would appeal to the *security* level of Maslow's hierarchy. Rewrite it so that it appeals to the *belonging* level; the *esteem* level; the *self-actualization* level. Determine which of the four ways would be the best; discuss how and why it might be the best. (If you do this as a group, one person might write the message aimed at *security*, another at *belonging*, and so on; then the group would determine which was most effective.)

3. Trace the history of research concerning dissonance (try speech communication journals such as the *Journal of Communication* and *Communication Monographs*, as well as journals in other fields such as the *Journal of Abnormal and Social Psychology*) and report to the class on your findings. What do we know about dissonance? Self-persuasion? Belief discrepancy?

4. Do the "letter to the editor" assignment (see number 2), but this time write a letter answering an editorial in the paper. Do it in a way that will cause dissonance for the editorial writer and then in a way to cause consonance. Submit both letters, using your own name on one and the name of another person on the other if your friend is agreeable. What happened? Explain to the class what you did and what the results were.

5
Content Premises in Persuasion

B esides the process premise, another kind of premise can serve as the raw material of persuasion: the **content premise.** This type of premise does not rely on personal preference for certain language choices or styles nor on the internal or psychological premises we have just discussed in Chapter 4. Instead, it assumes a good deal of agreement from situation to situation. For example, a group of persuadees believes that problems usually have causes. When causes are removed, the problem is reduced or even eliminated. This brings us to cause/effect reasoning. By drawing a strong link between a cause (say, the overconsumption of petroleum fuel in the United States) and the problems arising from this cause (for example, high prices, an unfavorable export/import ratio, national apprehension over the future, and so on), persuaders can influence behavior. We all try not to appear contrary or out of step with those around us. This encourages us to accept certain persuasive advice just because everyone else seems to think it is logical.

For example, with the worldwide economy in a precarious position at the outset of the 1980s, many people were persuaded not to buy a new automobile and thus go out on a limb in uncertain times. At the same time, the automakers argued that buying new cars might be just what the economy needed: "When Detroit sneezes, the rest of the country catches cold." Buying a new car will put people to work, they claimed, thus increasing tax receipts and cutting the government deficit. Further, they argued, the new models got better gas mileage—as high as 50 miles per gallon and even more. Consumers could save themselves the cost of the car in a short time and help cut down on oil imports, thus getting the country out of a slump. Government economists, on the other hand, might have argued that buying the car would just increase consumer debt and drive interest rates even higher. High interest rates had helped to cause the slump, and it would be far better for people to put their money into savings to help drive down interest rates.

Both the automakers and the government economists were using logic and not emotion to try to persuade. The cause/effect appeal is frequently used by politicians and government officials, in the courts, in business, and even in consumer advertising to some degree. It assumes that certain premises already in the audience's mind can be used as the implicit premise in an enthymeme. We call these premises content premises because they rely on the patterns by which the *content* of the messages is connected with what are believed to be accepted patterns of logical or rational thought. In other words, content premises "sell" because they are assumed to be logical. There are four dimensions of such premises:

4 dimensions of content analysis :

1. **The nature of content and proof:** What causes us to believe or not believe a persuader who is appealing to our intellect? Why do we sometimes believe with very little evidence presented and at other times demand much detailed evidence? How much proof is enough?

2. **The nature of evidence and reasoning:** What is evidence? What is reasoning? What are the basic modes of drawing conclusions or of linking information to action?

3. **Strategic and tactical levels of content premises:** What is the difference between the *over-all organization* of content-oriented persuasive messages and the *internal steps* used to get agreement with this over-all thrust of the message? Are there simple ways to describe and analyze both levels?

4. **Proving a point:** Does *self-persuasion* operate in all persuasion? If so, how? Is one kind of *evidence* better than another for the purposes of proof? Is one kind of *proof* better than another? Why do some methods seem more successful than others? Why is emotional or empathic evidence so persuasive?

With these questions and others in mind, let's look at persuasion as it occurs around us—on TV, in the newspaper, in the classroom, on campus, and in our homes. We know that we are persuaded many times each day and that we need to be persuaded in order to make choices in this confusing and complex world. But *how* are we persuaded?

What Is Content?

Suppose that you are confronted by a Campus Crusade evangelist on campus. He wants you to join the group and hopes to get a new convert. He tells you that you must go to the informational meeting in the student center lounge at 7 P.M. tonight. You have three options: you can do as he asks; you can reject him out of hand; or you can ask for good reasons for going to the meeting. The first two options are likely to be prompted by some kind of emotional response you have to the speaker and the topic. You might hate "holier than thou" evangelists and thus reject the persuasion. You might be a true believer already and so will warmly follow the advice. The last option, however, is the one that seeks further information. If you said, "Give me three good reasons," you would be asking for proof in the form of content premises—arguments or statements that would be convincing to most reasonable persons. The crusader could say, "Well, because you are attending the philosophy of religion class with me. This is a good way to add to your knowledge about that subject. You may even get information useful in writing that term paper we have to do." This would be a good enough reason for many people to give the informational meeting a try. You might be a little more demanding and say to the persuader, "That's one good reason, two more to go." If the evangelist hoped to persuade you, he would have to come up with more information that would be reasonably acceptable.

So the value of the content premise for persuaders is not in its ability to prompt an emotional or psychological response. Rather it elicits a logical or rational response—one that relies on the nature of the evidence presented in the argument and on the logic by which the evidence fits with the "widely accepted" content premise held to be reasonable or true by receivers.

What Is Proof?

Proof varies from *situation to situation.* What may "prove" a point to a weekly fraternity meeting may not "prove" the same point to the university administration. Several books in the last two decades have tried to "prove" that President Kennedy's assassination was caused by a complex conspiracy. They successfully persuaded some people but failed with others. So proof varies from *person to person* as well. In the early 1980s the Reagan administration tried to "prove" that Libya and the Soviet Union were the spawning and training grounds for many international terrorist groups. The proof worked for some people in the United States but didn't convince many people in Middle Eastern cultures. So proof can vary from *culture to culture.* In general, though, we can say that proof consists of *enough evidence that can be connected through reasoning to convince audience members to take the persuader's advice or to believe in what he or she says.*

Aristotle, an early student of persuasion, recognized three kinds of proof. First, there was the credibility, or **ethos**, of the persuader, which had two dimensions. One was reputation: Had these persuaders been reliable in the past? Could they be trusted? Were they wise? The combined answers to these questions constituted the reputation that the persuader brought to the speaking situation—courtroom or senate chamber. The other dimension of ethos was the credibility that developed as the speaker spoke. Credibility relied on the speaker's voice, gestures, eye contact, and so on. (We will consider this kind of proof in Chapter 6 where it relates to cultural premises that we hold.) The second kind of proof was **pathos**, or the appeal to the "passions or the will"—in other words, emotional appeals such as we have just discussed in Chapter 4. Third, there was a kind of proof called **logos**—appeals to the audience's logical or rational self. '

According to Aristotle, there are several ways to talk about logical persuasion, the foremost being syllogisms. A classic syllogism is usually expressed in three steps: *a major premise, a minor premise,* and a *conclusion.* For example: All men are mortal (major premise); Socrates is a man (minor premise); hence Socrates is mortal (conclusion). Since the time of Aristotle, the task of the persuader using logical persuasion has been to identify major premises that would be generally acceptable and then to offer minor premises *substantiated by evidence* that would lead to conclusions that would imply action or belief changes. That is also the focus throughout this book—to identify the stylistic, process, and content premises that are generally held by audiences and to which persuaders often appeal.

Most contemporary theorists agree that proof is composed of two factors: **reasoning** and **evidence.** In the proper mix, these two will lead persuadees to adopt the changes advocated by the persuader. Sometimes more evidence is needed. Sometimes very little reasoning is involved. For instance, in the musical comedy *The Music Man*, Professor Harold Hill sells an entire town on a need for a boys' band complete with uniforms (which he, by chance, happens to sell) on the flimsiest of logical appeals. He points out numerous symptoms of trouble in the town (kids are smoking, reading dirty books, cursing, dressing outrageously, and so on). He then concludes with these words, "That's trouble and that starts with T and that rhymes with P and that stands for 'pool.' " He goes on to point out that with a band to be busy with, the boys will make no more visits to the pool hall where the bad habits are all learned. In this example, an overkill of evidence enables the persuader to short-circuit the reasoning process. Hill's "proof" relies on a rhyme scheme—P rhymes with T, therefore pool means trouble. Usually the "mix" between evidence and reasoning is not so extreme as in Harold Hill's case. More often there is an evidence threshold that might be met, given consistency in reasoning. Let us look more closely at these two components of proof.

Evidence and Reasoning

There are several ways to look at evidence and reasoning. The way in which information is linked (that is, reasoned out) is the strategic element in discourse using content premises; and the information that is combined and the choice of it (that is, evidence) are the tactical elements in content premise persuasion. We are interested in *strategic* effect. By examining what persuaders do—how they operate—we can infer motives and discover what they are ultimately up to. For example, suppose I wished to persuade you that smoking causes lung cancer. The thrust of my message—the strategy of it, so to speak—is to create a cause/effect argument. I want to prove to you that a given effect—lung cancer—has a given cause—cigarette smoking. Along the way I might engage in a variety of *tactics* (for example, I might show slides of cancerous body cells; I might give vivid testimony of the pain and suffering involved in cancer deaths; I might offer statistical correlations; or I might do a variety of other things), but they would all be related to my general strategy, belief, motive, or intention. These tactics are the "stuff" from which proof will ultimately emerge for you as persuadee; somewhere along the line, I will reach the threshold for you and will have "proved" to you that you must stop smoking. In other situations, other elements will persuade you to stop—the key may not even be planned by a persuader but can still be the threshold for change.

By looking at the traditional rule-governed ideas about evidence and reasoning as the *strategic* level of persuasion, we are able to consider various kinds of "proof," ranging from direct experience to emotional description to intellectual consideration of data and statistics—all under the label *tactics* or *evidence.* When coupled with the notion of a threshold for persuasion, the set of terms suggested here for analysis offers the persuadee a maximum amount of flexibility in examining not only what kinds of content premises persuaders utilize in the persuasive attempts but also the ways in which they present these. The rationale behind these moves can indicate motive or intent and can again provide the persuadee with a powerful tool for critically examining and reviewing persuasive information before making a decision.

Types of Evidence

Earlier, we referred briefly to the varying strengths of bits of evidence: In some situations, statistics are strong; in others, pictorial evidence is most powerful; and in yet others, experience is the best evidence. In all these instances, persuasion relies on an assumption that one can learn and act on the basis of information gained indirectly and vicariously.[1] Even when we do not learn or are not persuaded by the experiences of others, our own experience usually is enough to cause us to change. The Sioux Indians were aware of this. As a baby crawled close to the campfire, they did not pull it away saying something like "Hot! Stay away, baby! Hot!" as we in our culture would do. Instead, they watched the baby's progress very closely and allowed the baby to reach into the fire and touch a hot coal, burning itself mildly. Then they quickly pulled the baby away and treated the burn. The experience "persuaded" the child to be careful with fire.

A more contemporary example of the persuasive potency of experience is reported by Hannah Arendt in her book, *Eichmann in Jerusalem: A Report on the Banality of Evil.*[2] Adolf Eichmann was one of the top Nazi war criminals who had escaped from Germany at the end of the war to live under assumed names in South America. He was traced to one of these countries, kidnapped by Israeli agents, and flown to Israel to stand trial for the murder of millions of Jews in the extermination camps of World War II. The jury heard many survivors of the camps identify Eichmann as one who came and inspected to make sure everything was working to maximum efficiency. The jury saw film footage of mass exterminations, of warehouses filled with the shoes and eyeglasses of the dead. And they heard many mind-boggling reports of the extermination plans drafted by Eichmann and others. When Eichmann was permitted to testify, the jury heard him say that he had never murdered anyone. It was true that he had "relocated" Jews and non-Jews and that he had "exterminated" Jews and other *untermenschen* (subhumans), but the jury should know that he had never killed a human

---

1. A good discussion of this premise (that we learn much of our knowledge vicariously) is presented in Mark Abrahamson's *Interpersonal Accommodation* (New York: Van Nostrand-Reinhold Co., 1966).

2. Hannah Arendt, *Eichmann in Jerusalem: A Report on the Banality of Evil* (New York: Viking Press, 1964).

being.[3] From that point on, the jury realized Eichmann's testimony would be laced with special language. "Special treatment" meant something quite different in Nazi minds than it did in normal prisons. So did "final solution," "experiment," and "resettlement camp." The singular experience of hearing Eichmann deny the humanity of Jewish people was indeed persuasive to the jury.

So, whether our experiences are real or only vicarious, they can "prove" things for us. Persuaders must use enough evidence to convince their audiences, but they must be careful not to overwhelm their audiences with too much or with too dramatic evidence. Generally, evidence falls into two categories—the **dramatic appeal** that aims at the imagination and emotions of the persuadee and the **rational appeal** that aims at the intellect. Let us look at these two types of proof—Aristotle's *pathos* and *logos*—in detail.

Dramatistically Oriented Evidence

Imagine the following situation in your class: A student stands and announces that he is going to give a speech on abortion. As an introduction to this speech, he turns on a cassette tape recorder, and you begin to hear an interview with a young girl who is dying in a hospital as a result of an illegal abortion. The testimony is being taken by a hardened policeman, and the young girl is weakly gasping for breath. Her voice rattles in her throat as she recounts the abortion scene, the amount of money paid, the instruments used, and so forth. She is clearly in pain, as indicated by her voice, and she is also obviously frightened and in need of comfort. As the details unfold, you feel yourself becoming sick to your stomach. When recorded this way, the bare facts are almost unbearable. The persuader is utilizing what most persons would call "emotionally laden" proof— some call it psychologically oriented. Clearly aimed at deep-set fears and dislikes, it is designed to cause revulsion in the listeners—and to persuade them that illegal abortions are horrible. Although the evidence is emotionally oriented, it is certainly not "illogical" to conclude, as a result of it, that illegal abortions are not desirable; in fact, it is *totally* logical to draw such a conclusion. Instead of labeling this evidence and reasoning as "irrational," "nonrational," "illogical," or "nonlogical," we call it **dramatistically oriented** evidence.

The point is that emotional responses to problems are often as logical as intellectual responses. One does not need to sift systematically through mounds of statistics on abortion. The conclusion is not based on intellectual ability but on human emotional response. This reality has been one of the points made by critics of today's American culture—that we do not respond emotionally often enough, that we rely too often on "intellectualized responses" to problems, thus neglecting human situations and feelings in favor of hard cold facts. Perhaps a single example of illegal abortion *is* enough evidence to convince any *reasonable* person that legalized abortion is needed to prevent human suffering. If the evidence is dramatic or emotional enough, persuadees will not ask for more; they will not engage

---

3. *Ibid.* See especially p. 22, where Eichmann is quoted as saying ". . . I never killed a Jew or a non-Jew, for that matter I never killed any human being"; and p. 84, where Arendt cites some of the "code names" for extermination, such as "evacuation," "special treatment," and "resettlement," and discusses the "language rules" of the Third Reich.

in philosophical discussions about first premises relating to the sanctity of human life. Instead, by vicariously suffering with the victim of the illegal abortion, the persuadees become convinced.

Perhaps it is that word "dramatic" that really is important here. Dramatistically oriented evidence invites and encourages vicarious experience on the part of persuadees in an attempt to persuade them to a certain course of action.[4] Such persuasion relies upon the persuadees' ability to project themselves into a context or situation described by the persuader—to "feel" what others feel, to live the problem vicariously.

If we were to look at historic persuasive speeches or at highly successful speeches of the present, we would undoubtedly find a great deal of emotionally oriented and dramatic evidence. The persuader presents a dramatic situation to the audience and then "invites" the listeners to participate in the drama—in their imaginations, to become actors themselves. There is no intellectualizing here; at the same time, one would be hard put to say that the audiences reacted "illogically" or "irrationally." They merely responded to dramatic evidence. This type of evidence encourages the persuadee to co-create proof with the persuader. The result is powerful, and probably long-lasting, persuasion.[5]

There are several types of evidence that lend themselves to this dramatistic approach. For example, a good way to use dramatistic evidence is through the **narrative,** or story. Most of the great preachers, orators, and politicians were also good storytellers. They could use the narrative skillfully. Often the narrative is used to capture the audience's attention and to draw it into the topic. This effect is reinforced with other evidence, and more narratives might be worked in to keep us interested. The final call for action or change may also be expressed in the narrative form—perhaps telling a story that parallels the one that opened the speech but now has a happy ending instead of the tragic one that first riveted audience's attention to the topic. Chances are that you have heard speeches or sermons in which the story or narrative was skillfully used. These are the sermons and speeches that seem to have the most impact and are remembered the longest. The parables of the New Testament are easy to recall while many of the other verses fade from our memory soon after we hear them. As a professor of mine once said, "The narrative will carry more persuasive freight than any other form of evidence."

Another type of dramatistic evidence is **testimony.** Now we are not telling the story or narrative about someone else—say the bride who didn't stop her new husband from drinking too much at the reception and who subsequently was killed in an auto accident while he was driving. The persuader who uses testimony

---

4. Several good discussions of the importance of the dramatic structure can be found in literature from various fields. For example, from the perspective of literary criticism on the power of the dramatic to cause persuasive motivation, see Kenneth Burke, *A Grammar of Motives* (Berkeley: University of California Press, 1970); Robert F. Baker, *Personality and Interpersonal Behavior* (New York: Holt, Rinehart and Winston, 1970)—see especially Chapter 7, "Describing Fantasy themes," pp. 136–155; Ernest G. Bormann, "Fantasy and Rhetorical Vision: The Rhetorical Criticism of Social Reality," *Quarterly Journal of Speech,* Vol. 58 (December 1972), pp. 396–407.

5. Good examples of the use of dramatistic invitations can be found in a number of speeches in recent times as well as in the history of public speaking. Some examples are Clarence Darrow's defense of joy killers Richard Loeb and Nathan Leopold, which "invites" the judge to join in the high drama of humanitarian change; and John F. Kennedy's Inaugural Address, which invites the listeners to do something for their country.

may read an eyewitness account or may recount events. Some use their own testimony as eyewitnesses to an event or problem. Sometimes, they use the testimony of recognized experts on the topic. Suppose we were interested in persuading Americans of Irish descent to stop sending funds to the terrorist I.R.A. We could read the testimony of a mother whose little daughter had been blown to bits by an I.R.A. bomb. Or we could give our own accounts of the trip we took to Ireland and of the fear people there expressed to us. Or we could report the testimony of some recognized expert on the problem—say Senator Edward Kennedy who, as a person of Irish descent, did research on the I.R.A. He concluded that support of it only made things worse for Northern Ireland, and he tried to persuade fellow Irish-Americans to stop sending aid. Testimonial is very similar to narrative, except that it is from the perspective of an eyewitness or a recognized expert.

The **anecdote** is a related form that can be used. Anecdotes are usually very short scenarios, perhaps only a sentence or two long, that tell of some event to make a point. For example, suppose we were complaining about the U.S. Postal Service, and we say we have an inside tip that turtle soup is a daily staple at the Postal Service employee cafeteria. Anecdotes are often humorous and are frequently hypothetical, so that they are quite different from the testimonial or the narrative.

There are several other ways in which persuaders can dramatize evidence. At an antismoking presentation, for instance, audiovisual materials can show cancerous lung tissue. The audience can participate by exhaling cigarette smoke through a clean white tissue and observing the chemical stains left behind. Sometimes persuaders dramatize using visual aids to demonstrate the problem and solution. One of my students spoke on the need to be aware when stress was building up and how to use jogging to reduce it. He displayed a large, deflated balloon that he said represented an average student at N.I.U. The "student" was inflated a little with the stress of settling into a new dorm room. Another puff of air was the stress of registration. More air went in for the first exams and fraternity rush. Soon the balloon was ready to pop. The speaker then called on his audience to release their stress through exercise. He ended the speech saying, "Or else do you know what could happen?" Whereupon he popped the balloon with a pin. The audience's attention never strayed from the balloon or the point of the speech. This kind of dramatization is useful and persuasive. You will encounter many kinds of dramatizations as you process the many persuasive messages aimed at you each day. Learn to recognize them and to respond to them wisely.

Intellectual or Rational Evidence

One might use dramatic evidence to persuade listeners to conserve fuel (for example, describe a cold, desolate North America with most of its population dead from exposure and those who are left huddled together in our southernmost states without electricity, conveniences, and so on). With topics like this, however, we are more likely to hear evidence that appeals to our intellect rather than our emotional needs. Most appeals urging conservation point out that we can save money by insulating, for example, or by avoiding jack-rabbit starts and speeding.

The persuaders assume that we hold a major premise—that it is good to avoid waste and hence to save money. By giving us a minor premise—that insulating or slow driving saves money—and by backing it up with numerous examples, the persuaders create a kind of syllogism:

Major premise—saving dollars is good.

Minor premise—conserving fuel saves dollars.

Conclusion—hence conservation is good.

This appeal is based on data that we can verify and not on some imagined distant setting or time. The persuader using this tactic asks us to draw conclusions from the evidence. Dramatistically oriented evidence, on the other hand, relies on people's ability to use their creative imagination and empathy; this ability is usually related to specific situations. To say that one is more or less logical than the other clouds the issue. It may be totally logical to respond to highly dramatic material or events. It may be totally illogical to stick only to advice that is intellectually oriented. Both methods work, but at different times and in different ways with different sets of persons. They both rely on the persuadees' matching data with beliefs or laws of reason that they hold to be true.

There are several kinds of intellectual or rational evidence that we are exposed to every day. For example, we often see or hear *statistics* cited in an advertisement, a speech, or a documentary. Usually, statistics are more persuasive if they are general or if they can somehow be visualized. It is hard to imagine our national debt when we see the figures written out. It is much more meaningful to hear that our national debt is so large that the income taxes paid until June pay only the interest on this debt. Statistics are often used to *compare and contrast* two or more different brands, politicians, ideas, solutions, and so on. We can say that the national debt rose twice as fast during one Administration as it did during the previous one. We might hear that solar energy could save the average homeowner over $400 per year in heating costs compared with oil or gas heat. Or we might learn that light beer from Michelob has only 76 calories per twelve-ounce can compared with 90 calories for Brand X.

Examples are another kind of evidence that appeal to the rational mind. A speaker trying to persuade you to take up skydiving might use an example that even people who are afraid to climb stepstools can become competent and safe skydivers. *Samples* can be used to *demonstrate* a product or a point. Telling people that cola drinks are bad for their health is not as effective as showing what the can of Coke did to a nail and a chunk of meat that had been left soaking in it overnight. And there are other kinds of evidence appealing to the intellect that you will encounter in our persuasion world.

Types of Reasoning

Remember that we said that proof was enough evidence that was *connected with reasoning* to convince an audience to believe or act on a persuader's advice.

"There are so many ways of entertaining the children. They're so well behaved here, and we're so relaxed."

Mike and Mary Lee Hurley discuss their third visit to Bermuda.

"Tennis, golf, beautiful seascapes, sightseeing. Whatever your passion is, you don't have to go far in any direction to find it."

"We had a panoramic view of the entire island. The beauty is incredible."

"It's the people on this island. They're part of it. Very fine, very pleasant."

Bermuda
Unspoiled. Unhurried. Uncommon.

See your travel agent or write Bermuda, Dept. 314, 630 Fifth Avenue, N.Y., N.Y. 10020
Suite 1422, 401 N. Michigan Ave., Chicago, Ill. 60611 or Suite 1010, 44 School St., Boston, Mass. 02108

Figure 5.1. The evidence presented here is very dramatistic. Following the persuader's advice may be totally logical even though the evidence doesn't demand that the persuadee generalize, categorize, or sift evidence. (Courtesy Bermuda Department of Tourism.)

So there is this second step in the process of logical persuasion—connecting the pieces of evidence by reasoning. Several patterns of reasoning that are deeply held in our culture form the unseen premises on which much logical persuasion is built. Persuaders don't identify these for the audience by saying something like "Folks, I am about to reason by the cause-to-effects pattern," but they do shape their arguments in accordance with patterns like cause-to-effects.

Cause-to-Effects Reasoning

Cause-to-effects reasoning is very powerful in our culture. Even our language is dependent upon it. For example, we rarely say "the ball was hit by the bat," which is a passive-voice clause. Instead we put the cause out front and let it create the effect. We say "the bat hit the ball" which is an active-voice clause. Persuaders frequently use cause/effect reasoning to identify events, trends, or facts that have caused certain effects. They tell us that if a cause is present we can expect certain effects to follow. If the effects are bad, and we want to do something about them, we usually try to remove the cause. For example, some argue that the cause of high crime rates is slum environments, which are occupied predominantly by minorities. If we permit slums to continue existing, we can expect more rape, murder, robbery, arson, and muggings. The way to avoid the disadvantageous effects is to rebuild the slums, find jobs for the unemployed, and provide day-care facilities for the inner-city working mother. The persuader's task in cause/effects reasoning is to provide some pattern, perhaps out of the past, to suggest that as the cause emerged, the effects followed. In the above example the persuader might show that in cities where there are no slums—Stockholm for example—crime rates are very low. Or the persuader could show a correlation between size of slums and crime rates; that as slums grow, crime rises.

Effects-to-Cause Reasoning

A less-used, and sometimes flawed, type of reasoning is called **effects-to-cause** reasoning. Here the persuader cites some known effects and tries to work back to the cause. For example, at an antihandgun rally in Chicago, posters and fact sheets cited these statistics:[6]

Handgun Murders, 1980—6 months

Great Britain	8
West Germany	42
Japan	48
United States	10,728

Here the persuaders cited effects—a tremendous number of handgun murders in the United States compared with other countries. They hoped to tie the effects to a specific cause—the large number of handguns in circulation and the ease with which one can go out and buy one. They hoped to persuade voters to approve of the upcoming handgun registration ordinance. The problem they had, of course, was in making the argument that handguns were the *sole* reason for the large amount of murders. For example, violence on TV may be a contributory cause of murder. Furthermore, their opponents might say that there were higher rates of (say) knife murders or strangulations and poisonings in those other countries or that the U.S. population is higher. This is the weakness in effect/cause reasoning.

---

6. *The Chicago Tribune*, October 25, 1981, Sec. 3, p. 2.

Reasoning from Symptoms

Persuaders sometimes identify a series of symptoms and then try to conclude something from them. This strategy is similar to effect/cause reasoning. For example, politicians may cite how much worse things are now than they were when their opponent took office—unemployment is up, inflation is running wild, and recent polls show that people have lost faith in their ability to control their own destinies. The hope is that the voters will blame the incumbent opponent for the troubles. Midas Muffler company recently ran an ad in which a pudgy, middle-aged, and obviously bushed man flops into an easy chair while his wife asks him about the new muffler job. "Did you have to wait long, dear?" she asks. His response is "I should've gone to Midas." "Did you get a guarantee?" "I should've gone to Midas." The wife is expressing a series of symptoms of a high-quality muffler job. Hubby is persuading us—go to Midas when you need a muffler.

Criteria-to-Application Reasoning

Another kind of reasoning is argument from **criteria to application.** With this kind of reasoning, the persuader sets up some criteria that are then applied to a specific case in order to prove something about that case. Consider the following set of hypothetical criteria for a good government social program:

1. It should be efficient in terms of numbers of dollars spent and the number of recipients served.
2. It should attempt to serve people while providing them with opportunities to become self-sufficient and ultimately free of the governmental aid.
3. It should be flexible in terms of the number of persons needing the social service.
4. It should be future-oriented, planning for tomorrow and not compensating for yesterday.

Not everyone would necessarily strongly agree with each criterion, but most people might be willing to accept them. So the persuader applies these criteria to some program to try to "sell" it. In Illinois in 1981 a $12 million program for support of day-care centers was targeted for cutting to zero dollars. Proponents of day care argued that the cuts should be restored for several reasons. First, over 6000 children and 3000 mothers were benefiting from the service. Thus, the costs were very efficient—only a little over $1300 per person or between $3 and $4 per day. Further, the mothers thus freed from staying at home to care for their young children were earning an average $7000 to $8000 per year—a total income of over $20 million per year. Sales tax alone returned over $1 million to the state treasury. Income taxes on the salaries provided more revenue to the state, so the program could be said to be "paying" for part of itself. If the day care were discontinued, the state would lose tax revenues from the mothers' incomes. Many mothers and children would have to go on some direct aid such as AFDC or Family Assistance. This would *cost* the state several million.

Given the criteria cited above, the program seems to be efficient in terms of costs. It certainly serves the mothers while providing the opportunity to become self-sufficient. It is difficult to tell how flexible the program is, since there are more applicants for day-care help than there are day-care facilities. But the program clearly is future oriented, helping its beneficiaries to establish themselves as earners and taxpayers not only for the present but for the future as well. Thus the program can be called a good one by the application of the four criteria. The only criterion not met by the program (flexibility) is one that would logically lead to budget increases.

Arguing from criteria to application can be a very effective way to persuade. Once the criteria are accepted by persuadees, skillful application of those criteria helps them persuade themselves. The missing *content premise* here is the logic that categorizes the day-care program as a good one, once it fits the criteria.

Reasoning from Comparison

Sometimes persuaders use **comparison** as their logical reason for some conclusion. In this form of reasoning a given example or situation is analyzed and described, and conclusions are then drawn about that example or situation. The persuader then compares example or situation number one with example or situation number two, pointing out similarities and reasons why conclusions about the first example or situation apply to the second. Let's look at a recent use of reasoning from comparison.

During the early 1980s governments of several small countries in Central and South America requested that the United States send military advisors to assist them in quelling guerilla armies that were attempting to overthrow them. Opponents of the assistance argued that this was precisely the kind of action that got the United States tied down in Vietnam twenty years earlier. That war, they argued, had cost fifty thousand American lives and billions of dollars in material and human resources. Some held that the Vietnam War was in large part to blame for the shortages of the 1980s, the rampant inflation that followed the Asian war, and many other societal ills. The government of Vietnam had been very similar to the Central and South American governments now asking for help. The countries were similar to Vietnam in other ways, too. They tended to have jungle terrain that made it virtually impossible to win guerilla-type war. Given these similarities, it would be unwise to send advisors, said the opponents. They were using reasoning by comparison or what is sometimes called the literal analogy.

Those who favored sending the advisors rebutted by pointing to *dissimilarities* in the two instances compared. They argued that Vietnam was an Asian country with a culture that made it very difficult for their citizens to work with the Americans. Their values were so different. Further, the guerillas in Vietnam had received massive support from other countries including China and the Soviet Union. This did not seem to be the case here in our own hemisphere, where it would be much more difficult for Far Eastern countries to send assistance to the guerillas. Thus the comparison wasn't accurate, and advisors should be sent. This set of persuaders were also reasoning from comparison but were finding *dissimi*larities that led to the opposite conclusion.

Deductive Reasoning

Deductive reasoning is familiar to most of us. It is the kind of reasoning that is frequently used in editorials, textbooks, law courts, and legislatures. It is usually defined as reasoning from the general to the specific. A persuader begins with a generalization. In court, for example, the prosecutor tells the judge and jury "The state intends to prove that defendant X knowingly and with intent to defraud his employer did on seven dates in 1983 take and conceal large sums of money totaling $3 million." The prosecution's case then goes on to provide the specifics— the dates when the money was taken, the amounts taken, and the methods of concealment. In a legislative body, a persuader might support a bill or a motion by saying something like "The legislation before us is desperately needed to prevent the state budget from going into a deficit situation." Then, the persuader goes on to provide the specifics. An editorial might begin, "Sycamore needs to pass this school referendum in order to save its extracurricular sports, its music and art programs, its newspaper, and its dramatics program" and then go on to describe the details. One of the problems with the deductive approach is that receivers who are in the least bit negative to the persuader's general point may "check out" and not pay attention to the specifics that are at the heart of the issue. Or the initial generalization may prompt rebuttal before the persuader has the opportunity to provide the details of the case.

Inductive Reasoning

specific ⟶ General

Inductive reasoning gets the specifics out on the table before bringing up the generalized conclusion. For example, in the school bond case the persuader might begin by saying, "Many of you know that it costs over $60,000 just to run the athletic program. The budget for the marching band was over $12,000 for travel, instruction, and uniforms. I was surprised to learn that it cost over $2000 just to pay the royalties for the spring musical. We have cut and cut until there is nothing left to cut. The last referendum increase was fourteen years ago—inflation has risen over 200 percent since then. Unless we pass this referendum, the district now faces elimination of these valuable extracurricular programs." With the specific evidence apparent, the generalization flows logically from it.

Stock Issues

Another kind of reasoning is the **stock issues** approach. The name stock issues derives from the circumstance that these issues *have to be addressed* any time a policy change is brought up. Two sides are usually involved: those who favor the change (sometimes called the *affirmative side*) and those who favor the status quo (sometimes called the *negative*). The affirmative side, which favors the change, is responsible for demonstrating, beyond reasonable doubt, that there is a *need* for such a change. This responsibility is called the **burden of proof.** When you face persuasion that involves some kind of policy change, ask yourself, "Who has the *burden of proof* here?" The answer can make things very clear to yourself and others considering the policy change.

A good example came up on my campus recently. Because expenses were rising and state assistance was being reduced, the athletic board had passed a motion requiring students to pay $1 per game for basketball tickets in addition to their regular $28 athletic fee. Following the summer recess, the student members of the board decided to try to rescind that motion because the athletic board department had had several windfalls totaling well over the amount to be generated by the surcharge. Who has the burden of proof here—the students or the rest of the board? The burden of proof falls *on the side wanting to change the status quo*—in this case, the students. They had to show that the windfalls would be likely to continue; that the anticipated surcharge income hadn't already been spent, and so on. In addition, they had to show that there was a *need* to rescind the earlier motion. For example, they might show the effect of the surcharge on the average student's finances. Maybe they would show how hard it was to get summer jobs during bad economic times. Or they might point out the reduction in student loans and other factors that would lead to the conclusion that change was needed.

In *stock issues*, the next stage would be the **plan for change.** Once a need for change has been demonstrated, most people would logically ask something like "OK, there is a need to change—but to what?" So the affirmative must present some sort of plan. In a court of law, for instance, having convinced the jury that a crime has been committed and that the accused is probably guilty, the prosecution must present a plan. Usually this is a request to the judge for a directed verdict of guilty. If that plan is refused, the prosecutor then asks the jury to find the accused guilty of the crime. For the students wishing to rescind the surcharge on basketball tickets, the *plan for change* would have to be related to how the athletic board would make up for this lost revenue in future years. It might include playing some home games in the large indoor sports center to increase the number of paid admissions. It might call for reduction in athletic scholarships. In any case it would have to be a plan with a reasonable chance for success.

A final stage in stock issues is for the affirmative to provide evidence that such a plan will indeed solve the problem. This stage is called **plan meets need.** The prosecutor might ask for life imprisonment with no chance for parole, arguing that this criminal should not be permitted back on the streets again. The students might cite statistics from other schools like N.I.U. that have cut athletic scholarships or have held home games in places away from campus to increase the paid admissions. All their evidence should lead logically to the conclusion that the plan will solve the problem and thus meet the need.

Content Premises: The Strategic Level

Having considered the theoretical nature of proof, evidence, and reasoning, we now face the task of seeing how these operate in practice. We will do that by looking at content premises on two levels: (1) the over-all thematic level, or *strategic level*, and (2) the more particular and specific, concrete level, or *tactical level*. In so doing, we must continually take the notions offered here and compare them with the persuasion presented to us every day. We ought to look for the strategic moves made by persuaders in editorials in the campus newspaper, in advertisements on TV, or by politicians trying to capture our support.

Again, we assume that the way people use symbols is indicative of their world view, their likely intentions, and their probable actions. This assumption applies not only to language use (see Chapter 2) and to how those language choices are organized and put together—but also to our interest here. One way to look at the strategic level of content premises is through the use of the syllogism as an organizational device, which is discussed in this section. Another way is through the system for argument analysis proposed by Stephen Toulmin, which will be discussed in the next section.

Types of Syllogisms

To begin with, there are three major syllogistic formats: (1) the *conditional* (if A, then B), (2) the *disjunctive* (either A or B), and (3) the *categorical* (since A is a member of category X and B is a part of A, then B is also part of X). Each of these formats has a number of varieties or hybrids and can appear and operate in several forms. At the root of these hybrids, however, a basic form predominates and forms the skeletal and strategic structure of argument.

Conditional Syllogism The conditional syllogism has as its basic form "If A is true, then B is also true." This is the *major premise* of the syllogism, and it makes a statement about a relationship assumed to exist in the world (for example, "if you add water to Kool-Aid, you will get a refreshing cool drink"). Now we might argue about the truth of these relational statements, but we assume that if proved "true" they will accurately describe a situation in the world. The next stage or step in the conditional strategy is to present data that relate to or make a statement about some part of the major premise—or, tactically speaking, to present evidence. The following sentence is an example of a *minor premise:* "A is known to be true by all world experts." When it is put together with the relational major premise, a *conclusion* (in this case, that B is also true) can be drawn. In the example cited, you could pour water into Kool-Aid powder or state that you had done so. Given these pieces of "truth," the persuadee and the persuader together draw the conclusion that a cool, refreshing drink is at hand.

In both of these cases, by affirming or stating the truth of the "if" part of the major premise (sometimes called the *antecedent*), we can also affirm the "then" part of the statement (sometimes called the *consequent*). One of the combination rules for the conditional syllogism is the "affirm antecedent–affirm consequent" form. Another form is the "deny consequent–deny antecedent" variation (for example, there is no refreshing drink around, so obviously no one poured water into Kool-Aid powder). These are the only two "valid" combinations that can be made with the conditional form.

Remember, however, that many persuaders successfully use *invalid* combinations to achieve their goals. For example, one invalid form is affirming the consequent and thereby affirming the antecedent (that is, because B is true, then A must also be true—there is a refreshing drink available; therefore, someone must have added water to Kool-Aid powder). This form is invalid because a third and unseen factor may have caused the observed effect (for example, someone could have poured water into lemon concentrate). Yet advertisers often use this form as a strategy and argue that because a person feels better the morning after taking cold tablets, those tablets cured that person. It is possible that sleep, a hot toddy, or a shot given by the doctor had something to do with the cure. Likewise, with the other possible variation on the conditional syllogism—deny the antecedent and deny the consequent. The flaw here is like the flaw in the other invalid line of proof—there may very well be an interceding and outside third factor or combination of factors that may cause the consequent, since we have no rational reason to consider the antecedent as the one and only cause of the consequent. Nonetheless, this invalid form is often used by persuaders. But "truth" enters in.

For example, Hanes stockings for women are frequently sold through an if/then conditional syllogism. The pitch is that if you buy Hanes, then gentlemen will prefer you. It relies on a major premise stated by the persuader—gentlemen prefer Hanes—reinforced by a minor premise in the form of the visual that is usually placed with the slogan/major premise. This visual is an unusually attractive woman who is the center of male attention even though other attractive women are also on the scene. Our prize woman is wearing Hanes stockings so.... Of course, the advertiser hopes that you women will visualize yourselves as attractive and hence as sought after as the model in the ad. The problem here is not with the logic that is used or with the *validity* of the claim-linking system. The problem rather lies with the *truth* of the claim that gentlemen do prefer Hanes. So *while a conditional syllogism may be perfectly valid in a logical sense, it may be largely untruthful.* This is the trap that the persuadee needs to be alert to. Persuaders may use a logically valid syllogism to camouflage untrue premises. Persuadees who find this strategy employed ought to search for other explanations and, in fact, will find that they are better able to engage in counterargument if they do look at syllogistic strategies in this way—searching for validity and truth and answering in accord with what they find. The conditional syllogism is, as you have probably noticed, similar to the cause/effect linkage described earlier.

Disjunctive Syllogism The disjunctive syllogism has as its basic form "Either A is true or B is true." This sentence is the major premise of a disjunctive syllogism and is usually accompanied by some set of proof or evidence that suggests the probable presence of A or B, or the probable absence of A or B. The conclusion is then drawn on the basis of these probabilities. In economically tight times like those referred to earlier, a school board might present voters with a disjunctive syllogism. They threaten to do away with extracurricular activities unless the voters approve a certain referendum increasing property taxes, saying *"Either you vote to increase property taxes or you lose the extracurricular activities."* The voters then provide the minor premise of the syllogism through their vote. The strategy is often effective because the case is such a clear-cut issue. However, the strategy may backfire because it seems like a threat. Refusing to be bullied, the voters may reject the referendum, leaving the school board in trouble. They can go ahead and cut the extras, thus angering the community and especially the students. Or they can seek other ways to lower costs, thus reducing their own credibility.

Most disjunctive syllogisms have another weakness as well. Very few situations present a clear either/or, even in cases of life and death. During the late 1970s, a widely publicized case involved a young woman who was in a coma from which her doctors declared she would never recover. Her parents wanted to remove her life-support systems, or "pull the plug." After numerous court rulings on whether the young woman was legally alive or dead, a final ruling permitted the parents to disconnect the equipment. To everyone's astonishment, the girl continued breathing and "living" without the machines. So, even in such a concrete area as life or death there is no easy answer. Strict either/or logic cannot take other belief systems or three, four, or even more alternatives in a situation. The persuadee needs to examine persuasion framed in the either/or mode to search for other alternatives or differing belief systems under which the disjunctive model would not work.

Categorical Syllogism The categorical syllogism is a *spatial* kind of reasoning. The persuader considers the world as divided into separate spaces—or sets and subsets, to use modern math terms. That is, every phenomenon is either a part of a larger kind or class of phenomena or the genus of some smaller set or species of phenomena. Thus, the major and minor premises in this form can be expressed in the sentence "All of A is included in category B." For example, a letter to the editor of *Playboy* magazine addressed itself to the debate about abortion. The writer stated: "I keep hearing about right-to-life groups. I presume these are the people working to abolish the death penalty."[7] The letter was a facetious jibe at the groups working to prevent legalization of abortion—groups like SOUL (Save Our Unwanted Lives), the Catholic Church, and others. These groups, at least in the letter writer's mind, were also likely to favor the conservative position of retaining capital punishment while promoting the equally conservative position of outlawing abortion. To the letter writer, there was an inconsistency in the two positions, best expressed in categorical terms: (1) Persons who want to retain capital punishment are not in the category of people who want to preserve human life; (2) persons who want to outlaw abortion are in the category of persons who want to preserve life; (3) therefore, persons who disavow abortion must also disavow capital punishment.

This kind of argument smacks of "guilt by association" or "you must be bad because you keep bad company." This kind of reasoning is often used in public persuasion dealing with political issues (for example, "since you look like a hippie, you must be a Commie because hippies tend to be Commies") as well as persuasion dealing with more mundane issues (for example, "join the Pepsi generation—and you will be going strong since members of the Pepsi generation all go strong"). Lewis Carroll used it even more cleverly in his descriptions of Alice in Wonderland—the pigeon tells Alice that she must be some kind of snake since she eats eggs and that is just what snakes do too.[8] All of these examples have the same characteristic flaw—to possess *some* characteristics of a group does not mean possessing *all* characteristics of the group.

Persuaders use and persuadees respond to the invalid "guilt by association" form of this strategy. Responsible persuadees must ask themselves, when they find the categorical syllogism operating as a skeletal structure in an argument, whether the categories are accurately represented. They must seek to discover whether membership in one category necessarily implies full membership in

---

7. *Playboy,* June 1972, p. 68.

8. Lewis Carroll, *Alice in Wonderland* (New York: Lancer Books, 1968), p. 58.

another. (Because one is a member of the category of persons with long hair and beard, does this necessarily mean that he is also a member of another category such as "pot heads" or "religious freaks" or "slobs"?)

Truth and Validity

As we can see from our brief investigation into syllogistic reasoning, there are some knotty problems here. First, true *(empirically verifiable)* statements can be linked logically or validly, but the same true statements can mislead the persuadee when they are joined in illogical or invalid ways. At the same time, untrue *(empirically unverifiable)* statements can be linked in logical and valid ways or in illogical and invalid ways. Furthermore, we seldom encounter clear-cut syllogisms in our everyday lives. Few persuaders, be they politicians, advertisers, peers, subordinates, or superiors, run around saying "If A then B" or "Either A is true or B is true but not both and at least one" or "All A's are B's and all C's are A's; therefore all C's are also B's." Instead, we find that persuaders arrange more extended pieces of persuasion, such as entire speeches or campaigns or complete advertisements, into syllogistic patterns. A classic example is the standard toothpaste, mouthwash, or deodorant advertisement saying that a person has bad luck on a date because he or she has forgotten to get shiny teeth, sweet breath, or dry underarms. We watch the product being used, then immediately we see a church wedding scene. The syllogism is an "if/then" conditional one. (*If* you use Toothbrite toothpaste, *then* you will have a lover's mouth and get your desired love object.) Perhaps the best each persuadee can do is to outline, formally or informally, the general point of the persuasion and then to search for the relationships the persuader is attempting to "sell." Having discovered these, the persuadee can look for the traces of syllogistic reasoning in the arguments and relationships.

Content Premises: The Tactical Level

As already noted, we seldom hear syllogisms formally stated and used by persuaders. Instead, they underlie larger pieces of persuasion. What do we typically hear in real-life situations? Typically, we hear statements of one of these categories or types:

1. Those that advise action or state conclusions.

2. Those that present bits of evidence to support conclusions or courses of action.

3. Those that explain why the evidence is related to courses of action or conclusions. (The "linkages" described earlier are good examples.)

These three kinds of statements make up what we hear on the **tactical level** of persuasion—they are the stuff of which persuasion is made. A British philosopher and logician, Stephen Toulmin, has identified and labeled these three elements as the *data*, the *warrant*, and the *claim*. The assumption is that persuaders present

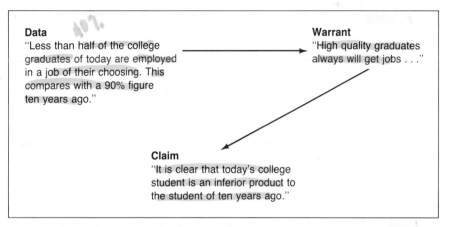

Figure 5.2. Toulmin system of analysis: sample argument.

data or evidence, which is linked by warrants or reasons to claims or conclusions. The sample argument diagramed in Figure 5.2 uses the Toulmin system.[9]

Your first response may be something like "Hey, that's not the whole story; there are other reasons for a bad job market—inflation, slowed government spending, and so on." On the tactical level, you do not have to search for underlying strategies. You are readily confronted with the real, immediate, and concrete elements of persuasion. You respond almost instinctively to them and have a sense for what ought to be said in response to the persuasive message. That is the point. We tend to respond to the smaller elements in persuasion rather quickly and automatically, but that is where the problem arises. Unless we, as persuadees, have first examined the strategy underlying the tactics, and unless we respond to the tactics we hear in more sophisticated ways, we are likely to come off as naive, argumentative, and sometimes stupid. You are probably all too familiar, for example, with those time-worn phrases parents use: "When you get a little real experience, then you'll see what I mean," or "Oh, all that baloney they teach you kids at college, it just isn't able to hold water," or "Well, that's just what you think."

Toulmin's system does afford us some opportunity to approach this tactical level of persuasion more specifically and systematically. So, let's look more closely at how the typical interpersonal attempt at persuasion flows or operates and then apply Toulmin's system to it.

Claim

Suppose that you want to persuade authority figures that they are overlooking important information that could affect decisions, which in turn affect you. Let's say that you want to persuade your teacher that he ought not give you an open-book midterm examination. You begin by raising your hand and saying something like "Why do we have to take an open-book test? Why not just have a take-home test? It's the same thing." What you have done, in Toulmin's terms, is

---

9. Stephen Toulmin, *The Uses of Argument* (Cambridge, England: Cambridge University Press, 1969). See Chapter 3, "The Layout of Arguments," pp. 94–145.

make a **claim**—that take-home tests and open-book tests are essentially the same. You hope he will draw the conclusion that there is no need for a test in class, that another paper will serve the purpose. Let's assume that your teacher listens and seriously considers your claim. He then has three options. He may, if you have been persuasive enough, agree to accept your claim as it stands and permit you to write up a take-home exam instead of an open-book one. Another option for him is to reject your claim out of hand; he might say, "Well, I run the class and I have scheduled the exam into the syllabus and have it made up already. We'll take the open-book test." His third option is to ask you to demonstrate further the reasonableness of your claim. He might say something like "Well, you may have something there and then again you may not. How do you know that these two kinds of tests are essentially the same kind of activity? What proof have you?"

Data

In Toulmin's terms, you are faced with a request for the **data** supporting your *claim*. Of the teacher's three responses, the first two typify immediate and spontaneous responses to persuasive tactics. The third response is closer to the critical and aware persuadee's response, at least on the content level of persuasion. Instead of making a snap *yes* or *no* judgment, the persuadee explores the issue further (in this case, the teacher decides to look into the comparison between two different types of examination) and suspends judgment. Unfortunately, most persuadees respond most of the time in the first two ways and not nearly often enough in the critical and reserved manner suggested by option three.

Warrant

Let us continue this interpersonal exchange. Suppose you have taken a course in tests and measurements and you have access to information about open-book and take-home methods. Your sources say that identical sets of subjects repeatedly scored essentially the same on take-home and open-book exams in an experiment conducted at several colleges. You tell this to your open-minded instructor, and he considers your evidence. Again, he has three options. He can accept your evidence as supporting your claim and agree to let your class have a take-home exam, or he may reject your data out of hand, saying something like "Well, if they are the same, then I may as well give the open-book exam as I had originally planned," or he might again follow the third option (remember, he is a very open-minded instructor) and ask for more proof. In this case, however, he asks you to tell him *why* that evidence leads to the conclusion that you should have a take-home exam instead of the regularly scheduled test. In Toulmin's terms, he is asking for a *warrant* to link the *data* you have presented in support of your *claim*. The flow then goes from claim to data to the warrant, where the real philosophical elements in the issue are likely to arise.

Let us see what you will do next. Suppose you say in response to the instructor's request for a warrant:

I assume that the most valuable asset we have as students and teachers is learning time together. Now the scheduled exam will take one entire class session and part of another in the critiquing process. We only have thirty class sessions together, and some of them are already eliminated by vacation days, convocations, and other matters. We can't afford not to have a take-home exam, since it is equivalent to the open-book test now scheduled.

That is pretty sound reasoning, and it seems to fit with your data and claim. The instructor may consider this sufficient evidence and agree to cancel his exam. He may want you to modify your request and agree to an open-book final exam if the midterm is a take-home, or he may be stubborn and refuse to reschedule or change his plans. In any case, he has the same three options—agree, disagree, or ask for more (in this case, for concessions in your request). If the issue is not as simple as this one, the persuadee may argue about the philosophical position inherent in the warrant. The interaction could then continue, but on issues central to the question and not on whether the experiments comparing take-home exams with open-book exams were carefully conducted. You would be discussing implications, not facts; and after all, facts are usually not very debatable.

Substantiating Elements

Toulmin's system has a number of secondary terms. For example, in the preceding case, the concession in the claim is called the **qualifier.** (Usually it is a simple qualifier—something like saying *"In most cases,"* or *"Probably* we don't have to take an open-book test," or *"It is likely* that open-book and take-home exams are parallel.") The point is that the term or concession qualifies or limits the claim; it allows for the possibility that this is not an "Either A or B" type of argument. The claim is *probably* acceptable and true, but there is the *possibility* that another factor may enter in and affect the final outcome. To continue our example, the qualifier to the claim would probably be something like "Open-book exams and take-home exams are *essentially* the same kind of test, *at least on the basis* of evidence now available."

Another minor term in Toulmin's system is the **reservation,** a statement attached to or related to the warrant. For instance, suppose, in the argument over examinations, it became clear that the instructor did not consider examination time to be an inferior learning activity but rather one that was just different from regular classroom activity. The warrant would then probably evolve into something like *"Unless there is reason to believe* that exams are a learning experience and not an evaluation experience, then class time for student/teacher interaction is the most important asset we have." Notice that the reservation states the conditions under which the assumptions and philosophical bases of the argument operate. This aspect of the reservation is often overlooked by persuaders and persuadees alike—they assume that both parties begin from the same point, from the same frame of reference. Only when we begin at the same point or when we make allowances (such as reservations) for these differences, can we really progress in any persuasive transaction. Coupled with the qualifier, the reservation allows for great flexibility in persuasion because both terms allow dialogue to occur; both provide the persuadee with the opportunity to object or agree to part but not all of the persuasion. As persuaders, we need to include these elements of flexibility in our persuasion. As persuadees, we need to request them of the persuaders who are attempting to get us to take action.

Unfortunately, history is filled with examples in which legislation, for example, has been destructive because of the deletion of qualifiers or reservations. The lack of a reservation in the 1964 Tonkin Gulf resolution gave to the U.S. President unrestricted power to wage war, thereby eventually costing the United States thousands of lives in Vietnam. Much earlier, a gag rule in the U.S. Senate prevented the issue of slavery from being discussed for nearly ten years while various territories were being added to the country, thereby necessitating continuous and informal negotiation and compromise. For several years the American automobile industry must have had a premise about not building mini-cars that could get good gas mileage. Somehow there must have been a reservation missing from that premise. Perhaps it should have been something like "*Unless* the public turns to foreign autos, we will make big autos like we always have." There is another danger also—the danger of having indefinite or vague qualifiers or reservations. For instance, the 1955 Supreme Court ruling on implementation of desegregation used the words "with all deliberate speed" to define the time frame in which to desegregate. As all of us know, this problem is still with us in the form of conflict over busing, racial quotas, and so forth. Clearly the phrase "all deliberate speed" had many meanings.

Advertisers are clever with the use of qualifiers (see Chapter 9). For example, the label on Cascade dishwasher detergent says that it will make your dishes "virtually spotless." Neat, isn't it? Not spotless, but *virtually* spotless, and who can say whether one spot or three spots or twelve spots qualifies being "*virtually* spotless"? So the persuadee needs to be aware of two problems connected with qualifiers or reservations. One is absence of them, which can lock us in to one course of action or belief. The other problem is with the too-vague qualifier, which may allow persuaders to wiggle out of any commitment to product, action, person, or idea. It is far better to be specific about qualifiers, as was the energy-saving legislation of 1975 and 1976. This allowed for something of a "fudge factor" on gasoline mileage but set specific mileage performance for specific dates. Persuaders may still try to interpret the qualifiers to their advantage, but it is much more difficult when specificity and details are given. Persuadees need to think twice when confronted with lack of details and lack of specificity in persuasive claims. If advertisers say that their tires will stop faster, we need to ask such questions as "Faster than what?" and "Under what conditions?" For all we know, they may be comparing the tires with wagon wheels or doughnuts.

The final element in Toulmin's system for showing the tactics of argument is called the *support*, or sometimes the *backing*, for the warrant. Toulmin observed that many issues hang on this element—that it justifies acceptance of the warrant. Suppose a persuadee does not consider the warrant to be true or doubts some part of it. The persuader must then provide some kind of proof that would *support* or *back up* the reasoning expressed in the warrant. In a sense, there is a whole separate argument with a separate claim, data, and warrant going on when support is offered for a warrant. Essentially persuaders claim that the warrant is acceptable because of the support or backing offered. The backing is really data for this second claim. This same process of claim-data-warrant within claim-data-warrant can go further and often does—and creates the complexity surrounding most controversial and philosophical issues. (Figure 5.3 depicts a persuasive argument in these terms: (1) *claim* made by the persuader, (2) *data* provided by the source and (3) emergence of the *warrant*.)

We can now see that the tactics of persuasion are not usually parts of simple syllogisms. Instead of making statements like "If A then B; A is true; therefore B is also true" or "Either A is true or B is true; B is false; therefore A must be true," most persuaders make claims that persuadees may (1) buy outright with no questions

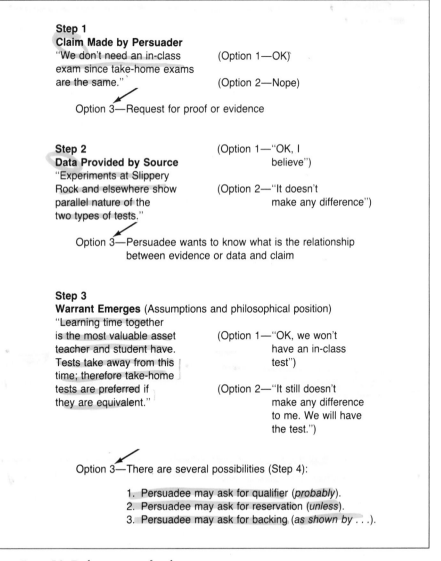

Figure 5.3. Toulmin system of analysis: steps in a persuasive argument.

asked, (2) reject outright, or (3) ask for proof. Persuaders then can provide data, which again can be accepted, rejected, or questioned. If the persuadee continues to request more, the persuader ultimately provides the warrant or reason for linking proof to request. Given enough time, three other elements may enter into the persuasive appeal:

1. The qualifier (which limits the force or universality of the claim or request).

2. The reservation (which states the conditions under which the warrant operates).

3. The backing (which supports or provides evidence to substantiate the validity of the warrant).

Some of you will be asking now how persuadees get their input noticed and considered. After all, there are thirty or more people in most classes, and not everyone will get a chance to participate; and the problem is compounded as time goes on and as the audience gets larger, as in political campaigns. Although that is true, you must also remember that in another sense persuadees *always* get input; they always are "heard" in a way. The persuader who knows anything about audiences will anticipate the kind of questions persuadees *might* ask if they had the opportunity. Furthermore, if not satisfied with the completeness of the argument offered by the persuader, the persuadees may decide not to follow the course of action suggested by the persuader, thus asking for more proof, reasoning, qualification, backing, or reservation. Finally, the function of the persuadee is to dissect the persuasion, knowing *when* and *whether* to be persuaded; it doesn't matter whether the persuaders are exposed to all of this analysis. They ought to catch on if fewer and fewer persons buy the product or vote or give rewards. What does matter is that persuadees are aware, critical, and fairly sophisticated and systematic as they are exposed to persuasion. Toulmin's system for analyzing the tactics of persuasion provides us with a simple but discriminating tool that operates well with the kind of persuasion to which we are exposed every day.

For persuaders there are a few simple pieces of advice, if they intend to structure persuasion with Toulmin's system in mind. First, they must anticipate the audience's probable response. Second, they need to provide data if a claim is likely to be questioned. Many persuaders merely restate a claim if it is not accepted—a more appropriate course of action would be to provide the persuadee with good reasons (data) for following the advice of the claim. If they wish to bolster their persuasion, they need to demonstrate reasoning, or the warrant of the case. Finally, the probability of getting audience acceptance for the case will increase to the degree that it is less dogmatic and is well documented. Therefore, it is wise to qualify claims, taking any reservations in the warrant into account, and to provide substantial backing for the data.

Now that we have looked at how persuasion operates on this rule-governed or procedural or *content* level in strategic and tactical ways, let us consider what we do know about logical thought processes and the human responses to various kinds and amounts of evidence or proof.

Experimental Evidence on Evidence

Since its inception, the field of speech communication has been interested in the nature of evidence—what it is, what types may occur, how much of it is necessary, who is most likely to be persuaded by certain types of evidence, and other similar issues. Aristotle, in his study of persuasion, categorized the types of reasoning and evidence into what he called *topoi*, or topics or *places* where arguments of a rational nature could be found. The philosophers of the New Science during the Renaissance tried to establish scientific methods of proving things to be true or false.

In its simplest form, evidence can be thought of as an example in some form. It is in support of or gives credence to an argument or conclusion. If the evidence is statistical, then the support is the result of compiling numerous examples. If it is expert testimony, then the testimony is an example of the point being made. If the evidence is an analogy, it is also a kind of example—a narrative that supports a premise or leads to a conclusion.

Researchers have tried various "scientific" means to test the effect of such things as evidence types, organization, and concreteness. A number of presumably typical persuadees (for example, several hundred college freshmen) are given varying degrees or types of persuasion and evidence (for example, emotional versus logical evidence, good delivery of evidence versus poor delivery of the same evidence). Following this treatment, the subjects' attitudes are evaluated, using an attitude measure. Then the results are compared with pretreatment scores on identical or similar measures, and the difference between scores is compared, by statistical methods, to determine the effects of the varying degrees or types of evidence characteristics.

Unfortunately, the over-all results of the numerous studies have not shed much light on the questions that were bothering the ancients (for example, what kinds of evidence persuade best? what amount of evidence is enough? when should you use what kind of evidence?). Rather, the results are often contradictory or inconclusive. Richard Gregg observed that the over-all results of these studies were disheartening when he noted that "the audience reaction to an argument may have little or nothing to do with whether the argument includes fully documented evidence, relevant or irrelevant evidence, weak or strong evidence or any evidence at all."[10] Yet we do know that people ask for evidence when in doubt. In spite of the pessimism suggested by Gregg, we do know some things about evidence, as a result of about a quarter of a century of behavioral study:

1. Evidence increases persuasive effects if the persuader is unknown or has low to moderate credibility.[11]

---

10. Richard B. Gregg, "Some Hypotheses for the Study of Psychology of Evidence," as quoted in James C. McCroskey, "A Summary of Experimental Research on the Effects of Evidence in Persuasive Communication," *Quarterly Journal of Speech,* Vol. 55 (April 1969), p. 167.

11. See the discussion on evidence by James C. McCroskey, cited in Footnote 18; and Gerald R. Miller and John Baseheart, "Source Trustworthiness, Opinionated Statements, and Response to Persuasive Communication," *Speech Monographs,* Vol. 36 (March 1969), pp. 1–7.

2. There seems to be little difference in the persuasive effects generated from emotional as opposed to logical evidence.[12]

3. Usually some evidence is better than no evidence.[13]

4. "Reluctant" evidence (that given by people against themselves or their own interests) is no more effective than biased or unbiased objective evidence.[14]

5. Good delivery can enhance the potency of evidence (but perhaps only when the sources are unknown or have low credibility, so that the delivery makes them and their evidence more believable and therefore more persuasive).[15]

6. Evidence can make persuasive changes more permanent.[16]

7. Evidence is most effective when the persuadee has not heard it before.[17]

8. The method of transmitting the evidence (live, on tape, and the like) seems to have no effect on evidence potency.[18]

9. People are likely to believe evidence that agrees with their own position more than evidence that does not.[19]

10. Highly dogmatic persons differ from persons who are not so dogmatic, in that the highly dogmatic are more affected by evidence.[20]

For the most part, these findings are not surprising or unpredictable. Many of them seem to be common-sense conclusions, and that has prompted many researchers to attempt to investigate the effects of evidence from a different perspective—that is, by observing persuasion as it operates in the "real world." After observing a number of both successful and unsuccessful persuasive efforts, the researchers draw some conclusions based on the general patterns observed. By now, you will have concluded that this is the admonition repeated in almost every

12. See McCroskey, cited in Footnote 18.

13. See the McCroskey summary cited below (Footnote 18); and Robert S. Cathcart, "An Experimental Study of the Relative Effectiveness of Selected Means of Handling Evidence in Speeches of Advocacy," doctoral dissertation, Northwestern University, 1953.

14. William E. Arnold and James C. McCroskey, "The Credibility of Reluctant Testimony," *Central States Speech Journal,* Vol. 18 (May 1967), pp. 97–103.

15. James C. McCroskey and R. Samuel Mehrley, "The Effects of Disorganization and Nonfluency on Attitude Change and Source Credibility," *Speech Monographs,* Vol. 36 (March 1969), pp. 13–21.

16. See the McCroskey summary cited above (Footnote 10).

17. See the McCroskey summary cited below (Footnote 18); and Karl W. E. Anatol and Jerry E. Mandel, "Strategies of Resistance to Persuasion: New Subject Matter for the Teacher of Speech Communication," *Central States Speech Journal,* Vol. 23 (Spring 1972), pp. 11–17.

18. James C. McCroskey, *Studies of the Effects of Evidence in Persuasive Communication.* Report SCRL, 4–67, Speech Communication Research Laboratory, Michigan State University, 1967.

19. Victor D. Wall, Jr., "Evidential Attitudes and Attitude Change," *Western Speech,* Vol. 36 (Spring 1972), pp. 115–123.

20. Gary Cronkhite and Emily Goetz, "Dogmatism, Persuasibility, and Attitude," *Journal of Communication,* Vol. 21 (December 1971), pp. 342–352.

chapter of this book—observe, search for a pattern, try to draw some conclusions about the persuader and the persuasion on the basis of these patterns, and then and only then respond to the persuasion confronting you.

Several patterns seem to emerge from the discussion in this chapter and from the assumptions underlying Chapter 2. First, *evidence is probably most effective when it encourages audience partipation.* Earlier we noted that, in using emotionally oriented evidence, persuaders are most effective if they can present audiences with a dramatic scene or setting and can then ask the audience to empathize with the character acting within that setting. By participating with their imaginations, members of the audience co-create the proof. They incorporate the proof into their own frames of reference—the persuasion thus achieved is more permanent and potent. In using intellectually oriented evidence, effective persuaders present claims and perhaps data to support them. They hope that warrants will be provided by the audience, but even if listeners do not supply the linkage that is needed and instead question the persuaders' conclusions, they are still participating in their own persuasion when they begin to play the game (that is, co-create a proof with the persuaders).

Consider the following extracts from an article in an admittedly white racist publication:

> Leftist forces have long waged a relentless battle to have the death penalty abolished. Jack Greenberg . . . is representing negro Lucius Jackson, Jr. . . . He was sentenced for raping a White doctor's wife . . . What the Jew lawyers . . . have failed to tell the court . . . is the fact that blacks commit over 80 percent of all forcible rapes in this country. Remember that negroes are only 13 percent of the population, therefore their crime rate is far out of proportion to their numerical percentage in this country . . . the negro constitutes by far the most dangerous criminal element in America. Over half of all black males are expected to be involved in some crime during their lifetime.
>
> There is no way to rehabilitate this entire race of people . . . We want to save White people from further murder, rape and plunder . . . Let's bring back peace, prosperity, safety, low taxes and all the improvements resulting from the elimination of slum ghettos and violent crime will be reduced by an astounding 85%.[21]

The publication then repeatedly appealed for help in promoting a "Back to Africa" movement to deport all blacks as soon as possible. For a moment, try to avoid having an emotional response to the quotation. Instead look at it as a piece of persuasion, which attempts to use both kinds of evidence discussed in this chapter. There is a clear-cut attempt to appeal to the emotions and biases inherent in the audience. At the same time, there is an attempt to appeal to the audience in intellectual ways (for example, citing statistics and giving examples).

In all likelihood, most nonsubscribers reading this newspaper article would

---

21. From an article entitled "Black Rape of White Women Grows." *The Thunderbolt,* February 1972, p. 2. The publication is published irregularly by the National States Rights Party, Marietta, Georgia.

not be persuaded by it. Yet it demonstrates some of the things that we have been talking about. The article creates a dramatic scene with great potential for action. It includes data in support of claims and even draws the conclusion in some cases (for example, "therefore their crime rate is far out of proportion to their numerical percentage in this country"). Why does it fail as persuasion? Examine it more closely. The situation drawn by the persuasion is dramatic, but it does not allow participation or empathy (except perhaps on behalf of the Negro defendant in the death penalty case). The audience is not invited into the drama—it is not asked to use its imagination. The same thing occurs with the intellectually oriented parts of the message. This passage is a good instance of not allowing auditors to participate in their own persuasion. The conclusion that black crime rates are higher than black population ratios is one that is easily drawn from the 80 percent to 13 percent figures, but the author insists on drawing the conclusion for you. The probable response to this kind of paternalistic persuasion is to question the con-clusion that is drawn. Persuadees want to get in on the action. Since there are no openings here, they find one on the opposite side of the case. They start asking questions about the data given (for example, "Isn't crime caused by environmental factors like poor home life?"). They look for faulty relationships or linkages. They wonder how lower taxes fit in with deporting people—it seems like an expensive plan at best. Sooner or later they reject the whole argument. It is doubtful that this particular passage could be doctored up to be persuasive in any meaningful sense; probably it is so extreme that it rules that possibility out. However, if the per-suader had not tried so hard to lead persuadees through the message, drawing conclusions for them and so forth, chances for success would have been better.

A second characteristic that seems to help, in using evidence for "logical" or content-oriented persuasion, is to highlight the evidence in one of two ways—either as part of a narrative or by use of some form of analogy. The earliest form of human ritual and entertainment was the *narrative* as it was used in dances, tales, and myths. As we noted earlier, the narrative is an extremely powerful form of evidence.

A Review and Conclusion

Content premises do not necessarily rely as much on the internal states of each individual persuader as do process premises. Instead, they rely more on universally agreed upon norms or rules, in contrast to individualized processing of bits of information.

Evidence tends to be either dramatistically oriented or intellectually oriented. Users of dramatistically oriented evidence may lead persuadees to a "logical" conclusion, drawn from a content premise, by creating a dramatic scene for the audience and then by inviting the audience to join in the drama. Persuadees thus "prove" the validity of the premise to themselves. Users of intellectually oriented evidence, on the other hand, may lead their persuadees to "logical" conclusions by presenting them with a set of data in support of a certain claim or content premise. The persuadees provide the connective between these data and the claim in the form of a warrant.

Both types of evidence rely upon a kind of self-persuasion on the part of the persuadee. Persuadees ought to participate in some way in their own persuasion, whether the evidence is intellectual or dramatistic—that is the basic principle. Some of the most fascinating research done in persuasion has focused on self-persuasion. Much of this research is based on Festinger's theory of dissonance, and studies usually ask persuadees to state arguments that are contrary to their own beliefs or attitudes (for example, why a dull experiment was interesting, why strange foods taste good, or why they might accept some group or idea that is counter to their beliefs). Having engaged in this kind of participation, the respondees tend to change their beliefs in accord with the false or counterattitudinal message they advocated. Though this issue has been plagued with problems in research measurement and design, the findings have been fairly consistent—when we engage in self-persuasion, even if it runs counter to our own beliefs, the effect of the participation is powerful.

From a strategic point of view, the traditional syllogism usually forms the skeletal structure of an over-all argument or content premise. Within this over-all structure, the tactics or particular arguments or premises are represented by claims supported by data and hopefully linked by audiences through warrants.

Finally, of the types of evidence available to the persuader, several seem more important than others. First, probably, are those that support the three major linkages: cause/effect, symptoms, and congruency. Also, evidence that provides perspective for the audience is probably more effective than evidence that does not. We have focused on two particularly effective methods of providing this perspective—the use of the analogy, which provides a comparative perspective, and the use of the narrative, which has the same ability to provide a perspective within a dramatic frame of reference. Both are also "artistic," in the sense that neither merely presents information; both depict evidence in dramatic or visual formats.

To sum it up, we are most effectively persuaded by our own experiences—real or imaginary. Successful persuaders will try to shape content premises, their linkages, claims, data, and warrants in terms of the audience's experience. If they can invite audiences to participate in the drawing of conclusions or with the drama of the proof, they will share in their own persuasion, thus being affected by it.

Questions for Further Thought

1. What are the three types of argument? Give examples of each from news advertisements, political speeches, or some other souce of persuasion.

2. Define proof. What constitutes adequate proof for you? Does it change from issue to issue? If so, in what ways?

3. Review some of the magazine commentary concerning a particular issue and attempt to identify the pieces of data that are offered. What kinds of evidence are they? Are they dramatic? If so, in what ways? If not, are they persuasive and why or why not? What is the underlying syllogistic structure inherent in the discussions of the issue?

4. Read a contemporary discussion of some ideological issue. Try to identify the claims put forth. What kind of evidence is used to support them? Do the warrants for linking data and claim appear in the text? Are there qualifiers or reservations? Where is the argument most persuasive and why?

5. Identify several forms of proof in the source used for question 4.

6. Identify various forms of proof (for example, intellectually oriented or emotionally oriented, analogical, dramatic) in an issue being debated on the editorial pages of your daily newspaper.

7. What is the difference between intellectually oriented evidence and emotionally oriented evidence? Give examples and explain how they differ.

8. Give examples of the following: (a) comparison and contrast, (b) example, (c) sign argument, (d) statistics.

9. Give examples from your own experience of (a) opinion, (b) attitudes, (c) beliefs, and (d) values that affect *behavior.* Give examples that do not affect behavior. Why is there a difference?

Experiences in Persuasion

1. Read the "Letters to the Editor" section of a popular magazine (for example, *Playboy, Ms., Time*). A group of letters will usually refer to an article included in the magazine's earlier issues. Go back to this earlier article and see what kind of persuasion and evidence seem to have prompted the letter writers to go to the work of writing to the editor. Were they emotionally or intellectually stimulated? Was their response based on intellectually or emotionally oriented evidence? If you were to answer the letter, how would you go about doing it? Try to compose an answer utilizing the same kind of persuasion or evidence used by the author of the letter, by the author of the article, and by the author of a competing letter if there is one.

2. Tape-record a discussion on a TV talk program involving people who are not entertainment personalities but who are associated with an issue. Trace the argument over the issue utilizing the Toulmin system of analysis. Retrace it using syllogistic analysis. What happened? How could it have changed? What kind of position and line of reasoning do you suppose would be used by the participants on other issues—such as using quotas for hiring minorities or refusing to register for the draft?

3. Involve yourself in a discussion with your parents, friends, or students in your dormitory over some emotional issue (for example, homosexual marriages or rising rates of venereal disease on campuses). As you discuss the issue, try to identify the path of the discussion. Does it go from claim to data to warrant? If not, try to make it do so by asking for clear articulation of claims; ask for evidence or data; question the philosophical basis on which these two are

related; and see if the resulting discussion leads to the addition of qualifiers or reservations to the discussion.

4. Rewrite a piece of intellectually oriented persuasion so that it makes the same requests but is emotionally oriented. Now rewrite an emotionally oriented piece of persuasion to make it intellectually oriented. Identify the rational or reasonable elements in both pieces of persuasion. After rewriting the two, be prepared to argue for the relative effectiveness of one version over another.

5. Make a collection of advertisements in magazines and newspapers that are good examples of:

   a. Persuasion designed to change attitudes.

   b. Persuasion designed to change behaviors.

   c. Persuasion that operates from the three content linkages discussed in this chapter.

   d. Persuasion that uses dramatistically oriented evidence or proof.

   e. Persuasion that uses intellectually oriented evidence or proof.

   f. Persuasion that uses the various kinds of evidence discussed toward the end of the chapter (for example, sign argument, analogy, narrative).

6
Cultural Premises in Persuasion

Whether or not we realize it, we are trapped by our own culture. Anyone who visits another culture, particularly a non-Western one, quickly becomes aware of this. Not only are values, language, and customs different, but there are hundreds, even thousands of little things that differ from our familiar American ways. For example, only one third of the world uses tableware to eat. Another third eats with chopsticks, and the rest eat with their fingers. Even in England, differences are apparent. People wait at bus stops in neat, orderly lines, or "queues." We Americans usually crowd around the bus door or the sale table at the department store. For some reason we only queue up for supermarket check-out lines or at ticket windows.

We are also becoming aware of cultural differences brought about by the recent influx of emigrants from other lands. Following the Vietnam War, hundreds of thousands of Vietnamese, Laotians, Thais, and others who became known as Boat People were admitted into the United States. At the same time, so many people from Puerto Rico, Cuba, and other Spanish-speaking areas gained entry that some observers predict that America will be a dual-language country by the end of the twentieth century. Your children may have to study and speak both English and Spanish.

Changes related to the native cultures of these various emigrants can be seen throughout our society. One look down the aisles of any supermarket will demonstrate a few of these differences. You will find soybean curd, bean sprouts, and wonton—products one had to go to Chinatown to get only a few years ago. You will find corn and flour tortillas in the freezer case and pita bread at the deli. These minor cultural differences are, of course, only the tip of the iceberg. The important differences between cultures are values, beliefs, and patterns of behavior that are trained into us from early childhood through our language, the myths and tales we hear, and our observations of how those around us behave.

This training that we absorb from our culture and language forms some of the premises we have been discussing. The cultural preferences we have, or the cultural myths we believe in, or the cultural values we embrace, are all missing premises in enthymemes that persuaders can construct. This kind of persuasion occurs at a low level of awareness. We often react subconsciously to various stimuli based on our cultural training. Consider the following instance of cultural patterning:

> Suppose that you are a member of an Eskimo-Indian tribe called "People of the Deer," whose sole food supply is caribou. You kill enough animals in the spring to last the tribe until the fall, when again the animals migrate south following the food supply. The tribal custom is to kill and preserve these deer in a period of a week or two. The tribes are perhaps 100 persons strong. Suppose that we have just finished our fall hunt. We discover that we face a severe winter without having killed enough caribou to feed the tribe until the spring migration. Death is certain without sufficient supplies of meat and fat. Imagine that you are part of a tribal meeting called to consider the matter. What would you do in this situation?

In several persuasion classes, students brainstormed for solutions to this problem and came up with these suggestions in this approximate order:

1. "Let's follow the deer and kill enough."

2. "Let's seek an alternative food supply—we can eat berries or fish or birds."

3. "Let's send a band of the tribe to get help."

4. "Let's ration food to make it last longer."

5. "Let's use all the parts of the deer—skin, horns, everything—in order to increase the supply."

6. "Let's send some of the people away to another place where food is more plentiful and thus decrease demand."

7. "Let's kill some of our tribe in order to decrease demand."

8. "Let's kill the most useless—the old first, and the very young next."

9. "Let's resort to cannibalism along with the killing."

The most practical solutions emerged first and then more desperate ideas until someone suggested cannibalism. The actual People of the Deer do nothing—they eat the food at their regular rates, knowing full well that they will not live through the winter. Then they sit and wait for death. The tribe simply does not enter into the problem-solving frame of mind typical of Western culture. They accept a problem and do nothing, while we try to find solutions for any problem even though it may be insoluble. We are trained to *do something.* In our culture, persuaders succeed if they outline a problem and suggest solutions. In other cultures, the same tactic would not meet with success.

The classic example mentioned in Chapter 5 is the Music Man, Professor Harold Hill. You will remember he came to River City, Iowa, to sell band instruments. He created a need for these instruments by creating a problem for the townspeople—trouble. By the time he was through, the people of River City were not about to sit still as the People of the Deer might. They wanted action. Their need for action was met by buying band instruments. A cultural premise formed a basis for Hill's appeal.

In order to see how these premises relate to persuasion in general, let us look first at how we get them (cultural training and pressure). Then we look at three kinds of culture premises: (1) cultural images or myths, (2) an American value system, and (3) nonverbal premises. Bear in mind that a *value* is an idea of the "good" or the desirable that people use as a standard for judging means or to motivate others. Examples of values are honesty, justice, beauty, efficiency, safety, and progress. Because our value system is a major source of persuasive leverage, you may want to see how persuaders link proposals and arguments to our values.

Cultural and Societal Pressure

I am sure that everyone has heard stories about the children of various Indian tribes who never cried because it was essential not to frighten off game. Anyone who has been around a newborn infant must doubt these stories. Children cry when they are lonely, hungry, or want exercise. How, then, did Indians train their children not to cry out?

During the first hour of life, whenever a Sioux baby cried, its mother clapped her hands over the child's mouth and nose. The hand was removed only if the child stopped crying or began to smother. If this was done within the first hour of life, the infant never again cried out loud. Of course, as the child grew, it saw a pattern repeated over and over again. Parents and the elders spoke of the power of silence. They valued quiet and stealth in stalking game. The Indian brave was tested and proved his courage by experiencing pain and not crying out. The most significant test was the Sun Dance, outlawed for 50 years. Here a leather thong was sewn into the shoulder flesh of a brave. The brave would be tied to a totem pole at the center of a tribal circle. The test was to dance away from the pole until the pain of the thong forced him to fall (usually after several days of dancing). The fall usually tore out the thong from the shoulder. The brave was then a full-fledged warrior. Later he could do the Sun-Gazer's Dance. This involved dancing while staring directly into the sun. Sitting Bull is supposed to have done this for three days, after which he had a vision of the future massacre of Custer and his soldiers at the Little Big Horn.[1] Thus the pattern introduced at birth was seen at work throughout life.

Each of us goes through such cultural training seeing values demonstrated, and as a result we adopt the values. They become rules for governing ourselves as we interact. We do not even notice that they are there. We respond instinctively to them. This training underlies each of the three cultural premises we are going to study. It lurks beneath our surface thoughts and acts. Sophisticated persuaders

---

1. For a good discussion of the trials by pain used by Indians, read *Black Elk Speaks* by John Neihardt (Lincoln: University of Nebraska Press, 1961). The Sioux's use of smothering to prevent crying is discussed in *These Were the Sioux* by Maria Santos (New York: Dell Publishing Co., 1961), p. 19.

appeal to these premises directly and cleverly. They can appeal to cultural and societal premises because they believe in them and can expect that their audiences do also.

Cultural Images and Myths

Every culture has its own myths and heroes who do things valued by the culture. For example, early Greek society developed a series of myths surrounding the sin of pride. Eventually the myths became institutionalized in such Greek dramas as *Oedipus Rex*.

Parts of the myths related to physical acts, like trying to control one's own destiny, that were discouraged. Greeks placed a high value on avoiding prideful action. They elected leaders who were modest. They valued modesty. We have similar beliefs. You probably know that the overproud student is less likely to be elected to office or chosen as team captain than the more humble person. We view the antics of a pompous person with disfavor. We ridicule needless pride.

What are some of the cultural myths or legends or images underlying American culture and society and how do persuaders use them? Can these images be changed? If so, how? Are they being changed at present and if so, how? Stereotypes and proverbs are good indicators of cultural myths. Let us consider a few of these cultural myths.

Wisdom of the Rustic

One of the legends in American literature with great persuasive appeal is the clever rustic. No matter how devious the opposition, the simple wisdom of the backwoods wins out. Numerous folk tales rely on this image. The Daniel Boone tales, the stories about the inventiveness of Paul Bunyan, and many Lincoln stories rely on the rustic image. We have faith in humble persons when we look for leaders. The small-town boy is chosen team captain. We believe in humble beginnings and we believe that difficulty teaches even the most uneducated of us to be wise in a worldly way.

Persuaders often use the image, portraying themselves as rustics who have wisdom. There are obvious examples—Abraham Lincoln, George Wallace, Charles Ingalls of *Little House on the Prairie*. Advertisements focus on clever rustics or comparable figures (for example, Mrs. Olson of Folger's coffee fame or Robert Young of *Marcus Welby, M.D.*). In these images are several cultural values: a faith in common sense; a belief in instinct (think of maxims like "trust your horse sense"); and a reliance on physical and mental prowess.

At the same time that we seem to value the simple, common-sense rustic, we have a set of norms that devalues the intellectual or the educated. Alexis de Toqueville, in his book *Democracy in America* written in the 1830s, observed the same distrust:

> The nearer the people are drawn to the common level of an equal and similar condition, the less prone does each man become to place implicit faith

in a certain man or a certain class of men [intellectuals]. But his readiness to believe the multitude increases, and opinion is more than ever mistress of the world. Not only is common opinion the only guide which private judgement retains ... it possesses a power infinitely beyond what it has elsewhere.[2]

Richard Hofstadter also wrote about this anti-intellectualism in several places.[3] Persuaders often use the reverse side of our value in the wisdom of the rustic. The intellectual is often the brunt of jokes. Advertisers often have the rustic win out over the smart guy. Politicians frequently emphasize their humble roots.

Possibility of Success

The Horatio Alger myth is based on several novels written by Alger in the nineteenth century. They always told of a young man who through hard work, sincerity, honesty, and a faith in the future was able to make good. He might even rise to the top and own his own company, have a beautiful wife, live a fine life, and be able to do good for others. The myth has appeal and was believed by immigrants, the poor, and the downtrodden. They passed it on to their children, admonishing them to work hard and achieve success. One of the slogans on college campuses today is "Get a degree, get a job, and get ahead." That slogan is part of the Alger myth, which parents reinforce over and over, as the Indian tribal elders reinforced the value of silence.

In a sense, this myth—the possibility of success—links up with the wisdom of the rustic myth. If you follow the advice of the common man and use common sense, with sincerity and hard work, you will be a success. It has the values of hard work, sincerity, honesty, and law and order. Some persons claim that the myth was established to enslave the common people and to keep them on a treadmill. If you think that you have a chance to achieve success, you will not risk questioning authority figures. Instead, you will submit to them and try to gain power for yourself. Again, this myth was observed by Alexis de Tocqueville:

> No Americans are devoid of a yearning desire to rise; ... All are constantly seeking to acquire property, power, and reputation. ... What chiefly diverts the men of democracies from lofty ambition is not the scantiness of their fortunes, but the vehemence of the exertions they daily make to improve them. ... The same observation is applicable to the sons of such men: they are born ... their parents were humble; they have grown up amidst feelings and notions which they cannot afterwards easily get rid of; and it may be presumed that they will inherit the propensities of their father, as well as his wealth.[4]

You probably can see your parents and your relatives in this description. If Tocqueville was right, you may see yourself also. You are ready for persuasion

2. Alexis de Tocqueville. *Democracy in America* (New York: Mentor Books. 1965). p. 148.

3. Richard Hofstadter. *Anti-Intellectualism in American Life* (New York: Alfred A. Knopf. 1963).

4. Tocqueville, pp. 156–158.

aimed at the possibility of success. If you follow the myth—work hard for your grades or job or pay, and if you have the faith and stamina, you will succeed. This myth was used by Richard Nixon in his 1972 campaign and by Jimmy Carter in 1976. It will probably be used by one candidate or another in elections to come. As a persuadee, you should expect to hear appeals made for the myth. Persuaders will offer success as just around the corner, if only you will follow them and not the false prophets. They will offer the "big break" and the chance to have a better life for you and your children. Whether it is a speed-reading course, a body builder, or a weight watchers' club, the carrot is always the same—try and you will succeed.

Coming of the Messiah

Americans expect to be saved from disaster by great prophets or saviors. Let us investigate the values of this image.

First, what does the myth claim? Well, there are times so difficult, confusing and chaotic, that escape seems impossible. For the unemployed during the Great Depression, it was the total lack of job opportunities and the prospect of more of the same. For the 1950s, it was the increasing Russian domination. For America in the late 1960s, there were two problems: (1) a serious breakdown of traditional values and lifestyles, seen in civil riots, the use of drugs, common-law marriages, and communes, and (2) the seeming inability of public opinion to deter the war policy of the Johnson and Nixon administrations. In the 1970s, the problems clustered around energy, inflation, and the ability of the country to live up to its promises of security for the elderly, health care for the masses, and equal opportunity for all.

The first element of the messianic myth is a problem perceived as insoluble. The second element in this myth is a person believed to have answers and solutions. In the 1930s he was a person with a common touch who displayed great vision tempered by adversity—Franklin D. Roosevelt. There were others who sold similar qualities—Huey P. Long of Louisiana, Floyd B. Olson of Minnesota, and Father Charles E. Coughlin, for example. In the 1950s there were would-be prophet-messiahs like Senator Joseph McCarthy, who charged that the State Department was riddled with traitors. All of these prophets claimed to have the insight and wisdom to be the savior of the country. The 1950s must not have demanded as much as the 1930s, for we chose a reluctant war hero—Dwight Eisenhower—and a witty intellectual—Adlai Stevenson—as major candidates. In the 1960s, other messiahs emerged to solve the insoluble—George Wallace, Eugene McCarthy, Barry Goldwater, Robert Kennedy, and George McGovern. Again the situation was evidently not bad enough to warrant the election of any of these saviors. In the 1970s, the messiahs were technology and clever amateur inventions to create new fuel sources. One fellow invented an engine for cars or trucks that would run off the methane gas emitted from chicken manure!

The messiahs of the 1980s seem to be different. Like Ronald Reagan, they have been hard-nosed, bite-the-bullet types. In state after state in the early 1980s, budgets were slashed. Advertisements promoted austerity and toughness. Actor John Houseman, a grumpy old-fashioned type, became a very popular spokesman for financial firms in their advertising after becoming well known for his portrayal of a demanding, back-to-basics law professor in the TV series *Paper Chase*. Other messiahs emerged in other contexts, but they always demonstrated the same kind of image—the no-nonsense type who seemed to be saying "Enough is enough!" as they drew a line in the dust and dared the opposition to cross it. This image spread into foreign policy as the United States actively opposed guerilla wars in many Latin American countries and refused to negotiate with the Soviet Union until certain conditions were met. In industry, people like Lee Iacocca of Chrysler took the helm, and in the autoworkers' unions, new wage pacts were hammered out with lower wages for workers in return for more job security. Bank presidents went on TV to urge a return to the old values of thrift and balanced budgets. So, while time and circumstances may change, Americans seem to be always waiting for another messiah to come down the road and save them from one big, bad wolf or another. The back-to-basics messiah of the 1980s will probably not be the messiah of the 1990s, but there will be messiahs of one kind or another when the 1990s do arrive.

Presence of Conspiracy

Another cultural premise is the belief that big problems don't have simple causes. Richard Hofstadter calls the belief the paranoid style. This is a belief that when problems appear great, the only reasonable explanation for them is that a powerful group has conspired to cause them.[5] This conspiracy argument has recurred throughout our history in the form of alleged Papist conspiracies, Masonic conspiracies, and Populist conspiracies, among many others. Franklin D. Roosevelt used the argument in connection with the Great Depression: Money interests and the great banking houses had caused the depression and should be "thrown out of the temple." McGovern claimed that a conspiracy was behind the bugging of the Watergate headquarters in 1972. Later, Richard Nixon, trying to deny Watergate charges, accused elements in the CIA of being behind the plot. At one point in the scandal he said that a "sinister force" was against him. The energy crisis is sometimes blamed on an OPEC conspiracy. We can expect to see conspiracy theories from time to time in the future as well.

Though the conspiracy myth does not really carry values of our culture, it does trace a pattern of response. If you hear a conspiracy argument (whether there actually is a conspiracy or not), chances are the persons using the pattern hold these views:

1. They have something of value to lose. They are in possession of some kind of power or property.

2. They see themselves in danger of losing some or all of this power or property or as already having lost some of it.

3. They see themselves as helpless to prevent loss.

---

5. For a more complete discussion of the conspiracy argument, see *The Paranoid Style in American Politics and Other Essays* by Richard Hofstadter (New York: Vintage Books, 1967).

It is easy to see how these beliefs could link up with the messiah. The messiah can defeat the evil conspirators and thus save the culture. Here lies one of the dangers of the conspiracy argument—it invites mass hysteria and charismatic leaders.[6] In times of trouble and confusion, we may see the rise of mass movements following leaders who are believed to be heroes or saviors.

Value of Challenge

Associated with the messiah or savior myth is another myth or image—the value of challenge. The myth is fairly simple and may parallel tribal tests of strength and character. The myth suggests there is a kind of wisdom gained only through great challenge and testing. There is a rite of passage or initiation that gives one power, character, and knowledge.

You are probably now going through such a test in college. People say that going to college is a test of endurance more than a training ground for a specific job. College graduation shows that you can meet a challenge and handle it, that you have matured, that you have learned how to learn. Employers hire college graduates and then train them for a job after college. Boot camp offers another example of belief in the value of overcoming difficulty and in meeting challenges.

The more dramatic the challenge, of course, the more persuasive is the myth, and the appeals to it become more potent. Good examples of past uses of this myth are Hitler's references to his imprisonment as a test, the reminders of Roosevelt's testing when he was crippled with polio, and Ted Kennedy's references to his brothers' assassinations.

The rite of passage or the meeting of a challenge underscores several values that persuaders use as appeals in our culture. First, it suggests that there is something good about suffering—you learn from it and grow emotionally as a result of it. Persuaders say that though the going might be rough, the lessons learned along the way are worth it. Remember your parents telling you how good it was for you to suffer through trigonometry or Latin? Second, the myth suggests that there are certain signs of maturity. One is the ability to behave with character when under duress. Finally, the myth suggests that greatness needs to be tempered under fire. No one who ever was great became so without suffering and lots of scars from the hurly-burly of battle. The battleground might be politics, athletics, or the grueling hours of training for artistic successes. All the suffering prepares the person for greatness tinged with a humble nature. Try to identify the places in your life where the challenge has been brought up to motivate you or others around you.

The "Man's Man" and the "Woman's Woman"

Another popular myth is that for a male to be a success, he has to be a man's man. The schools, the family, and television told children that important male persons were people who did macho things. They competed in sports, talked tough, owned guns and heavy-duty equipment, drove four-wheel-drive vehicles,

---

6. For a good discussion of the degree to which persons will follow charismatic leaders, see Eric Hoffer, *The True Believer* (New York: Harper & Row, 1951).

never showed their emotions, and died with their boots on. Girls, on the other hand, were dainty, fussy, prissy, and spent a lot of time in grooming. These myths of course affected the way we valued certain things children did and devalued others. It was unwise for a female to engage in any sport except tennis, golf, or swimming; it was unwise for any male to take up gourmet cooking, needlepoint, or flower gardening (vegetables were OK). Boys shouldn't cry. Girls always did. This myth of the distinctions between the sexes is changing, however. Probably because of dependable birth control and the Women's Liberation Movement, we now see young boys and girls playing soccer together in neighborhood leagues. High schools and colleges have women's field hockey, basketball, and baseball teams and rivalries. In many towns, you will find girls' softball leagues for seven-, eight-, and nine-year-olds. Phone company ads show women climbing poles. At the same time, it is becoming permissible for men to take to the kitchen and to become house-husbands. Roosevelt Grier, the ex-football bruiser, even does needlepoint.

At the same time, the old myths do not die easily, for we still see many examples of the macho male and the perfectly "feminine" woman. The Lite beer ads feature retired athletes engaged in a man's world, bragging to one another over beers. The sponsors for L'eggs pantyhose know that dancer Juliet Prowse epitomizes femininity. Perhaps the differences we are now seeing as a result of the Women's Movement relate more to what students of persuasion have called *ethos* or *credibility*. We no longer "believe" the housewife who keels over in surprise at the neighborhood "hen-party" as the hostess reveals that the chips aren't really chips but Pringles. Likewise, the housewives who compare one another's whites at the laundromat fail to convince.

Persuaders will have to continue to adapt as Americans shift their values and as they shift their concept of the kind of person who is to be believed. Perhaps as the over-all American population ages and as the traditional two-parent, two-child American-home ceases to be the norm, we will come to view older citizens and single parents as credible or as having high ethos.

Image or Ethos as a Cultural Premise

Sometimes persuaders are successful because of their image, or as we sometimes call it, their charisma. We know that we should believe them because they are so convincing and dynamic in their presentation or because they have a reputation for being truthful or knowledgeable. As we noted earlier, this kind of proof was recognized by Aristotle, as well as others. He called it *ethos* or ethical proof. In more recent times, researchers have worked at identifying exactly what it is that causes or creates high ethos in some persons and low ethos in others. Their technique was to have audiences rate various speakers on a variety of bipolar scales that had sets of opposing adjectives at either end.[7] Figure 6.1 shows a set of such scales.

---

7. For a full description of the development of the Semantic Differential, which was the central measuring device for research on ethos, see *The Measurement of Meaning* by Charles Osgood, George Suci, and Percy Tannenbaum (Urbana: The University of Illinois Press, 1957).

This speaker is (mark scale at the spot you feel best fits):

Fast	....	....	....	....	....	**Slow**
Light	....	....	....	....	....	**Heavy**
Powerful	....	....	....	....	....	**Weak**
Open	....	....	....	....	....	**Closed**
Truthful	....	....	....	....	....	**Untruthful**
Sincere	....	....	....	....	....	**Insincere**
Biased	....	....	....	....	....	**Unbiased**
Graceful	....	....	....	....	....	**Clumsy**
Dumb	....	....	....	....	....	**Smart**
Unstable	....	....	....	....	....	**Stable**

Figure 6.1. Audience rating scale for evaluating ethos.

The researchers used several hundred such pairs of terms and then tried to determine which kinds of traits seemed to typify speakers who were considered persuasive and believable. They discovered in repeated tests that the choices seemed to cluster around three kinds of traits or three dimensions of what came to be called **source credibility.** The first dimension was finally called the *expertise* component of source credibility. In other words, highly credible sources were perceived of as having knowledge and experience regarding the topic they addressed. This makes sense. We tend to put more store in the ideas and advice that come from an expert than those that come from a nonexpert. Whom would you listen to for advice on auto racing, the winner of the Indy 500 or the kid down the block who drag races on Friday nights? The clustering of items related to expertise was later verified by a number of experiments in which a variety of groups listened to the same tape-recorded speaker giving the same speech. The speaker was introduced to some of the groups as an expert—say, the Surgeon General. These groups believed the speaker much more than did others to whom the speaker was introduced as a college senior.

Another dimension that emerged as being focal was *sincerity*. The word itself comes from the Latin *sincerus*, which literally means without wax. This had a dual meaning in ancient times. The first referred to the use of wax coatings as preservatives. To be without wax was to be fresh, pure, or unadulterated. The second meaning referred to a practice of unethical pillar carvers, who used wax to cover up their mistakes or to hide imperfections in the marble. Only after decades of weathering did the wax fall out to reveal the deception played by the by now long-gone carver. So a sincere person was the genuine article, or *without wax* or uncamouflaged. This was the idea to which the *sincerity* dimension of the credibility scale related. Words like truthful or honest or genuine differentiated the sincere speakers from the insincere. Perhaps the audiences felt speakers were sincere because they maintained good eye contact or didn't shift back and forth on their feet or didn't have a tremor in their voices. Or maybe the respondent judged sincerity from the person's reputation. Some studies showed that a well-known singer of the 1940s and 1950s, Kate Smith, had great credibility with audiences who heard her appeals to pledge money to various causes. She was associated with the song *God Bless America* and usually closed her shows with it. Perhaps audiences felt anyone who sang *God Bless America* had to be sincere.

A final dimension of credibility as a form of cultural proof was identified as *dynamism* or *potency*. This is probably as close as the studies came to identifying the quality we call charisma. Dynamic speakers didn't necessarily move about or wave their arms to give off dynamism cues. They just seemed to take up a lot of psychological space. They entered a room and people expected them to be in charge. The kinds of words associated with the dynamism dimension were words like fast, powerful, potent, or quick.

There are probably other dimensions of source credibility that could be investigated, and there are others that have already been studied.[8] We know, for example, that a taller speaker is, generally speaking, more likely to be believed than a shorter one. Timid or shy and reserved persons are likely to have low credibility, while authoritative and self-assured ones will have high credibility. Bossy and egotistical persuaders lose credibility, while pleasant and warm persuaders do not. These and many other dimensions of source credibility probably interact and affect the three fundamental dimensions of *trust—sincerity, expertise*, and *dynamism* or *potency*.

These values are not shared by all cultures. In some cultures where the bribe or "backsheesh" is the order of the day, people are presumed to be *untrustworthy*. Haggling over prices in the bazaars and markets of other cultures is based on *insincerity*, not sincerity. Many cultures value the *undynamic* persuader who is cool and calm. And in some cultures, a religious leader, who perhaps lacks expertise in economics and diplomacy, becomes the head of state while the experts are ejected from government. So credibility or ethos is also culturally dependent.

Presence of an American Value System

The myths we have just examined are actually fantasy forms of deep and enduring values that most Americans hold. They are expressed in myths in order to simplify them. This makes them seem less lofty—more down-to-earth and ordinary. For example, we have a belief or value in this country that all persons are to be treated equally and that in the eyes of God they *are* equal. This value has been debated for more than two centuries through such issues as slavery, women's suffrage, civil rights, desegregation, and affirmative action programs. The value is acted out or dramatized in the possibility-of-success myth. We see the myth acted

---

8. For an excellent discussion of various studies conducted on source credibility, see Calvin David Mortensen, *Communication: The Study of Human Interaction* (New York: McGraw-Hill, 1972), pp. 142–159.

out in TV commercials. A middle-aged wife says, "We've worked hard for what we have and now we are going to take care of ourselves, too—we use Geritol." The film *Rocky* depicted a man rising to a championship boxing match through hard work. Many politicians say they have come up the hard way.

One of the early speech-communication studies that explored values was conducted by Edward Steele and W. Charles Redding.[9] They looked at the communication of several political campaigns and tried to extract core and secondary values. These were the core values observed by Steele and Redding:

- **Puritan and pioneer morality**—the willingness to cast the world into categories of foul and fair, good and evil, and so forth. Though we tend to think of this value as outdated, it has merely been reworded. The advocates and foes of present marijuana laws and of legal abortion both call on moral values such as just/unjust, right/wrong, and moral/immoral to make their cases.

- **Value of the individual**—the ranking of the rights and welfare of the individual above those of government and as important in other ways. This value seems to persist. All politicians claim to be interested in the individual. Cosmetics are made especially for you. We praise the house decorating scheme that expresses individuality. Burger King lets you "have it your way."

- **Achievement and success**—the accumulation of power, status, wealth, and property. There was a short period during the 1960s and 1970s when young Americans seemed to reject this value. They joined communes, would not dress for job interviews, and so forth. Those people are now often the classic models of success-minded organization types. Literally millions of dollars are spent every year on self-help products or courses designed to make success more possible for you. All these appeals rely on the value we place on achievement and success.

- **Change and progress**—the belief that society develops in positive ways measured by progress. Though this value is probably the one most often questioned today (General Electric does not claim that "Progress Is Our Most Important Product" any more, and environmentalists want to know the cost of progress), it still has a good deal of persuasive potency. Recall the frequency of maxims suggesting "You can never stand still; if you do, you fall behind." Again, even the most vehement ecologists still want change and merely define progress as the movement away from technological change and toward change and progress in lifestyle. Most auto advertisements suggest the value of change and progress.

- **Ethical equality**—the view that all persons are equal in a spiritual sense and ought to be in a realm of opportunity. Though the "equal in the eyes of God" aspect of this value has changed since the 1950s, the opportunity element remains potent. Affirmative Action programs were built on the power of this value. Most revival movements appeal to this value.

---

9. Edward D. Steele and W. Charles Redding, "The American Value System: Premises for Persuasion," *Western Speech*, Vol. 26 (Spring 1962), pp. 83–91.

Effort and optimism—the belief that hard work and striving will ultimately lead to success. This value is clearly incorporated in several of the myths discussed above—the value of challenge and the possibility of success, for example. Retirement programs are ballyhooed with this value.

Efficiency, practicality, and pragmatism—the value placed on solution-oriented as opposed to ideologically oriented thinking. A key question often asked of any piece of legislation is "Will it work?" This value extends to other parts of our lives, too. We want to know if a microwave oven is energy efficient, if it is practical or handy. We want to know if the diesel engine will save money and run longer and cleaner. We want to know if our schooling will lead to a job. In other words, we value what is quick, workable, and practical.

Even though these values were catalogued over thirty years ago, they still have a great deal of relevance. This, if nothing else, suggests their basic quality. The fact that political position has less to do with the strength of these values than the method of enacting them seems to underscore the probability that these are core values for Americans. Our culture has been effective in instilling a set of values in all, or very nearly all, of its members—radicals, moderates, and reactionaries all believe in the same things, but just operationalize them differently. The power of a social system or culture to train its members is immense, even though the members do not often realize this as they react to the dictates deeply ingrained in them.

Does this mean that values remain essentially static and cannot be changed? Not necessarily. It only means that values are so deeply ingrained in a culture that its members often forget how strong their pressures are.

Use of Nonverbal Messages and Cues

A final kind of cultural or societal predisposition for persuasion relates to symbolic behavior that is not spoken or articulated. The whole field of nonverbal communication is relatively new, and the research is extremely broad—far too broad to be adequately covered in part of one chapter. To limit our consideration here, we will not consider those nonverbal signal systems that seem to be biologically oriented. Instead, we will just look briefly at the kinds of nonverbal signals that seem to be culturally related—that differ from culture to culture and that can increase or destroy persuasive potential. We will look at the use of artifacts or objects, the use of space, and the use of touch.

Use of Artifacts

We humans are probably not so far removed from animals, but there are some differences. Though birds feather their nests with bits of string, straw, hair, and wood, they do it for purely functional reasons—to keep their nests intact and cozy. We humans feather our nests not only for those reasons but also for highly

Figure 6.2. Ads like this can be found in almost every magazine. They play on our need for achievement and success.

symbolic reasons. The best way of discovering how this happens is to look at your work area in your dorm room or at the work area of your roommate or spouse. It is not arranged only so that work can get done; people feather their nests with objects—artifacts—that symbolize them. Arrangement is also symbolic (certain kinds of people have messy desks, while others have extremely neat desks, with each pencil sharpened and papers stacked in neat piles). Our culture has taught us to react in certain ways to the artifacts of others and how they are used. These patterns of responses form premises for persuasion.

A common type of artifactual cosmetology is revealed in the objects surrounding a persuader in a message situation (for example, in a public speech situation the banners, the bunting, the use of flags, the insignias)—all contributing to the ultimate success of the persuasive attempt. Another type of artifact is clothing. What people wear sends signals about what they are like (think of the differences between casual sports clothes and a tuxedo), what they believe (for example, a priest's collar or an army officer's uniform).

Another type of artifact is exemplified in the personal objects surrounding a persuader. Consider how you feel when you go into a doctor's office with diplomas on the wall—no art, no colorful posters or any other kind of decoration—just diplomas. What cultural signal do you receive about the kind of person the doctor is likely to be? Compare that with the feeling you have as you enter a college professor's office with posters or abstract art on the walls. The artifacts symbolize the kind of persuasion you will be likely to hear—in one case, professional, concrete, and probably prescriptive, and, in the other, abstract.

Large objects like furniture can also give off signals. We can expect a certain kind of communication to occur when we are told to sit down at a table and the persuader sits at the opposite side. Persuaders who put a lectern between themselves and the audience will probably engage in a certain kind of communication—probably very formal. If they step out from behind the lectern or walk around while talking, they may well be more informal. Types of furniture can also symbolize certain characteristics. What kinds of persuasion and what kinds of persons would you associate with French Provincial furniture? What kind of persuasion is likely to occur in a room with industrial metal furniture? What kind in a Danish Modern room? Or Early American?

Proxemics: The Use of Space

The way people structure the space around them is also a factor in communication that seems particularly related to cultural training. We can, if we wish, signal to our fellow communicators that we feel superior and that formal communication is called for. We can suggest that informal communication is called for, or we can suggest that intimate and extremely frank communication is called for. Edward T. Hall notes four general distances used by persuaders in American culture.[10]

Public distance—distances we often find in public speaking situations where speakers are 15 to 25 or more feet from their audiences. Informal persuasion probably will not work in these circumstances. Persuaders who try to be informal in a formal situation will probably meet with little success.

Social or formal distance—the distances used in formal but nonpublic situations like interviews or committee reports. The persuader in these situa-

---

10. Edward T. Hall, *The Silent Language* (Garden City: Doubleday & Co., 1959), *The Hidden Dimension,* (Garden City: Doubleday & Co., 1966), and "Proxemics—A Study of Man's Spatial Relationships" in *Man's Image in Medicine and Anthropology* (International Universities Press, 1963) all provide further insights to the use of space.

tions, though formal in style, need not be oratorical. Formal distance runs about 7 to 12 feet between persuader and persuadee. You would never become chummy in this kind of situation (regardless of whether you were persuader or persuadee), yet you would not deliver a "speech" either.

Personal or informal distance—the distance used when two colleagues or friends are discussing a matter of mutual concern. A good example might be when you and your roommate are discussing this class or a problem you both share. In these situations, communication is less structured than in the formal situation; persuadee and persuader are both more relaxed and interact often with one another, bringing up and questioning evidence or asking for clarification. Informal distance, in our culture, is about 3½ to 4 feet—the eye-to-eye distance if you sit at the corner of a teacher's desk, as opposed to the formal distance created when you sit across the desk.

Intimate distance—the distance people use when they mutter or lovingly whisper messages they do not want others to overhear. Persuasion may or may not occur in these instances; usually the message is one that will not be questioned by the receiver—he or she will nod in agreement, follow the suggestion given, or respond to the question asked. When two communicators are in this kind of close relation to one another, their aims are similar, in all probability. The distance ranges from 6 to 18 inches.

When distances are used to encourage or discourage a certain kind of persuasion or when a persuader oversteps the boundaries "agreed upon" by the persuadee, results can often be startling. For example, during the 1972 presidential campaign, George McGovern, after being heckled during a speech, walked up to one of his hecklers and when he was in intimate distance said to him "kiss my ass" and walked away. The message—an intimate and certainly not a persuasive one—was overheard by some members of the press and then written up in the evening newspapers and related over the television news—a public kind of exposure. The response did not help the candidate's image.

In studies of communication flow and its relation to ease of conversation, leadership emergence, and a number of other variables, researchers discovered that the most used communication channels at a conference table (see Figure 6.3) were those across the corners of the table (or informal distance); the next most often used channel was directly across the table (or about the distance we have called formal distance); the third was down the length of the conference table (or about what we have called public distance); and the least used was between persons sitting next to one another (or about what we have called intimate distance). In conferences, we feel fairly comfortable to converse, to discuss, to persuade in informal ways; we do not often engage in intimate conversation and thus avoid speaking with those next to us. Most people form few intimate relationships and probably feel uneasy responding *as if* in intimate relation with another person. Think of what you do in the front seat of an auto when there are three passengers or at a banquet table when you must talk to the person next to

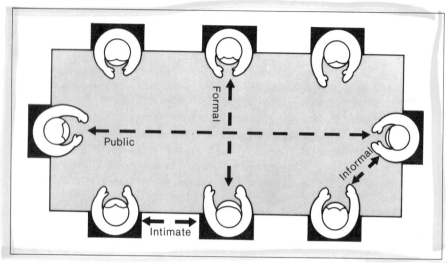

Figure 6.3. Communication channels at a conference table.

you. You probably move away from that person's face or you speak to a spot in midair—perhaps the windshield of the car or a centerpiece on the banquet table. You rarely allow yourself to communicate in intimate distance unless you are on an intimate basis with a person.

If you want to encourage communication flow, try to arrange informal spaces for persons to use; if you want to discourage communication, arrange intimate spaces for persons to use. Be alert to persuaders who are adept at using space this way and to persuaders who seem to have misjudged their relationship with a listener. In either case, the use of space indicates something about the persuader.

Recently, people in the real estate business became interested in the communicative power of correct and strategic use of space. Industry publications discussed questions like how close the real estate agent should be to the prospective buyer during a tour of a home or whether the agent should lead or follow the buyer. In many other contexts—offices, hospitals, banks, prisons, and factories—serious consideration is given to the use of space as a communicative device or as a communication facilitator. Try to be alert to the uses of space in your life. How have you arranged your room or apartment? Does the arrangement facilitate or deter communication? How do various people with whom you interact use their space? Do foreigners use space differently? You will soon discover how important this nonverbal channel of communication is to persuasion and to other kinds of communication as well.

Chronemics: The Use of Time

There is a saying in our culture that goes, "Time is money—don't waste it!" Time can communicate many things to others. Let's suppose that you have set a time and reserved a place for a meeting of a work group in one of your classes. Since you are arranging the meeting, you show up ten minutes early to make sure things will go well. You want to be sure there are enough chairs and that there are appropriate materials for the meeting. A few minutes before the meeting is to start, two members of the group arrive and begin to chat. Right on time, to the minute, comes another group member. Now only two people are missing. You will probably say something like "Let's wait a few minutes before starting—people might have had a hard time getting served at the cafeteria." After five minutes, one of your missing persons shows up and you start the meeting, promising the rest of the group that you will see to it that the missing member gets the information. Nearly a half hour after the meeting has started, the missing member arrives with no excuses for the lateness. What has each person communicated to you? In our culture, it is permissible to arrive at a meeting up to five or six minutes late, but arrive later than that and you'd better have a good excuse like a flat tire, a stalled elevator, or a speeding ticket. By coming late, you "persuade" the others that you really don't care much about the appointment; that you are a thoughtless person; and probably that you are also a pretty arrogant prima donna. If, on the other hand, you are invited to a party, be sure to show up at least twenty minutes late or you will be early. Only losers show up on time at parties. The host or hostess may still be in the shower at the appointed starting time. If you really want to put people in their place, make sure that they have to wait to get in to see you—that's a favorite trick of some college profs. Most importantly, begin to observe how time works in your culture, and don't be surprised if it doesn't operate that way in other cultures or even in subcultures within our culture.

Tactics: The Use of Touch

One of the strange inconsistencies in American culture is the way we regard physical touch between human beings. One often sees the heads of state in various European countries hugging and kissing one another when they meet after trips. Can you imagine what the press would do with a televised and photographed incident in which our President and Vice-President hugged and kissed after the President had returned from a trip abroad? In spite of new freedoms granted to homosexuals, public opinion would probably not be in favor of physical suggestions of homosexuality between public officials, even if there were no doubt in anyone's mind about the relationship. At the same time we have no strange feelings when the wives of the President and Vice-President hug and kiss. Touch is perfectly acceptable between two men on a football field or between two grade-school chums or between a man and a woman. Certainly touch is one of the most important systems of communication with infants—the sureness of a mother's or father's touch can calm and soothe an infant in distress.

Generally, in Western culture touch between men is limited to shaking hands or backslapping. Persuaders who are too "touchy" with persons around them (for example, with fellow candidates for office, with other people on interview shows, or with other members of the board of directors) are likely to offend not only the person touched but also the persons observing the touch. Credibility can be drastically undermined if persuaders misread a relationship and respond inappropriately with touch.

Examples of misread physical touches abound in the literature of politics and social relations. Robert F. Kennedy is supposed to have been extremely touchable as a candidate, often in a day of campaigning losing several pairs of cufflinks and ending the day with clothing torn and hands and shoulders bruised by the "press of the flesh." At the same time he hated being touched in a formal situation such as a dinner or reception. I once worked with a group of firemen in a communication training program. For this group, the only acceptable touch from another male was the handshake or backslap. I wanted them to understand the importance of touch as a communicative device. A fireman must sometimes calm frantic men, women, and children to get them out of a burning building. They resisted rehearsing any kinds of touches. Not until we played a game in which one of the men was trapped and ordered to break out of a circle formed by the others linking arms and waists did the group begin to accept the idea of touching one another. The game gave them a culturally acceptable way to hold one another's arms and waists. Once past this initial barrier, we could talk about how touch could be used to calm people in crisis situations. The laying on of hands used in some religions is sometimes given credit for conversions when it is possible that touch is persuasive enough to prompt people to come forward and convert.

On the other hand, touch is extremely important and facilitates certain kinds of communication. Terminal cancer patients need more touch than other patients, according to some experts. Touch helps to express sympathy when one attends a funeral service. Recent studies showed filmic evidence of the importance of touch. Strangers were asked to give information to a researcher who was being secretly filmed on a street corner. In half of the cases he lightly touched the stranger before saying "Excuse me, but I'm sort of lost. Can you tell me where. . . ?" The researcher got much more information and even conversation when using the light touch. Observe the printed ads in magazines. Look at the kinds of touches that are used in them. You will discover the persuasive potential of touch has many dimensions.

Dialect

We learn dialect culturally. It can communicate many things about us and can affect our persuasion too. Many of my students come from Chicago or its suburbs—often from the South Side. They get angry with me when I tell some of them to stop "talking like steelworkers." They do not hear themselves saying "dis" for this and "dat" for that and "dem" for them. Yet they will be discriminated against if they keep their dialect. At the same time, others from the North Side and some suburbs have another dialect that may cause equal problems for them. They talk what I call "Skokien" because of the predominance of this dialect in the suburb of Skokie. They say "dubbie" for Debbie, "shovie" for Chevy, and "new-ahth" for north. This dialect is associated with the values presumed to be held by people from Skokie, a predominantly Jewish upper-middle class community. Of course, it would be easy to document the kind of discrimination that occurs when black or Spanish dialect is used. Be aware of your responses to various dialects and see whether people respond to your dialect in certain ways. I still have a Minnesota dialect and get certain responses because of my frequent use of "Yup" and "You betcha." People start looking for hayseeds in my hair.

Norman Heap, communication professor, suggests a way to look at the impact of dialect.[11] He observed that we tend to regard dialect as signaling educational background and communication context, resulting in a four-category system. These categories are:

Formal context/educated speaker—proper pronunciation and usage like that we hear used in the courtroom, in governmental bodies, and by news announcers on television.

Informal context/educated speaker—proper pronunciation but accompanied by slang usages, perhaps, which signal the informal context. Those might include localisms like my "You betcha" or profanity. Once this usage is exposed in formal contexts it is sometimes viewed as unacceptable, as was the case with the release of the taped conversations in the White House during Richard Nixon's Watergate problem.

Formal context/uneducated speaker—attempts at proper pronunciation and usage such as we might hear when an uneducated person testifies in court or at some sort of governmental hearing. It is like the charwoman saying at a fine dinner party, "This spoon is entirely too large for my mouth." The speaker is almost trying *too hard* to sound correct.

Informal context/uneducated speaker—pronunciation and usage such as we might expect in steel mills: the "dese" and "dem" and "dose" pronunciations. These will vary from locale to locale but usually can be associated with blue-collar job settings or informal outings. Educated speakers can lose credibility by being too formal or correct in such settings. Imagine the college professor asking the salmon snagger during the fall run: "The salmon is an andronomous species isn't it—I mean it atrophies after the spawning run doesn't it?"

So while people are entitled to their own particular dialect, we need to remember that dialect signals a variety of meanings, including one's background, regional origins, and the kind of context that is presumably in effect.

Other Nonverbal Message Carriers

There are other carriers of meaning that do not use words and that are peculiar to our culture or various parts of our culture. Duration of words, for example, is often a cue to the end of a sermon in black congregations. The preacher will say, "And for all of this we can thank Jeeeeeessssssuuusss!" emphasizing the last word not only by increasing volume but by stretching it out. In other cultures this emphasis would seem out of place. This characteristic of the Negro church service was picked up by the Civil Rights Movement. Martin Luther King Jr., in his last speech before he was assassinated during the Memphis garbage workers' strike, finished his speech urging workers to a final rally and march. He

---

11. Norman A. Heap, Trenton State College, private correspondence.

said, "Mine eeeeyyyyyeeeesssss have seen the glory of the coming of the Lord," stretching the word "eyes" out as a signal to his audience that he was finishing and that they ought to join in with "amen" and "right on." Eye contact or the lack of it can signal important messages in our culture. We say people should be able to look us straight in the eye if they aren't lying. If they happen to have artificial eyes or visual handicaps that do not allow direct eye contact with both eyes, we are uneasy. We sometimes speak of a person's having lively eyes and associate this attribute with high spirits, a good sense of humor, and ambition. The raised eyebrow asks a question or expresses doubt. The rate of eyeblinks one has is associated with one's level of conscious awareness of the world. Vance Packard reports a research study that found that the eye-blink rate in supermarkets slowed down to a near hypnotic state for some shoppers. A person who is very tense will blink about once a second compared to the normal rate of twenty-five to thirty times a minute. Packard's shoppers dropped to an average of fourteen blinks a minute.[12]

A researcher named Ray Birdwhistell has catalogued numerous facial movements that carry meaning. He can describe literally hundreds of combinations of mouth, eye, cheek, and brow movements that carry meanings common to most people in our culture. The furrowed brow, for example, usually signals concern, worry, or anxiety. Couple this with a high degree of lip tension and perhaps a repeated wetting of the lips, and a pretty consistent message comes across. Birdwhistell even claims to be able to tell what part of the country one comes from by looking at facial position while speaking. New Englanders, for example, keep the upper lip pulled in and pressed tightly against the teeth—the grandpa who sells Pepperidge Farm bread is a good example. Of course, his regional accent reinforces his regional facial expression.

Smell may also have a message-carrying quality. We all recognize the power of the smells of fine foods being cooked. The homey smell seems to have a persuasive quality. Certainly the use of deodorants, perfumes, after-shave lotions, and powders is meant to be persuasive. Some recent research suggests that we have a dominant nostril just as we have a dominant hand if we are right- or left-handed. We turn the dominant nostril slightly into any situation that we are encountering for the first time. Our language suggests the power of smell—"It doesn't smell right to me," "Something is rotten in Denmark," and so forth. The persuader and persuadee need to become alert to the power of this nonverbal device.

Using Nonverbal Behavior

Again, we need to emphasize that nonverbal behavior—like the other cultural predispositions for persuasion—occurs at a very low level of awareness, almost instinctively or automatically without our being aware of it. Nonetheless, we respond to nonverbal uses of objects, space, touch, and other symbolic cues like facial expression; we feel at ease with what has happened or with what we observe if the observed actions are consistent with what our culture has taught us and if they seem sincere. We began this discussion of nonverbal cues in persuasion

---

12. Vance Packard, *The Hidden Persuaders* (New York: Pocket Books, 1964). See Chapter 16.

by saying that though humans may not be far from animals, they engage in the symbolic use of artifacts, touches, and space when they attempt to persuade. The same notion applies as we receive messages—we trust our nonverbal reactions because of what we believe these unspoken messages symbolize about the persuader. We do not look at clothing or the use of touch as happenstance; we see these things as intentional, even if only at a low level of awareness. There is "leakage" in nonverbal cues—though we may try to pretend or to fake nonverbal signals, we are unable to prevent our true motives from seeping through. The perceptive and sensitive persuadee will be on the alert for these cues.

Obviously, the artifacts, space, and touch are not the only nonverbal dimensions with persuasive impact. In evaluating persuasion, you should also consider the roles and meanings of such nonverbal cues as tone of voice, directness of eye contact, facial expressions, and gestures. In a persuasive situation, what meanings may be attached to silence on the persuader's part?

A Review and Conclusion

As you have probably felt by this time, the world of the persuadee in an information age is not an easy one. There are so many things to be aware of—the persuader's self-revelation using language and stylistic choices, the internal or process premises operating within each of us, the interactive rules for content premises, as we have called them—and now we have glimpsed societal and cultural predispositions for persuasion that may also act as premises in persuasive arguments. Persuaders, either because they have studied and analyzed our cultural predispositions or because they instinctively appeal to these trends, rely on the societal training and shaping of belief and action in the people they are trying to reach. On at least three separate levels, this training has an effect on each of us—in the cultural myths or images we respond to, in the sets of values we consciously articulate, and in the nonverbal cues we respond to (uses of artifacts, space, and touch, to mention a few).

Questions for Further Thought

1. What are the three types of culturally or socially inculcated predispositions for persuasion? Give examples of each from your own experience.

2. How does culture or society train its members? Give examples from your own experience.

3. You are in school for a reason: What is it? How did you become motivated to come to college? Why? Is this related to any particular myth or image repeated to you? What were the elements in it? (For example, as the child of immigrant parents, I was repeatedly told that though "they" could take away your house and job, "they" could never take away an education—it spelled success in America.)

4. How do you rank the core values mentioned in this chapter? How do you put them into practice? Are there other values in your own value system not mentioned by Steele and Redding? What are they? Are they restatements of the core values? If so, how? If not, how do they differ?

5. How do you use space in the classroom? How far does the teacher in your favorite class stand from the members of the class? In your worst class? In classes in which you were most successful when it came to grades, what kind of distance was used most often (for example, social, intimate)? Which are you most familiar with or most at ease with? How do you use space when you interact with people where you live (observe your behavior at mealtime, in conversations, and the like)?

6. How much do you touch others? Try to increase the number of touches you use and observe the responses of others. Does the increase cause a different effect? If so, how?

7. What artifacts do you surround yourself with? What do they mean to you? (Some students have reported that the first thing they do after unpacking for dormitory living is to purchase "conversation pieces" or artifacts that symbolize themselves.) What about your roommate? What artifacts does he or she use? Do they symbolize him or her? What about your family members?

Experiences in Persuasion

1. In a group of four or five, observe a television talk show without turning on the sound. Concentrate on one participant and his or her nonverbal gestures and movements. Report on the nonverbal interaction between guests and host and between other guests. (This exercise is particularly revealing if the show is a controversial one in which emotional behavior is exhibited.)

2. Observe the entertainment page of a newspaper from a town or city other than your own. What kinds of values might you predict for the inhabitants of that city based on your observations? Justify your conclusions.

3. Rearrange the personal artifacts and space of your roommate or a family member. Observe and record his or her reactions. Interview the offended person after your experiment and see which objects mean most to him or her. Find out why. Report on your findings.

4. Interview foreign students on campus. Try to find out what their culture inculcates through the use of myths or images, and through values. How does their nonverbal system differ from yours?

7
The Persuasive Campaign or Movement

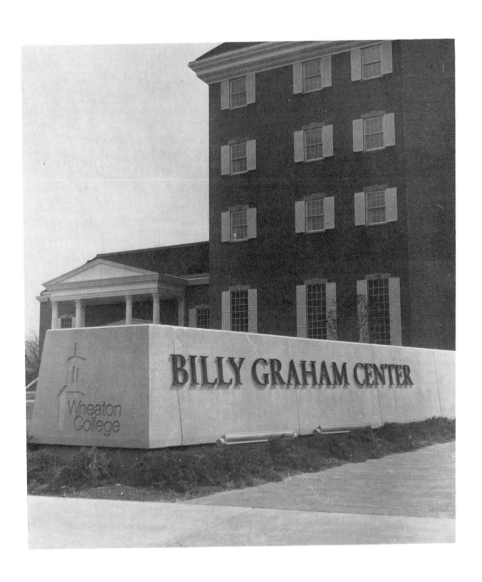

$\mathbf{M}$ost changes in attitude, behavior, belief, or action are not the result of a single message. If they were, it would imply that people are so fickle that they bounce from pro to con minute by minute. It would be hopeless to try to persuade them, for at any time another persuader could happen along, deliver a single message, and undo all. People do not sway from pro to con and back again on the slim basis of single messages. They reflect at length before acting. Of course, all of you can think of instances in which you were persuaded by a single message—in an instant, so to speak. Perhaps you decided to date a certain person as the result of a single visit with him or her. A particular teacher was able to open a whole new perspective to you in a single lecture. Most of the time, these instances are not really the result of the single incident you recall. Rather, you were ready for the message that changed you. You were exposed to many pieces of data, and the combined effect was your change of mind. You were the recipient of a series of messages that could be called a **campaign.** The series led to your decision, not the single message. Most persuasion occurs as the result of many message inputs, as the result of a campaign or movement and not a single speech. This chapter focuses on the campaign. We look at how it works, how it develops, and how we can listen to and evaluate the campaigns and movements that occur around us.

Aspects of Campaigns and Movements

In considering persuasive campaigns, we need to look at why campaigns and movements differ from other methods of persuasion. The elements that we shall consider are common to all campaigns. Generally, they can be grouped into two categories: (1) the **functional** aspects of individual campaigns, or the strategies that make them work and that shape and direct the thrust of the campaign; and (2) the **formal** aspects of campaigns, or those characteristics that are common to all campaigns. We will explore seven functional aspects of campaigns, covering things like the stages through which many campaigns pass, the dramatic aspects of campaigns, and so on. We will focus on one formal aspect of campaigns—the importance of designing the campaign as a *communication system* rather than (for instance) as a series of propositions or arguments.

Functional Aspects

A campaign is not just a series of messages, all dealing with the same issue. Nor is it a debate over an issue. What makes the campaign different? One of the differences is that campaigns and movements are *developmental* in nature. They move from stage to stage. They have a beginning, a middle, and an end, so to speak. Also, if they are to succeed, campaigns must create a sense of the dramatic in the mind's eye of their audiences. Movements or campaigns need to depict their cause as one of historic magnitude. Then they need to invite others to join and share in the great cause in some real or symbolic way. Campaigns also need to communicate so that audiences align themselves or identify themselves with the person, product, or idea being promoted—because all persuasion involves self-persuasion to some degree. The audience members have to become involved in their own persuasion. They must add something to the persuasive mix for change really to occur. Getting them to identify or align with the campaigner's goals or purposes is a step toward such participation or co-persuasion.

These two functional characteristics work well together, for the ideal developmental format is one that is also dramatic. Viewing a TV serial is like following movements or campaigns. Each of the daily dramas leads to the conclusion of the serial. Each episode adds to the over-all result of the campaign or movement. Though the episodes can stand alone (each has its own beginning, middle, and end), they draw on one another. They rely on one another. They meld into one another until a collage is completed.

Formal Aspects

As already noted, a campaign or a movement is not just a collection of messages about the same topic. The thing that makes campaigns differ is the systematic flow of information through four basic steps. These four steps are like those of a computer system as it works. There is (1) programming, (2) information input and dispersal, (3) re-formation of the information, and (4) the end product of the newly arranged information—the representation to the audience of the campaign's central cause.

You may want to explore campaigns in much more depth than we will here, read accounts of campaigns, participate in one, or perhaps even plan and conduct one. Discover how you are persuaded by campaigns. In finding how we are affected and swayed by campaigns, we ought to be able to see trends we can use in our own campaigns. We may feel a need to object to a college or university policy. A campaign can help elect a member of the student senate who will work to change minds and actions of people. A campaign can get parents' support for the purchase of a car or for the right to live your own lifestyle.

Types of Campaigns

Three kinds of movements or campaigns predominate: (1) the *politically oriented* campaign for office, (2) the *product-oriented* advertising campaign, and

(3) the *issue-* or *cause-oriented* social movement or campaign. At first glance, you may think the first and last types are not really different. Political campaigns focus on people. They are campaigns with the goal of winning voters to believe that one candidate is more sincere, wise, or active than another. The issue-oriented movement or campaign gets audiences to support a certain course of action or to embrace a certain belief.[1] As such, the issue-oriented campaign does not rely on a single leader. Its leadership may shift. No single person speaks for the cause. We might distinguish between the three types of campaigns by saying that the first tries to convince people of the value of a person. The second tries to convince them of the value of a thing or object. The third tries to convince them of the value or goodness of an idea, a belief, or an ideology. "Person," "thing," and "idea" are the three key words. Many of the characteristics of person campaigns and idea campaigns relate to product campaigns, and vice versa.

Developmental Aspects of Mass Movements

The information discussed here can be used and thought of in connection with campaigns for particular offices in student government organizations or in groups like fraternities or perhaps in organizations like the campus newspaper. It also relates to those campaigns promoting a certain philosophy. The campaign to keep legal abortions on the law books is one example; the countercampaign to outlaw abortion is another. Idea campaigns seem to come and go in cycles depending on the times. If things are bad—the economy is down, there is a war, there is a lot of crime, and so on—and you have a charismatic leader like Hitler, FDR, Churchill, JFK, or maybe Ronald Reagan, an idea campaign can develop. Both elements are essential. The charisma of Churchill, for example, was not successful in persuasion until the times had become nearly catastrophic. In fact he did not become prime minister until England was hanging on by a thread in World War II, and he himself was sixty-five years old. Hitler was unsuccessful during the early reconstruction years of the 1920s after World War I, but when inflation was rampant in Germany ten years later, he was elected to office. Reagan tried three times to be nominated for the Presidency—once in 1968, again in 1976, and finally in 1980 when the times were economically bad with high inflation rates and high unemployment, and he himself was seventy years old.

Who Joins Them?

One theorist, Eric Hoffer, has pointed out that "true believers" who are followers of idea campaigns come from groups of disaffected people. These are the undesirables, the minorities, the poor, the social or physical misfits, students, sinners, the bored, and the selfish. These people see the idea campaign as a way to

---

1. A good discussion of the differences between the issue and the image of candidates for political office and what that difference implies is available in "Political Myth: The Image and the Issue" by Dan F. Hahn and Ruth M. Gonchar. *Today's Speech*, Vol. 20 (Summer 1972), pp. 57–65. Hahn and Gonchar conclude that the image may well be the best indicator of a candidate's future behavior. Issues change and fade, they maintain, but image indicates a pattern of behavior independent of issues.

move up from the bottom.[2] Such people are most likely to be disaffected during tough times. This explains why the black power and student power movements developed in the 1960s and 1970s. The Vietnam War threatened both groups through the military draft. It explains why the Moral Majority was able to affect elections at the same time that pornography was increasing, marriage was decreasing, divorce was common, and so on.

What Motivates Them?

Hoffer reports that the followers of mass movements have several motivations for joining. First, they see the movement as a way for them to lift themselves from their poverty, degradation, or difficulties. Usually they have nothing to lose and everything to gain from joining the movement. A second motivation is that some of the potential joiners are bored with their present status and way of life. This explains why some people from affluent homes join ideological movements; it is a way for them to gain identity, to rebel, or to be excited. The movement is a game for them. A final motive for joiners of mass movements is to symbolically reverse some social or individual sin. For the Nazis, it was the social sin of the Treaty of Versailles, which economically hamstrung Germany in the years after World War I. For the individual joiners there were individual sins that had to be expurgated. Himmler, the number two man in the Nazi movement, was an unsuccessful chicken farmer. The propaganda minister, Goebbels, was physically deformed with a clubfoot and was unusually short. Hess, a ranking member of Hitler's inner circle, had been a street thug. Goering, who headed the *Luftwaffe* or air force, was a drug addict and had other perversions. Nazism gave these men individual chances to atone for or to get revenge for their individual sins. The urge for atonement or revenge is associated with other ideological movements in history and will probably be part of the appeal of similar movements in the future.

What Are Their Strategies?

In their book *The Rhetoric of Agitation and Control*,[3] John Bowers and Donovan Ochs describe several stages or strategies through which most ideological movements pass before ultimately failing or succeeding. In the first stage, agitators **petition** the sources of power (the government, the school district), making demands that are constructed to just barely exceed the level that the power source can or will give up. This makes the power source appear unreasonable and assists the agitators in their second stage, which is called **promulgation** or the marketing of the movement. Using handbills, leaflets, or rallies, the agitators spread their movement by informing outsiders of the unreasonableness of the power source. At this stage the movement hopes to gain recruits and to get publicity that will attract even more recruits. If this stage is successful, the movement grows and moves into a third stage called **solidification.** Now the newly recruited members

---

2. Eric Hoffer. *The True Believer* (New York: Harper & Row, Perennial Book Edition, 1966), pp. 26–56.

3. John Bowers and Donovan Ochs. *The Rhetoric of Agitation and Control* (Reading, Massachusetts: Addison-Wesley, 1971).

are educated and hyped up through songs (e.g., "John Brown's Body," "We Shall Overcome," or "Solidarity Forever") and through powerful symbols like the swastika or the peace sign, uniforms, and salutes.

With a now committed and educated following, the movement leadership seeks to **polarize** the issue. This fourth stage attempts to force uncommitted observers either to join the movement or to support the power source. Debate and demonstration focus on some "flag issue"—the use of napalm, the extermination of some species of fish or bird, the development of some nuclear site, and so on. Another approach is to identify a "flag person." Past flag persons have been national leaders like the late Shah of Iran, government officials like a local sheriff or mayor, or other people in leadership positions (college deans, leaders of opposition parties or groups, and so on). Usually this is done through the use of emotional language like Pig, Scab, or Uncle Tom. Polarization forces the uncommitted to choose between "us or them." In stage five, **nonviolent resistance** is used. Police all call in sick in what is called the Blue Flu. Students occupy a building, claiming that they have "liberated" it. There is a rent strike. There is an illegal march. These and other devices call attention to the mass movement and hopefully prompt some sort of response by the power source. Agitators hope that the power sources will call out the army or police, and that the press will cover this. Then agitators can claim repression or gestapo tactics. Usually this leads to some kind of public confrontation, or the sixth stage—**escalation,** which is intended to increase tension in the power sources. Perhaps threats are made—rumors of planted incendiary bombs or public displays of weapons. Perhaps some violent act occurs.

At this point, the power sources may feel compelled to act. Perhaps they declare martial law or institute a curfew. The agitative forces may then display a division of strategy. One faction calls for guerilla warfare while others preach calm and negotiation. Bowers and Ochs call this stage **Gandhi versus guerrilla.** Usually the nonviolent segment of the movement goes to the power source and argues that unless the power source gives in, the guerrillas will take over. Depending on the outcome of this stage of the model, the final stage may or may not emerge. This last stage is **revolution.**

We have seen this set of stages reenacted over the last decades in the Civil Rights Movement, the Anti-War Movement, and revolutions in various countries. Being able to recognize these stages is useful for receivers, especially as they may very well find themselves being members of the large group of uncommitted observers at whom much of the rhetoric of agitation is aimed.

Product Campaigns

The campaign to promote a product has been with us since the first snake-oil pitchman loaded his wagon and headed for the boondocks. The goal then and now was to flimflam the gullible yokels out on the frontier. He would usually come into town with much hoopla, leaflets, and ballyhoo. Often the next stage of the campaign was some form of entertainment—an Indian show, magic, music, or oratory and dramatics. Once a sizable crowd was gathered, the huckster would begin to sell the product, using on-the-spot demonstrations, testimonials, and so forth. Frequently, listeners sampled the product. Finally, the flimflam artist talked about his need to be moving on and suggested that they had better take advantage of his offer right then and there. It was their last chance to get a bottle of the Formula X elixir to cure warts, baldness, hot flashes, and anything else that might ail anyone. Things have not really changed that much, when you think about it. The Incredible Hulk is brought out to fight for justice. That is the hoopla and ballyhoo of the medicine show. Then we are entertained by the show, just as the snake-oil pitchman entertained the audience. At intervals during the entertainment we get the sales pitch. Most contemporary products promise almost as much as Formula X did. Platformate in Shell gasoline gives longer engine life, better mileage, less pollution, and a quieter running engine. Purina Puppy Chow not only "makes its own milky sauce" but provides the extra protein and iron needed to build strong muscles during puppy's important first year of life. It also helps build strong teeth and bones.

Despite their differences, the three kinds of campaigns have many similarities. Many parallels lie in the kinds of communication strategies that they use to sell their person, product, or idea. The persuadee who wants to be aware of the "snake oil" that is being pushed, who wants to spot doublespeak, needs to be aware of these strategies. The next section looks at several such strategies, which we can see as we examine the mass-media culture we live in and its many campaigns. Those discussed below are by no means all the communication strategies that could be cited but are only representative ones.[4]

Stages of Successful Campaigns

One of the communication strategies that occurs in all three types of campaigns is that they are **developmental.** They do not run on the same level or pitch throughout. They do not repeatedly pound away at the same bits of information. They do not always have the same strategy at various times in their existence. Instead, they grow and change and adapt to audience responses and the emergence of new issues. You might think of a campaign as a fishing expedition in which the strategists of the campaign try in various ways to get the attention of the audience. They use different methods or lures. If one method does not succeed after some use, they try another and perhaps another. As the mood of the audience develops, the mood of the message must also change. The whole thing must be planned so that each shift follows from what came before.

For instance, suppose you are hired to establish product X (say, a new kind of building material) in the public eye—to get across the idea that this is the greatest, most impressive development in construction since the steel beam. What would you do first? You would not blindly go about trying first this method and then that method. Instead, you would outline the major points you want to make about this

---

4. Some of the strategies arise out of communication research, others out of theory and research in other areas—history for example—but all of them have been verified in numerous campaigns. At Northern Illinois University, we have looked in depth at more than 800 different person, product, or idea campaigns. Not all of the strategies occur in each campaign but those listed seem most prevalent.

new product. What kinds of people would be buyers? What are their values and beliefs about construction? How to reach them? Now suppose, after your first advertising attempt, you discover that you failed. People are not buying the durability of the product. They are more impressed by its cost. You will have to shift your strategy. You would never have discovered the discrepancy between what you thought was important and the actual key factor if you had not first tried to focus on durability. The discovery will affect your next ads for the product. Campaign planners adapt to audience responses.

Five Functional Stages of Development

Well, how do campaigns develop? There are several possible answers to this question, depending on the theory you begin with. In 1960, Theodore H. White believed that presidential campaigns developed by the careful use of a mass media–created "image" that could be elected. A campaign could be traced by looking at the candidate and his or her relation to the information media.[5] Four years later, in 1964, White saw the political campaign as the ongoing challenge to the daring of the voter.[6] Four years later still, he saw the political campaign as somehow linked to the ability to explain, step by step, the chaos and change surrounding the audience.[7] He had changed his perception again by 1972 and again by 1976. The power of money (1972) and the critical mistake (1976) seemed to best explain those campaigns. By 1980, White was no longer analyzing individual campaigns but published an overview of a quarter-century of campaigns in which he stressed the way in which the mass media and TV in particular had intensified image campaigning.[8] Strategies shift with time, and events sometimes make certain strategies null and void.

The important thing to note is that most critics seem to agree that a campaign must demonstrate change, growth, or development. One theory comes from study of the development of emerging nations.[9] There are five steps in the development of a national image or character: identity, legitimacy, participation, penetration, and distribution. Each stage must occur before the next can emerge and develop.

Identity   For instance, suppose that Transylvania has just declared itself a nation. The first step is to characterize itself. It needs an insignia, an **identity** that will distinguish it to the rest of the world. Transylvania may design a flag. It may develop hero myths. Or it may fight wars or have building projects.

---

5. See Theodore H. White's *The Making of the President: 1960* (New York: Atheneum, 1961). This volume was the first to deal comprehensively with the candidates in a presidential election. It won the Pulitzer Prize in 1961.

6. See Theodore H. White's *The Making of the President: 1964* (New York: Atheneum, 1965).

7. See Theodore H. White's *The Making of the President: 1968* (New York: Atheneum, 1969).

8. See Theodore H. White's *America in Search of Itself: The Making of the President 1956–1980* (New York: Harper & Row, 1982).

9. Leonard Binder, et al., *Crisis and Sequence in Political Development* (Princeton: Princeton University Press, 1971), especially Chapter 1. I wish to thank William Semlak for calling this source to my attention; Mr. Semlak utilized the suggestions offered by the volume to analyze the campaign of George McGovern.

A movement must do the same thing to show its identity. It needs some kind of handle or label by which it can be identified. The Black Power Movement developed such things as a flag, a salute, a handshake, a hairstyle, and a style of dress.

In 1974, a new football league called the World Football League (WFL) was established. It got identification by changing the rules. It permitted more players in the backfield than did the National Football League (NFL). The goalposts were moved to make field goals easy. Team names were not animals like bears or lions as in the NFL. Instead they were tied to the home cities of the teams—such as the Chicago Fire, the Shreveport Steamers, and the Honolulu Suns. These plus the team songs and colors were all identification devices. The league and the teams all achieved this first step in the development of campaigns. Later they failed, but, in this first stage, there was a high degree of success for the WFL and its teams.

Candidates for political office also need identification and use many of the same tactics. They choose color codes—Jimmy Carter, for instance, was known as the green-and-white candidate during the 1976 primaries and maintained that combination after he had won the nomination. Most politicians think that red, white, and blue are the only colors that can be combined, but other combinations have been used in campaigns at all levels of government. The candidate also usually chooses a slogan. The slogan "He Has the Guts to Do What's Right" was used to help reelect a Republican from a very conservative part of Illinois even after he had voted to impeach Richard Nixon. Slogans are often tied to the logo or emblem of the campaign—an American eagle in flight, the ecology symbol, or some other trademark. Politicians usually have theme songs or campaign songs that are used to identify them to voters and supporters. Products have jingles that do the same thing.

So, all three types of campaigns use similar tactics for the important stage of becoming identified in the minds of the target audience.

Legitimacy   The second of the five related stages is to establish a **base of legitimacy.** Transylvania may seek alliances, admission to the United Nations, and so forth. All of these give the country a legitimacy or a kind of credibility. This signals that Transylvania is not a fly-by-night operation. It is a force to be reckoned with. Legitimacy is another way of saying that the movement or campaign

Figure 7.1. Many devices are used to gain product, person, or idea identification in campaigns. Logos, like the one above, are one kind of device. Why is the winged foot of Mercury used? What does it communicate? Why put it between Good and Year? Answers to these questions help explain how product image or identification develops. (Courtesy The Goodyear Tire and Rubber Company.)

has power. For the product, a certain amount of sales may be the key. Volkswagen became a "legitimate" threat by selling half a million vehicles a year. The U.S. auto industry began to design its own compacts. The Black Power Movement of the late 1960s demonstrated that it had power by destruction in ghettos. Legitimacy of the Student Power Movement was shown by the "occupation" or "liberation" of pieces of university property—classrooms, offices, files, flags, and deans. A political campaign shows legitimacy by being tied to power figures or centers. The candidate usually is seen with important members of the party leadership. Candidates may also choose to demonstrate how power works. They have rallies. The student hoping to live in an off-campus apartment gets legitimacy or power through a summer job that will cover the costs or by joining ranks with several fellow students to share costs. The student running for fraternity president establishes legitimacy when fellow group members begin to support him.

In political campaigns, incumbents have automatic legitimacy unless they have bumbled and botched the job, so challengers have a major task. They must try to discredit and erode the legitimacy of the opposition and develop their own. Further, they may have to do this while running in primary elections against fellow political leaders who are also emphasizing the shortcomings of the incumbent. The "mudslinging" in a political campaign is usually an attempt to destroy a candidate's legitimacy. A challenger finds out that the incumbent gave government contracts to friends or used the office for self-advancement. The incumbent points out the nasty tactics of the challenger and shows his or her lack of experience in office. The real question is which candidate the voters will consider the most legitimate.

Products have to show legitimacy, too. The patent medicine show demonstrated that some of the claims made for the product were at least partly true. The pitchman showed a thick head of hair that the "cure" had supposedly produced or had someone give a testimonial about the product. Today's products frequently use similar tactics to establish legitimacy. Football players use the product, so it should be durable—or at least compatible with a strong he-man image. Beautiful women use the perfume so it must enhance feminine sex appeal. Sometimes before our very eyes we see how Top Job cleans a filthy wall with just one simple wipe of a sponge. This stage of a campaign is crucial, for it leads to the third and highly involving stage, the participation stage. In participating, scores or hundreds of people get in on the action by working, voting, or buying.

Participation   The third stage of a campaign is like the second stage in that it involves more and more people in the campaign in actual or symbolic ways. People are invited to join. They may be asked to fly the flag or to join the army or to open their houses to tourists. They may be asked to share in some project like a five-year plan.

The distributors and users of products *participate* in the use and profit of the product. Coupon offers are made to product users. They buy and use the product and get money or gifts. In some instances, stores are paid to allow some of their space to be used for special displays of certain soaps, wines, and so forth. The dealer may get an extra discount for pushing a certain product. Similarly, a movement may urge participation in real or symbolic ways. Women stopped doing

A comparison of projections from manufacturers' treadwear ratings under the new government Uniform Tire Quality Grading System indicates that on a government-specified course:

Uniroyal Steeler projected to last 15,000 more miles than comparable Goodyear or Goodrich tires.

The U.S. Department of Transportation recently gave the public a standard yardstick to compare tires by.

Now, each tire company is required by law to grade its tires in three areas. Traction. Temperature resistance. And treadwear.

And then to emboss the resulting grades on the side of the tires.

When compared, most of the similarly priced steel-belted radials in the chart fared equally well in the traction test. Same for temperature resistance.

But one tire pulls ahead of the pack when it comes to the important grade that indicates the relative wear rate of your tire.

That tire: the Uniroyal Steeler.

In fact, when you translate its 220 rating into projected miles on the government-specified course, you see it was no photo finish.

On that course, the mileage projection for the Uniroyal Steeler is 66,000 miles.

That's 15,000 miles longer than the Goodyear, Goodrich, General and most Firestone ratings in the chart would project.

And 24,000 miles longer than Michelin's rating would project.

These mileage projections (including those in the chart) should be used for comparison only. You will probably not achieve these results. Actual treadlife will vary substantially due to your driving habits, condition of vehicle and, in many sections of the country, road conditions and climate. See your Uniroyal dealer for details.

UNIROYAL

Clip and take this to your Uniroyal dealer:

MANUFACTURERS' RATINGS FOR U.S. GOVERNMENT QUALITY GRADING SYSTEM			PROJECTION OF MILEAGE ON GOVERNMENT-SPECIFIED TEST COURSE
Manufacturer/Tire:	Traction and Temperature Resistance	Treadwear	
UNIROYAL Steeler	B/C	220	66,000
GOODYEAR Custom Polysteel	B/C	170	51,000
FIRESTONE 721 (13" & 14" sizes)	B/C	170*	51,000
GENERAL Dual Steel II	B/C	170	51,000
B.F. GOODRICH Life Saver XLM	B/C	170	51,000
MICHELIN XWW	A/B	140	42,000

*Most 15" Firestone 721 tires rated 200 which projects to 60,000 miles.
Source: U.S. D.O.T., 12/19/80.

For a free booklet on grade-labeling, please send your name and address to: Uniroyal, Inc., Tire Advertising Department, Middlebury, Connecticut 06749.
©1981 Uniroyal, Inc.

When you compare, you want Uniroyal there.

Figure 7.2. How does Uniroyal achieve legitimacy in this advertisement?

housework in a one-day strike. The slogan of one such strike was "Don't iron while the strike is hot!" In other situations, people may be asked to wear arm bands or badges, to yell slogans at rallies, or to put signs around their houses or on their automobile bumpers. During World War II, it was hard to get bread sliced at bakeries, supposedly so electricity would be conserved for the war effort. The power thus saved was never really devoted to the war effort, but participating in this way increased commitment of the average citizen to the war. The same sorts of stories are told about saving tinfoil, lard, and tin cans. People running for student body president may ask others to participate in their campaign by canvassing dormitory floors or student groups. For a Campus Crusade for Christ rally, many students were asked to distribute leaflets and urge others to attend. This kind of activity gets people involved in the campaign or movement. It guarantees further active support. People who put bumper stickers on their cars will vote for the name on the sticker most of the time. Movements ask supporters to do something, even if it is only symbolic. They can march, hold a vigil, or salute. The effects of this are to increase commitment to the cause. It activates the kind of self-persuasion discussed in Chapter 4.

Political workers are asked to wear campaign buttons, to use campaign pencils, nail files, or matchbooks. All these are designed to give support to the candidate and more importantly to get people involved. I once offered to purchase all ten barbecue tickets in the book, if only I did not have to go to the rally—or approach others to get them to buy tickets. The offer was refused, and the explanation was that that would do no good. No one was making money on the barbecue. It was a break-even affair—its purpose was to get people involved. The purpose of the participation stage is twofold; not only does it get people involved and thus committed, it also demonstrates legitimacy. First, it gets people involved and committed to the cause. Second, it shows the legitimacy of the campaign or movement.

Recent innovations to get audience or customer participation include "scratch and sniff" ads that get potential customers to "sample" a perfume, cologne, or room deodorizer. The age-old "free sample" or "free trial" also attempts to get customer partipation with the product prior to purchase. My spouse and I once went to new car showrooms during a diet to keep ourselves preoccupied and to avoid being tempted to snack. The car salesmen usually urged us to take a test drive in one of the new models. Ten days after starting the diet, we had lost a few pounds and had purchased a new sport model that we really didn't need. The use of participation is a powerful persuader in campaigns because by scratching and sniffing, by clipping the coupon, by wearing the candidate's buttons, or by taking the test drive, we have already symbolically purchased the product, voted for the candidate, or adopted the idea.

Penetration   Stage four—the *penetration* stage—is the most difficult to explain. Think of it this way: Suppose that you have been totally unaware of some movement—say, consumerism. Then you are exposed to it. You probably first hear about the movement after the first three stages have already taken place. You are part of the mass of people who will never engage in the movement. You will never be the person who brings consumer charges against the manufacturer of a product. You will never organize a boycott of an inferior or dangerous product. Instead, you merely get the messages of the movement. Nonetheless, the movement needs your silent support. Without it the people involved will remain a minority. This minority status, shared by all movements and campaigns, must lead to large-scale support among the people. Various terms have been coined for this stage, such as "the grass roots," "a ground swell of support," and the "silent majority." The fourth stage of a movement or campaign builds a general public attitude toward the movement—preferably favorable, of course. People reflect this attitude in some way. They respond on a poll, recognize the name of a product, are aware of the issues, or perhaps agree with the goals of a candidate. In a sense, this stage is getting through to a good-sized part of the market. In the film industry, for instance, penetration means creating enough identification, legitimacy, and participation so that even the people who only see three or four films a year turn out to see whatever is "in" that year. In a school bond referendum in which extracurricular activities are at stake, it means making sure that even those inclined to stay home will show up at the polls. For products, it means capturing a sizable portion of the market. In the toothpaste business, for instance, an overwhelming share of the market was controlled by Gleem and Crest during the 1950s and 1960s. Then, in the mid-1970s, Maclean's began marketing a product that promised to make the teeth whiter and sexier instead of using the anticavity pitch of Gleem or Crest. Within a few months, a significant and sizable share of the market was buying the whiter and sexier promise. Thus Maclean's had achieved *penetration.* In this stage, we often see competing products, candidates, or ideas picking up the tactics of the successful penetration. So, not long after Maclean's, we began to see other toothpastes pitching the whiter and sexier aspects of their products, too—Ultra-Brite, Pearl Drops, and so on.

Though these steps seem distinct and clear, they often merge and flow from one to another. The progression is logical, but there are times when stages may merge so smoothly that they become indistinguishable—often in very rapid sequence. Every campaign aims at the penetration stage. The real point at which penetration occurs is when the movement or campaign has succeeded and has power. Candidates for public office may become identified as certain kinds of characters and may even demonstrate legitimacy by having large rallies or winning primaries. They may identify with power personages or power organizations. They may also get wide participation, with hundreds of volunteers. However, until significant numbers of the large mass of voters support such candidates, effective penetration has not yet occurred.

A movement may go through the same initial stages of getting an identification and a kind of legitimacy or power, coupled with highly active participation on the part of some of its followers. Until a large part of the masses support it or until the movement gets the change in the status quo that it desires, it too fails to complete the penetration stage.

In a different situation, a majority of persons in the United States probably supported the changes started by President Franklin D. Roosevelt in the 1930s. Though he did not really overthrow the status quo, he did achieve a ground swell of public support for significant changes. He achieved penetration. This stage may also be reached in the campaign for an off-campus apartment when your parents begin to offer less and less resistance to the idea and when they begin to identify reasons of their own for allowing you to live outside the dorm (it's cheaper, handier, and so forth).

Some products establish a penetration stage rapidly. For example, Tide, the washing product, was the first detergent to come on the market in the 1950s. The difference between Tide and soap products was so obvious that it quickly became the top-selling wash product, thus establishing penetration in a short time. The same thing occurred with the first low-sudsing washday product—All. It penetrated the market quite fast. Soon we were using the words low-sudsing detergent when talking about other similar products. Similar effects occurred with products like Jell-o, Kleenex, Xerox, and Hershey's, which have such great market penetration that their names are frequently used to stand for all gelatin desserts, facial tissue, photocopies, and chocolate bars.

Distribution   In the fifth and final stage of development—**distribution**—the campaign or movement becomes institutionalized. Having achieved the control they sought, the leaders of the campaign or movement must now live up to their promises in some way. They must signal to the people that change is going to occur. The likely moves are the designation of subgroups of the campaign staff or the movement's leadership to positions of power with tasks to complete. These tasks fit with the promises made in the campaign and with the goals of the movement. This stage does not always occur in the campaigns involving products that are being sold. However, such things as rebates, money-back coupons, and incentives to store owners are kinds of distribution that we see in product campaigns. In an emerging nation, the new government begins land reform, court reform, changes in the social structure, and other changes to show that power is now being divided and shared with the people, the faithful, the party, or the movement leaders.

Unfortunately, this stage is rarely instituted except in symbolic ways. The end of the Civil War in 1865 did not result in a change in the status of most Negroes in the South. Black Codes were instituted, and reconstruction officials neglected to institute much meaningful change in the daily lives of most former slaves. Following the overthrow of the Batista regime in Cuba by Fidel Castro, little land redistribution actually took place. The distribution stage, so it seems, often contains within itself the seeds of its own destruction. By setting itself up into bureaus, the new movement opens itself to the same kinds of criticism leveled at the old order. Perhaps that is why most people are cynical about political party platforms and why many people say, "It doesn't make any difference who gets in; politicians are all crooks, anyway." Or, as Cicero put it over 2000 years ago, "Politicians are not born; they are excreted."

The first of the functional aspects of campaigns and movements, then, is that they are developmental in nature. They go through stages, each of which is logically related to the others. Usually these stages flow in order, but at times they may meld into one another. The first four stages must occur for a campaign or movement to be complete.

As you observe campaigns for public office or movements to change social thought, you ought to be able to identify their stages. The real difference between campaigns and movements is that while the political campaign focuses on the image of a person, the movement develops acceptance of an ideology or lifestyle. The advertiser develops acceptance and use of an object or service. All three follow the stages of identification, legitimacy, participation, penetration, and distribution. Many campaigns and movements never reach full bloom; typically they die out at the participation or penetration stage. Social and political movements, upon reaching this stage, usually distribute only superficially the power and privilege wrested from the opposition. Thus, as a movement or campaign develops, it sets for itself not only its next stage of development but ultimately the raw material for a countermovement or countercampaign. This development aspect of campaigns is particularly suited for the second functional characteristic of campaigns—their reliance upon the dramatic metaphor.

Invitation to the Drama

We have already talked in several places about dramatic impulse in human beings. We see the world and identify its forces in ordered ways. The most common form of ordering is the dramatic episode. It is interesting to observe in our own lives how often we tend to structure the world in episodes. We see meals as having a "plot line." Mealtime starts with a prayer in many homes. Certain foods like salads are followed by other courses in a neat, orderly progression to an after-dinner liqueur with coffee. We see our workdays as divided into episodes: first-hour class, opening-the-mail time, lunch at the dorm, and others. We see our weeks ordered the same way. Wednesday is called humpday, since it is the halfway point. We see those around us as actors in the drama. Our parents may be villains and our friends may be heroes and heroines. Our fellow workers are classic stereotypes—the gossip, the bitter old-timer, the apple polisher, the good-natured fellow, the footloose-and-fancy-free jokester, and so on.

This impulse for the drama is deep and powerful. It is one of the universals that link movements and campaigns. In fact, unless a movement or campaign can create a drama or pseudoevent, it has little chance of getting the support of the people it needs. The success of a movement or campaign depends upon its ability to create in the minds of its audience the sense of a momentous event or series of events that must be lived out or else the whole world and all people involved will suffer. Given such a drama, the movement or campaign succeeds to the degree that it can also invite the audience to participate in the drama in real or symbolic ways.

Let us look at the dramatic impulse. What is it that creates a sense of drama? How are dramatic elements used by persuaders? How do they occur? What effects do they have?

The first thing we need is a setting or **scene,** to use Burke's term (see Chapter 3), with dramatic potential. For instance, someone's backyard may have dramatic possibilities, but they are limited. A posh New York nightclub or an impressive apartment or perhaps a deserted junkyard all obviously have dramatic possibilities much broader than the backyard scene.

Given a dramatic scene, we now need the second element—**characters.** To keep it simple, let's limit ours to the good guys and their helpers and the bad guys and their helpers. We need to see our dramatic scene filled with opposing forces that are going to do battle. So in a political campaign it may be the politicians of compassion and understanding versus the politicians of special interests. In many washday products it is the good character—Mr. Clean—versus the baddies of dirt and grime. Television commercials for STP motor oil have played this bad guys/ good guys theme out in a familiar drama. A poor distressed auto engine is shown surrounded by four villains—dirt, heat, cold, and rust dressed as attacking Indians. They are spotted by four cans of STP coming over the brow of a hill dressed as cavalry. A bugler sounds the charge, and the cavalry gallop down onto the plateau and chase off the nasty villains to win the gratitude of the coy engine, which is now safe. In an idea campaign, the forces of good and evil may be personified or they may be hooked to certain groups. For example, a factory safety campaign may focus attention on the evil represented by the bored worker who becomes careless and causes accidents. The campaign to end pollution of the Fox River may see its villains in the boardroom of U.S. Steel. In any case, a drama necessitates opposing forces—of good and evil, of wisdom and folly, of youth and age, or the like. Going back to the stylistic attributes of persuasion in Chapter 3, we find that Weaver's notion of God terms and Devil terms relates here. Persuaders create the dramatic mood they desire by choosing hierarchies or families of terms that delineate the good guys and the bad guys in the drama.

The third element of the dramatic characteristic that is common to movements and campaigns is a **plot.** Most movement or campaign plots are also simple. The weak are exploited, and a hero arises in their midst to lead them to liberty. Another variation may be the one in which members of a group are being enslaved or exploited. Through some event or other means, they become aware of their grievances and then try to overthrow the bad guys. The Women's Liberation Movement used both of these plot lines, with men being the exploiters and women needing to take aggressive action to avoid slavery. Sometimes the villains are institutions that cleverly hide the slavery. Banks, for example, do not allow women to lift the heavy bags of coins at the tellers' windows at the end of a working day. There was a time when management argued that anyone who could not do the whole job really could not become a bank officer, so few women, until recently, ever moved up to executive positions. "Once conscious of the trick, you can fight it, so raise your consciousness" is a theme of a campaign using the second variation. We could cite numerous examples of dramatic plots, but generally they are subplots of three or four major lines of action:

1. The **overcoming of odds** by some group under the leadership of a hero or a speaker of some cause like reform of marijuana laws, civil rights, the right to life.

2. The **quest for a goal** like success, power, prestige, or respect. In many of the television soap operas the quest is easily as important as the actual goal itself.

This plotline underlies the quadrennial promises by politicians to reduce inflation or to achieve energy independence.

3. The **purgation** of some kind of symbolic sin in our midst or the removal of some evil enemy or foe (industrial pollution, big government, over-regulation, bias).

4. **Outwitting a mastermind** at deception. We frequently hear the spokesperson for certain movements like the KKK or the Moral Majority claim that the enemy—perhaps left-leaning liberals—have been so clever that they have practically sewn up all opposition except for the followers of the movement. But the leaders and followers of the movement will win out and reestablish power where it should be—with them. The Wilderness Society, for example, launched a movement to oust the "fiendish mastermind" who was, they claimed, out to steal away the birthrights of millions of our citizens—then Secretary of the Interior James Watt (see Chapter 2). The basic plot puts the villain in a very powerful position. It attributes immense knowledge, trickery, and resources to the villain while limiting the people to meager resources if acting alone but real power if united under the movement.

If the raw materials of the drama are at hand in the setting or situation, in the characters, and in the plot, the persuader uses these elements to invite the potential supporter of the movement or campaign to enter into the dramatic setting, to do battle with or to lend support to the characters of the drama, and to act out a part of the plot line. In this way, the participation stage mentioned earlier is fulfilled. Supporters of the movement or campaign feel that they share in the victory. Their actions result in ego rewards as they see payoff in election returns or as they see authority figures lose their tempers because of wisecracks, comments, or chanting. In other words, the supporters' actions become part of the whole theme of the movement or campaign. They engage in the drama as in a work of art.

Many movements must fight off competing dramas, and their own dramas never really take hold. At other times, leaders of the movement or campaign do not invite participation. They prefer to dwell on ideology or on praise for themselves. The mudslinging campaign, though interesting for its conflict aspects (everyone likes to watch a fight), is a risky kind of campaign to run. There is a high risk that it will backfire. The audience may oppose the persuader who calls names or tries to set up a dramatic "fight" for persuasive purposes. At the same time that mudslingers besmirch the adversary, they seem to be praising themselves. Both arguments are called *ad hominem*—to the personality or about the person. Audiences suspect people who attack others and then praise themselves. In 1982, the governor of Illinois supposedly accused his opponent of being a "wimp" and as a result lost a commanding lead during the campaign.

Some dramas fail to be fully played out in the audience's minds because the campaigners choose to dwell on issues of philosophy. People want to see ideas acted out. They do not want to be preached to. For example, the American Indian

Movement (AIM) failed at first by preaching its ideas. It succeeded later by acting out demands when AIM members captured the entire Pine Ridge Indian Reservation in South Dakota. The setting had the drama needed. It was not far from the site of Custer's last stand. It included the site of the massacre of Indian women and children at Wounded Knee, South Dakota. There were two types of villains—the Bureau of Indian Affairs and government officials who would not deliver on various demands. The Indians were easy to depict as underdogs. There were various subplots that could be played out as well—such as the ruin of the Indians when they went to the cities, and cheating whites who tricked the Indians by giving them firewater.

A second characteristic of movements and campaigns, then, is their tendency to succeed when they focus on the dramatic—when they act out their ideology instead of preaching it. When action invites the audience to the drama in real or symbolic ways, the movement becomes vital and attractive. It succeeds to the degree that it is able to avoid overstatement and being preachy and to the degree that it can present historic dramas. Hitler invited the German people to join him in finding Germany's "place in the sun." Martin Luther King Jr. invited others to join in his "dream." Ronald Reagan invited voters to work "Together—[for] A New Beginning." The Wilderness Society invited potential joiners to a dramatic vigil as it asked financial pledges to support a Wilderness Watch.

When a movement gathers speed and power and begins to have effect, the receiver can hear other dramatic invitations. Though many persuasive campaigns do not focus on high drama so obviously, they do nonetheless rely on dramatic raw material. Students trying to get a trip to Europe subsidized may outline the dramatic dangers of staying home during a boring summer, or they may highlight the dramatic potential of exposing oneself to other cultures and languages and of possible advantages that might accrue from exposure (for example, they may be able to write columns for the home-town newspaper, or they may get a better job later because of the experience). Many product campaigns rely on dramatic input also—many commercials are, in fact, mini-dramas. For example, a girl rushes out of a restaurant crying because her boyfriend has told her that she has horrid-smelling breath. Her friend produces a bottle of Breathsweet and saves the day. The final scene is at the party where the two lovers gently nuzzle one another. The story is a minor adaptation of the overcoming of great odds, a plot line already noted.

There are, then, *functional* aspects of campaigns and movements that shape and direct their course. They are the strategic moves campaign leaders make to attract support. Though there may be many of these functional aspects, two of them—already discussed—are of interest here. They provide us with a means for examining movements or campaigns. They are the developmental nature of the campaign or movement and the need for a dramatic invitation to be extended to the audience. These two aspects work well together, for the developmental flow of movements and campaigns seems well suited for dramas. At the same time, there are formal aspects of campaigns and movements. We will consider only one: the use of communication in systematic ways.

Formal Aspects of Campaigns

The Communication System

Campaigns seem to succeed to the degree that they communicate systematically.[10] We are not saying that movements succeed by communication as such, but that *they succeed when communication is systematic.* Let us look into this aspect more deeply.

What is a communication system? Begin with what happens in a computer and think about the flow of information from input to output. The computer is a system with great power. It communicates with itself and with its users or audience. The planner establishes a path or program for the flow of communication in the machine. The programs tell the machine to "think" in a certain way— to accept and process data in certain steps. The next step is to introduce data as input, which begins to flow through the program. Next comes the processing of the data—the computing and coupling of the many small bits into a complete picture. At this stage, data may be stored in a "memory" to be held till needed, or bits of data may be sent to some other part of the machine, for example, to the printout mechanism or CRT screen. Once the data have been sent to parts of the system, they are considered and combined in new ways. The data are "discussed" by the machine and the program. In a final step, the data are abstracted and sent out of the system in the form of a printout. The printout does not contain each of the data bits. It does not contain the program of the machine. Nor does it contain the combinations of data. It contains a new product based on all of the forms of information but distinct from them.

The system in a campaign or movement is like this. At the early stages, planners of the campaign or movement establish the routines by which data will be combined and considered. For instance, in a political campaign the candidate's staff and advance crew establish the ways in which messages will be presented to the public (radio, TV, papers, and the like). They set up speaking tours and arrange for proper publicity. They prepare pamphlets; they arrange for rallies, press conferences, and news releases; and they coordinate the candidate's activities. In other words, the staff teams—with the candidate—program the campaign.[11] The same thing occurs in a product campaign when an ad agency staff is charged with selling a certain product. They, too, program media, style, and the timing of messages.

Even in smaller campaigns, we can see a system at work. For example, one of the ways to conduct a campaign to get a date with a certain person is to let a friend of the person know of your hopes. This data input is thus programmed. Taken with the dropped hint, the meeting of the date, and the offer of assistance on a class project, it acts to move the data through the system. Of course, success will be measured by what goes on in the potential date's mind. This same process can

10. I wish to thank Professor Ernest G. Bormann of the University of Minnesota and the students in his 1972 summer seminar, "The 1972 Presidential Campaign as a Communication System," at the University of Minnesota, for many ideas discussed in this section.

11. For a good discussion of the details of this situation in political campaigns, see Dan Nimmo's *The Political Persuaders* (Englewood Cliffs, N.J.: Prentice-Hall, 1970).

occur when one wants to convince a teacher to change the date of an exam. Several people can come to the teacher at different times, with varied reasons for changing the date—there is to be an assembly that day, the debate squad will be out of town, there are a lot of exams planned for that day, and so forth. There is a program to get data into the system. (In idea campaigns the systematic aspect of the campaign is not so clear-cut. The supporters of the factory safety campaign are not likely to get much direct payoff, and so they are not so committed as advertisers or politicians. The resources available to the safety campaign or the United Fund campaign are usually limited. Their budgets are small, and they have to rely on volunteer labor and free publicity. In short, the programming aspect of idea campaigns often is loose.) Once a program has been established, data can be distributed—the local offices of Citizens for Senator Fogbound can begin passing out leaflets, meeting voters, running TV and radio spots. Most of the local campaign headquarters for a presidential candidate do not know what the candidate's stands on issues are, and lack of this information limits their scope of action. In the dispersal stage, however, the candidate's views are made available. The same thing occurs in product campaigns. The local grocer does not know the details about a certain soap that is being introduced on the market. The manufacturer provides displays, posters, coupon advertisements, and TV spots to disperse these data to buyers. In a movement, the plan is not so strict, but pieces of data still flow into the system and are sent to sectors of it. A group in one of my classes decided to try to get student support to pass a local school-bond issue. A key element in the campaign planning of the group was how to disperse data. They used many means to get data spread throughout the student body (door-to-door visiting, sing-along meetings, access to the local cable TV station, and broadcast of a TV "documentary" on the condition of schools).

One of the key elements in the dispersion process is the use of media. This applies to movements, campaigns for political office, and product campaigns. The mass media are channels for the flow of data from program through dispersal centers and to the public. As far back as 1896, the power to control these channels became important in presidential politics. In 1896, large numbers of business interests poured in support for the faltering campaign of William McKinley. The interests feared that William Jennings Bryan would take the country off the gold standard if elected. The money was used to purchase newspaper space. In the 1930s, with the advent of radio and the widespread use of cars, men like Huey Long were able to disperse information using handbills, posters, newspapers, and the radio. In fact, because of his media skill in 1936, Long was a threat to the two major parties. He planned to run for the presidency on a third-party ticket. George Wallace in the 1968 and 1972 campaigns used the media with great skill. Persons in favor of his candidacy had to *pay* for the campaign messages they displayed (buttons, bumper stickers, posters, and so forth). Many people were shocked at this, but by that time people were beginning to be glad to pay to promote a product if the product name was printed on a T-shirt or hat. The dispersal of campaign messages had become pop art, and with them we spoofed our world of ad gimmicks. You can probably see such promotional T-shirts, hats, and so on on your campus every day. Of course new media and adaptations of them will continue to emerge, as they are bound to, and successful campaigners will quickly adapt to and use them. They can be expected to utilize the emerging cable systems, electronic games, various computerized media, the videodisc and videotape industries, and others to pitch their messages. Consider what happened with the advent of television.

In the 1950s, only about 10 percent of American households had TV sets—there were 4.2 million sets. By 1967, 95 percent of American households had them (there were 54.9 million sets and 58.2 million households). Furthermore, these sets were being used from three to six hours a day.[12] Clearly, since Americans spent from a sixth to a third of their waking hours receiving TV messages, this machine had to be the key channel for message dispersal. Although we deal with the power of this medium every day, it wasn't so familiar to campaigners in the 1950s when the television revolution was just catching on. In fact most politicians were reluctant to use it during their campaigns because it might be seen as being unethical. In the 1952 election, it was not until the final weeks of the campaign that candidate Eisenhower agreed to use television spots, and even then he insisted that they be at least five minutes long so as not to seem to be dealing with image instead of issues. Today we see many 60- and 30-second spots for candidates that are clearly focused on image and not on issues. We will have more to say about various media and especially TV later. Suffice it to say here that, in the dispersal stage, TV is a potent channel. Various movements, persons, and groups try to attract the attention of TV cameras, which testifies to the power of the medium. This power explains the tactics and strategy behind the use of violence, bizarre events, costumes, and other attention-getting devices (the staging of fights, the burning of flags, the use of nudity).

In campaigns or movements, programmers have least control over the third stage—or when data are "discussed" and recombined. In a computer, recalling information—putting it together in new patterns—is highly controlled. In a campaign, however, the data are combined with other information, past history, and other factors in the audience. Computers do not have this kind of problem. In campaigns, data are considered and combined, but not before they have been compared with many parts of a persuadee's image of the world. Clearly, the campaign or movement planners cannot control the audience's image of the world. All they can do is hope that by being exposed to the same or similar pieces of data a number of times, members of the audience will fit all or part of the message into their image of the world. Of course, the information becomes more or less central in the minds of voters or buyers, depending on the data they are exposed to, what their own self-interest happens to be, and such uncontrollable factors as personal problems like a traffic ticket or a fight with a spouse. In movements, the philosophical view of life held by audience members plays a part. For instance, some women oppose the Women's Liberation Movement because they believe women's proper role is to be subservient. Others oppose it because they may feel that the movement threatens their femininity. In political campaigns, elements other than the candidate may sway voters. Some people voted against Thomas Dewey in

---

12. As quoted in *The Image Candidates* by Eugene Wyckoff (New York: Macmillan, 1968), pp. 12–13.

1948 because he had a mustache and looked like the little groom on the top of a wedding cake. In 1980 some people voted against Jimmy Carter because of his brother Billy. Some may have voted against Ronald Reagan because his son was a ballet dancer. A classic case of image over issues was seen in a senatorial race in Oklahoma in the 1960s. The Republican candidate was Bud Wilkinson, former coach of the Oklahoma football team, a repeated national champion. He had natural appeal and thus had an advantage over the unknown Democratic candidate, Fred Harris. Faced by his opponent's huge lead in the polls, Harris tried to find out what Oklahomans had as the image of a senator and used that information to win. In 1966, Senator Harris asked the staff who had run his campaign to find out what kind of candidate would be on the Democratic ticket for governor. The letter quoted below shows how TV and film images were used by the advertising agency to determine the appropriate image. The letter was written to me personally by Ross Cummings of Oklahoma City, advertising agent for Senator Harris.

> Dear Dr. Larson:
> Thank you for your letter of March 12. For the most part, Bill Carmack's recollection is accurate.
> Having served as the advertising agency for Fred Harris' successful campaign in 1964 to fill the unexpired term left by Bob Kerr's death, we were very interested in trying to determine who the Democratic nominee for governor was likely to be in 1966, when Fred would have to run again for a full six-year term.
> Most polls conducted by politicians are done on a name basis. They select a number of likely names, attempt to rate them in various degrees of public awareness and acceptance, and match them against each other.
> As though advertising did not exist.
> We had just helped our candidate prevail over two former governors (one an incumbent Senator) and the greatest popular hero in Oklahoma since Will Rogers. Polls taken 60 and 90 days before election day had shown Fred as an unknown and an ignominious third in a field of three seeking the Democratic nomination.
> We knew that images can be affected during a campaign, but only during a campaign does the public become sufficiently interested to let an emerging public figure gain massive acceptance. So how can you measure something like this before a campaign starts?
> We were not attempting a serious study of issues, since candidates most often join each other in embracing identical issue positions. We only wanted to know what sort of *identity* the people of Oklahoma might prefer for governor.
> We had seen "young men's years," when the public swept out the old guard politicians, and other years when established businessmen with mild messages had the greatest appeal.
> We first considered a questionnaire describing candidates by personal traits, but discarded that as too wordy and awkward. We then decided to use identities everyone would know—and this led us to the use of TV and movie characters.
> We used James Bond, Perry Mason, Ben Cartwright, Andy Griffith, and Gomer Pyle. . . . Our known political contenders fit these characters loosely. . . .
> Well, Ben Cartwright won handily, garnering some 60% of the votes, and pointing toward a tendency on the part of the voters to favor an older candidate. Andy Griffith did poorly even in "Little Dixie," indicating a pull-back from an unrelieved rural image.

James Bond ran last, indicating dissatisfaction with handsome young playboy types. Perry Mason was second, but far enough behind Ben Cartwright to indicate that rugged, patriarchial directness was a more desirable characteristic than urbane, articulate competence.

We decided the likely winner in the Democratic primary was probably Preston Moore. Although he still had touches of Perry Mason about him, he fit fairly well with the Ben Cartwright character. We speculated that Raymond Gary's rural image would hold him back under circumstances indicated by the survey. David Hall, the urbane young Tulsa county prosecutor, did not seem to be favored by the results, but a strong possibility for public acceptance if he would avoid being too "country" would be Clem McSpadden, a glib senate leader and linear relative of Will Rogers.

We picked Moore to win the primary and he did. However, in his campaign he failed to show the frontier wisdom of the head of the Cartwrights, and in the fall he was defeated by a Tulsa oilman who never developed a real image of his own, Dewey Bartlett. This candidate, defeated for reelection as governor but beating Ed Edmondson in 1972 by characterizing him as a liberal, is a protest candidate whose victories grow from public dissatisfaction with his opponents. I don't believe our polling method could have picked him up on the radar screen.

. . . I would not seek to palm myself off as a political witch doctor but as a professional communicator.

On second thought, there are some unbelievable fees in being a witch doctor.

Sure enough, a candidate who resembled Lorne Greene (the lovable "Pa" Ben Cartwright of *Bonanza*) intensified that image and won. The same kind of image-making occurred in the campaign of 1960, when John Kennedy built an image that whittled a 16 percent lead by Richard Nixon to a 0.5 percent edge for Kennedy. At any rate, in the final stage the re-formation of data takes place in the audience's mind, where it is combined with other input—none of which is *exactly* what the planners had in mind.

While the re-forming occurs, parts of it are seen in two kinds of images of the campaign or of the movement's cause. The first is that held by the audience members. The second is that held by the planner. These images are a shadow of what was fed into the system but only that—a silhouette that resembles but is not the original. At this step, the "computer printout" is not neatly tapped out by a daisy wheel but emerges in unclear and abstract terms. At the end of a campaign, we know more about the product, but we do not know all; and we are certainly in error about some of the things we believe. For instance, Richard Nixon was often thought to be "tricky" owing to his image at the end of campaigns early in his career. This image was probably true in part, but the "new Nixon" image of 1968 and 1972 was of a master technician. That image was later shattered by Watergate. The end product, then, consists of an image about a candidate, product, or cause. Part of the image is true, part of it is part-true, and part of it is false. All three parts yield the final image and also change the initial image the campaign planners were trying to build. After a campaign, even the planning staff sees their candidate differently. They see a combination of their original image, their experiences with the candidate, and the image the public holds.

The same thing happens to causes or issues in movements. At the end of the movement for women's suffrage, for example, women's role was different from the early view of that role. To start with, the suffragettes fought for the right to vote. At the end of their campaign, they saw the need to carry women's rights further—jobs, birth control, and so forth. In this sense, a movement is never really over because the fourth communication step—representation—is just that. It presents the cause or issue in a new light.

At the end of a campaign, such as to have a date with a certain person, you may be disappointed with the outcome, not because you never got the date but because the prize changed as a result of the campaign. We all know what it means to work to attain a goal and then find that it was not what we thought it to be. A good example might be what sometimes happens to people who have their hearts set on certain jobs. They go through job interviews. They write letters to the employer. They follow up by telephone. They may seek ways to get further input into the decision-making process. They send recommendations from prestigious persons. They pick up hints from people who already work for the company, and soon, after struggling to land the job, they may discover that their image of the company has changed. It may be much better than they had thought it was because they had to fight so hard to get the job. On the other hand, it may be less than they imagined because the campaign may have been frustrating or for other reasons.

Other Communication Characteristics of Campaigns

There are several other characteristics of campaigns that relate to how they communicate—what messages they send overtly and what messages they send less openly. In many cases this second kind of data is much more potent in persuading than data that are clear and easy to observe. Take a product like prunes, for example. What can we say about prunes on a real, sense-data level? They are black, they are kind of gooshy and sticky, they don't smell too bad, and they taste pretty good. That is the *reality* of a prune. However, in the buyer's mind there is another set of information. Crabby people are called prunes. Scout leaders always made you eat prunes at breakfast when you were on a field trip. When you get stewed prunes, one is always split open and is leaking. People are always making jokes about prunes and their laxative quality. One of Dick Tracy's villains was a guy called Pruneface who was ugly and wrinkly. Those are the subconscious dimensions of prunes. Both sets of data—the real prune and the *symbolic* prune—have persuasive potential, but buyers usually do not sense the reality inputs as they purchase. That is, they do not usually touch, taste, feel, smell, or look at prunes, though they might try to recall what prunes feel, smell, taste, or look like. They do, however, go into their storehouse of symbolic data and use those data in making a decision. That is probably why the National Prune Institute went to so much trouble to build a new image for prunes using humor ("These prunes aren't for me. They're for a friend").

So the symbolic messages that are sent in a campaign are processed at a very low level of awareness. They may be the key message factors in a campaign because voters, buyers, and believers rely on these more than on reality-based data. Part of Jimmy Carter's appeal in 1976 was tied to the choice of colors for his campaign message—green and white. Green has all sorts of symbolic meaning—

life, lushness, fertility, safety, cleanliness, and so forth. Most voters did not consciously process those meanings, but the color surely had effect. Let us briefly look at some of these kinds of campaign factors. Most of them work on the storehouse of potent symbolic meanings that we carry with us and which can be prompted by a clever campaign. Most of them relate to some communication theory that operates in many places. Only the way in which the theory is put to work has changed when it is used in a campaign.

First Characteristic *Successful campaigns usually communicate a sense of credibility about their product, person, or idea.* We follow the advice of those in whom we have faith—those whom we feel we can believe. I have never bought Imperial margarine because I cannot believe that it will make me a king in my own family. Yet some people are influenced by the TV spot in which Mr. Average Guy gets a crown for biting a muffin with some Imperial margarine on it. The campaign has plucked some source of symbolic data in many people. These data may not make sense to you or me, but they do to Imperial buyers. Credibility relates to a number of factors discussed earlier. They are *dynamism, trustworthiness,* and *expertise* or *competence.* Perhaps the Imperial folks have sent a message of simple trust in their character Mr. Average Guy.

In other instances, persuaders build credibility by emphasizing the potency or dynamism aspect discussed in Chapter 6. The Marlboro Man is weathered, lean, and active. Billy Martin gets his comeuppance in Lite ads from macho types. Hamm's beer used to associate their product with a backwoodsman and his macho willingness to cavort around with his pet—an 800-pound grizzly bear. He would fly the bush country, canoe, ride trail horses, and walk miles in the wilderness. He was dynamic. If he drank Hamm's, it had to be pretty good stuff. You could be like him if you join the big beer (bear) drinking brotherhood of Hamm's. Some candidates communicate credibility by showing how expert they are on some issue— farming, defense, or whatever. Others develop credibility by referring to their trustworthiness. "I'll never tell a lie" was Carter's key tactic. Others simply act dynamic. They are athletic, rugged, attractive, and articulate. The end result of all these tactics is to make the persuadee believe and follow the advice of the persuader. The source is credible.

Second Characteristic *Successful campaigns hook their messages into the prevailing climate of opinion.* Times change. That is a cliché that passes for folk wisdom, and it is accurate. In 1976, Americans probably elected a politician who said he would not lie because we were soured by the lying of the previous administrations. It was *in the times* to look to an outsider who did not have ties to cronies. By 1980, the world seemed out of control, with soaring inflation rates making it impossible for young people to even think of buying a house. Unemployment was rising, and the President couldn't even deal with a nutty religious leader in Iran. It was natural for the challenger to suggest that the country start "A New Beginning."

Products also need to be marketed according to the prevailing climate of opinion. For instance, in the late 1960s, the makers of 7-Up were on the verge of bankruptcy when they asked a national advertising agency to develop a new image for the soda. They discovered that 7-Up was thought of as medicinal. You got 7-Up when you had the flu. It came in a green bottle like many medicines. That image was hard to sell or even change, so the agency suggested using *concept advertising*. In concept advertising the product is not directly promoted. Instead, the central focus is on a concept, and the product is only incidentally attached to the concept. In the late 1960s the prevailing climate of opinion was one of revolt. People demonstrated against the war or pollution. Beards sprouted on young men's chins. Many young women went bra-less. Four-letter words became acceptable in casual talk and class lectures—and even in some sermons. There were full-scale and mini-riots in the streets, on campuses, and in corporate boardrooms during stockholders' meetings. Seven-Up hooked their message into this prevailing climate of opinion by suggesting that you could revolt by buying the Uncola. Other products followed suit, urging people to join the Dodge Rebellion, or to take up a new lifestyle with Dr. Pepper or Pepsi. Again, the times were fit for that kind of appeal. As times changed, Uncola had to show you that you could "See the Light" and later that you could "Undo it." Dodge's rebellion lasted only a few years. Then "Mean Mary Jean" took over and featured physical fitness and Dodge. By 1977, M.M.J. was through and you could be "car-napped" by Dodge Magnum. With the rise of gas prices, both rebellion and carnapping fell by the wayside: X-cars, J-cars, and K-cars took over. Even their names were economical. Idea campaigns, more than others, rely on timing to fit their campaign goals to the prevailing climate of opinion. The civil rights campaigns of the 1950s and early 1960s gave way to Black Power, which in turn gave way among blacks to a much lower profile and a focus on economic equality. The times changed; so the movement had to change its appeals. As a persuadee, you will want to see if your feeling for the mood of the times matches up with what persuaders appeal to in their campaign messages. What does this politician seem to think the mood is? What does that advertiser think? Do the current idea campaigns fit the times—the Equal Rights Amendment? racial quotas, pro or con? other campaigns?

Third Characteristic *Successful campaigns seem to aim their messages at opinion leaders.* Studies done in the late 1940s to discover how farmers adopted new farm methods (contour plowing or crop rotation) found an interesting phenomenon. Most farmers did not respond to direct appeals from the Department of Agriculture. Instead they seemed to adopt the new methods only after a highly respected farmer or an opinion leader did. This pattern was labeled the *two-step flow* theory of communication.[13] We are most persuaded when an opinion leader does something in response to what a persuader says. Later studies demonstrated that this flow had many layers or levels and the two-step notion was elaborated to a *multi-step flow* of information. The Successful Farmers, who followed the lead of the Super Farmers, were leaders in turn to the Good Farmers, who were opinion

---

13. An early reference to this phenomenon is found in P. E. Lazarsfeld, B. Bevelson, and H. Gaudet, *The People's Choice* (New York: Columbia University Press, 1948), which identified two-step flow in the 1940 presidential election. Later elaboration to a multi-step flow can be seen in J. N. Rosenau, *Public Opinion and Foreign Policy* (New York: Random House, 1961).

leaders to the OK Farmers. Even OK Farmers were opinion leaders to the Dumb Farmers. Of course there were some Zero Farmers who never adopted the new methods. They knew that corn planted in the ground grows and could be harvested but that was about as complex as they could get. Crop rotation didn't fit into their scheme of things.

In other campaigns, this targeting of opinion leaders also occurs. Politicians will use TV spots of themselves listening to well-known and respected farmers, shop stewards, union leaders, leaders of women's groups, and others. Products are shown being used by people who would be opinion leaders to us if we knew them—daring mothers who are scientific researchers recommend Tang. Parachutists who sky dive drink Blatz. Famous people do not have problems getting credit if they have an American Express card, and so on. Ideological movements also rely on the use of opinion leaders to prompt action. Famous movie stars are asked to support the drive against muscular dystrophy. The names of well-known supporters of the United Fund are printed in the ad appealing for donations. The American Indian Movement had supporters from Hollywood.

A problem that everyday campaigners may have in using this third characteristic is the identification of opinion leaders. A little research will usually help, however. Suppose you wanted to market C.B. radios to long-distance truckers and needed success figures. Most truckers dream of someday becoming independent and having their own rig, and the most successful independents are those with the newest, shiniest, most expensive tractor and trailer. You might want to give free sets to such owner-operators and use interviews with them about the C.B. set in print ads or TV spots. In this way the image of the successful trucker would be conveyed to other truckers, and the product would be associated with this image. How might you determine who the opinion leaders are on your campus? In your town? In other contexts? Asking yourself questions like these can alert you to persuasion that appeals to the prevailing climate of opinion.

Fourth Characteristic *Successful campaigns make the ordinary seem unusual; the banal becomes unique.* One TV ad depicts an ordinary housewife fixing dinner for hubby. She is busy at work on the salad, and it is a pretty humdrum salad until . . . Chef's Delight! As she opens the foil package, a symphony begins to play. The lights dim as the camera cuts to an elegantly set table. By candlelight, hubby pours the vintage wine from a towel-swathed bottle. In the final shot, he romantically eyes humdrum housewife, who now is a knockout. All human effort—cooking, voting, working, learning, and so forth—has some humdrum aspects. The clever persuader takes these boring events or routines and makes them unique. The banal aspects of life are dressed up to become really special, and this shift draws our attention in potent ways. We enjoy the out-of-the-way, the special, the unique things in life. The clever persuader tries to tie the product, candidate, or idea into such unique or special events or moments. Hundreds of times each day on TV, ads like the one for the salad seasoning make many mundane things unique, such as washing clothes, brushing teeth, making coffee, mowing your lawn, or driving your car. Politicians make themselves unique through their actions. In our town, one rode a horse along the route of a proposed freeway to "visit" with the angry farmers whose land was to be used. Others might announce that they have children who are handicapped. Some make themselves unique by dressing in costumes such as a western-style shirt, cowboy boots, and a Stetson.

Fifth Characteristic *Successful campaigns have messages that make persuadees feel* OK. Thomas Harris, in his book *I'm* OK—*You're* OK, noted that all humans want to feel OK, but that most of us do not.[14] This relates to the many years during childhood when we were not able to do the things needed to support ourselves. For instance, we were too little to drive or cook. This feeling of NOT OK is deeply recorded in our minds like a kind of tape recording, says Harris. It forces us to find ways to feel loved, content, witty, well liked, and so forth. The campaign offers rewards for taking action that will make you feel OK. These rewards make us feel OK in lots of ways. The woman who fears that her husband is losing interest is advised "Want Him to Be More of a Man? Try Being More of a Woman. Use Emeraude Tonight." The reward for using the perfume is shown in a photo of a very handsome male model nuzzling a very lovely female model who has presumably just applied Emeraude. So you can be made to feel more OK about your sexual role by using certain products.

You can feel more OK if you follow certain ideologies. Mirabel Morgan in her book *The Total Woman* tells women that they will be more sexy and will get their way with their husbands if they do certain things. She suggests that a wife might try meeting her husband at the door wearing only some Saran Wrap—if he does not notice her then, she must be NOT OK. We can also be made to feel OK about our work roles or social roles. The working mother who feels guilty is assured, by the makers of Tang, that even a woman truck driver gives her children Tang to make sure the kids get off to a healthy start on the day. Dad is advised that he will move up to a penthouse suite of offices if he works late at night and drinks Johnny Walker Red Label scotch, the sign of an OK executive. Consider the following ad in a Cupid's column in my town:

> One-Owner, Used Man—1946 model. No body rust. Not fast. Top is showing some signs of wear and smokes a bit, but lots of good miles left. Could be a classic someday. Write to Box L for a free test drive.

Not only does the ad demonstrate its author's sense of humor, it also suggests to the target audience that she is OK to him even if she, to, is showing some signs of wear. The goal to link rewards or OK-ness to a persuader's advice is likely to aid in the success of a campaign. Persuadees need to observe when and how they are being made to feel NOT OK or when their NOT OK state serves as an internal premise for the persuader.

Sixth Characteristic *Successful campaigns usually rely on information, experiences, or memories that are already inside persuadees rather than trying to*

---

14. Thomas A. Harris, *I'm* OK—*You're* OK: *A Practical Guide to Transactional Analysis* (New York: Harper & Row, 1967).

"teach" the audience to follow advice. In his book *The Responsive Chord,* Tony Schwartz advises trying to make your message ring true with or resonate with feelings that the audience has.[15] In the campaigns of 1972 and 1976, he served as an advisor to the McGovern and Carter campaigns. He often gave advice that showed this *resonance approach.* For example, he advised buying TV time during *Monday Night Football* in 1972 in which to challenge Nixon. Football viewers are primed for a fight in reaction to the game. They have seen and heard smashing blocks, battering tackles, helmet slaps, bump-and-runs, and so forth. Plugging into this set of experiences on the Monday night before election day can be very useful. The persuader does not try to approach the audience in order to get data across or to "teach" listeners about issues. Instead the resonance theory approaches audiences in order to see what can be gotten out of them. A good way to sell a drain cleaner is to show someone sticking hands into a stopped-up sink full of greasy water that is filled with food bits, coffee grounds, and the like. Most people have had to do that at least once in their lives and so already have the feeling imbedded in their experiential storehouse. Then someone pours in some Liquid Plumber, and we watch the sink drain out as the faucet pours out clean fresh water to wash away the grime. This is another great clean feeling that those of us who have had to unclog sinks can relate to. In this ad, the persuader gets the meaning *out of* the viewer. Contrast that with the commercial that explains how traps in sinks get clogged with grease and hair. The ad then shows a cutaway of such a trap and goes on to explain that the grease can be cut by either an acid or an alkalyde. Since acids can damage plumbing, the announcer suggests that we use Drano, an alkaline base, to dissolve the grease and unclog the sink. The ad then shows that happening. This ad is busy trying to *get something into* the viewer.

As noted, there is no persuasion that does not involve self-persuasion. We must agree to be persuaded and then find good reasons for doing so. Studies show that the most careful readers of a Chevy ad will be recent Chevy buyers. The sixth pattern of successful campaigns, as well as Schwartz's theory, shows the power of this kind of self-persuasion. Consider Figure 7.3. There are several details in the ad that help to prompt experiential memories out of the reader. Of course, not every reader of the ad has dated such glamorous people, but everyone has at least imagined experiences like the one depicted here. Meaning is gotten *out of the persuadee* in this ad, for the ad copy doesn't even vaguely suggest a seduction. Only the hints in the photo and the combined real and imagined experiences of the consumer reading the ad lead to that conclusion. This is the kind of ad that Schwartz would say is *resonating* with its reader.

A Review and Conclusion

You will notice other communication patterns that seem to be associated with the successful campaign—things like timing, choice of theme music or score, and

---

15. Tony Schwartz, *The Responsive Chord* (New York: Anchor Press/Doubleday, 1973).

Figure 7.3. What meaning is the persuader who developed this ad getting out of you? (Used courtesy General Wine and Spirits Corp.)

clever uses of colors in print and TV ads. Noting them is the most useful thing that you can do, even if you don't verify them through some high-falutin' scientific system. You will be tuning your persuadee's ear to the kind of doublespeak that will be spewed out at us all in campaigns seeking new buyers, new voters, or new joiners.

We have seen here the process of stages that most campaigns seem to go through. We have looked at how a system is needed to direct the flow of messages in a campaign. We have also looked at several communication patterns that go hand-in-hand with successful campaigns.

Questions for Further Thought

1. Define each of the developmental terms and identify examples of the first three stages in some magazine or newspaper campaign.

2. What stage of the campaign or movement is represented when we vote for or against a particular candidate or proposition? Why?

3. We have been told more and more lately that cutting spending for social programs like welfare, Social Security, and school lunches is a valuable thing to do. Suppose someone felt this trend needed to be changed through a persuasive campaign. If you were trying to change the average American, what would you do for identification? How would you get audience participation? How have our government officials done these three things? Rate their success or failure and try to determine why they succeeded or failed and at what stage.

4. As we are exposed to more and more TV series like *Archie Bunker's Place*, we are probably being exposed to an informal and vague campaign. Nonetheless, these programs do change ideas and beliefs. At what stage is Archie Bunker as a persuasive symbol at the present time? Is he clearly identifiable? How would you justify your answer? Does the program have legitimacy? Justify your answer. Has it achieved any sort of audience participation? How? Has the point of the program penetrated?

5. Identify a movement of recent times (for example, the consumer movement or the E.R.A. movement). Trace its development. Where was it most dramatic? How was this achieved? How effective was or is the movement in communicating its messages? Explain.

6. What elements of the drama are successful in capturing audience attention? Look at your local newspaper as well as at national news events and nationwide ads. Who are the heroes of the dramas? Who are the villains? Are there common plot lines? values? settings? and so forth.

7. Give examples in which you identify the six patterns of successful campaigns. How do they differ from campaign to campaign? Are some better with one kind of campaign than others (for example, the person, thing, or idea categor-

ies)? Why or why not? Create a campaign message that tries to use some or all of the patterns.

Experiences in Persuasion

1. Trace the history of some recent movement (for example, the Women's Liberation Movement or the anti-abortion campaign). Use your library resources, and if the movement is still going on, establish a clipping file to gather coverage of the movement in newspapers. You may wish to collect radio and TV spots of the movement or campaign by contacting TV or radio stations and by recording off the air. Once you feel that you have enough material to give you a good idea of what the movement or campaign is like, begin to search for a pattern. Ask if there is a drama. Is there a plot? Are there characters, villains, heroes, settings? Are there favorite metaphors (see Chapter 3 for help in identifying metaphors)? Ask if the campaign or movement follows the stages outlined in Chapter 7. If so, at what stage is the campaign or movement? What has it done at various stages? In short, do a complete analysis of the campaign or movement.

2. Research a movement of past history (for example, the suffrage movement or the Populist movement). Use all materials available to you from libraries, interviews, and other sources. Then do the same kind of detailed analysis outlined in project 1. Look at historical novels focusing on the same movement (for example, *T.R.* by Noel B. Gerson, which deals with Teddy Roosevelt as a populist). How does the dramatized version compare with the historical facts you gather?

3. Join a campaign or movement on campus. Keep a communication diary of the experiences you have while you are a member of the movement or campaign staff. Look for dramatic and developmental aspects of the campaign. Try to identify metaphors, plots, and so forth. Report on your findings.

4. Read the reports of various campaigns (for example, any of Theodore H. White's *Making of the President* books on presidential campaigns). Do the kind of analysis already outlined. Ask what stages the campaign or movement is in or has passed through. Where did the movement or campaign appear strong and most persuasive? Why? What was done to exploit this? When was it weakest? Why? How was this used?

5. Research one of the questions raised about persuasion in this chapter. For example, you might want to look at other sources on the use of TV and its powerful impact or on the usefulness of metaphor—how to identify it and how to interpret metaphors—or the importance of the dramatic format in modern society. Reanalyze the campaigns or movements sketched out in Chapter 7.

6. Research the journals in communication and other areas to see what has been done concerning political, advertising, and ideological campaigns or move-

ments. Look for the common assumptions used by the researchers. Are there trends in the ways the researchers describe campaign strategy? Report on your findings.

7. As a class, try to develop a mini-campaign on your own campus. Set your strategy to develop in stages. Build in a feedback method to see whether you are being successful. Try various methods suggested here. (*Note:* In the author's course, several groups have run members of their group for office— alderman, student senate, and even a delegate to the Democratic nominating convention. They have also tried to persuade administration and student associations of the need for bicycle paths, no-profit bookstores, and other projects.)

psychiatry

psychiatic views all through out this book.

8
Becoming
a Persuader

very pragmatically oriented chapter

Knowing Your Audience
    Demographics and Audience Analysis
    Rhetorical Visions and Audience Analysis
    Determining Audience Needs

Shaping Your Message
    Forms of Organization
    Forms of Proof
    Building Your Credibility
    Stylizing Your Message

Delivering Your Message
    Delivery: The Persuader
    Delivery: The Channel
    Delivery: The Audience

Some Common Tactics of Persuasion
    The Yes-Yes Technique
    Don't Ask If, Ask Which
    Answering a Question with a Question
    Getting Partial Commitment
    Ask More, So They Settle for Less
    Planting
    Getting an I.O.U.

Our over-all focus in the first seven chapters has been on training our receiver skills, or learning how to recognize doublespeak in our world. Now we'll briefly turn our attention to learning how to be persuaders ourselves. We all have to persuade others. Salesmen have to do it every day—so do most teachers. Every one of us will have to persuade our own particular audiences. Husbands persuade wives and vice versa. Parents persuade children to follow advice, and as they grow older, children need to persuade parents to allow them freedoms. We will all probably have to persuade a complaint manager at some department store to let us return a piece of merchandise. Some of us will be asked to make persuasive presentations to larger groups—the ad department may need to persuade the marketing staff to use more print media and less TV time. Computer programmers will need to persuade a sales staff that a new system will sell. A YMCA coach will want to persuade the board of directors to build indoor tennis courts, and so on.

Our personal attempts to persuade do not have the drama of the political campaign, nor are they so well financed as ad campaigns, but they will be as important to us. You become a persuader through three stages or steps: (1) knowing your audience, (2) shaping your message, and (3) sending your message. Throughout the first seven chapters of this book, you have been training yourself to "discover the available means of persuasion" that are being used *on* you. These means can also be used *by* you. Try to think of a formal kind of presentation you might have to make someday (though what we discover can apply to interpersonal and informal contexts as well). Perhaps it will be the persuasive proposal made in a sales department meeting or the speech in favor of a certain motion at a student association meeting or the attempt to sell fraternity brothers or sorority sisters on some new way to build the float for the homecoming parade. This possible attempt to persuade can serve as your model of the three stages in persuasive message building.

Knowing Your Audience

Of course it is common sense to say that you have to know your audience before you can expect to persuade them. However, the problem is "How do I get to know my audience?" There are lots of ways to do this. We have already learned about some ways to address this problem. We listen to persuaders' language use—their key terms—to understand how they are trying to persuade us. But we also listen so that we can persuade *them* should the need arise. So listening is one way to get to know your persuadees. Recall what kinds of things they have said in informal talks, in letters or memos, and in their attempts to persuade others. Chapters 2 and 3 are useful for attuning oneself as persuadee and as persuader. Then you can see what process, content, or cultural appeals persuaders make and adopt the same approaches. We all assume that if it would persuade us, it will persuade others. Take me, for example. I am persuaded by examples and stories. When I try to persuade others, I load the message with examples and stories or jokes. A clever persuader who listens to me can spot my weakness. This persuader can get to me through the story or narrative.

Demographics and Audience Analysis

One way that persuaders in advertising and marketing analyze their audiences is through a method known as **demographics.** Every one of us shares certain attitudes, traits, habits, and circumstances with others. We may be of the same sex, religion, race, or political party. We might make about the same amount of money or live in a community or neighborhood that is like the neighborhoods of other people. We might share the same ethnic background or the same values. All these commonalities could be considered demographically. What the advertiser does is to go out and research facts like those mentioned and then group the market into segments that have certain things in common—beliefs, backgrounds, and so on. Advertising can be slanted toward those shared items to appeal to the targeted segment of the market. Often these surveys of demography are very sophisticated and complex. At other times they are quite simple.

For example, trying to market some kind of money-making scheme to the members of the Goodview Golf club will be tough, since the members already are quite well-to-do and have good jobs. The persuader will have to focus in on some other value that they share. Maybe the persuader's research reveals that the club has a young mothers' group that meets twice a week before playing a round of golf. Young mothers are likely to share values, experiences, and beliefs that can be used in a pitch about the money-making scheme. Maybe the group would like to

FRANK AND ERNEST   by Bob Thaves

Figure 8.1. Frank knows his audience's preference for certain kinds of words. (Reprinted by permission of NEA.)

have child-care facilities at the club and the money-making idea would help them finance it. Probably the advertiser would have to spend quite some time interviewing members of the golf club to hit upon this key piece of information. But if the product being sold is related to the interests of most golfers, the task will be much simpler.

Suppose you were trying to market a Mercedes diesel, which costs $40,000. Given what you know about the members of most golf clubs, what kind of appeals would you make? The golfers probably share many common values about auto ownership. But for them, cars are likely to be status symbols, so you might want to stress the status value of the Mercedes—only the most "in" intellectuals and prestigious members of the community own Mercedes. Maybe owning a prestige auto that is also fuel efficient will balance any discomfort they might feel about being wealthy. So, as you become a persuader, try to get at the demographics of your audience. Search for those significant factors that audience members share.

Significant Factors The first step is to decide what you need to know about your audience, given your topic. Clearly, average age will be well worth knowing if your topic is "Tax Planning for Retirement." It will not be if your topic is "Scrap Reduction." Sex will be a key factor if your topic is "Support ERA" but not so important if it is "Improving Our Company Image." Average income is central if you are trying to persuade someone to install expensive solar-heat devices. It will matter little if all you are asking is to use caulking and weather stripping to conserve heat. So your first task is to determine which demographic items will influence your topic, time of presentation, and so forth. Let us suppose you have been asked to speak to an alumni group. Your purpose is to convince the alumni to support the building of new handball courts on campus. Which of the following will be among the factors you will want to explore about your audience?

1. **Average Age?** Will it matter if they are all over fifty or if they are all under thirty-five? Probably.

2. **Income?** Will it matter if they are well-to-do or just struggling along? Probably not so much, since it is the group's money that will be used and not personal income. However, handball is a costly sport. Most people have to rent a court. It will be good to tell about the value of handball for off-season times for members of the baseball team. The moves in handball are similar to those needed in fielding a baseball, so the court could serve several purposes, cutting the cost per user. You can sell your idea on more than one level here.

3. **Sex?** Are your alumni likely to be male or female and does that matter? Say that 90 percent are male, and that will matter.

4. **Religion?** Are Jews, Catholics, or Protestants more likely to favor handball? This factor is one you can ignore for the most part.

5. **Family Size?** Will it matter if your audience members have zero, two or five children?

6. **Political Party?** Will it matter if they are Republican or Democrat? No, but if you had reason to believe they were Socialists, that might make a difference. They might oppose handball as a sport for the elite that is identified with expensive health clubs and spas.

Of course there are other factors that you would like to explore, but the key thing is to determine which factors are most central to your topic. If your audience is from the Chicago area and they went to a public university, don't tell any Polish jokes. Chicago has more Poles than Cracow, and many of them go to public colleges. They will be in your audience in large numbers. If you are dealing with a Minnesota alumni group you would not have this problem, but you might have others—don't knock Swedes or Danes.

Once you know the key demographic factors for your group/topic/context, the next stage is to explore them. The president of the alumni group will be able to tell you about some of these. Membership lists will show you where alumni tend to live. That can cue you to income and age. Past actions—maybe even old yearbooks—can be useful in finding out if they prefer certain projects. If they have turned down past requests from students, you need to know why. If they have not funded athletic requests, you need to explore that, too. Sometimes, just talking to one or two typical members of a group before you begin to persuade can be helpful. I once was asked to speak to a group of hairdressers. I expected to see the chairs filled with overelegant men and dolled-up women. The group was mainly made up of middle-aged black women from Chicago who ran beauty shops out of their homes. I learned to ask ahead about my audience after that! Knowing the make-up of your target is valuable as a first step in becoming a persuader.

Rhetorical Visions and Audience Analysis

Each member of an audience probably has a personal vision of what a perfect world would be like. For me, it would be in the Boundary Waters Canoe Area of my home state of Minnesota. I would be bronzed from many days in the outdoors, and my fishing skills and luck would be phenomenal. Everyone in the area would be envious and would come to my campsite with little gifts in hope of prying some fishing secret from me. Because I have this vision, persuaders can get me to purchase all sorts of gear for camping and fishing.

Recently, several communication scholars have tried to discover the details of people's fantasy worlds by getting people with similar interests and occupations together and asking them to discuss their combined hopes for the future.[1] How do they expect their businesses to develop? What would they have to have to consider themselves successful? What are their goals? These and other questions prompt the group of subjects to enter into a common or shared view of the "perfect world," as the discussion continues, group members add in details like those in my vision of a fishing paradise. The researchers look for common themes of connection.

1. John Cragen and Donald Shields. *Applied Communication Research* (Prospect Heights, Illinois: Waveland Press, 1980).

For example, suppose the researchers were working with college students. I think that on my campus, most students would describe a lifestyle combining great freedom, a good income, the chance to travel widely, a smashing wardrobe, lots of attention from members of the opposite sex. Researchers would probably be able to record sentences detailing the travel—sentences about the beach life in Florida or the ski resorts of the Rockies. These sentences could be grouped together according to their central themes, and the group fantasy thus constructed would be used to analyze similar audiences. Just as the clever promoter can sell me depth finders, ultra-light canoes, durable backpacks, and knock-'em-dead lures once the details of my fantasy are known, promoters using the research about the college students can pitch their products to the student population.

The sentences gathered in rhetorical vision analysis are rated by a second sample of the target audience using a technique called Q-sorting. Subjects are asked to rank the sentences according to their agreement or disagreement with them. The results can then be factor-analyzed to discover where the sentences are clustered. The clusters indicate concepts that will be highly persuasive to a similar audience and those that will be highly dissuasive. Combining these analyses with demographic data, advertisers can develop messages that not only appeal to an audience's demographic needs but also appeal to the audience's rhetorical or communication preferences.

Using this technique, two communication scholars—John Cragen and Don Shields—created the ideal political speech during a recent presidential campaign. They fed sentences into a computer, which analyzed and assembled them according to the preferences of the audience—citizens of Peoria, Illinois, which is supposedly the most typical town in America. The computer-written speech was designed to appeal to the greatest possible number of typical Americans and to offend as few as possible.[2]

> I'd like to take the opportunity here in Peoria to set forth clearly and specifically my position on foreign policy. In order to do that I'd like to explain how I see the world today and indicate to you what I believe America's role in world politics should be. First of all let me say that the U.S. is not a failure. For 200 years we have provided the world, through the great experience of democracy, a model—a model that the world is free to follow, but one that we will not impose. Ideally, we would prefer merely to be this model. Unfortunately, the pragmatic realities of the international scene force us to play other roles. . . .

> Now please do not misunderstand me. A policy of detente with the Soviet Union does not mean that we're "Uncle Sucker." I recognize that it's foolhardy to unilaterally disarm, but I also know that it's easy to talk in a mock and tough way and run the risk of war. Neither response reflects my position. . . .

> I don't intend to "flip-flop" on any foreign policy issues. Nor do I intend to speak in glib generalities. I came here to talk specifically about American

---

2. *Ibid.*, pp. 117–137.

foreign policy and that's what I mean to do. First of all, the lesson of Vietnam. The lesson of Vietnam is one of indecision. . . .

Which brings me to the issue of possible future U.S. interventions. I believe that intervention is a diplomatic tool that is needed even if it is only a threat to maintain a balanced international scene. Intervention is not right or wrong. But, it may be used rightly or wrongly. . . .

On terrorists, my position is clear. International terrorism, such as bombings and hijackings is deplorable. Yet, the U.S. should not put itself in a position committed to meet such actions whenever and wherever they might occur. I will go to the United Nations and get an international law against terrorism.

I should not leave Peoria without stating my opinion on grain sales. First of all, I think the embargoing of food is immoral given the starving millions in the world. Second, whether we sell or do not sell grain to Russia will not alter her behavior in international affairs.

As I stated in my opening remarks, the U.S. is not a crippled giant. We have not lost confidence in ourselves. We are a proud democratic nation that must play a major role of leadership in international affairs. I trust you will agree that my foreign policy is based on a realistic and mature view of how to maintain world order and peace.

The technique was of course designed for creating advertisements, public relations campaigns, and so on. But you can use it, too, as you prepare to persuade. Of course you can't do such a technical analysis of your audience as that described above, but you can still try to tap into your audience's ideal world. Spend some time thinking about what they hope for. Ask yourself what kinds of details this ideal world would have. If possible, talk to members of the audience and prompt them to describe their goals and aspirations in detail. Look for clusters of details, and then prepare your message with those factors, as well the demographics, in mind. If you are going to deliver a speech to the class, you may even be able to test out your clusters of sentences. You don't need to mimic the audience by using their exact words, but you can appeal to them by approximating their language. As we've seen many times in earlier chapters, most persuasion is really self-persuasion. It involves *getting messages out of people* instead of putting messages into them. Using the rhetorical vision of your audience can help you get those messages out.

Determining Audience Needs

We touched on audience needs in Chapters 2 through 7 when we looked at the kinds of premises that people hold. Some are emotional, some are logical, and some are cultural. Looking at the motives likely to persuade our target audiences will have to be guesswork. We are not like advertisers with their sophisticated techniques for getting at people's underlying needs, the kinds of deep needs many persons have (for example, Packard's hidden needs, which are discussed in Chapter 4). Advertisers can test out certain ads by showing them to people and then interviewing in depth. The Leo Burnett agency used this method and found out that the Jolly Green Giant had better stand still in ads. People said they were afraid for the valley dwellers when ads showed the giant moving. Burnett invented the Sprout to allow for movement in the ads. Sprout is a *baby* giant and so will not squash anyone if he walks around.

End-needs analysis is a technique using a series of cartoon balloons. People are asked to fill in a balloon to complete a statement like "I use Sta-Pruf on my husband's shirt and that is good because. . . ." The answer written down is carbon-copied to the next page where it becomes the new response. For example, suppose Mrs. Homemaker completes the first statement by saying "that is good because his shirts look crisp and white." "His shirts look crisp and white and that is good because . . ." becomes the next statement to be completed. Interviewees complete as many such chained answers they can. The result is an *end-need* around which an ad can be built. Let us suppose Mrs. Homemaker ends up saying in her *final* answer "and that is good because my mother will love me." The ad-exec can then build a message around a mother visiting her daughter on laundry day and oohing and aahing over the crispy white shirts.

Although we cannot usually get into such complex analysis, the work that has been done by others—usually ad agencies—is there for us to use. You can identify audience needs that are being appealed to in TV commercials today. One type that seems to sell well is the cure for a general feeling of incompetence. Many ads give people a way to feel more competent. Mrs. Olson uses Folger's coffee to make more competent wives. Shell gives maintenance hints to women to give them the sense of competence they may lack when it comes to fixing cars.

Let's get back to the question of how these data can be used when we try to persuade the alumni group. There are several ways. We could focus on this need for being self-confident and try to sell our handball courts on the basis that athletes are self-assured because they do *something* well. Now the alumni can give others the same feeling by opening up the handball option. Or we could talk about body image. We need to keep in good shape in order to be healthy in our minds—"and more than 50 percent of hospital beds are for persons who are having mental problems." All these appeals and many others hook into key needs in today's world, if we judge by present advertising strategy.

All audiences have some sets of shared experiences. People my age can tell you exactly where and when they first heard of the murder of John Kennedy. It is an experience that can be used by a persuader dealing with people born before 1955 or so. All parents know what it is like to fret over the first baby. During the hellish first two months, a baby goes through dozens of diapers a day, never seems to stop crying, and just is not very lovable, smiley, or clever. That two-month ordeal can be a prime source of examples if you are trying to convince parents to treat themselves to a night out, for instance. McDonald's did this for years with their slogan "You Deserve a Break Today!" People who have been to college share memories of the madness of registration for classes, making grades, dealing with stubborn profs, dorm food, and so forth. All these stored data can be building blocks when someone tries to persuade you to pay $499 to go to Florida over break.

So in the process of audience analysis we can also try to locate the key experiences that relate to our topic or goal. In this way, we will *get a message out of the audience*, in Schwartz's terms (see Chapter 9), instead of trying to get something across. The next time you need to persuade someone, try to list the experiences that he or she has likely had. Can some of these be tied into your message? If so, try to work them in.

Another factor in audience analysis is also suggested by Tony Schwartz. In his book *The Responsive Chord*, he favors messages that are built for the time and place, when and where they will be heard.[3] If you were an ad agent trying to send a message to people telling them to vote for someone and you knew that they would hear it on Labor Day weekend, how would you design the message? You would want to plug into the picnic mood, the out-of-doors, and the family fun that people are having on that weekend. You might have the candidate talk about conservation for us and for our children or about the need to make it easy for friends to be together. Schwartz calls this the "task-oriented" approach to persuading. You can use it, too. But first ask yourself if your goal fits with the audience's ability to follow your advice. If you are going to ask them to quit smoking, you'd better do it in such a way as to make it easy for them. Give them brochures that offer helpful hints on quitting. Advertisers ask what their market targets are going to be doing when they receive the message. So can we. The same thing applies to the state of mind of our persuadees—the alumni, the sales force, and the job interviewer. What is the likely mood for the alumni? They will be relaxed. They will remember old times. They might be bragging to former classmates. Take these things into account and design your message to do its task, using the good mood, nostalgia, and the feel of success. Remind them of the good feeling of competing with classmates on the athletic field and how that feeling served them in later years. Remind them of the new people they met. Then tell them that there is a chance to make that kind of feeling available to more students through the handball courts. Though you will be only guessing at the mood of your listeners in this stage, your guesses can be more than random-chance flings if you spend some time getting to know the audience. They will help you to shape your appeal.

Shaping Your Message

Once we know something about our target group and how its members feel toward our topic, we can begin to shape the message, be it speech, interview, ad, or rally cry. There are many aspects to the shaping process. First, we need to *organize* the message in the most useful way. People recall things that are well organized better than things that are helter-skelter. Since we want the audience to

3. Tony Schwartz, *The Responsive Chord* (Garden City, N.Y.: Anchor Press/Doubleday, 1973), pp. 40, 88–91, and 100–105.

remember our speech, clear organization can help us achieve our goals. Then we need to *support our claim*. In Chapter 5 (Content Premises), we said that each claim has a kind of minimum threshold of proof needed to convince people. So we need to select those items of proof or support that have the most effect. A third step in shaping the message is to *judge our believability* and what can be done to improve it. Finally, we need to consider what might be the *best style* to use. Are the listeners likely to respond to the pragmatic or to the unifying style (see Chapter 3)? Will they accept or reject figures of speech? Will they prefer a down-to-earth, "lay your cards on the table," straightforward style? Or are they more open to a less blunt approach? Once we have thought about all of these factors, we can shape the message and prepare to send it with a good chance of success. Let us explore each of the four factors in the shaping process in a little more depth.

Forms of Organization

There are a number of ways to organize messages to make sure they can persuade and are easy to remember. We will look at five such formats here—the topic format, the space format, the time-frame format, the stock issues format, and the format called the motivated sequence.

By Topic The **topic format** is most useful when the message that you want to convey seems to fit into several topics or issues. For example, let us suppose that you want to persuade a company to hire you for a job. You will have a chance to persuade during the talk you have with the company representative. Your message will not be a public speech, but it can still have organization. Since there are several reasons why you think that you would be a good person to hire, the topic format is the best. It allows you to group your reasons for being hired. It also allows you to present part of it—say, past work experience—during a single phase or exchange in the interview. Another—say your educational background—can come during another phase. Your résumé probably has grouped data by topic. Your presentation will reinforce what is in the résumé. Your topics might be the two already noted plus your own interest in the firm, the good things you have heard about it, the pay, and the location of the firm. Employers want to keep the people they hire. Thus you can persuade on two levels using the topic format. First you will give them good reasons to hire you. Then you lead them to believe you will stay. Your format might look like this:

Topic 1: Past Work
    Sold products as a youth
        Christmas cards, driveway sealer, and others
    Sold in retail store in high school
        Clothes and florist (gift items and service)
    Sold ads for college paper
        Top seller three of nine months (eight others in sales)
        Dealt with major accounts (Dayton's, Minnesota Twins, and others)
        Dealt with major ad agents (layout, copywriting, logos)

Sold film programs to students
    Student Center Board—ad director
    Film coordinator (ads, posters, etc.)
Other sales experience
    Paper
    Intern at ad agency
    Fraternity rush

Topic 2: Education
    Majored in speech communication
        Courses in persuasion, interpersonal communication, and campaigns,
        among others (G.P.A. 3.7 in major)
    Minored in marketing/sales
    G.P.A. 2.9 in minor

Topic 3: Interest in Sales
    Sales is relied on for success of any firm
    Salespersons make higher salaries if successful
    Salespersons are promoted faster

Topic 4: Interest in Foursquare Company
    Growing industry
    Good salaries and fringes
    Friend gave good recommendation
    Located in a major city

You might not take the outline with you. It is probably better to keep it in mind and perhaps open the interview by saying "I think there are four good reasons why you should add my skills to the Foursquare Company." The topic format here lets the interviewer recall you and your reasons when reviewing the day.

By Space The **space format** is useful when you try to persuade others of the size of a problem or solution. It is like that analogy since it allows other people to visualize the topic. They can recall its parts because they can see it in their mind's eye. Suppose you want to persuade local businesses to form an evironmental agency for the town. You might tell them about the size of the problem. How much water pollution is in the county? How much air pollution? How much other pollution? What part is due to schools and what part to the town? How much is caused by visitors and industries? What is the effect of the new K-Mart store and the Ford plant likely to be? Each of these is a factor—a slice of the pie. A graph could present the amounts accounted for by city, campus, and so on. You might ask the businesses to think of the pollution as a map of the United States. The eastern states up to the Ohio River are the part of pollution due to townspeople. Up to the Mississippi River is due to the campus. Up to the Rockies is due to industries and visitors. The rest is from other sources (trains, buses, and cars). The picture changes when we look at nuclear pollution, though. Maine is the part due to townspeople, the campus, and others. All the other states are due to industry. Being able to see the problem helps you understand and recall it. The use of space is helpful when you want the audience to see differing dimensions.

By Time Frame Sometimes we want to persuade people that it is time to take action. The goal is to make them aware that time has passed, and things have happened that need attention. The **time frame format** is most useful here. It traces an issue or problem across time. For example, suppose that you hope to persuade your parents to let you bum around eastern Europe next summer. They have a whole set of biases against this idea. They are afraid you will be arrested by Communist secret police. They know you do not speak the languages of those countries. You need to persuade them that you and the world are different now. This is not the 1950s or 1960s. You could trace what has happened across the past fifteen years to you and to eastern Europe. You could trace your own growth as a travel veteran. Your first trip away from home was when you were eight and took the train to Duluth. Then you continue the time tracing, noting your walking trip across canoe country and your hitchhike trip to the West Coast. You can bring them up to date, reminding them of your bike trip through western Europe last year and Mexico before that. Time tracing could also be done for eastern Europe. More and more people tour eastern Europe. Now they have English lessons over state TV and radio. Almost everyone speaks English now. The time tracing lets them see that their early ideas were wrong—that they need to change their view of the world. That change leads to your taking the trip.

Stock Issues Sometimes we want to change a policy. Since the policy is in place and working, and since people are used to it, it will be hard to change. The **stock-issues approach** works best in this kind of situation. It has three steps. The first is showing a need for change, usually by citing symptoms of a problem and causes. A second step provides a new method or plan that can handle the problem. Finally, one offers data showing that the method will work, perhaps by noting where it has worked. Suppose that you want your college to change its late-add period. This makes it easier for people to join classes that are under way. Your speech to the add-drop committee might begin with statistics as to the number of late-adds at present, the number denied, and so on. This shows a need for change. You also show a cause of the problem—the stringent one-week deadline for adding a course. Your new plan is to extend the late-add time to two weeks, with teachers asked to provide newcomers with notes and an update.

The Motivated Sequence Another organizational pattern that resembles the stock-issues approach is the **motivated sequence** suggested by communication scholars Alan Monroe, Douglas Ehninger, and Bruce Gronbeck.[4] It has five parts and is often used by persuaders to get persuadees to attend to their message, to feel a need to follow the advice of the persuader, and most important, to take action related to the advice. Thus the motivated sequence is a good pattern to use in sales, recruitment—say, for the armed forces or some organization—in politics where the action step is the vote, and in many other instances.

The first part or step in the motivated sequence is the **attention step**. No

4. From *Principles and Types of Speech Communication*, 9th edition, by Douglas Ehninger, Bruce E. Gronbeck, Ray E. McKerrow, and Alan H. Monroe. Copyright © 1982 Scott, Foresman and Company. Reprinted by permission.

persuader can be successful if the audience is uninterested in the persuasion. So, capturing the attention of the audience is the first task. There are hundreds of ways to do this. A persuader might begin the message with a startling statistic, for instance—"Over 70 percent of the heart attacks today are related to the kind of person you are—type A or type B. Today you can decide for yourself what kind you want to be."

The persuader might use a joke or humorous anecdote. We often hear this on the after-dinner speech circuit and even in sermons. Another approach used by political persuaders is to make an important announcement in the first few moments of the message. The president announces settlement of a strike or a new peace initiative in the Middle East. A senator gives a "Golden Fleece" award for wasteful government spending. It is also used by advertisers who make startling announcements or offers to capture attention. You can "get the fourth bar of Lifebuoy Free!" announces the store label. Or an advertiser states that *Motor Trend* magazine has declared the Plymouth Horizon to be the "Car of the Year."

All these tactics and many others are useful in capturing the attention of the audience. Dramatic actions also draw attention; shooting off a pistol to start a speech on gun safety would complete the attention step. As you prepare to persuade, try to think of your audience as a group of bored and uninterested people who need to have their attention drawn to your message. Then set about designing an attention-getting device.

The second part or step in the motivated sequence is the **need step.** The task here is to demonstrate to listeners that they have a specific unfulfilled need that can be met by listening to your advice. Again, there are many ways to demonstrate this need. The best ones usually flow from the attention step. For example, take the speaker on gun safety. Following the attention-getting step of shooting off the pistol, the persuader might say, "Three of the persons in this room are going to be shot with handguns in the next year. Two of the shootings will be because someone was not trained in gun safety. Each of us is in danger of falling victim to accidental shootings as the number and variety of handguns increase."

By trying to relate the attention step directly to the audience, the persuader begins to create a need in the audience. This need can be satisfied by following the persuader's advice. As persuader, you describe symptoms of a problem. Your receivers may be only dimly aware of the cause for the problem and the symptoms. By doing this you begin to create a need in your receivers. The encyclopedia sales representative gets attention by offering to "place" a set of books in your home. This attention-getter is followed by showing you how much you need the books—libraries in schools are out of date and crowded and refuse to lend reference books; sometimes you need your information *now* and not when the library opens; or the set of books is increasing in price from week to week, and this alone is reason enough to buy the books today. With each argument, a need is created. Try to create needs in your audience—needs that can be met only by listening to you and your advice.

Steps three and four—**visualization** and **satisfaction**—are often interchangeable, depending on the persuasive purposes. For example, suppose you are trying to get people to protect their health by eating more fiber or roughage in their diet. You can get attention by noting the United States has the highest rates of cancer of the colon in the world. Then you can work to create a need by telling your receivers of their chances of getting cancer and other diseases of the intestinal tract. Then you can choose to offer either a dramatic visualization or satisfaction step (like a plan in the terms of the stock-issues approach) relative to the need that you have just created.

For instance, you can ask the receivers to picture themselves in coffins and to imagine what their loved ones will say at the funeral. Stop-smoking clinics often use that tactic; it causes the persuadees to visualize the need. Another approach is to describe a hypothetical case. "Joe first found out that he had colon cancer on his twenty-seventh birthday. He was told he had three years to live. But he didn't really live during those three years. He had painful colon radiation treatments. These involve. . . ." The verbal picture of the need that you paint can make your point vividly.

In the alternative approach, the persuader offers the satisfaction of the need first, then visualizes it. Suppose I am selling new cars. I might get your attention by offering some special premium or opportunity to get you into the showroom. (In Chicago, one car dealer regularly has past Playmates of the Month from *Playboy* magazine as guests on weekends. They offer autographs and pinups. The traffic created this way leads to a need in the customer—to buy a new flashy, sexy-looking car.) In selling cars I would probably also offer a free road test. You begin to feel the need as you compare the smell, feel, and handling of the new model with the rattles of your old car. After your road test, I might try to visualize what your satisfaction might be like if you follow my advice. I might say "In that car, you'll be able to take that trip up to Lake Geneva and feel like you own the place. You'll be the hit of the tennis club, too. I'll bet your weekly sales level will rise just because of the image this GT will give you." Thus I visualize not the *need* as with cancer of the colon but the *satisfaction* of the need. Whichever approach you choose, be certain to get your receivers involved in picturing themselves either in trouble or well satisfied. Get them to visualize these things as vividly as possible. A professor I once had said that we get 80 percent of what we know about decisions we have to make through our eyes and our ears. Too often we forget to use the sense of sight in verbal persuasion.

Finally, the persuader who uses the motivated sequence or similar patterns must offer an **action** step. It is not enough to get attention by citing a statistic on colon cancer, then to create a need by vividly depicting the stages of the disease, then to offer a preventive—getting more roughage into the diet. These will not get action. The persuader needs to suggest some specific action step that is reasonable and that can be taken soon and easily. A good one in the colon cancer case might be eating whole wheat bread instead of white bread daily. This action step might be verified by citing statistics to show that as little as one slice will provide the daily minimum to prevent this disease. The action is specific, reasonable, easy, and effective. Given the attention, need, visualization, and satisfaction steps that preceded it, we can reasonably hope that the persuadees may follow our advice.

A common action step used by students in persuasive speeches is to suggest that class members write letters to their elected representatives. Though this is the single most effective thing people can do to affect legislation, few of them actually ever write. Even the staunchest suporters of the Equal Rights Amendment in my district of Illinois—advocates and officers of women's rights groups on campus and in the communication profession—had not contacted their legislative representatives at all before a crucial vote in 1978 in which the proposition was defeated by two votes. Perhaps this action step seemed to them too mundane or even useless. A persuader had to capture their attention—"Did you hear about the representatives in our district on ERA?" Then the persuader had to create a need—"They are wavering on ERA, and I know you support ERA, don't you?" The satisfaction step followed in this case—"You can register your opinion in the short time remaining by using the telephone, you know. Why don't you?" This satisfaction was then visualized—"You can call their toll-free Springfield offices or their local offices and tell the person who answers why you support ERA. You might even get to talk to the representative yourself or the administrative aide. They are both easy to talk to and will really probe you for your reasons for supporting ERA, and that's the kind of opinion that needs to be fed in, don't you think?" The visualization will lead nowhere in many cases unless the persuader provides the easy outlet or action step—"Here is a slip of paper with the toll-free and local numbers of the two representatives in our district who are wavering on tomorrow's vote. Call them now and register your opinion."

Though some receivers, even those who claim to share the need you have sketched out, will opt out of this action step, more will choose to follow your advice on this telephone option than will write letters. It takes time to remember to pick up writing paper, envelopes, stamps, and so on. Then it takes effort to compose the letter, type it error free, and send it off. The form-letter response that usually results reinforces the commonly held notion that letters are usually filed in the wastebasket. Legislators can tell the difference. They discount the identical letters and postcards produced by organized campaigns, but they do pay attention to communications individually thought out by constituents.[5]

In effective persuasion, it is essential to give the persuadees a realistic action step, whether it is signing the sales contract, phoning the representative, or boycotting the non-union food market. Build such steps into your persuasive attempts at sales, recruitment, and so on, and you will find your percentage of success increasing dramatically.

Forms of Proof

We want good reasons for changing our attitudes, actions, or beliefs. Even if we are sure that the change advocated is a good one, we still need to have proof. Usually this proof comes in the forms of data or evidence that were discussed in Chapter 5. Let's briefly review these here. In Chapter 5 we looked at forms of support mainly from the receiver's point of view. From the persuader's point of view they take on new import.

---

5. In research I conducted in 1980, legislators in Illinois unanimously confirmed this. The most important and effective ways to communicate with them are via the personal visit, letter, or phone call. Resolutions or petitions are virtually ignored.

Statistical Evidence Sometimes the most effective kind of support is statistical. For instance, car buyers are interested in gas mileage. They will be more persuaded by the Environmental Protection Agency (EPA) figures than by all the reassurances from the sales staff that the car is a real gas saver. Statistics are most useful when they are simple and easy to understand. When persuaders decide to use statistics, they need to make them clear. They need to provide a reference point for the numbers. For example, the car salesperson needs to say that the 21.5-cubic-foot trunk on the Fairlane is twice what you will get in the more costly Volkswagen Rabbit. The comparison makes the cubic feet meaningful. When we decide to use this form of support, we need to make it clear and simple.

Narratives and Anecdotes We have noted the power of drama, stories, and jokes. The narrative makes examples come alive. It makes them easy to recall and relate to. The persuader who tells of a person rising from rags to riches will have more success than one who relies on statistics.

Testimony We suspect people who try to convince us of a certain idea if it is based only on their own feelings or brainstorms. That is why the testimony of another person is so useful. Even if the person testifying is unqualified, the testimonial still has influence. Of course, it is much better to have an expert witness to the wisdom or folly of the idea, person, or product. Even better is testimony of a hostile or reluctant witness. This has impact because it runs counter to the self-interest of the witness to speak in favor of the product or idea. A recent ad features a top executive at American Express Company. He advises you to get yourself a Carte Blanche credit card. It is counter to his self-interest as head of Carte Blanche's biggest competitor to say such things. As a result the ad had double impact. Actually this strategy works to the advantage of both credit card firms. It will increase sales for both American Express and Carte Blanche.

Visual Evidence We have noted how useful it is for an audience to see or experience evidence. This is why visual aids are used in sales work. If you have ever walked into a department store where a salesperson was showing a veg-o-matic or pasta machine, you know the power of visual data. You see the product at work, and seeing is believing! This was also the most powerful kind of data for the tribal medicine man, who made sure to add visual proof to his magic—smoke powder, and so forth. Sometimes I think my doctor does a lot of razzle-dazzle for the same reason—to persuade me that I am getting my money's worth. Though you may never be so dramatic in your persuasion, you can use visual aids like graphs, charts, or even cartoons to reinforce your ideas. A student in one of my classes used Snoopy drawings to highlight the points of his speech on safe driving habits. It was easy to recall and organize the data he gave us. We considered it in depth with Snoopy there to help.

Comparison and Contrast Sometimes it is hard to really see a problem in perspective. We see the issue from a single viewpoint and cannot really judge it accurately. So it is wise to provide something with which to compare or contrast the issue, product, or action. For example, we might point out that the new graphite body on Ford is 1250 pounds lighter than that of a comparable Chevy. It sounds like a lot but would not be much if each car weighed 50,000 pounds. However, if the source says that this is one third less we can get an idea of how important the reduction is. If the source extends the comparison saying that this will add 30 percent more to gas mileage and 15 percent more space in the passenger compartment and 50 percent more space in the trunk, the comparison makes it easy to favor Ford when we shop for a new car. Candidates often compare with their opponents' records their own records in Congress or their positions on a variety of issues—defense, farm prices, and the like.

Analogy We discussed the analogy as a form of proof in Chapters 3 and 5. It is a useful but risky form of support to use. As a special kind of comparison, the analogy has two types—figurative and literal. The figurative type compares a familiar idea or object with an unfamiliar idea or object. The literal analogy compares two nearly identical ideas or objects. Candidates might compare their accomplishments with those of their opponents. They might stress that both have been in office the same length of time, have been on the same number of committees, and so on. Yet Jones, he says, has a much better record than Smith.

Building Your Credibility

All the evidence in the world, organized perfectly and delivered well, will not persuade if listeners do not trust the speaker. This happens time after time in politics. Presidents will all suffer from a credibility gap. We see it in the world of sports when coaches and players come out of long meetings over salary or during trades. They *say* that everyone's happy, but we know better. You do not fight over your future and come away without any bad feelings. Surely, in many product appeals, credibility suffers. It is hard to believe that we can have an instant change in personality, social life, and sex appeal due to hair dye or after-shave lotion. We accept some of this "incredibility" as part of the game, but in matters such as persuading the boss to give us a promotion or parents to let us marry before graduation, credibility is a key factor. What makes some people credible while others are not? How can we build our own credibility before and during persuasion? Let us look further at some answers to these questions.

Remember that we discussed this idea of credibility in Chapter 6 using Aristotle's ideas about the reputation of the speaker, the speaker's delivery during the speech, and perhaps the audience's response to the speaker's image or charisma. In more modern times this translated into several dimensions of credibility—reputation was roughly equated with the known *expertise* of the speaker. Attribution of a speech is important. For example, when an identical speech was attributed to experts in some cases and to novices in others, the speech attributed to an expert was always more persuasive than the novice version. Delivery and charisma seem related to sincerity and dynamism. Audiences don't seem to believe speakers who cannot maintain eye contact. Tall speakers seem to have more persuasive potential. Speakers who are animated in their delivery seem to be able to persuade more effectively than those who are frozen at the podium. Exciting language usage in a speech usually helps make the speech more persuasive. A well-groomed speaker will probably be more persuasive than one whose clothes have that slept-in look. The interpersonal persuader who is disheveled will have more difficulty persuading others than the persuader who is neat, bathed, and mouthwashed. You would think that most of these points would be obvious, yet these "obvious" hints are overlooked daily by sales reps, politicians, spouses, teachers, students, and parents. Here are some examples from everyday life in which the elements of credibility can be and are used.

Trust We trust people for many reasons. We trust them because they have been trustworthy in the past. We trust them because they give off trustworthy cues—direct eye contact, a calm voice, and so forth. We trust them because we know it would not be in their self-interest to betray us. A good example of this might be airplane hijackers, who trust the passengers and crew not to gang up on them—to do so would endanger all their lives. Usually, it is the first two kinds of trust that we wish to communicate. We want to tell employers that they can trust us because we have been constant in the past. We want to tell voters to support us because we have been faithful to campaign pledges in the past. Or we tell customers that they can trust antiseptic Listerine because it has been around since Grandma's time. We also try to give off cues of trust. We look at our persuadees directly. We try to sound sincere, even if we are not (though this isn't always effective—our nonverbal messages "leak" and tell that we are lying). Persuaders who want to have a trust relationship with the audience need to remind them of the past record for trust. They need to refer to times when it would have been easy to break trust. Sometimes this can be worked into the persuasive speech or exchange early. For example, the worker tells the boss, "You'll recall the times I had to take charge of the cash receipts for the day. Sometimes we had over $20,000 in cash." The husband reminds his spouse that "there were lots of chances for some action on the side at work." The youth reminds the parent that "there was plenty to tempt me not to study at the dorm. There will be no more at the house I hope to pledge, I'm sure." We communicate our trust during the speech. We look at receivers eye to eye; we have relaxed posture; we speak with a sure voice. All these devices help to develop credibility and trust.

Expertise How do we know if someone is a true expert on a topic or job? Mostly we look for data from past success at a task. If a person was a good treasurer for the Luther League, he or she will probably be good for the student council. Sales representatives who did well in the Midwest should also do well in the larger and more complex East. A person who has had experience in many areas of the company—shipping, sales, and so on—is much more credible to workers than the person who has had experience only in one area of the company. So a persuader can refer to past experience. As in the job interview situation discussed earlier in this chapter, applicants can show that they are experts in sales and can refer to past successes. Sometimes we refer to our expertise during the persuasive presentation. At other times a letter, résumé, or even a verbal introduction can cover the topic. Some people believe that you can make yourself look like an expert by giving off competence cues. John T. Molloy, clothing researcher, has written several books and a syndicated column dealing with how one's clothes can give off messages that say, "I am competent and in charge," or "I am a threat."[6] Molloy says that the color of our clothing communicates, too. To project a power or "take-charge" image, one should wear three shades of blue. To project sincerity and warmth, browns are the key. The subtleties involved are very complex. So speakers should consider what they wear as an element in the expertise they communicate. Of course there are other nonverbal signals that relate here and which can further develop our credibility along the expertise dimension. Finally, you can signal expertise by being well prepared, by suggesting that you really know about the topic (constantly referring to or reading a manuscript of the speech shows that you are unfamiliar with the topic), and by being willing to engage in question/answer sessions when you have finished speaking.

Dynamism The factor of **dynamism** is elusive and even mysterious. It is sometimes related to physical appearance. The taller candidate seems to win more often. Attractive persons hold attention better. This kind of dynamism is sometimes labeled charisma. It probably cannot be developed very much. Some cosmetic techniques can be used (for example, through clothes or the use of proper makeup and choice of color when on TV, as in the Nixon-Kennedy debates of 1960). There are people who are not large or attractive, but who have charisma. They take up a lot of psychic space when they enter a room or speak up. They have stage presence. Perhaps something they have done makes them appear more dynamic, more central and important. They speak with authority. We can learn to project better or to speak with more volume. That will add stature to our image. We can improve our image by associating with dynamic persons or by referring to them as friends. Politicians are often photographed with sports figures and thus "borrow" a dynamic image from them. Doing active things can signal dynamism. Referring to one's athletic interests might be an example here. Again, politicians work hard at getting pictured *doing* things. We like to follow men and women of action. Certain words can give off a sense of dynamism, and if they are used the image of the source is improved. McCulloch chain saws feature the word "power" in their ads and refer to things like "triggers" and "revving up" the machine. So, a statement with high-energy, powerful words can help develop a dynamic image for a speaker. This image along with trust and expertise can be of help in achieving persuasive goals. Persuadees want persuaders to be credible. They rely on the three dimensions of trust, skill, and dynamism to judge that credibility.

Stylizing Your Message

In Chapters 2 through 5 we covered style from the *persuadee's* viewpoint. Let us now look at what a *persuader* can do to develop style. Most persons are affected by dramatic words and styles. They react to stories and to exciting words and phrases.

---

6. John T. Molloy. *Dress For Success* and *The Woman's Dress For Success Book* (Chicago: Reardon and Walsh, 1977).

Rewriting messages is a good way to improve style. We often rehearse our words before saying them. Sometimes we do this silently. As you wait to get the floor during a meeting, you "practice" what you are going to say. During this rehearsal, we can edit and work on style. Would the word "smash" be better in talking about our goal of defeating the other sales staff or would it be better to use "destroy" or some other word? Try out different options as you rehearse in silence.

Using a **narrative** as an introduction to a message can also improve style. We all listen to a story and can then be drawn along into the rest of the message.

Figures of speech are useful, given the right time and place. In a group of union men debating the new company offer on wages at the local bar-and-grill, flowery words would backfire, but a strike leader could successfully urge a vote of "no" on the new contract by using a figure of speech. He could say, for example, "Give them a message they can't ignore"—or a more earthy version of the same idea.

Finally, **nonverbal aspects of style** can be used by the persuader. We can dress persuasively. We can decorate the setting with an eye toward our goals. John T. Molloy has also shown that the label a woman executive puts on her door signals her image. Mary L. Smith was more effective than Mrs. Mary L. Smith, which was better than either Ms. Mary L. Smith or last-place Miss Mary L. Smith. A paneled office with leather-covered chairs and a filled pipe rack prepares a persuadee for a certain kind of message. That message is not expected in a ceramic-tiled office with metal desk and chairs. Albert Scheflen described the meaning attached to some thirty postures. For example, when people want answers to their statements, they raise their heads slightly at the end of a statement.[7] Of course, we cannot rehearse and plan all these movements in detail, but paying some attention to them can add to our hoped-for effects.

Parallel structure can add a memorable style to one's speeches. By returning at the end of the speech to an example or narrative that was used to begin the speech, the speaker seems to tie things up nicely. The audience finds that it remembers the speaker's point more easily. Internal summaries or foreshadowings also add style and help the audience to retain more of the message.

In conclusion, the second stage for persuaders—shaping the message—has several dimensions that can affect the final outcome of a message. These include organization, forms of support, using credibility, and, finally, stylizing a message to fit our needs. With a well-planned message, a persuader can focus on delivery. Here the advice is simple and straightforward.

Delivering Your Message

Usually we think of delivery as a source issue. That is, it is something that only the source itself can affect. To some degree, this is true. However, there are at

---

7. Albert E. Scheflen. "The Significance of Posture in Communication Systems," *Psychiatry,* Vol. 27 (1964). pp. 316–331. Scheflen also noted that the "bowl gesture," or holding one's hands like the ad for Allstate insurance, was persuasive.

least two factors in the process—the channel and the audience—that can affect the message and that sources often overlook. The careful choice of channels used to send the message is often important. Would the ad be better on TV, radio, or billboards? Should we ask for the raise over the phone, in a letter, or in person? The state of mind of receivers can also affect the final impact of a message. They get the pitch sent by the colorful package in the store, but they may be too relaxed by the soothing piped-in music to buy the item. So we need to pay attention to all three elements in delivery. The source is clearly the one over which we have most control and that will have the greatest effect.

Delivery: The Persuader

Among the factors that a persuader can adjust before and during delivery are posture, eye contact, bodily movement and gesture, articulation, and vocal quality. Other factors that are under the speaker's control are the use of visual aids and other nonverbal signals.

Posture We have all seen persuaders who are so nervous about their speeches that they cannot stop pacing back and forth. When they do stop, they stand so ramrod stiff that it looks like they might freeze into statues. At the other extreme we have seen speakers who are so relaxed that they do not seem to care at all about their messages. They slouch lazily across a podium or they slide down into their chairs during a meeting. They rarely look up, and you wonder if they will nod off in the middle of a sentence. So, it is clear that posture can signal to the audience that you are either too relaxed or too nervous. The ideal posture lies somewhere in between. The persuader should be alert and erect. The shoulders should not be tensed, but neither should they slump. There should be no visible signs of nervousness or tension. I wiggle my toes, but no one can see that. Over-all, the message should be one of confidence. Try to observe persuaders in differing contexts—interviews, speeches, arguments, and so on. You will see that the effective ones avoid both the nervous and the "nearly asleep" extremes.

Eye Contact There is some truth to the folk wisdom that a person cannot lie to you and also look you straight in the eyes. It is true most of the time for most people. We are believed better if we get eye contact with our audience. We do not need to look at everyone, but we need to look at various areas in the audience. Polticians know this and use devices like Teleprompters to enable them to read a speech and appear to be looking around at the same time. In a one-on-one context, you will want to have repeated eye contact with your persuadee. Again, politicians make sure to look directly into the TV camera and hence to have apparent eye contact with each viewer. In a meeting, you will want to have eye contact with many persons or maybe even everyone at the meeting. It is clear that eye contact can effect persuasion.

Body Movement and Gesture We can move during a speech, if the movement is not likely to distract. We can likewise gesture during a speech, if we do not distract by doing so. During a meeting, we can gesture or pound the table for effect. In an interview, we might include gestures or facial expressions, which can have impact in all three contexts. Again, the rule is to be natural and to avoid the extremes, as with posture. Vigorous arm-waving by speakers distracts. Frozen and inanimate people seem bored with it all and so lose effect. People whose faces are expressionless come across as dull. Those who have eternal smiles pasted on signal insincerity. For most people, facial expressions happen naturally and without forethought. Those gestures are probably the most useful.

Articulation and Vocal Quality Everyone has heard persons who have speech defects or who pronounce words or sounds incorrectly. What is the result of these kinds of errors? Mostly we focus on the error and not on the message. In other words, the mistake distracts us from the message. Persuaders who succeed listen carefully to themselves and try to work on articulation. Listening to ourselves on tape pinpoints our own careless articulation and can help us to focus on our vocal quality. Another good idea is to transcribe your articulation from a tape. If you know the phonetic alphabet, your mistakes will become crystal clear. Vocal quality—nasal-sounding, wheezy, breathy, or a voice pitched too high—can be improved by using some of these methods as well. If you are really interested in persuading others, you will spend some time working on your voice and your articulation.

Delivery: The Channel

In a campaign that I once studied, the candidate put much of his money into billboard space. I was surprised because I assumed that in a television age, the major cost would be TV. The reason for the apparent mistake relates to the factor of the communication channel. His district was a large one, stretching nearly half the length of the state. No single TV channel reached all of the district. To use TV would mean paying a triple load to get a single message across. However, everyone in the district drove. The district was large, and residents had to drive to do shopping, business, or farming. Thus the billboard was a channel that could touch nearly all the voters in the district. The candidate was careful to choose the key spots for his signs. For example, he did not want to buy space next to a billboard for his opponent or just before a shopping section along the road or by an X-rated theater. The best billboard channels were at stoplights; cars had to wait. A good spot was on the way out of most towns where drivers would see signs after the distractions of the downtown area.

The same kind of care ought to be taken when persuaders make up their minds to succeed in a conference, in an interview, or with larger audiences. Again Schwartz's notion of creating a task-oriented message comes into play. What is the best way to tell the boss that he is being undercut by his assistant? Perhaps dropping a hint might work best. Maybe using the grapevine through the departmental gossip would work. Or maybe going in and telling the boss outright would work best. You need to be as careful about choosing your channel as the politician is about choosing the spots for billboards. A good place to start is by listing all channels that you could use to send your message. The list will vary from task to task. Identifying the channels gets you thinking in the right direction. Then locate which channels you can control. Then try to "psych out" your persuadee in terms of which channel will be most useful in getting his attention. Finally, shape your messages to fit your channel and to hit your target. Clever use of channels can make the difference between success and failure.

A student who wanted to get a job in the mass-mail industry used a receiver approach. He had been in the business before and knew that mass mailers were impressed by paper quality. So he had his résumé printed on the best parchment paper. It cost $400 to print the résumé. He also knew that mailers like simple design and a lot of white space. He made the résumé open like a folder with only a phrase on each panel so that the unfolded brochure simply and clearly stated his past job experience. He was clever to leave the fact that he had been thrice decorated for gallantry in battle until last for full impact. Within two weeks of mailing 100 résumés, he had more than half a dozen job offers, several of them starting at more than double the average. His use of the right channel to the right people with the right message spelled success. Spend some time thinking about the effects of various channels on your message as you get ready to persuade.

Delivery: The Audience

It is not easy to get the audience to help you with your delivery, but when speakers are able to do this, the results are impressive. For example, speakers can get audiences to respond to questions. The speaker says, "Eighty-seven senators voted for the Medicaid bill"; the audience roars, "But not Senator X!" Members of the audience feel that they are part of the speech—that they are delivering it too. So the clever use of questions and active feedback can get persuadees involved. Though not so dramatic as before a large group, the question can also be useful in the informal meeting. The persuader might ask a direct question of the audience (for example, "What is the problem here? Bill? Bob?"). Or we might let the receivers "fill in" for us by beginning to list examples and then letting our listeners provide some of their own. We could say, "So there are a lot of ways to save heat, like weather-stripping your doors and windows and by. . . ." The persuader can try to shape the situation to make the audience feel like being persuaded. In some situations, we can do this with lighting, music, setting, and so forth. A minister of the largest Lutheran congregation in the world had a control switch in the pulpit so he could bring up the lights during the bright spots of his sermon and dim them on the hell and damnation parts. At other times, we can use the introduction to get people in the mood. One speaker I know always gets the audience on their feet to get the blood going in the first minute or so. He says this increases his success ratio. W. Clement Stone, the originator of P.M.A. (Positive Mental Attitude) asks his audience to stand up and shout, "Yes, I can!" You can be creative in setting the mood for persuasion. Consider what would make your persuadees want to be convinced. Then try to get them involved in their own persuasion.

Some Common Tactics of Persuasion

If you think about the key emphasis of the chapters you have read so far, it is that the *strategy* of persuasion is to find out what the audience already believes.

Then speakers need to take that common ground and build on it, tying their own goals into what the target group or person thinks. What follows are some *tactics* for doing this. Tactics are the working tools that put strategy into action. These tactics are by no means the only ones that you can use.[8] You can add to this list as you try new techniques of persuasion in your own life.

The Yes-Yes Technique

A common tactic used in sales and other persuasive appeals is the technique called **yes-yes.** The source attempts to get the target group or person to respond "yes" to some of the parts of the appeal, holding the key request until last. Having agreed to most parts of the appeal, the target person is somewhat tied into saying "yes" to the key and final request. For example, suppose that you were trying to sell a lawn service. The service provides yearly fertilization, raking, and weed-killing. You might ask the homeowner, "You would like to have a beautiful lawn, wouldn't you?" The answer is going to be "yes"; all homeowners want nice lawns. Then you ask, "And you'd like the weeds removed?" Another "yes" is likely. You might follow up with, "And wouldn't it be nice if these things could be effort-free, huh?" A "yes" answer is likely again. Now that the homeowner has accepted all your points in favor of the service, it is nearly impossible to respond with a "no" answer to the final question. So you ask, "Then you'd like to be one of our lucky customers?" By accepting the "yes" pattern, the buyer will be more inclined to fall into agreement with your final request. The same technique could be useful in a meeting as a persuader gets the group members to agree with all but the final point in favor of the change in work schedules, for instance. They agree that flexibility is good, that more free time for workers is good, and so on. They are almost bound by the need to be consistent to agree that the change is a good one. A politician might ask if we want to lower jobless rates, if we want to stop high fuel imports, and if we want to cut inflation. It follows then that we may be inclined to favor that politician's plan of action to combat the weakness in the status quo.

Persuaders can and do use this technique to slowly lead their target group or person through stages to a final "yes" answer to the request for purchases, change, or votes. Persuadees need to be alert to this tactic so they do not get trapped into making unwise choices just because they agree with parts of the pitch.

Don't Ask If, Ask Which

Suppose you run a small company. You want to ask an elderly department head to take early retirement. This is a common problem in all organizations. Now suppose your persuadee is evasive. He is not available when you phone. He finds excuses to avoid conferences. He refuses to discuss a retirement date. You need to

---

8. These and many other tactics are mentioned in texts and books of advice for persuaders. For example, see the following, which mentions many of the tactics noted here: Clyde J. Faries. "Teaching Rhetorical Criticism: It's Our Responsibility." *Journal of the Illinois Speech and Theatre Association.* Vol. 33 (Spring 1977), pp. 7–15. See also Ernest G. Bormann, William L. Howell, Ralph G. Nichols, and George L. Shapiro. *Interpersonal Communication in the Modern Organization* (Englewood Cliffs, New Jersey: Prentice-Hall, 1969), pp. 233–241.

get some kind of action. So you use the **don't-ask-if, ask-which** technique. This tactic asks the person to make a choice. There is no option other than the ones given. In the retirement situation, you say, "I need to have a meeting with you. Is Tuesday better or Wednesday?" There is no room for an answer like "I don't want to meet at all." The person can try to shift ground by saying, "Neither of those is good." This can easily be met with the same tactic. You ask, "Which day this week is good then?" You will eventually nail down a definite day. You can follow with "Your office or mine?" or "Two o'clock or three?" and thus force the action. Once the meeting is set, the tactic can go on as you ask if this June is better or would July be a good time to retire. There may be need for an interim step such as "Have you thought about retirement or is that something you haven't considered?" This sets the stage for your suggestion.

Salespersons often use this tactic, asking, "Which suit is best on you—the brown or the blue?" They follow with "Would you like a matching shirt and tie or just the suit for now?" Politicians ask "Who do you want to lead this great state, a party hack or myself?" TV and print ads often ask "Which wax cleans best—Pledge or the lemon-oil brand X?"

Though the don't-ask-if, ask-which tactic can be very manipulative, it has the value of forcing action when buyers, voters, or others are stubborn and try to avoid making decisions. Persuadees need to watch for this tactic in order to avoid being trapped into a poor decision.

Answering a Question with a Question

A tactic that some people use to throw you off guard is to respond to a request by asking a question. For example, they say, "Why do you think I would like to do that?" or "What gave you that idea?" or a similar response. We are expecting them to come to the point, to make a statement that relates to the discussion or the request. This throws us off pace and may leave us speechless for a moment. Then the initiative is gone. What is a good counter to this approach? The tactic of answering a question with a question is useful here. For example, a sales prospect responds to a sales pitch about a new car with a question, saying, "Aren't new cars awfully high priced these days?" The salesperson sputters, unable to say "yes" or "no." Cars are high priced but to admit this weakens the sales pitch. The best tactic for the seller is to ask, "What do you mean by high priced?" or "In relation to what? A new house or your tax bills?" The buyer must answer the question in some way; but the initiative is back with the salesperson, who has the added advantage of having time to think. Politicians often use this tactic. A voter at a rally asks, "Why is the treaty a good one for us if we own the Panama Canal anyway?" The politician counters with "What do you mean by the word own'?" and is back in the driver's seat. The tactic is not often seen in the ad world, but you do run into it sometimes. The ad says, "People have been asking why Mr. Coffee is better. We ask why are they willing to throw away flavor."

This tactic is most useful in question-and-answer sessions and when the target person or group uses the tactic of asking to throw us off pace. We do not often see this tactic used against us unless we are using the question to stymie those who are trying to persuade us. The person who uses the question to throw persuaders off is more frequent. Persuaders need to know how to deal with the questioning tactic. "Answer one with one" is the best advice.

Getting Partial Commitment

Evangelists often close their pitch by asking members in the tent or auditorium to bow their heads and close their eyes for prayer. This gets a partial commitment from all the audience. The preacher then asks in the prayer for the Lord to enter the hearts of all and can then ask those who want God to come into their lives to raise their hands or to stand up. This is a second act by which people commit to part of the request. The final request may then be "Those of you with your hands up come to the front and be saved." The tactic is seen elsewhere, too. A sales pitch may include asking if you could afford to give up one pack of cigarettes a week to help put the Great Books series into your home. This willingness to commit oneself to a part of the deal can be continued until the sale is made.

Of course there are other kinds of commitment that are used to persuade. Ads offer a free sample of the product. You try it and have taken the first step in the purchase process. You get a free taste of cheese or sausage or yogurt in the supermarket and you will be more likely to commit yourself to buying the product. A politician can ask you to sign a petition to put his or her name on the ballot. The act is a form of commitment to that politician.

This tactic resembles the yes-yes technique but uses acts instead of words to lead the persuadee to the final request. Persuaders can use it with neutral or negative audiences. We need to watch ourselves as we make commitments. It is possible that we are being led to a major decision that is not the one we would make if it were the only thing we had to decide.

Ask More, So They Settle for Less

This tactic tries to set a price or level in people's minds that is higher than what the source really wants; when the persuader backs off, the buyers or voters feel as if they are getting a special offer. For example, suppose I bring in a set of test scores to my class and write on the chalkboard the curve that the computer suggests. Now I pass back the answer sheets; students moan because the curve is so high. Then I say that since I am so kind and sweet, I am making my own curve. I write it on the board, and it is a lower curve. Students cheer and sigh with relief. Then I tell them that the one-to-three-point essay can be added on without changing the curve. I set a high expectation. Then I back off from that high level and though my curve may be stringent, compared with the machine curve, I am Santa Claus. Government officials often use this tactic as they ask for more appropriations than they expect they will get. The whole sales field is built on the notion of giving prices that you can mark down.

Persuaders can use this tactic when they have a product or goal that is hard to sell. Better to ask for more than your audience will stand for, so that in compromising, you will persuade. Audiences need to watch for this tactic and test the source's real bottom line.

Planting

The device called **planting** uses one of the five senses to open a channel to the memory. We want the target group or person to recall our product, idea, or candidate. Memory responds best, it seems, to messages that have sense data as raw material. Thus the key factors are sight, sound, smell, taste, and feel. For instance, take the classic series of ads for bathroom tissue. Which is the softest tissue on the shelves? Why, of course it is Charmin. How do we know this and what makes us respond as one to the question? The source cleverly used the sense of touch to plant the Charmin message in our minds. We know that Mr. Whipple is always caught red-handed squeezing the stuff because it is so soft. The appeal to the sense of touch and the unique personage of Mr. Whipple created a long-lasting image in our minds. The source could appeal to the sense of smell instead. Then Mr. Whipple would be caught sniffing the packages of perfume-laden Charmin. Or the sense of sight might be used as Mr. Whipple is dazzled by the bright whites of Charmin. Candidates try to relate with audiences by referring to their local foods, reminding them that they have eaten Iowa corn or Maine lobster. Sight is also used. The candidate tells of the beauty of the Blue Ridge country. Sound might be useful if a candidate mentioned the deafening sounds of the drop forge to steel-workers. In each situation, the senses would be the key factor in getting the message planted in the voter's memory. In informal contexts, how might you make your points "stick" by using the tactic of planting?

Getting an I.O.U.

Sometimes called the swap or trade-off tactic, the technique of getting an I.O.U. aims to get your listeners to feel as if they owe you something. For instance, the insurance rep spends several hours doing a complex assets and debts analysis for a buyer. The goal is to prove to the buyer that he or she needs more insurance. The sales rep then spends hours explaining the figures to the husband and wife, perhaps taking them out to lunch or dinner. By the end of all the special treat-ment, the couple may feel that they really *ought* to buy something, even though they may not need it or cannot afford it. They need to cancel out the obligation— the I.O.U.—that was built. Hare Krishna members used this tactic at airports until police made them stop. They were giving away a costly book that details their beliefs. If you took the "free" book, you felt duty-bound to listen to the Krishna pitch. After all, they had been nice enough to give you the "gift." Many door-to-door sales schemes use the same tactic. The seller may give you a vegetable brush, a sample of hand lotion, a plastic letter opener, or a set of steak knives to force you into an I.O.U. In order to clear the debt, you feel obligated to listen to the pitch. Ads sometimes include offers that try to build the swap or I.O.U. tactic.

Persuaders find this tactic useful when it is hard to make a first contact with buyers, voters, or joiners. We need to note when a source tries to get us into debt through free gifts, samples, or offers of help. The old adage that "there's no such thing as a free lunch" is a pretty good warning in our doublespeak world. All these techniques and others offer sources many routes to success when the goal is to persuade others to action. As you develop your skills to persuade, you can try some of the tactics cited here and some of the others that you will meet. As a persuadee, you need to observe these and other tactics in use, often in sales but also in advertising and politics.

A Review and Conclusion

We all have to persuade at some point. The problem we have when we try to persuade is that we are careless when we go at it. We do not spend enough time planning how our format will affect the message. We do not often spend much time developing our forms of support and thinking about which would be most useful. We do not spend enough time trying to control factors in delivery. We need to use *source factors* like posture, eye contact, and so forth. *Channel factors* are subject to our control. *Receiver factors* can be used to get the target group involved in its own persuasion. As you are called on to persuade, use these skills in preparing. Rely on the kind of audience analysis that the receiver-oriented approach teaches—listen to your audience in order to *get messages out of them, not into them.*

Questions for Further Thought

1. Where does humor fit into the persuasion process? Give examples of sources who use humor. Does it relate to the audience? How?

2. What are the demographic factors you can locate for the people in your class? In your dorm? In your church? Elsewhere?

3. What is a task-oriented message? Give examples from ads in which persuaders have done a good job of this. Where have they failed?

4. What are the forms of organization discussed above? How do they differ from the forms of support? What might be other ways to organize a message?

5. What are the factors in credibility? Name a person who really has each of them. Find an ad that relies on each of them. Share these in class.

6. What factors in delivery are most often used by our President when he wants to persuade? By your teacher? By your parents? By your special friends? What factors are not useful with these people?

Experiences in Persuasion

1. Attend a persuasive meeting on your campus. There are numbers of them—Campus Crusade, transcendental meditation, political rallies, and so forth. Identify the demographic profile of the audience. See if the persuader seems to be sensing the same things you do. Study the speaker's organization, forms of support, style, and delivery. Focus on strengths and weaknesses. Report back to the class on your experience.

2. Do the same thing as in project 1 above, but for a set of magazine ads (for example, the Pepsi ads as they run in different magazines).

3. Buy a magazine that you usually do not read. Carefully look at the ads, at the letters to the editor, at the articles, at the cover, at the editorials, and at the features. Judging from these things, describe the target audience.

4. View a TV program you do not often watch. Using factors like the spots tied to the show, type of program, complexity of plot, development of character or setting, and so forth, describe the target audience.

5. Identify a persuasive presentation that you will face (for example, the job interview). Go through the steps outlined here—analyze your target, consider format, locate sources of support, work on style, plan your delivery. Prepare a report on your project or actually try to persuade.

6. Become a print persuader by writing a letter to the editor of your campus or home-town paper. Go through the steps outlined in this chapter and in project 5 above. Send the letter off to the paper.

9
Modern Media and Persuasion

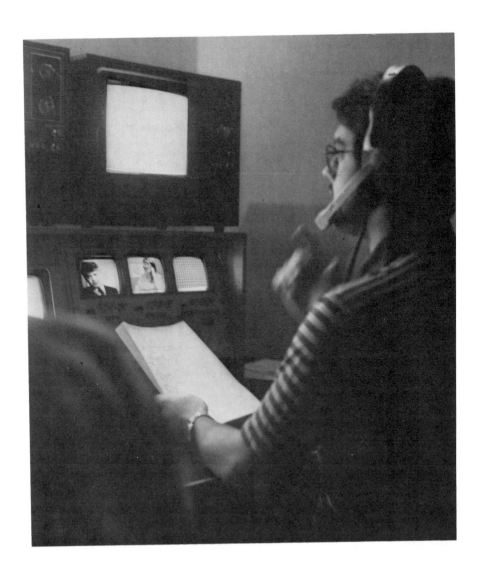

So far, there have been four major communication innovations in the history of humankind. Each of them was momentous; it shaped and changed the world and the destiny of humanity forever after. Each permitted us to view the world in new ways and to interact with one another in new ways. Each of these communication innovations involved the use of a new medium of communication.

Media Innovations

The Spoken Word

While we were still only *hominoids*, or humanlike creatures, grunts and gestures were our only means of communicating. Over thousands of years, we were able to develop the first communication innovation in human history—the power to speak and to symbolize. That permitted humanity to gather into groups or tribes. Speech also allowed us to develop labor specialization, rituals and religions, and a history, even if it was embodied only in myths, ballads, and legends.

We can sense the immense power of this development in the reverence with which the spoken word is held in most religions and in our everyday lives. For example, in the Book of Genesis, the story of the Creation indicates that with each creative act, God *spoke*. The *speaking* was the catalyst for the creation of night and day; earth and seas; fishes, animals, and birds; and ultimately man and woman. Later in the Old Testament, God again *speaks* to various characters— Jacob, Moses, and David. In the New Testament, almost all of Christ's miracles are brought about by His *speaking* some words, and Christ is also referred to as the "Word made flesh." In our daily social life, this religious attitude toward the spoken word continues. We must be sworn in to *testify*, or to *speak* to the court. At baptisms, the child's name must be *spoken*. At weddings, the vows must be *said*. The judge must *speak* the sentence before the defendant can be taken to jail. And even at death we *speak* words of absolution and commit the body to the grave using the *spoken* word.

The Written Word

The next major communication innovation was the development of the phonetic alphabet or an alphabet tied to *speech* sounds and not an ideographic one tied to vision. It had equally profound effects. With the alphabet, one could collect knowledge and store it. Advances of various kinds could be based on these stored records of what others had tried to do and how. The written word allowed us to develop complex legal systems and to assign or deed land and other possessions. That led to the centralization of power. Knowledge was power, and it was obtained and held by those who controlled the written word—kings, emperors, popes, and conquerors.

The written word also allowed us to organize nations rather than tribes. Consider what happened to the American Indians when they confronted a society that controlled the written word. They signed away land and belongings through treaties that they thought were "worthless pieces of paper" because the Indians relied on the spoken word.

The Printed Word

The third major communication innovation was the invention of printing in the late 1400s. The effects of spreading the power of the written word to the common people were immense. Within a short time, the release of this power led to the Renaissance. Because information could be spread and shared, science developed out of alchemy and astrology. Scientists could read about one another's work and build on what others had done. Such knowledge was no longer limited to clerics. Religion itself was greatly affected by the printing press. Before printing was developed, religious documents had to be hand-copied by monks whose life's work may have been to produce one single copy of, say, the Bible. With the printed word, many copies could be made fairly quickly, and the chance of error, once galley pages had been properly proofed, was essentially nil. An added advantage was that the printed word was much cheaper than the written word. Thus it could be shared widely. It is likely that the Reformation was dependent on the printed word. Luther's objections to the Roman Catholic Church could be printed up and distributed. The words of Wesley and Calvin could likewise be disseminated. Thus the power of the word that had been held by the Catholic Church was diluted. This led to the inevitable splits that ultimately led to Protestantism. Governments were not immune to the power of the printed word, either. Soon they had to legislate against careless printing of critical tracts.

In the Thirteen Colonies, the British delegated the responsibility for censorship to the publishers and printers of newspapers, leaflets, or books. In the famous John Peter Zenger case, Zenger (who was the printer of statements critical of the colonial Governor Cosby) was accused of criminal libel against the government. He had not even written the critical articles. He had merely printed them. Curiously, a similarity exists today in the use of the photographic copier. Copyright laws may be infringed if an unauthorized copy of a book page or magazine article is made. The person held responsible, however, is not necessarily the person who asked that the copy be made—a teacher, for example. Instead it is the person who *operates* the photocopier who is responsible for protecting copyrights—a secretary or student, perhaps.

However, the power of the printed word has diminished to some degree. While the number of newspapers published in the United States has risen since the advent of radio and television, readership of newspapers and newsmagazines is down. Though we have a cliché saying that people "will believe it when they see it in print," no one wanted the White House's *printed* version of the Watergate tapes. Instead, groups sued for the right to *hear* the *spoken words* on tapes themselves.

The Electronic Word

The electronic word begins in 1844 with the first demonstration of the telegraph and continues up to the present, with new advances being made almost daily. The telegraph converted written words into electrical impulses that turned a telegrapher's key on and off, thus allowing words to be sent as a series of dots and dashes. Then, in 1876, came the telephone, which transformed the spoken word into electronic impulses. Shortly thereafter came the radio or wireless telegraph, which transformed written and later spoken words into electronically produced sound waves.

More recently we have had television (which transforms written and spoken words into electronic words and pictures) and the computer (which transforms written and spoken words and numbers into electronic impulses of "on" and "off" much like the telegraph). All these electronic words had and continue to have immense impact on society. For example, consider video games. As of this writing, the city of Chicago is considering an ordinance that would make it *illegal* for anyone under age eighteen to play any electronic game that requires money. The reason? Parents and educators are concerned that Chicago schoolchildren spend their lunch money at electronic game emporiums. Further, they say, these games are highly addictive. (Imagine what a clever advertiser could do with these games. Before being permitted to play "Astro-Space Shoot-Down" for free, you could be required to watch a commercial for a product on the screen and answer several questions about the product.)

Likewise, many people are concerned over the amount of television being watched each day by the average American child. We worry about the effects of violence on television. We wonder if America's youth may go prematurely deaf because of the volume used on stereo sets and radios. And people regularly complain about the way society is becoming depersonalized by electronic technology like the computer.

Continual innovations spell more changes in our way of doing things. It is now possible to circumvent AT&T's long-time monopoly on long-distance phone calls by means of commercial computer/satellite linkages by which your long-distance call is in effect a local call at less than the AT&T rates. Many people are investing considerable money in cable television linkages, their own video cameras, and devices for recording off the air. George Lucas, the originator and producer of *Star Wars* and its sequels, vows that he will soon by-pass the Hollywood system by producing all his films by computer and satellite technology. This saves expensive studio time, and most important, it avoids the tightly held distribution system that the studios maintain. Lucas says he will make the facilities of his Skywalker Ranch, his own computer, and perhaps a private satellite available to young film-makers for experimental work. This may revolutionize the film industry and certainly promises that the average American citizen will be faced with new options for his or her leisure time. Surely it is necessary for us as receivers of persuasive messages to take a close look at the use of modern media in persuasion.

The most common kind of persuasion that we receive is advertising—in TV and radio spot commercials and in print ads. As noted before, most college freshmen have seen more than 22,000 hours of TV programming.[1] We live in a world in which media messages are common. The careful receiver needs to be alert to ways in which advertisers use the power of the media to achieve their goals. Researchers have only started to study the processes by which we receive and use media in our lives. Results are either speculative or sketchy. One thing is clear, however, and that is that the mass media are the most effective ways to persuade people of certain things. Mass media persuade us to buy products, to vote, and to take up causes. Why is this? One reason may be that since there is no real feedback in mass message systems (you cannot question, applaud, or respond), certain ploys work here that will not work in an open arena. In this chapter we will look at ways in which media may work. We will also discuss some common appeals that lend themselves to mass media. These should begin to alert you to the doublespeak that is used when persuaders employ mass media.

Schwartz's Perspectives on Media Use

We have mentioned Tony Schwartz in an earlier chapter. His theory and book *The Responsive Chord*[2] have both been used by sources ranging from a presidential media staff to hundreds of firms and ad agencies selling anything from baby powder to barrels of booze. He offers two competing models of the way media work to persuade. The **evoked recall** or **resonance model** is one, and the *transportation* or *teaching* model is the other. Schwartz favors the first approach and offers reasons why.

The evoked recall or resonance approach works on the idea that it is better to get a message out of receivers than to try to put one into them. In other words, it relies on the set of experiences and memories that people have stored in themselves. The basic tactic in getting these data out is to cue them in some way. Using this approach, persuaders might want to think of the kinds of problems people have with, say, a stalled car. Often a stall occurs when we are most rushed. The stall is sometimes a result of some minor bit of repair that we neglected. Maybe it was ice in the gas line or a dirty air filter. Knowing that the potential buyer of the product—an AAA membership—has been through at least one stall, the source

1. David Burmeister, "The Language of Deceit" in *Language and Public Policy*, ed. by Hugh Rank (Urbana, Illinois: National Council of Teachers of English, 1974), p. 40.

2. Tony Schwartz, *The Responsive Chord* (Garden City: Anchor Press/Doubleday, 1973). See also his recent book, *Media: The Second God* (New York: Random House, 1981).

can build a message around the feelings you have when your car stalls. Actors in an ad can show frustration. They can signal the anxiety you felt when you knew that the stall would make you late. The music or score can heighten the feelings. The voice-over can come on in a soothing way at the end to say, "When you've got to be there, AAA gets you there." Schwartz observes that most experiential meaning is not cued symbolically since it is not stored as a symbol. Instead it is stored as a feeling—a sense of ease or dis-ease. The best way to cue these feelings out is drama. The source acts out the feeling in the listener's head. Many times the cueing is done by music, color, sound effects, the actors' facial expressions or tone of voice, the acoustics, or some other message. So, we need to be aware of the many messages that are coming at us at the same time. They are prompting messages out of us.

The Verbal Script

Of course, Schwartz's idea runs counter to what many ad agencies believe. It is also counter to much of the theory about persuasion that emphasizes being specific, logical, and clever with words. That view looks only at the verbal script, which *is* the message. Ad agencies test their ads, and do just that. They ask people to look at ads and then to respond by recalling the words, numbers, and names that are in the ad. Rarely are viewers asked about their feelings or about the characters in the ads. It is often a quirk of fate that brings out data like the people who resented their suitcase because it survived a plane crash.

The Sound Script

The TV spot is more than just its verbal script. It includes a sound script—things you hear that are not words. For instance, the good feelings we have about keg parties can be cued out by the sounds of a keg being tapped. As we hear the thunk of the tap being punched through the cork, the spin of the wing nut bolting down the tap, and the gurgle of the first mug being filled, the good times come back. Then it is fairly easy to add words: "We've got beer in a can that's as good as beer from a keg—Hamm's Draft in the new aluminum can." The can is shaped like a barrel or keg to reinforce the good feelings most people have about past keg parties. So the sound script can be a key means of cueing feelings out.

The Sight Script

The sight script is also important as a source of such cues. The sight of the beer can in a keglike shape is a good example, as is the packing of certain cleansers in drum-shaped bottles to give the feeling of heavy-duty power. There are other ways by which the sight script can cue feelings out of us. Camera angle often has a cueing value. A low angle that "looks up" to the leader distorts size somewhat and "says" that this person is one to be looked up to—a cut above most people. A wide-angle shot with crowds of people thronging to see the leader and shouting salutes sends the message that this is a great leader of a great movement. Hitler used this technique in the famous Nazi propaganda film *Triumph of the Will.* It was outlawed in Germany for many years after World War II because of its power to raise the emotions and feelings. Close-up or zoom-in shots of people "say" that we need to get a closer look, to find out what kind of stuff they are made of and what sort of people they are. Editing can call out feelings, which can then be used to persuade. Many news films of battle situations depend on clever editing to build a sense of action. They use quick cuts from one action shot to another. Tanks shoot across the screen. Then we cut to planes diving. Then we cut to troops running across a field firing all the way, and so on. The quick cut makes the viewer feel that there is a lot of effective action. It looks like "the good guys" are making raceway progress across the land of "the bad guys." Of course anyone in the Army knows the truth in the old maxim about the Army's way of doing things—hurry up and wait. The quick cut can build the same kind of sense of action in other contexts. We see a snowmobile leaping across the screen and cutting through a snowdrift. Then we cut to a downhill racer carving a trail in new snow. We are ready to hear about "Lake Geneva—where winter isn't going to get you down."

Other aspects of the sight script keep getting messages out of us. Many newscasts convey a newsroom atmosphere. The teletypes clatter, people rush around the set carrying pieces of paper meant to be news flashes, and so on. The network anchor persons are then superimposed on the set from another studio giving the visual impression that they are in the middle of the hustle and bustle. You get the impression that you won't miss any news if you stay tuned to that channel. The background shots for political candidates can be part of the sight script and can prompt out feelings, too.[3] The same thing happens on spot ads and even entertainment programs. Feelings are cued out of viewers through the background setting. These and many more elements in a visual script can be used to evoke or recall feelings, the real stuff of persuasion, according to Schwartz. As we receive media messages, we need to be alert to the verbal script or the substance of the message, and also to the sound and sight scripts and their varied messages—the messages of color, camera angle and movement, background, sound effects, and musical score.[4]

McLuhan's Perspective on Media Use

Marshall McLuhan was another theorist who studied media use in our times. His ideas in many ways are like those of Schwartz. In fact, the two were friends and often drew on one another for examples and insights. McLuhan felt that we relate to media in two ways. First, every medium is an extension of one of our senses or body parts.[5] Second, media can change our way of thinking about our world. For example, the telegraph gave people the idea that they could communicate quickly across long distances. There is some reason to believe that this perception caused several key miscalculations just before the declaration of war in

3. For some interesting examples see David L. Swanson's "And That's the Way It Was?"—Television Covers the 1976 Presidential Campaign," *Quarterly Journal of Speech*. Vol. 63 (October 1977), p 245.

4. A fuller discussion of how to criticize those elements is found in "Media Metaphors: Two Perspectives for the Rhetorical Criticism of TV Commercials," Charles U. Larson, *Central States Speech Journal* (Fall 1972).

5. For a full discussion of these ideas, see *Understanding Media: The Extensions of Man*, by Marshall McLuhan (New York: Signet Books, 1964).

1914. Ultimatums were sent by telegraph with the assumption that diplomats could travel equally fast. The invention of the wireless helped bring David Sarnoff, past president of NBC, to power. As a young man, he was broadcasting from high atop a hotel on the night the *Titanic* struck an iceberg and slowly sank. He served as a key middleman between important people aboard the ship and their families, business associates, and attorneys. Essential directions about where wills were located, what to buy and sell, and so on were exchanged through Sarnoff.

Television led to the eyewitness coverage of events, to quiz shows and quiz show scandals, to the Muppets (today's equivalent to Walt Disney's world of animation), and to the two-minute drill in football. And of course the home computer has led to a myriad of changes in the way we look at our lives. McLuhan said that often the media themselves are the real messages.

One of the ways in which media tend to affect the way we look at our lives, according to McLuhan, is by their *form* or *fidelity*. Some media signals come to us in a complete, high-fidelity form. Others come to us in an incomplete or low-fidelity form. The high-fidelity forms require little of us in assembling the signals into complete messages. The low-fidelity forms require us to use our senses and to convert incomplete signals into complete messages. The telegraph would be such an incomplete, low-fidelity form or signal, whereas the radio would be less so. The same message sent on the two forms would be different, according to McLuhan. The high-fidelity form, by requiring little participation, would result in *little physiological* or *sensory* involvement. The low-fidelity form, requiring much participation, would result in *high physiological* or *sensory* participation. McLuhan called the high-fidelity or complete message signals "hot" and the low-fidelity or incomplete messages "cool."

Hot Media

As we have noted, "hot" refers to media and messages that have high fidelity or definition. These media are easy to perceive. Their images are well drawn or recorded. We do not have to work to get the image or the sound. It is sort of like the difference between the old wind-up phonograph that scratched out the sounds of the 1920s and the quad sound that makes you feel as if you are right in the middle of the orchestra. The quad set-up is hot because it has high fidelity or definition. It is easy to perceive. Messages have the same kind of quality. Hot messages are clear, distinct, easy to understand or get. We do not have to work at them. A good example might be the advertiser who comes on during the late movie and tries the hard sell about three rooms of carpeting for only $599.99. The message is distinct and comes through crystal clear. This is a hot message. Or consider the hot politician who comes on strong and does not pull any punches but blurts out his message in simple words. Ronald Reagan would be an example of a hot speaker appealing in a kind of gut-level language. It has often turned many voters off, though it does appeal to certain sets of people. This is the kind of politician who, Schwartz says, will "blow out" viewer fuses. Howard Cosell, the controversial but able sportscaster, does not seem to be a very pleasant guy. He is a hot message, too. The persuader presents hot messages by means of both hot and cool media, and conflicts occur. McLuhan says that TV is not a hot medium since it has such low fidelity. Only half the screen is active at any moment. Half the lines are on and half are off at any moment. Now we put Howard Cosell on TV, the cool medium. Who should appear with him? Would you pick another hot person or a cool one? *Monday Night Football* seems to suggest that a cool one works best. Dandy Don Merideth and Frank Gifford have been matched with Cosell—perhaps to cool down Howard's hot personality. When Cosell hosted his own cool variety show without any co-host, it flopped. Yet he seems to antagonize other hot figures like Alex Karras or Fran Tarkenton.

Cool Media

Conversely, cool media have low fidelity or definition. We have to work to process these messages. We have to put together the half-images we see on TV. We have to imagine a lot of sound quality into the wind-up Victrola. Low-fidelity sounds come out of a telephone. What kinds of messages are best for these media? McLuhan says that cool media breed cool messages, or messages that are vague and ill defined. He saw the politician of the TV-dominated future being abstract, fuzzy, shaggy around the edges. There is no need for this type to say everything at gut level. Instead, this type lets the voter fill in or put together a meaning or image. If McLuhan is right, we should have seen a growth in image politics since the theory was first presented in 1964. Until 1980, that is exactly what happened. The politicians who seem to catch on are those with an easy-going approach. They are abstract to the voter, not distinct. Likewise we ought to be seeing more TV commercials that rely less on words or scripts than on giving a mood or feeling. Then viewers can add to or subtract from what they watch to get a final meaning. Think of the many commercials that do this through the use of music or sets or lighting. We hear the sounds of a Broadway-musical love ballad. Then we see a well-dressed man and woman slowly walking down the stairs at the opera house. The man asks the doorman to signal for his car. Up drives a Volkswagen Rabbit. Only then do we hear the voice-over tell us that the "VW is in good taste anytime, anywhere." We fill in or add to the message we have received.

So, in today's world, we need to be alert to how we add to cool media and cool messages. We need to note the media mix that results when hot media carry cool messages and vice versa. Being aware—even if it is only on a part-time basis—can help us to sense doublespeak in the mass-media world. Refer to Table 9.1 for examples of hot and cool media.

Table 9.1 Hot and Cool Media

Medium	Source of information	Definition	Participation	Type of medium
Television	Lighted dots	Low	High	Cool
Books	Completed letters	High	Low	Hot
Cartoons	Dots on paper	Low	High	Cool
Photographs	Image on film	High	Low	Hot
Telephone	Low-fidelity sound wave	Low	High	Cool
Movie	Moving image on film	High	Low	Hot
Telegraph	Dots and dashes in sound	Low	High	Cool
Stereo	High-fidelity sound wave	High	Low	Hot

So, whether we look at our media-filled world from the Schwartz or McLuhan perspective, it is clear that modern media have great persuasive impact through words, sight, and sound. As receivers we need to remember that we are being appealed to in highly sophisticated ways. Let's explore some of these tactics, looking at how words and claims can deceive us.

Language Use in Media: Wrighter's Model

We have been looking at how the media work with images. This focus ignores the use of words in media messages. We know that symbols are the basic raw material of persuasion. We know words are central carriers of symbolic meaning. So we need to look at how clever persuaders can use words and at how these work in mass-media messages. Carl Wrighter, a former adman, in his book *I Can Sell You Anything*[6] focuses on some of the key words that he thinks are used to deceive us. He calls them *weasel words* because they allow the persuaders to seem to say something without ever really saying it. These words let sources weasel their way out of a promise. Let us look at a few of these. They are key tip-offs to the kind of pitch we need to guard against.

"Helps"

The word helps is a clever one. It seems to offer aid or perhaps even a cure. We hear that Listerine mouthwash *helps* prevent colds. Even if you get a cold, it *helps* you feel better right away. What is the promise here? Can you expect that you will feel better in a few days if you use Listerine? If you did, could you say your improvement was due to the *help* Listerine gave? These questions point up the problem with a word like helps. We need to be alert to this often-used weasel word. Ads for products use it. Politicians promise that they will *help* get this country moving again. Those who try to advance a certain idea or ideology promise that boycotting a certain chain store will *help* establish new hiring policies that will include minorities.

"Like"

Another weasel word used in mass-media ads is the word like. For instance, there on the TV screen is poor Mrs. Housewife. Her house is so dingy and drab. She wonders if hubby will come home or will he go out with the boys instead? Then out of a bottle of floor and wall cleaner comes a white tornado. We hear that Kleenstuf cleans *like* a white tornado. Now how does a tornado of any color clean? Does it scrub, brush, mop, or scour? Further, do white tornadoes clean better or worse than red ones? You can easily see the deception that can be floated with a word that has as many loopholes as the word like. In newscasts, we hear that this or that event is *like* some event in the past. Brooke Shields is supposed to be *like* young women all over the world. Soap operas claim to be *like* real life.

Perhaps that is the secret key to so many of the words we see and hear in

---

6. Carl Wrighter, *I Can Sell You Anything* (New York: Ballantine Books, 1972).

print and broadcast ads. They are loaded with escape hatches so they can promise without really giving. Think of the many promises that are given with the word *like*. A certain stereo component will create sound that will make your listening moments almost *like* being there. A prepared food tastes just *like* homemade. A jug wine tastes *like* the expensive French wines. A facial cream acts *like* "a thousand busy fingers massaging your face." Geritol will make you feel *like* you are a kid again. A K-car hugs the road *like* a cat.

"Virtually"

The weasel word virtually resembles like except that it seems to promise even more. The new cotton chamois shirts are *virtually* indestructible. Anyone want to bet?—try putting them into the furnace or through the table saw. Leatherette feels *virtually* like cowhide. As noted earlier, Cascade leaves your dishes and glassware *virtually* spotless. The promise seems so specific. There is only a tiny loophole. That loophole widens as much as is needed when the consumer says that the chamois shirt wore out after several months' wear or when we find out there are a few spots here and there on the dishes and stemware. If the product did what is claimed, the word virtually would not be needed. The same thing applies to the politicians who ask for support for their programs that will *virtually* wipe out discrimination. This weasel word appears in fund appeals, too. The fund is *virtually* within sight of its goal for the new year, so give a little more.

"As Much As"

The weasel words as much as tell you *the most* you can expect from a product and then suggest that *the most* will be everyday. Many thought that the policy of publishing Environmental Protection Agency (EPA) mileage estimates in every auto ad would assure honesty. The estimates were what you could expect under best conditions—perfect roads, good weather, fine tuning of the engine, and so forth. You were promised *as much as* 38 miles per gallon in city driving in a Dodge Colt, but you were not *promised* 38 miles per gallon.

A politician promises to cut taxes by *as much as* 20 percent. We find that this applies to few people. The newscast says there will be *as much as* 10 inches of snow. We hear that *as much as* 40 percent of the town was destroyed. All these uses of this weasel phrase aim to maximize the drama of the promise or event to get us to fall for the flimflam.

"Stronger," "Faster," or "Better": The Dangling Comparison

"Anacin fights pain *better* than ordinary aspirin." The impact of that claim lies in the comparison being made. What we are *not* told is how much better or better in what ways. The makers of Anacin might answer, "One tenth of one percent better." They could say ". . . better because it melts quickly." However, they persuade us because the message limits our options. We can compare Anacin only with all other *ordinary* aspirins. In what way are they ordinary? Instead of having a choice of ten we now have a choice between two: Anacin and the others. So the weaseling has two effects. It intensifies the advantages of one brand. At the same time, it limits the options that we consider. The candidate says that a program for health insurance is *better*. All other programs are lumped into a single category just as Anacin does with all ordinary aspirin tablets.

"Everyone" says that we have a *better* system of government. In what ways? Compared with what? These are the questions to ask. Entertainment programs imply that it is *better* to be sexy, rich, into sports, and so on. Why? In what ways? Compared with what?

Wrighter discusses several other weasel words in his book. You will be able to identify many others as you focus on media messages. A good way to find them is to search for words that sound like promises. They often have loopholes—"Feels like . . ." or "It is literally . . ." or "Can be effective in . . ." or "Easier than . . ." and many others. Sometimes the "faster," "stronger," or "easier" message is only implied, as we see that car number one can travel *farther* than car number two using the same amount of gasoline in the demonstration. Or we see two cars trying to stop on wet pavement, and the one with the Uniroyal radials stops *faster* than the other. In these cases we have the dangling comparison. We really don't know what is being compared with what (Figure 9.1). We need to ask key questions like "Under what conditions is Product X better, stronger, faster, or safer?" to dig out the key information that will help us make our purchase decisions. A good classroom activity is to identify claims such as those discussed above and write to the manufacturer asking the key questions or requesting the details of their advertised "test results." We need to be alert not only to weasel words but also to other uses of language that imply a promise while hiding a loophole.

Deceptive Claims in Media

Another kind of deception to which we are exposed in media ads is found in the claims that are made. We discussed content claims in Chapter 5 and spent most of our time looking at how the claim was supported and at the logic behind it. Now we need to focus on the wording of the claim. Clever sources use claims to attract our attention and to prompt us to buy, to vote, or to adopt certain practices. Let us look at several kinds of such claims.[7]

The Irrelevant Claim

Some persuaders use media messages to make claims that sound impressive but are really irrelevant if you look at them closely.

You will be exposed to such claims whenever you turn on your TV, open a magazine, or tune in your radio. The basic tactic is to make a truthful claim that has little to do with the purpose of our product, plan for change, or idea. Then we dramatize that claim in such a way that the people link the claim with our product, candidate, or movement. The key to spotting such a claim as that of Figure 9.2 is to ask yourself why you would want to have quality X? Why, for instance, would you want to have a Jensen Quadrax in your car? Of course it is a fine sound system, but would you really trade a Rolls Royce for it? That's what the ad implies.

---

7. See Wrighter, Chapter 3, "A Baker's Dirty Dozen of Claims," pp. 41–76.

Figure 9.1. The dangling comparison. Twenty-two percent more than what? (Used courtesy Kawasaki Motors Corp., U.S.A.)

J&B scotch claims to be "rare" and "natural." Why would you want "rare" Scotch? What is "natural" about J&B? Are other Scotch whiskeys unnatural? If you can't find an answer, chances are you have identified an irrelevant claim.

The Question Claim

Wrighter notes a kind of claim we often see beamed at us through the media. This is the claim that is hidden by a question. "If you can't trust Prestone, who can you trust?" "Why not buy the original?" "Why not send the very best?" "Would a bunch of guys really go at it this hard just for a Michelob?" "Why not catch a lunker—with Stren monofilament?" These are all examples of the question claim. Notice that the product advantage is only implied. Trusting one's antifreeze is OK, but the question implies that dependability is *only* to be found in Prestone. But we know that other brands of antifreeze are also dependable. Why buy the original? It may be overpriced. Maybe the volleyball or hockey players are going at it for fun, and the Michelob is just an afterthought. Will using Stren guarantee that I'll catch a lunker? When you see or hear a question claim, the best response is another question.

The Advantage Claim

Wrighter noted the claim that seems to offer some advantage for a product or idea. Mother's noodles claim to be fortified in a certain way. This is a supposed advantage over all other brands. We are asked to assume that fortification with vitamins is good and that it is exclusive to the Mother's product. Neither of these assumptions is 100-percent true. Government regulations force all product sellers

Figure 9.2. The question is, "Wouldn't you *really* rather have a Rolls?" (Used courtesy Jansen Sound Laboratories.)

to fortify certain foods. Compare the levels of vitamins in several types of breakfast cereal. You will discover that they are all about the same. Most of the nutritional value comes from the milk and not the cereal. Thus there is no advantage in Corn Chex's claim that they are "Fortified with 6 Important Vitamins and Minerals!" These are advantages that aren't.

Politicians often claim to have come from humble beginnings, and this is supposed to be an advantage. Perhaps this myth goes back to the legends about Abraham Lincoln being born in a log cabin and rising to greatness. Humility may be a virtue, but it is by no means guaranteed by humble beginnings. What's more, this advantage may be a disadvantage. The politician from humble beginnings may have had an inferior education and preparation to be a leader. Lincoln was apparently not a very successful lawyer—his partner Billy Herndon kept their firm afloat. Richard Nixon came from humble beginnings. They may have made him insecure enough to want to win to the point of breaking the law.

The advantage tactic is used in many idea campaigns. The National Organization of Women (NOW) tried for nearly a decade to get the ERA passed in Illinois. Their opponents pointed out that the national amendment was actually weaker than the equal rights clause in the Illinois constitution. Thus the national amendment was not advantageous, they said. The strategy apparently worked, as the amendment never did pass in Illinois.

Whenever we are faced with a person, product, or idea that claims some significant advantage, we need to ask whether the advantage is real; whether it is exclusive to that person, product, or idea; and whether certain disadvantages might not accompany acceptance of that product, or person, or idea.

The Hazy Claim
The hazy claim confuses the buyer or voter. If persuaders can confuse you, you will follow their advice just to be on the safe side. Consider the ad for Dannon yogurt shown in Figure 9.3. It confuses the reader by refusing to promise a chance at long life and then by making the promise that there might be a chance after all. As you read more of the ad copy, you see that the only health claim Dannon can make is that their yogurt, unlike some others (how many? off brands? so what?), has active cultures. The consumer does not know whether it is good to eat Dannon yogurt, yogurt of any kind, or no yogurt. Out of this confusion, Dannon persuades through its slogan: "If you don't always eat right, Dannon yogurt is the right thing to eat." We ought to ask "Why is it right?" "Who says?" and "With what proof?" when a hazy claim appears.

Again, we can see this claim widely used in the world of politics. A politician says that he supports the economic policies of free trade and protective tariffs. These policies are 180 degrees apart. The result for voters is confusion. If voters watch images, the problem becomes worse. What does it prove if a politician kisses babies or plays baseball or talks about the price of pork? These activities do not tell us much about an elected official's ability to construct policies on education, leisure time, or farm prices. They are likely to confuse the voter and draw attention away from the issues. The unclear or hazy claim leaves you not really sure what is being claimed because the source is never clear about it. This is designed to draw attention away from the real nature of the product or candidate.

The Magic Claim
Wrighter calls this the mysterious claim because it refers to a mysterious ingredient or device that makes a better product. I prefer the idea of magic instead because most of these ingredients or devices are not touted as spooky or myste-

Dannon Yogurt may not help you live as long as Soviet Georgians. But it couldn't hurt.

Bagrat Topagua, age 89.

His mother.

There are two curious things about the people of Soviet Georgia. A large part of their diet is yogurt. And a large number of them live to be well over 100.

Of course, many factors affect longevity, and we are not saying Dannon Yogurt will help you live longer. But we will say that all-natural Dannon is high in nutrients, low in fat, reasonable in calories. And quite satisfying at lunch or as a snack.

Another thing about Dannon. It contains active yogurt cultures (many pre-mixed or

Swiss style brands don't). They make yogurt one of the easiest foods to digest and have been credited with other healthful benefits.

Which is why we've been advising this: If you don't always eat right, Dannon Yogurt is the right thing to eat.

By the way, Bagrat Topagua thought Dannon was "dzelian kargia." Which means he loved it.

Dannon Milk Products, 22-11 38th Ave. Long Island City, N.Y. 11101.

Figure 9.3. The hazy claims about longevity and yogurt may confuse the persuadee enough to try the product to be on the safe side. (Courtesy Dannon Milk Products.)

rious. We are told that there is 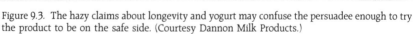 "a magic drop of retsyn in each Clorets tablet." The retsyn is just salad oil that helps bind the tablet together, but the ad implies that retsyn has magic power to destroy bad breath. Or we are told that Shell gasoline has the special stuff called platformate in it, which results in greater mileage. We get a demonstration. Two identical cars are hooked up to bottles of gasoline that contain exactly the same amount of fuel. The two cars are then driven at identical speeds until one runs out of gas and the other goes on farther. Which car had the platformate? You guessed it—the one that went farther. You are told that a certain model's dress should look purple on your TV screen and another's hair should look red and certain flowers shown us by another model should look bronze. If they do not, then you really are not getting the kind of color you deserve. RCA's new color gun can give it to you. It is designed to spread color signals to more of the special receiver modules fixed on an RCA screen. The model flicks a switch and the camera zooms in. Magically the colors are true. The dress is purple. (Cut to next model.) The hair is red. (Cut to next model.) The flowers are true bronze. Surprisingly, the colors are "true" even when you see the ad on your non-RCA set!

The mysterious claim is used by religious evangelists, too. If you really believe and do your converting in our magic way, then you, too, can be saved. That is the standard format for such appeals. Various groups insert their own dogma, relics, or rites. Each touts its own belief in a kind of magical act that yields salvation. Politicians do not usually brag about any magical quality but sometimes create a dramatic atmosphere around one of their ideas. For instance, the President requests prime time from the TV networks. Then we hear his announcement concerning energy. Then a leak reveals that he intends to replace his energy secretary. The tension is built up, but there is nothing magical about replacing a cabinet officer. Or a president or governor announces that he is going to reveal his new plan for economic recovery in a televised address next week. There is much speculation about what it will focus on. Will he increase taxes or cut them? Will he improve the roads or spend more on defense? Will he deregulate some industry or sell off government lands? All the speculation creates a sense of drama. The plan takes on magical qualities, and suspense builds. All the while the politician has center stage to the disadvantage of his opponents. The plan when revealed may not be any better than the last one.

When you hear that something magic will happen if we follow a certain course of action or that there is a secret ingredient in a given product, you can bet that nothing too special exists. If they had a real secret ingredient, they would not tell about it. Spies might find out what it is and sell the recipe to the competition. So if there is turtle oil in a face cream, the oil might be a good binder and not a wrinkle fighter.

Many other kinds of claims are made through the mass media. Wrighter's book points out some. You will discover others as you begin to evaluate the mass-media messages you receive. The important thing is to maintain a critical attitude. Ask key questions of the claim.

Hugh Rank, who originated the intensify/downplay model discussed in Chapter 1, has outlined a five-stage quiz that consumers of persuasion can use to analyze ads, in particular the radio or TV spot. Rank's quiz can be useful in analyzing printed ads as well as political speeches and pitches that ideological persuaders are throwing at us. Rank's "30-Second Quiz" is shown in Figure 9.4. Use this quiz to analyze radio and TV spots as well as printed ads and other "pitches" aimed at you.

the
30-SECOND SPOT
quiz

Based on *The Pitch* © 1982 by Hugh Rank

How to Analyze Ads:
Use this 1-2-3-4-5 sequence of questions, (see next page) to focus
on the *"skeleton"* underneath the *"surface variations"* of radio
and TV commercials, newspaper and magazine ads.

Recognize that a 30-second-spot TV ad is a **synthesis,** the end product of a complex process in which scores of people (writers,
researchers, psychologists, artists, actors, camera crews, etc.)
may have spent months putting together the details. TV commercials are often the best *compositions* of our age, skillful combinations of purposeful words and images. Be patient and systematic:
analysis takes time to sort out all of the things going on at once.
We perceive these things *simultaneously,* but we must discuss
them *sequentially.* Use this 1-2-3-4-5 pattern of "the pitch" as a sequence to start your analysis.

Recognize "surface variations": in 30 seconds, a TV spot may
have 40 quick-cut scenes of "good times" (happy people, sports
fun, drinking cola); or 1 slow "tracking" scene of an old-fashioned
sleighride through the woods, ending at "home" with "Season's
Greetings" from an aerospace corporation; or a three-scene
drama: a problem suffered by some "friend," a product/solution
recommended by a trusted "authority," and a final grateful smile
from the relieved sufferer. But, the structure underneath is
basically the same.

Recognize our own involvement in a mutual transaction. Persuaders are *benefit-promisers,* but we are *benefit-seekers.* Most
ads relate to simple "trade-offs" of mutual benefits: consumers
get a pleasure, producers get a profit. However, investigate
issues relating to any non-consumer ad; these are paid presentations of only one side of an issue, often involving more than a simple purchase transaction.

Understand that advertising is basically persuasion, not information nor education, *And not coercion!* Many important moral and
ethical issues (concerning intent and consequences, priorities, individual and social effects, truth and deception, legal and
regulatory problems) are related. The more we know about the
basic techniques of persuasion, the better able we are not only to
cope with the multiple persuaders in our society, but also to consider these ethical issues.

Figure 9.4. The 30-Second Quiz by Hugh Rank. (Used courtesy of Hugh Rand.)

What ATTENTION-GETTING techniques are used?

Anything unusual? Unexpected? Noticeable? Interesting? Related to:

☐ **senses:** motions, colors, lights, sounds, music, visuals (e.g., computer graphics, slow-motion)

☐ **emotions:** any associations *(see list below):* sex, scenery, exciting action, fun, family, pets.

☐ **thought:** news, lists, displays, claims, advice, questions, stories, demonstrations, contest.
(*Popular TV* **programs** *function as* attention-getters *to "deliver the audience" to advertisers.)*

What CONFIDENCE-BUILDING techniques are used?

☐ Do you *recognize, know* (from earlier repetition) the **brand name? company? symbol? package?**

☐ Do you *already know, like,* and *trust* the **"presenters"**: the endorsers, actors, models?

☐ Are these "presenters" **AUTHORITY FIGURES** (expert, wise, protective, caring,)? Or, are they **FRIEND FIGURES** (someone you like, like to be, "on your side'"; incl. "cute" cartoons) ?

☐ What key **words** are used? (*Trust, sincere,* etc.) **Nonverbals?** *(smiles, voice tones, sincere look)*

☐ In **mail** ads, are computer-written *"personalized"* touches used? On **telephone:** tapes? scripts?

What DESIRE-STIMULATING techniques are used?

(Main part of ad)

Consider (a) **"target audience"** as (b) **benefit-seeking;** and persuaders benefit-promising strategies as focused on (c) **product claims,** or, (d) **"added values"** associated with product.

☐ a. **Who is the "target audience"?** Are *you?* (If *not,* as part of an unintended audience, are you *uninterested* or *hostile* toward the ad?)

☐ b. **What's the primary motive of that audience's benefit-seeking?** Use chart at right. Most ads are simple acquisition *(lower left).* Often, such motives co-exist, but one may be dominant. Ads which intensify a **problem,** (that is, a "bad" already hated or feared; *the opposite, or the absence of,* "goods") and then offer the product as a **solution,** are here called **"scare-and-sell"** ads. *(right side).*

To keep a "good" (protection)	To get rid of a "bad" (relief)
To get a "good" (acquisition)	To avoid a "bad" (prevention)

Figure 9.4. (continued)

☐ c. **What kinds of product claims are emphasized?** *(use these 12 categories)* what key words, images? Any *measurable* claims? Or are they *subjective opinions, generalized* praise words ("puffery")?

SUPERIORITY *("best")*	STABILITY *("classic")*
QUANTITY *("most")*	RELIABILITY *("solid")*
EFFICIENCY *("works")*	SIMPLICITY *("easy")*
BEAUTY *("lovely")*	UTILITY *("practical")*
SCARCITY *("rare")*	RAPIDITY *("fast")*
NOVELTY *("new")*	SAFETY *("safe")*

☐ d. **Are any "added values" implied or suggested?** Are there words or images which associate the product with some "good" already loved or desired by the intended audience? With such common human needs/wants/desires as in these 24 categories:

"basic" needs:
FOOD *("tasty)*
ACTIVITY *("exciting")*
SURROUNDINGS *("comfort")*
SEX *("alluring")*
HEALTH *("healthy")*
SECURITY *("protect")*
ECONOMY *("save")*

"certitude" needs:
RELIGION *("right")*
SCIENCE *("research")*
BEST PEOPLE *("elite")*
MOST PEOPLE *("popular")*
AVERAGE PEOPLE *("typical")*

"territory" needs:
NEIGHBORHOOD *("hometown")*
NATION *("country")*
NATURE *("earth")*

love & belonging needs:
INTIMACY *("lover")*
FAMILY *("Mom" "kids")*
GROUPS *("team")*

"growth" needs:
ESTEEM *("respected")*
PLAY *("fun")*
GENEROSITY *("gift")*
CREATIVITY *("creative")*
CURIOUSITY *("discover")*
COMPLETION *("success")*

Are there URGENCY-STRESSING techniques used?

(Not all ads: but always check.)

☐ If an urgency appeal: What words? *(e.g. Hurry, Rush, Deadline, Sale Ends, Offer Expires, Now.)*
☐ If **no** urgency: is this **"soft sell"** part of a *repetitive, long-term ad campaign* for standard item?

What RESPONSE-SEEKING techniques are used?

Persuaders always seek
some kind of response!)

☐ *Are there specific triggering* words used? (Buy, Get, Do, Call, Act, Join, Smoke, Drink, Taste, etc.)
☐ **Is there a specific response** sought? (Most ads: to buy something)
☐ If **not**: is it **conditioning** ("public relations" or "image building") to make us **"feel good"** about the company, to get favorable public opinion on *its* side (against any government regulations, taxes)?

Based on *The Pitch* © 1982 by Hugh Rank   (Teachers may photocopy for classroom use.)

Figure 9.4. (continued)

Observe. Understand. Judge. (In *that* sequence!)Observe closely what is explicitly said and shown; consider carefully what may be implied, suggested either by verbal or nonverbal means.

Anticipate Incoming Information. Have some way to sort, some place to store. If you know common patterns, you can pick up cues from bits and fragments, recognize the situation, know the probable options, infer the rest, and even note the omissions. Some persuaders use these techniques (and some observers analyze them) consciously and systematically; others, intuitively and haphazardly.

Categorize, but don't "pigeonhole." Things may be in many categories at the same time. "Clusters" and "mixes" are common. Observers often disagree.

Seek "dominant impressions," but relate them to the whole. You can't analyze *everything*. Focus on what seems (*to you*) the most *noticeable, interesting,* or *significant* elements (e.g. an intense "urgency" appeal, a very strong "authority" figure). By relating these to the whole context of "the pitch," your analysis can be *systematic, yet flexible,* appropriate to the situation.

Translate "indirect" messages. Much communication is *indirect,* through metaphoric language, allusions, rhetorical questions, irony, nonverbals (gestures, facial expressions, tone of voice), etc. Millions of specific concrete ways of communicating something can be grouped in the general abstract categories listed here as "product claims" (3c) and "common needs" (3d). Visuals imply.

Train yourself by first analyzing those ads which explicitly use the full sequence of "the pitch," including "urgency-stressing" and a specific "response-seeking." Always check for this full sequence; when it does not appear, consider what may have been omitted: *assumed* or *implied.* "Soft sell" ads and corporate "image-building" ads are harder to analyze: *less is said, more is implied.*

Practice. Analysis is a skill which can be learned, but needs to be practiced. Take notes. Use print ads. Videotape, if possible; replay in slow motion. No one can "see" or "understand" everything during the actual 30 seconds while watching a TV spot. At best, we pick up a few impressions. Use the pattern of "the pitch" to organize your analysis and aid your memory. Such organization helps to avoid randomness and simple subjectivity.

Are ads worth all of this attention? Ads may not be, but *your mind is* . If we can better learn how to analyze things, to recognize patterns, to sort out incoming information, to see the parts, the processes, the structure, the relationships within things so common in our everyday environment, then it's worth the effort.

Professor Hugh Rank Governors State University Park Forest South, Illinois

Figure 9.4. (continued)

Agenda Setting by the Media

Mass-media theorists talk about the ability of the media to set the agenda for the nation, state, or locality. In other words, *mass media do not tell us what to think; they tell us what to think about.* There is some truth in this theory. How do mass media get us to attend to certain issues and not others?

Suppose that you were in charge of programming at a network. You want to push some idea—say, the meatless diet. What kinds of things could you do to promote your idea? You could run a series of documentaries on personal health. One of them could focus on nutrition and the value of meatless diets. That way your idea would be hidden in the series as a whole, but you could get your message across. Then you might refuse ads for meat products. You might have a show for gourmet cooks and use a vegetarian natural-foods advocate to host the show. Cooking shows do not get much of the market, but it might be worth a try. You could also try an editorial. Probably the single most useful thing to do would be to get your news staff to investigate slaughterhouses across the state and nation. Tell them to highlight stories in which food poisoning or contamination came from meat. All these tactics would help get people ready for your meatless ideas. None of them actually urge people to change from meat-eating to vegetarian habits. That has to be done more overtly, in situations where fewer people are being persuaded. Instead, you would get people to think about the vegetarian way versus meat menus. In other words, you would tell people what to think about, not what to think. You put meat-eating on the public agenda. Let us look at some of the tactics that help set our agendas.

Humor

The two cartoon strips shown in Figure 9.5 demonstrate how humor can be used to set the agenda of a community, state, or nation. The cartoons appeared in the *Chicago Tribune* just before consideration of the earlier-noted ordinance that would make the playing of electronic video games illegal for persons under age eighteen. The cartoons appeared one day apart, with the first one showing Kudzu angrily deciding to put ten dollars' worth of quarters into the game. Several other cartoons relating to video games also appeared later. As noted earlier, parents were becoming convinced that such games were accounting for loss of lunch money by schoolchildren and that the games were also addictive. The humorous approach of the cartoons helped steer community discussion to the ordinance. We often see such uses of humor to set the agenda of a city or state or nation on the editorial pages of newspapers and weekly newsmagazines. Certain comic strips like *Doonesbury* have helped to set the agenda sometimes. Finally, humorous jibes made by television talk show hosts, newscasters, and other media personalities identify items that community leaders need to consider. Usually humor as an agenda-setter is most effective if it is aimed at opinion leaders who fear a loss of "face," or prestige.

Figure 9.5. Humor is often used to set an agenda. (Reprinted by permission of Tribune Company Syndicate, Inc.)

Editorial Commentary

The editorial itself is a powerful agenda setter. Often, editors force an issue on the public agenda. In some cases only one or two powerful editorial pieces are needed. Take a look at any copy of the three newsweeklies—*Time, Newsweek*, or *U.S. News and World Report*. They all have guest and regular editorial columns. Compare the columns from the three magazines for several weeks and see if the Congress, some regulatory agency, or some public officials won't respond to some of the agenda items suggested. Sometimes these editorials are followed up in local newspapers, thus increasing pressure upon governing bodies or officials to take some action or to place the issue on the agenda. Often the editorial part of the evening television newscast brings up agenda items. In Chicago, one particular editorial broadcaster—Walter Jacobson—specializes in pointing out the foibles of the city's politicians and of the legendary patronage system. He isn't always successful in prodding the mayor or aldermen to take action, but on numerous occasions he and others like him have effected change. Not only does the editorial bring up issues, but in doing so it also pushes other issues to a lesser priority simply because they don't get attention. This pushing of issues to the back burner is as much an agenda-setting device as is the bringing of an issue to attention.

Dramatizing

We have discussed the power of drama in several places. It also is a potent device that the mass media use to set agendas and to gain support for certain agenda items. Dramatic evening news programs or headlines focus our attention. We hear or read about political bribes. This information leads to sentiment for further investigation and later follow-up reports. Public feeling runs against the politicians. In a final stage, perhaps the drama results in resignation of officials or court cases. The key factor that keeps attention focused is the reported drama of the situation. In 1977, a New York City man killed a number of young couples in their parked cars. He was nicknamed the .44-Magnum Killer in news accounts. Later he was called Son of Sam. Before his arrest, the press focused on the killer, his choice of weapon, the similarities among his victims, his letters warning of his need to spill blood, and so forth. Son of Sam became a major item on the New York City agenda and on the agenda of the nation as well. The drama of the killings and of the mental problems of the killer turned everyone into a detective looking for the .44-Magnum Killer. The citizens of New York City became a vigilante force. This is how the killer was finally caught. Some people reported descriptions of a car that had been parked near the murder sites. It belonged to a man who had been reported as a suspect by neighbors. He looked like the artist's drawings made from victim and witness descriptions. The news media led the successful search for Son of Sam. They injected a lot of drama into the number-one agenda item.

Another thing we need to do as receivers is to look carefully at the dramas that are played out in the evening newscasts and in the daily headlines. Sometimes they will build agenda items that need attention. Sometimes they will overdramatize a problem and make us use undue effort to solve it. Perhaps the Son of Sam case shifted attention from the scores of other murders that occur each year in New York City. Sometimes they may focus us on problems that do not deserve agenda status. Dramatizing can also push an issue into the international spotlight, thus helping to establish a national or even worldwide agenda. In the early 1980s, a newly formed organization called MADD (Mothers Against Drunk Drivers) used first newspaper publicity and then the full range of campaign tactics, including TV talk shows and even teenage auxiliaries, to put strengthening and enforcement of drunk-driving laws on the national agenda. Earlier, antinuclear rallies begun in Europe gradually had influence around the world. Even in the United States, where there had been long-standing support for the government's plans for nuclear energy, public opinion was finally shifted by the early 1980s. Ultimately this forced the postponement of nuclear power plant construction.

Of course, drama is the stock-in-trade of the entertainment programs that we see on TV and hear on radio. Here the dramas are simple and require less critical viewing. They may persuade us to follow a certain lifestyle or to adopt certain slang expressions. However, they rarely set agendas for us. The more important thing that these dramatizations do is to provide us with role models. They show us day in and day out that crime does not pay, that attractive people succeed, that wives and mothers are at home in the kitchen and laundry while fathers fly the friendly skies, and so on. These messages may have a more enduring effect on society than all the various policy questions that the news programs put on our local and national agendas.

Role-Modeling and Media

In earlier times people learned to model themselves after the patterns shown by those with whom they worked or lived. Girls learned to be good housewives by watching their mothers. Boys learned to be farmers by watching their fathers and the other farmers in the community. Today, the media exert a much more potent force on role-modeling than the world around us does.

As we enter into the many contexts in which we work and play, we are forced to adopt various roles. These roles are patterns of acting and talking that signal many meanings to people around us. We act like a stuffy teacher and that sends messages to students that lead them to treat us as stuffy. We come on as the hale, hearty, extrovert type, and people expect us to have good jokes, to be easy to talk with, and so on. These roles shift from place to place and time to time. I do not often swear in church, but I am quite good at it on a canoe trip. You act the humble student when you are trying to get the teacher to let you do extra credit to make up for the low grade on the midterm test.

We adopt such roles in two ways. First, we may take on a certain role because the scene or setting demands it of us. For example, certain roles are called for at funerals while others are called for at weddings. These are *assigned roles*. A President may suffer a personal tragedy but should not show its effects too obviously in public. The scene assigns a President the role of leader, and shows of emotion are not called for in leaders. At other times, the setting may demand a role that we do not accept, and we choose another role. For example, a pro-football player should be tough and burly. He should make a show of proving that he is "all man." Big, tough, burly he-men don't hurt and they don't cry. The scene of the football field assigns this role. However, suppose that players know that a team-mate is dying of some disease, as was the case with the Chicago Bears a number of years ago. Now the tough guys show emotions and cry at the end of the final game of the stricken player's final season. These actions come from roles dictated by the players, not the scene. These can be called *assumed roles*. They are taken at the will of the role-player and often run counter to the demands of the scene. If you return to Burke's dramatic pentad, the assigned role is a result of the scene:agent ratio and is a situation in which the scene dominates. The assumed role flows out of the same ratio but here the agent dominates. Again and again through all our lives, we choose between these two options—the assumed and the assigned roles. We have varying degrees of success and failure in playing roles, and we learn from them. How do we learn which roles are called for and which are not?

Here is where mass media come in. Unlike our ancestors, even our grand-parents, who learned roles mostly from people around them, we learn about roles from mass media. Ask yourself what a working mother is like? Your responses may come from watching your own working mother, but they will also come from characters in ads or in situation comedies or in other TV and radio programs. You read newspaper or magazine stories featuring working mothers and your role-model grows.

This is why the critics of the mass media are so concerned about programs, ads, and other messages that feature sex or violence. Suzanne Somers is a good example. When she was first featured on the sitcom *Three's Company* she skyrocketed to fame. Some thought her shape had something to do with the rise to fame. Women's groups objected to featuring her body in almost every episode of the series. They argued that an innocent female public was being persuaded that the way to be successful in love and on the job was by using one's body. Eventually this led to outcries and even product boycotts against "jiggly" programming. Scripts were rewritten for entire series. *Trapper John*'s nurse was given the chance to display brains as well as her body. The opponents of violence on television make equivalent claims. They say people see violence on television and then go out and mimic it, thus accounting for rising crime rates. Dirty Harry has shot someone with his trademark weapon—a .44 Magnum pistol—in virtually every movie about the character. This caused violence opponents to make an even more direct claim. Remember the .44-Magnum Killer noted earlier in this chapter? Some blamed his choice of weapons on the role-model provided by the Dirty Harry movies.

How does a child learn about the social graces? Again, the mass media play a part. Children learn from the media that successful people drink cocktails, lust, smoke, and sometimes do unethical things. So, role-models train us to act in certain ways long after we have forgotten that we have ever seen the model. Thus, in a mass-media age, we need to be on guard so that all roles do not become assigned ones—assigned to us by the role-models to which we are exposed daily through TV, radio, newspapers, billboards, and so on. The critical persuadee needs to be aware that ads are not the only persuasive messages in mass media. Role-models are acted out and sometimes even prescribed to us in all the communications media.

Finally, we can note briefly that dramatization is often a key factor in mass-media advertisements. The dramas are endless, even though they follow very similar patterns (a person who is down and out buys the product and makes good, or conversely a person is doing well and does not buy the product and ends up a loser). We have seen thousands of washday dramas where dirt gets defeated and hundreds of marriages that have been brightened up by a new kind of prepared food or a certain kind of perfume or foot powder.

Subliminal Persuasion and the Media

Subliminal persuasion is a controversial topic. The idea behind this means of persuading is to present a message that is either so brief or so disguised that it is not consciously processed by the receivers. For example, the soundtrack of the film *Jaws* had shrieks recorded at the precise points where the film-makers expected real screams from the viewers. The subliminal cue or recorded scream triggered screams in the theatre audiences. Of course, persons who saw the show told their friends about how many people screamed during the film, thus advertising it better than any newspaper, radio, or TV ad could ever do. In other instances, hazy messages are included in films, photos, and soundtracks. These enter our subconscious mind and prompt us to action.

This idea of subliminally persuading an audience has been tested. In one of its early trials, "buy popcorn" was momentarily inserted in several frames of a movie. Audiences stormed the popcorn stand when the supply was sold out. The message registered in the viewer's subsconscious, where it created a compulsion to buy popcorn. Finally, the frustrated viewer *had* to act. At another time, viewers were exposed to a hidden message to call a certain phone number. The lines were supposedly busy for days and callers reported that they felt compelled to call that number even though they did not even know what it was for. The technique seemed to be so powerful that it was barred from use.

Recently the controversy was heightened by Wilson Bryan Key, an advertising researcher and college professor. Key decided to look at the possibility that messages could be "imbedded" into the visuals used in magazine advertising. He was struck by the need to touch up by airbrush in certain magazine advertisements. For example, Key notes that most liquor ads need airbrushing because the ice cubes in the glasses melt under the hot lights needed for magazine-quality photos. As long as the persuaders were airbrushing in the ice cubes, Key reasoned, why wouldn't they consider airbrushing in a subtle message like the words buy or good? Now, most magazine ads in major weekly or monthly publications cost tens of thousands of dollars. Given the investment, the persuader needs to get maximum impact for the advertising dollar. We know that basic human needs are the most motivating and that themes of sex and combat are central in most people's fantasy worlds.

Operating from those premises, Key felt that it was likely that ad designers would try to imbed sexual messages into ads to arouse readers. He tested his hypothesis with a Gilbey's gin ad in which the word SEX seemed to be airbrushed into the ice cubes and in which other parts of the layout continued the seduction theme. He thought he detected phallic symbols, reflections that depicted various stages in seduction, and so on. Now, seeing these vague airbrushed words and symbols might all have been in Key's head, so he tested 1000 people by showing them the ad and asked them to put into words the feelings they had while looking at the ad. None of the 1000 was told what to look for, and none had heard of or knew of subliminal techniques. Although 38 percent did not respond at all, the remaining 62 percent reported that the ad made them feel "sensual," "aroused," "romantic," "sexy," and even "horny" in several cases.[8] It is possible that this finding was accidental, but Key claims to have replicated the test with several ads with similar results. It is also possible that the advertiser does not consciously put subliminal messages into his ads—that they are accidental. I suppose it really does not matter as long as there are receiver effects. The point of persuasion is to get people to change their behavior or beliefs. We assume that any changes ought to be in source-intended ways, but the effect can be accidental and not related to the

---

8. Wilson Bryan Key, *Subliminal Seduction: Ad Media's Manipulation of a Not So Innocent America* (New York: Signet Books, 1973), p. 4. The book also has several sample ads in which Key claims to have identified "imbeds." More recently Key has added to his claims in two subsequent books, *Media Sexploitation* (New York: Signet Books, 1977) and *The Clambake Orgy* (New York: Signet Books, 1980).

source. Of course, if the advertisers really were trying to persuade by manipulating the subconscious, that would raise some ethical issues, as we shall see in Chapter 11. However, if an advertising agency did use subliminal techniques, they would probably deny it, as many agencies have done since the publication of Key's book. So whether the messages are there as a strategy of the source or not, the message has effects that correlate with Key's hypothesis that symbolic imbeds (usually sexually oriented) affect audiences. Key advises us to become critical receivers by looking beyond the surface message in any ad and searching for elements in the background, in the lighting, in the potential symbolic messages that could be generated. That will alert you to an ad's hidden meaning and may train you as an "imbed spotter." He says that the ad copy, layout, and characters should tip you off to any potential imbeds. Whether you see the imbedded sex symbols or not, you can get cued to possible subliminal persuasion by looking at ads more critically and by trying to determine what they suggest without saying.

Consider the two perfume ads in Figures 9.6 and 9.7. The first ad is called "The Promise Made." The second is called "The Promise Kept." Use Key's technique to see if you find any subtle messages here. First, note the actual words that are included in the ad. Then see if they may imply dual meanings. If so, search for visual clues in the ad that would substantiate the implied meaning. Observe what has changed between "The Promise Made" and "The Promise Kept." The champagne bottle is empty, the phone is off the hook, the fire has died down, the woman's shoes are on the dias, the flowers on the left seem to have bloomed in the heat, and the woman's earrings are off as is her stole.

In the early 1980s, the "dancing" logo of the Danskin Company was "hidden" in each of its ads, much as *Playboy* "hides" its rabbit motif on each cover of the magazine.

Another use of subliminal persuasion is unrelated to selling sex and then attaching merchandise to it. This product, called The Black Box, is a device used to discourage shoplifting. It uses a subliminal message in the piped-in music in department stores. Under but through the music comes the message "I won't steal. I will get caught here if I take something" and so on. Store owners who use this subliminal device claim to have reduced theft by thousands of dollars annually.[9] Although this use of subliminal audio material seems benign enough, it doesn't sound very far from the thought control that George Orwell depicted in his novel *1984*. There, subliminal audio messages were used to keep the populace meek and controlled. The messages were beamed over the state-operated radio and television, which was always turned on. Sounds unlikely? It has been reported that during the Nixon administration, the Pentagon proposed to the then President that every TV set in the country be fitted with a device that could be used by the President to turn all the sets across the country on simultaneously and to tune them to his message and his message alone. The White House wisely turned the proposal down because people might "misinterpret the intentions" of those proposing it.[10]

---

9. *The Wall Street Journal*, November 25, 1980, p. 33.

10. Jerry Mander, "Arguments for the Elimination of Television," *Penthouse*, March 1978, pp. 54–58.

"The Promise Made."

Figure 9.6. What kind of promise is being made? (Courtesy Lanvin Parfums Co., New York.)

Figure 9.7. What subliminal messages imply the promise was kept? (Courtesy Lanvin Parfums Co., New York.)

There are several sides to the subliminal controversy. The ad people say they never use the stuff, and people like Key say that our world is loaded with subliminal seducers. Interested observers also differ. Some say that Key is like the man who responded with "sex" in a Rorschach test to every inkblot presented by the psychiatrist. When accused of being preoccupied with sex, the patient countered that it was the doctor who collected all the dirty pictures. My position is that if it can be done (that is, if you can persuade through subliminal messages—sexual or otherwise), then someone is probably doing it. In a world where persuasion bombards us so often, we need to be aware of any kind of persuasion that might occur. Taking a second, hard look at ads for imbedded messages cannot hurt us. We will be almost guaranteed of being less likely to fall for as many pitches. We can learn about the kinds of things that are put into ads that persuade us on a conscious level—background objects, furniture styles, the kind of jewelry that the models wear, and so forth.

News Manipulation and Persuasion

In his book *Don't Blame the People*, Robert Cirino makes the point that there is a news industry in our country and that its business is to do business with business.[11] After all, the media stand to profit from the success of their clients and customers. Does news manipulation really occur or are people like Cirino supersensitive and paranoid about the power of the networks, the wire services, and the major newspapers and newsmagazines? Any answer to that question only leads to debate between those who espouse a free press and free speech and those who denounce the profit system. A better way to react to the question of news fixing is to say, "There may be cover-up, shading, and other ways to shape the news." If there are, persuadees ought to acquaint themselves with the possible tactics that can make or unmake news. That will allow us to have an extra safeguard against possible "hidden persuasion" in news programs. Let us look at some of these tactics and at our news system.

There are basically three wire services to which you are exposed in mass-media news programs or reports. They are United Press International (UPI), the Associated Press (AP), and Reuters. These three channels pour out most of the news you hear and read. Go through your daily newspaper and see how many stories are run from any of the services. You will find that most of the items come from the central three wire services. That means that, in a way, we are all getting the same news. There is nothing wrong with that, as long as the news is accurate and as long as the key news items get printed or broadcast. That is the problem. The key items are not always the ones on the front page, as we noted with agenda setting. The problem is worse with broadcast news. The "evening news" on TV contains only about twenty-two minutes of news. Furthermore, the messages are sent through the aural/oral channel. We speak and listen at speeds much slower than those used for reading. The speech speed on broadcast news is about 125

---

11. Robert Cirino. *Don't Blame the People* (Los Angeles: Diversity Press. 1971).

words per minute or less. That means that you will hear a maximum of about 3000 words of news, weather, sports, and editorial comment on the "half-hour" nightly news. If you read at a speed of, say, 400 words per minute *you could read what you hear in about seven or eight minutes!* Clearly, a lot is going to pass you by if you rely only on TV or radio. So the problem has two facets—the centralization of news and the short supply of it even if it is fair. Beyond the problem of supply is the more serious problem of shading the news, which happens more often than most of us realize.

Cirino observes that if the poor and hungry in this country controlled CBS, ABC, NBC, the *New York Times,* and so forth, hunger would be a major daily news item. Hunger simply is not what we hear or read about night after night. How is it that problems like this slip by with so little notice?

And even this shortened version of the news has been diluted and distorted because of the need of TV stations to capture a share of the market. As Ron Powers points out in his book *The News-Casters: The News Business as Show Business,* the ratings game has led to what we call "happy news." Powers writes, "The biggest heist of the 1970s never made it on the five o'clock news. The biggest heist of the seventies *was* the five o'clock news. The salesmen took it. They took it away from the journalists."[12] In their attempts to capture a greater and greater share of the audience, station managements went all out to entertain rather than inform their audiences. The trend began with the "anchors." Stations tried using former beauty queens, handsome lads, and kindly father figures. The trend soon affected weather and sports reporters. Logically, this led to the idea of a "news team." The news team was really a *personality team* with "uniforms"—matching blazers and ties or designer blouses and scarves—to identify the players. Research was done to discover public preferences in settings and a host of other variables—not, says Powers, to determine what was newsworthy and important for the populace to receive, but to identify:

> What did people want (not need but want) under the rubric of "news"? What pleased them most? Amused them? Gratified them, charmed them, or provided them with the sort of vicarious cheap thrills that kept them mesmerized during prime time entertainment? What colors did they like? What faces, voices? Conversely, what did viewers *not* want to know? What sort of news displeased them, threatened them, bored them, impelled them to switch away. . . ?[13]

The end result of all this research was "people" news—news that caters to the wants of the public:

> People did not want complicated, disturbing newscasts any more. . . . People were sick of unpleasant news. The new "mood of the country" . . . was no

---

12. Ron Powers, *The News-Casters: The News Business as Show Business* (New York: St. Martin's Press, 1978), p. 1.

13. Powers, p. 2.

longer "issue-oriented" but "people-oriented." The very term "Pee-pull" to denote a news genre became oracular; it was spoken in hushed italics; it bore the tintinnabulation of cash register bells.[14]

The result is a news *program*, not a news *broadcast*. The "news" is manipulated, selected, shaped, and massaged to attract the largest share of the audience—to please the most and offend the fewest. How is this manipulation done?

Ignoring

One tactic is simply to ignore the news item and not print or broadcast it at all or to hide it away on obscure inside pages. A good example cited by Cirino is the information about the Kennedy assassination. Available data indicated that things were not so simple as the Warren Report said. Mark Lane's book *Rush to Judgment*, which was the first to really get media exposure on the killing and on the idea of a conspiracy, was ignored by mass media for several years. In fact, it took Lane nearly fifteen months to find a publisher for it. For months before publication, he was refused interviews by the news industry, or if he was interviewed the interviews were never reported.[15] So, a critical receiver of mass-media news needs to look at what is hidden on inside pages and to wonder about what is not exposed at all. You ought to learn to rely on many sources for your news—papers, radio, TV, newsweeklies, and so on, and to look for the underplayed stories as well as at the headlines.

Sponsorship

Another thing to look at is who sponsors the news and what kind of play that business or group gets. It is easy to turn aside a story on smoking if 20 percent of your income is from ads placed by tobacco companies. This is a more long-term kind of news research that receivers need to do. We need to keep track of the kind of treatment advertisers get from the paper or station. Few media outlets wanted to feature Ralph Nader's report on the unsafe Corvair. It was not just chance that General Motors spent heavily on advertising in all those media.

The Pseudoevent

Daniel Boorstin first coined the term **pseudoevent.** It means creating news where there is none. Business has done it for years. For instance, it is not really newsworthy that on a certain day the new models of autos are available. It certainly does not deserve front-page space or time on the evening news. Yet, year after year, the auto companies trumpet this date with press releases, billboards, luncheons for reporters, and ads. As a result, many papers and stations do human interest stories on the new models. Announcement of a stock dividend or a contract settlement can also be a pseudoevent. Mass movements hitchhiked on this idea by creating events such as rallies, bra burnings, strikes, vigils, and so on.

---

14. Powers, p. 3.

15. Cirino, p. 284.

Only then did the news industry really take note of the movements—and only then did criticism of the news programs start. Even the military knows how to use the pseudoevent. Most military units have people called Public Information Officers who handle public relations for their units. They send news releases telling of new weapons, planes, awards, and so on. The press is invited to see the test flight or the parade or the maneuvers and thus an event is made into news.

Bias: Verbal and Nonverbal

We have mentioned two kinds of bias already. The first bias is in the source of the news or the wire services, networks, and key papers that control the flow of news. A second kind of bias is in the selection of news, or agenda setting. But there are other kinds of news bias of which receivers need to be aware. A skillful journalist can interview with bias and can thus shade and slant the result. As the controversial black leader Malcolm X put it: "I don't care what points I made . . . it practically never gets printed the way I said it."[16] Some journalists lead interviewees into topics where they can be trapped. Mike Wallace of CBS once asked a media advisor to Democrats, "Then you're a gun for hire?" How do you answer that? If you say "yes," you look sleazy. If you say "no," Wallace can follow up and ask if you get money for advising candidates.

Another kind of bias is in appearing to be unbiased. We set up a program we call a news show—*60 Minutes, 20/20,* or *Issues and Answers.* Then we control the content of the show and come off getting the persuasion done while appearing fair and decent. Why are some people featured on these shows and not others? Why do some questions get asked and not others? These are questions that receivers need to ask about the news features.

Bias can also be seen in photo selection and captions. Richard Nixon was never popular with news media people, including photographers and picture editors. Published photos often showed him in poor poses. Sometimes he was caught glancing at his watch as if to brush off the important people he was talking to. His nose got good play from various camera angles as though the press wanted to remind the reader of what happened to Pinocchio. During Gerald Ford's Presidency, cameramen delighted in putting every misstep and stumble on record, making him appear the klutz of all time. Clever captions can do the same kind of persuading. A photo on a coal strike for instance might be captioned "Miners Warm Up While Nation Freezes," thus giving the union a black eye. *Time* once captioned a photo of a black civil rights leader with the words, "As qualified as Attila the Hun," thereby reducing his ethos.[17]

Finally, the language of camera angle and movement and editing can create bias. If we see a person from a low camera angle, that figure appears larger than life. Long shots persuade us to believe in great size. Zoom-ins ask us to take a closer look—things are not as they seem. Quick-cut editing gives the effect of

---

16. Cirino, p. 147.

17. Cirino, p. 170.

great speed and activity. Montage superimposes two conflicting images—say strikers and strikebreakers or angry housewives and angry farmers. Though the people pictured are not actually angry at one another, the montage tends to persuade us of the conflict. There are other ways in which bias in news coverage can be created by the news industry. Ask controversial people about their news coverage, and they will tell you that you ought to believe half of what you see and less of what you hear and read.

In the 1980s, the rapid growth of cable TV and satellite broadcasting is affecting news broadcasting as well as entertainment. All-news TV channels will offer opportunities for more extensive and informative news coverage. Whether they provide it or go the way of all-news radio remains for persuadees to find out.

A Review and Conclusion

We have the statistics that the average eighteen-year-old American has seen 22,000 hours of television and hundreds of thousands of commercials. Remember that TV is just one media channel being used for persuasion. Most of us are affected by billboard persuasion. Films persuade us; magazines and newspapers frequently persuade us through their ads and their stories and editorials and cartoons. Further, labels, bumper stickers, T-shirts, and other paraphernalia seem to be increasingly used for persuading. Although on the average, Americans buy less than one third of a book per person per year (we don't know if they are ever read), books may sometimes persuade us.[18] All in all, we live in a highly persuasive, media-rich environment. We cannot hope to provide you with enough tools to filter out all these messages, and maybe that would not be good anyway. You need to be persuaded about some things, and media persuasion is sometimes the best way to get information about your choices. One thing that we all can do, though, to protect ourselves from all persuasive attempts made by the media is to begin to look beyond the surface meanings in media messages. Look for the responsive chords that are being plucked and decide whether the messages that elicit them are hot or cool. Look for the agenda items that are being set up. Identify the deceptive language and claims being used by persuaders. Finally, you might want to consider the possibility of the subliminal messages imbedded in media. This chapter is just the tip of the iceberg—you will want to research the role of media in persuasion much further.

Questions for Further Thought

1. What kinds of things that are in you could be evoked by persuaders and then tied to their product, idea, or candidate? Think of favorite experiences you have had that could be tied to a product. Or try to recall some unpleasant

18. Schwartz. p. 6.

experiences that could be used. What about your responses to certain songs? Could they be tied to products, candidates, or ideas? How?

2. What is a hot medium? Give an example. Why is it hot? What kinds of messages seem to go best on a hot medium or doesn't there seem to be a pattern?

3. Why is television a cool medium? What kinds of responses do people have when you disturb their TV watching? Does that suggest high or low involvement? Why?

4. What is now on the political agenda for the nation? For your state? For your local government? What about on campus—has the campus newspaper or radio station set an agenda for the administration or for the student government?

5. What kind of language is being used in ads you see or hear? Can you identify any deceptive use of language there? If so, give examples.

6. When Folger's claims to be the coffee that is "mountain grown," what kind of claim are they making?

7. When Goodyear calls its snow tire The Gripper, what kind of claim is being made or imprinted?

8. When Top Job ballyhoos its "Ammonia D" as an ingredient, what kind of claim is being made? Give other examples of this kind of claim.

9. What is subliminal persuasion? Can you identify some examples of subliminal messages?

Experiences in Persuasion

1. Write up a media persuasion logbook, keeping track of how many persuasive messages you process in the space of one day and which medium is used by you as a persuadee most often. Identify the message that is most effective during that day. See if it is reinforced through several channels. Try to determine how that message is working on you.

2. Collect samples of the various kinds of language deceivers discussed in this chapter. You may use magazine ads, speech excerpts, editorials, cartoons, and so forth, as your examples.

3. Make a similar collection demonstrating the various kinds of claims that persuaders can make through the mass media.

4. Read Carl Wrighter's book *I Can Sell You Anything* and report to the class on the other language deceivers he discusses. Tell about the various kinds of demonstrations that can be conducted by persuaders in order to get you to buy.

5. Read any of Wilson Bryan Key's books on subliminal persuasion *(Subliminal Seduction, Media Sexploitation,* or *The Clambake Orgy)*[19] and make a project in which you report to the class on the issue. For example you might want to prepare a scrapbook containing examples of subliminal seduction or prepare a slide show. You may want to report in a paper on the views of both sides of the controversy—those who believe subliminal persuasion is occurring and those who do not.

6. Develop a campaign for getting an item of concern on the agenda of your college or university administration. Report to the class or go ahead and conduct your campaign and observe and report the results.

---

19. See Footnote 8.

10
The Techniques of Propaganda

O
ne of our problems in discussing the techniques of propaganda in the 1980s goes back to the ways in which the word itself has been used in the past.

What Is Propaganda?

We think of propaganda as a kind of evil body of tricks used to force the stupid masses into monolithic conformity. We imagine "propaganda" as the work of nasty little Russians behind the walls of the Kremlin who plot day and night to keep the poor "comrades" pumped full of the Party line. In the good old U.S.A., of course, the closest thing we have to propaganda is the Voice of America beaming the "truth" to millions of people around the world who huddle under the covers every evening with a secret short-wave radio telling them about "freedom." Our history books, our news sources, and scores of late-night World War II movies have shaped our image of propaganda, and that image is totally negative. But if this view is inaccurate, what *is* propaganda? Let's look at what some people have said about it. Then we can try to formulate a definition of propaganda that will distinguish it from persuasion, from education, and from other types of communication—if that is possible.

Twentieth-century interest in propaganda goes back to World War I, when it was used to stir up war fever in many countries, including America, over the supposed atrocities of "the Huns." After the war, interest in propaganda and its techniques increased with the development of modern media of communication (see Chapter 9 for more on this point). With the advent of the loudspeaker, radio, film, and later television, unique persuaders and demagogues learned to turn these media to their advantage. In America, people like Huey P. Long of Louisiana, Father Coughlin of Detroit, and Franklin D. Roosevelt used these new media to gain the support of millions. Elsewhere, Franco in Spain, Hitler in Germany, and Stalin in the Soviet Union were among those who used the new technology to great advantage. Scholars and social critics soon became concerned over the impact of propaganda when coupled with electronic media.

These early investigators of propaganda defined the object of their study in various ways. For example, L. W. Doob, a sociologist who was world-famous in the middle third of this century, said that the use of **suggestion** was the key. If suggestion was used ". . . then this process may be called propaganda, regardless of whether or not the propagandist intends to exercise control." On the other hand, Doob said that if the same result would have occurred with or without the use of suggestion ". . . then this process may be called education regardless of the intention of the educator."[1] So, perhaps what you are doing in your persuasion class right now is propaganda.

J. Driencourt, a French student of political science, defined propaganda this way: "Propaganda is everything."[2] Of course that isn't very helpful in distinguishing propaganda from other communication forms. To Joseph Goebbels, the Nazi Minister of Propaganda, it had to be covert—"Propaganda becomes ineffective the moment we are aware of it."[3] J. A. C. Brown, a scholar interested in the use of propaganda in the brainwashing process, put it this way: "Education teaches people *how* to think. Propaganda teaches them *what* to think."[4] And we could go on with other definitions. On the one hand we would find those who limit propaganda to those appeals that are emotional and camouflaged. On the other hand there would be those who say it is everything—like Jacques Ellul,[5] who says that propaganda is contemporary culture. (Ellul's views are discussed later in this chapter.)

For our purposes, propaganda is first and foremost **ideological.** It tries to sell a *belief system* or *dogma*. So, propaganda can be religious, political, or economic. Secondly, propaganda **uses some form of mass communication** to sell ideology. Speeches; documentary programs on films, TV, and radio broadcasts; posters; billboards; mass mailings; and so on could all be used in the propaganda process. Postage stamps, coins, paper currency, music, art, and drama have all been used to propagandize. Finally, one or some combination of the following must be **concealed from the target audience:**

1. The **source** of the communication.

2. The source's **goal.**

3. The **other side** of the story—various perspectives.

4. The **techniques** being used by the source in sending the message.

5. The **results** of the propaganda if successful.[6]

---

1. L. W. Doob, *Propaganda—Its Psychology and Techniques* (New York: 1935) as quoted in *Film Propaganda,* by R. Taylor (New York: Barnes and Noble, 1979) p. 20.

2. Taylor, p. 19.

3. Taylor, p. 23.

4. Taylor, p. 25.

5. Jacques Ellul, *Propaganda: The Formation of Men's Attitudes* (New York: Vintage Books, 1965).

6. Taylor, p. 23.

This definition allows us to begin to make distinctions. For example, most commercial advertisements are not propaganda under this definition because they are not ideological, and we usually know the source and its goal. We are free to look at other sides or other products and so on. However, *some* advertisements might be propaganda. If Reverend Moon's Unification Church uses an advertisement to promote its ideology under the guise of offering an "Awareness Weekend" sponsored by CARP—the Committee Aimed at Researching Principles—that is propaganda. The pitch is ideological, and the true goal of the program, other sides of the story, the source, the techniques being used, and the end results—joining the church—are all concealed.

Triumph of the Will, a classic propaganda film, clearly tries to sell an ideology—Nazism—while it conceals its techniques of influence by labeling itself as a documentary. It reveals no competing perspectives, nor does it convey the final results if the film is successful. An equally political film—*All the President's Men*, which retells the story of the unraveling of the Watergate scandal—is probably not propaganda. It doesn't seem to sell an ideology. We know the source, goal, and the outcome of the scandal. The warning on cigarette packs isn't propaganda—it isn't ideological, whereas the road sign warning you to "Prepare to Meet Thy God—Repent!" is propaganda. What about the following:

A bumper sticker that says: "Guns Don't Kill—People Do!"?

A billboard that says "55 m.p.h.—A good speed for America"?

A postage stamp commemorating the President's inaugural speech?

A film about the development of unions in the coal mining industry?

An advertisement from Chrysler that says "Stop Inflation! Buy American Made Products!"?

What about a poster like the one I turned up on my campus recently? It said "Dynamic Sex—Unlocking the Secret to Love. Hear Rusty! Sponsored by Campus Crusade for Christ International—A Student Movement." Perhaps by trying to determine whether these and other examples qualify as propaganda, you can begin to get a sense of what it is and of how to identify it. If you can, and if Goebbels was correct in saying that recognizing it is to defeat it, then you can begin to defend yourself against it. Let's look at how propaganda works and at what devices can be employed by the propagandist.

The I.P.A. Devices of Propaganda Analysis

Because of the importance of propaganda used by all sides during World War II, an organization known as the Institute for Propaganda Analysis (I.P.A.) tried to disseminate information about the devices of propaganda.[7] Many teachers picked

---

7. Clyde R. Miller, "How to Detect Propaganda" in *Propaganda Analysis* (New York: Institute for Propaganda Analysis, 1937).

up the Institute's list of tactics and taught about them in the public schools. Some of you are probably already aware of them. Nonetheless, they are a good place to begin the study of the techniques of propaganda.

Plain Folks

The **"plain folks"** tactic is used to convince the audience that a public figure or the group that person represents are not well-trained, shrewd, and manipulative people but just "plain folks" like you and me. Politicians are using this device when they put on bib overalls and clodhopper boots and wipe their brows with a red bandanna while talking with a back-country drawl. Sometimes the technique is as simple as using common language to appeal to the audience. It might employ plain, everyday actions like washing one's own car, splitting wood, or sewing one's own clothes. The device uses pretense to create identification between source and receiver. Such sources are really not plain folks at all. Instead, they are trying to manipulate the audience into following their call through a false feeling of kinship.

Testimonial

The **testimonial** is a familiar device in today's world. We see it used daily in both the print and electronic media. A well-known and supposedly expert source gives testimony about the usefulness of a certain product, the honesty of a certain person, or the wisdom of a certain course of action. Sally Struthers tells us how good it felt for her to adopt a child through the Save the Children Federation. During the controversy over the guerilla war in El Salvador in the early 1980s, a supposed eyewitness to a guerilla atrocity was introduced at a State Department news conference. When the eyewitness began, he denied the original story, saying he had been coached by the CIA. The CIA later denied this, accusing the man of being a propaganda tool of Fidel Castro, who was said to be behind all of the disruptions then occurring in the Caribbean.

In both these examples, the audience cannot tell whether the people giving the testimony are actually reliable sources of information. Perhaps they have been hired to give the testimony because of their celebrity status. Or they might be dupes of some government. Furthermore, we do not know for certain what the goal of the source is. Is Sally Struthers actually interested in the adopt-a-child program? Is the program a front for some religious group? Did the eyewitness want to "prove" himself to his Cuban masters or was it his intent to embarrass the CIA? Was he a planted agent assigned to making the Reagan administration look like bumblers? Also, what is the outcome supposed to be if we believe these testimonials? Will we be promoting some unseen cause or religion? Should we withdraw from Central America so that Cuban insurgents can communize the area? All these hidden elements make these two instances of testimonials potential or actual examples of propaganda at work.

Bandwagon

Propagandists, like some advertisers, try to convince the audience that it is *almost* too late to take advantage of the offer... to join the organization... to follow the fad... to vote for the candidate... to be contemporary... to "get on the **bandwagon.**" The history of the word bandwagon gives us a clue to the basic intent behind the appeal. When the circus came to town in the nineteenth century, part of the hoopla used to attract customers was the circus parade along the village main street. The parade gave the population glimpses of what they could expect if they bought tickets to the show. The first wagon in the parade was always the bandwagon. The circus musicians would toot and hoot loudly to get attention and draw a crowd. Reference to the bandwagon became synonymous with being a leader—a person who was "out in front" of an idea or a fashion. Suppose you receive a pitch like this: "Only three more days left to support our cause. Sign the petition now! Help us stop the utility rate increases! Commonwealth Edison is a monopoly! Send a message to the legislature! The people's rights before the rights of capitalistic corporations!" Those phrases are tipoffs. The time limit and the stress on joining "the people" suggest that everyone is getting on the "bandwagon"—don't miss out.

Card-Stacking

Building an overwhelming case on one side of an issue while concealing another, perhaps equally valid side from the audience is called **card-stacking.** Of course, few persuaders try to *tell* both sides of a story, but responsible persuaders at least suggest that there *are* other sides. In fact, we frequently see advertisers, for example, comparing their products with the competition in taste tests, mileage comparisons, tar/nicotine statistics, stopping power for tires, or starting power for batteries. In card-stacking, this is not done. Instead, the other side may not even be recognized. Or it may be downplayed or possibly denigrated. At the same time the cards are stacked in favor of one position.

Again, the history of the words gives us an idea as to the intent of this device. Crooked gamblers learned to be adept at shuffling cards so as to insert the cards they wanted for themselves or for a confederate into the deck at the appropriate spot—say every fourth card in a four-handed game. The cards were then said to be stacked. Naive or unknowing players could not win. The card-stacking described by the I.P.A. works the same way. Facts, figures, witnesses, and maybe even the judges or supposedly innocent bystanders are all inserted into the proceeding according to a prearranged scheme. Sources know beforehand that they can count on certain evidence being brought out. They know beforehand that they can expect "spontaneous" hurrahs for their side and maybe equally planned catcalls for their opponents. The cards are stacked against the opposition and against the informed decision of the innocent audience.

Transfer

As we have noted earlier, the credibility or ethics of persuaders is important in determining whether they will be successful. Credibility comes from image, reputation, and delivery. It is this second source of credibility—reputation—that lies at the root of the power of the **transfer** device. Transfer is an attempt to build or destroy credibility by reputation-building or reputation-destroying techniques. Transfer associates the preferred speaker or position with other high-credibility sources, thereby "borrowing" their credibility. For example, if someone mentions that he or she has friends in high places or went to a prestigious law school or can call on well-known and respected persons or organizations for help, *transfer* is being used to build credibility. If on the other hand, the opposition is associated with people of low credibility or with an organization that is thought of as subversive or dishonest, *transfer* is being used to destroy the opposition's reputation or credibility: "He still maintains his ties with the Americans for Democratic Action—a well-known Communist-front organization." Remarks like "Last week I was speaking to the Chief Justice on this matter, and he reminded me of the Blue Ribbon Panel we both served on for the American Bar Association and . . ." borrow or transfer the ethos of the Chief Justice, the panel, and the Bar Association to build the reputation of the speaker. Again, this device is a common one in contemporary American politics and advertising. It is also frequently heard at cocktail parties, fraternity and sorority rush functions, and professional conventions for college professors.

Glittering Generalities

Abstract language, highly charged with emotion and cultural values, is used by propagandists because of its power. Such words seem to "glitter" with high purpose and energy that can short-circuit people's reasoning process and make them jump to conclusions. Take words like "justice," "freedom," "dignity," "equality," "patriot," "integrity," and "wisdom." Such words are actually not very specific, yet they pluck at powerful emotions in audiences. Who hasn't heard some political speaker introducing the candidate who is *"dedicated* to the continuance of *justice* for all in this great nation of ours; who has worked *diligently* for our *freedom* and *dignity,* fighting for *equality.* My friends, I give you a *patriot* of great *integrity* and *wisdom*—SENATOR FOGBOUND!!" Later, of course, the voters may discover that Fogbound drinks too much, slips off to the strip joints on D Street, and has been videotaped taking bribes from an Arab oil sheik.

The glittering generalities of the world of advertising are only slightly less emotional and vague. Some examples are Heavy-Duty, Youthful, Vitality, Jumbo, Old-Fashioned, Homemade, and Glamorous. No one has ever heard of a *light-duty* battery or a *medium-duty* motor oil, just as no one has ever heard of a *small* or *medium* olive—they come only in three sizes: Colossal, Mammoth, and Jumbo. Leaf through any popular magazine and you will find hundreds of glittering generalities like these.

Name-Calling

The other side of the glittering generalities coin is **name-calling.** It uses terms or words that are charged with negative emotion and often have very specific meanings or referents. Calling someone a Fellow Traveler during the 1950s meant that he or she was a Communist agent, since this term was frequently associated with the trials of convicted agents. Hundreds of actors, screenwriters, directors, producers, and others in the entertainment industry were "blacklisted" or boycotted from employment as "fellow travelers"—even though the charge might never have been substantiated or even formally investigated. Calling the Germans "Huns" in both world wars identified them with brutal, almost bestial motives and actions. Calling the North Vietnamese and Viet Cong "slants" or "slopes" or "gooks" identified them with low intelligence and deviousness. The purpose of name-calling is always the same—to link some individual with a negative group, action, or idea in order to diminish that person's position, reputation, or opportunities. This, too, is a familiar and ancient device; Aristotle called it the *ad hominem* or the argument against personality.

Although these seven devices are well known and can be usefully applied to propaganda analysis, almost any scholar interested in propaganda would agree that we daily see examples of transfer, glittering generalities, and so on that could by no means be called propaganda. Testimonial, for example, is used to sell everything from gas to "light" beer to mouthwash—hardly propagandistic endeavors! So while we can keep the seven devices of propaganda in mind (for they are sometimes used to ideologize communication or the arts), we need to look elsewhere to identify the distinguishing characteristics of propaganda.

Jacques Ellul's Perspective

Jacques Ellul is a French social critic and scholar whose interest in propaganda flows from his investigation of contemporary technological society. His book *Propaganda: The Formation of Men's Attitudes*[8] is well known and is a unique approach to the topic. Propaganda, according to Ellul, is far more than promoting lies and half-truths by tricky little devices. Propaganda is an integral part of our technological society; it is everywhere, and it is not going to go away. Nor is it just "tall tales." Frequently it is a set of facts reported in an unbiased way. To Ellul, the fundamental characteristic of propaganda is *interpretation for ideological purposes*. Propaganda, explains Ellul, is by definition *totalitarian*—that is, infused in every aspect of our lives: school, church, and work; books and newspapers; fraternal organizations; government; stamps, coins, and currency. It is usually *secretive*, so we are generally unaware of its presence. Its purpose is to *indoctrinate* us into some way of thinking and behaving

Soviet and Nazi Propaganda

Propaganda varies from culture to culture and reflects each culture's basic values. For example, Ellul notes that Soviet propaganda is rarely aimed outside the U.S.S.R. itself. There is no "Voice of Russia" broadcasting propaganda messages to Western Europe; Russian propaganda is meant to indoctrinate the Russian people. Its aim is to condition people to react to national symbols, to certain persons or groups, or to certain ideas in predictable ways. At work, through the media, and at local Party meetings, the propaganda seeks to create stereotypes—the commissar, the dissident, the Jew, and so on—in order to elicit desired responses such as fear

8. Ellul, *op. cit.*

or respect, opposition, or hatred. In this way, Ellul says, Soviet propaganda is Pavlovian; it relies on the conditioned response.

Nazi propaganda, on the other hand, tried to stir up responses with a high emotional charge. These weren't necessarily so predictable. Nazi propaganda used powerful words and symbols—blood, fire, steel, the swastika. It stressed erotic and sexual matters. Hitler told the Germans that their problems were related to breeding—non-Aryans had mated with true Aryans and had thus "mongrelized" the race. To Hitler, the crowd was like a woman who had to be seduced. Ellul says that this kind of propaganda is typically Germanic and flows from psychological theories developed primarily in the Germanic countries. It is based on Freud's ideas on repression and the libido.

American Propaganda

American propaganda, according to Ellul, is equally totalitarian. But it is based on our own psychological innovations—largely those of learning psychologist John Dewey. Consider the following ideas that Dewey stressed and see how many of them are built into our churches, our schools, our government, and other elements of our social structure. Dewey taught that when faced with a problem, groups or individuals should engage in **reflective thinking,** an essential tool of learning through discovery. First, you should define the problem—its history, its limits, its effects, and so on. Then you should devise several different possible solutions, each one stressing, perhaps, a different aspect of the problem. Next, you should weigh them one against the other and find the best solution. Then you try that "best" solution out and see if it solves the problem. If it doesn't, you go back and redefine the problem. By repeating this series of actions, the problem will finally be solved.

If groups are involved, Dewey said, they might divide up the tasks of defining the problem and seeking solutions. But when it comes to choosing the best solution, they should behave *democratically. All participants* should have a chance to say how they think and feel before finally, in some kind of *"one-man-one-vote"* procedure, a decision is made and put to the test. Dewey's views on democratic education stressed motivating the child to *learn* to solve problems by using a form of "scientific method," experimenting with various solutions. Children would expose themselves to experiences, literature, and people who would help. To Dewey, education was a process of self-discovery, a highly *individualized* business.

In this "democratic" way, we Americans make political, economic, social, religious, and other policy. If we have been properly indoctrinated, Ellul would say, we would believe that this is the best—the most logical—way to make decisions. Furthermore, we might expect people of other countries and cultures to behave in this same way. We would believe, for instance, that Third World countries must be democratically governed. Well? Do we see this pattern in our daily lives? In faculty senates? In fraternities and sororities? In student councils? In church organizations? In our state, local, and national governments? Ellul says "Yes." Probably, he would add something like "You never knew you were being indoctrinated by your American brand of totalitarian propaganda, did you?"

Basic Propaganda Devices

All propaganda, according to Ellul, relies to some degree on two basic psychological devices, the **conditioned reflex** (or the automatic, "knee-jerk" response) and the **myth.** As we noted before, Russian propaganda relies heavily on the conditioned reflex, but other propagandas do, too. For us, "Let's put it to a vote!" might stimulate a conditioned response. The stereotypes such as the prissy Englishman, or the impatient and emotional Italian, or the authority-driven German, or the inscrutable Oriental might also be used to evoke conditioned responses. By a myth, Ellul means "an all-encompassing image: a sort of vision of desirable objectives . . . [which] pushes a man to action precisely because it includes all he feels is good, just, and true."[9] Examples he notes are the myth of race, the myth of productivity, and so on.

According to Ellul, both the conditioned reflex and the myth are part of a *prepropaganda phase* in which people are prepared for action by being conditioned into accepting the values of a culture. When the time comes for action, the leader or the "establishment" can prompt a reflex response by appealing to people's mythic beliefs. For example, our American culture treasures the myth of democracy, which says that the wisdom of the people, when operating in a democratic fashion, is the best and will prevail. American reactions to the repression of the Polish labor union Solidarity in the early 1980s were based on this myth. We and our political leaders, ministers, educators, and editors believed that the "will of the people" as represented by Solidarity had been thwarted. By definition, this was bad—it contradicted the myth of democracy. It may have been that the requests by the Polish union would have brought economic chaos on the country, and that thus the "will of the people" was foolhardy. The myth ignores this possibility, concentrating on Solidarity's popular origin and not on the content of its proposals.

Eight Characteristics of Propaganda

Ellul's theories of propaganda were analyzed by Michael Real and Clifford Christians in the *Journal of Communication.*[10] On the basis of their analysis, Ellul's work can be summarized around eight central ideas.

1. Propaganda is always associated with industrialized societies in which *la technique* (or the quest for ever more efficiency through technology) supersedes human social interaction. Thus a "communications expert" may simply be a salesperson for complex telephone set-ups and may know nothing about the human interaction that is the essence of communication.

2. Propaganda is not a set of tricks but is an ongoing, ever-present, interrelated system of methods, technologies, or "techniques" that pervade modern society

---

9. Ellul, pp. 30–32.

10. Clifford Christians and Michael Real, "Jacques Ellul's Contributions to Critical Media Theory." *Journal of Communication* (Winter 1979), pp. 83–93.

Figure 10.1. Here is an early use of propaganda: a depiction of the Boston Massacre engraved, printed, and sold by Paul Revere. It tells only one side of the story, and Revere's goal is not clear. (Courtesy The New York Historical Society, New York City.)

and become increasingly dominant as the society becomes increasingly totalitarian (or centrally controlled).

3. Propaganda inevitably occurs in societies where people are depersonalized and unknowingly forced into *masses* while they are being isolated as individuals. They derive their identity from the mass, which is united through propaganda. You may be an isolated individual on a large college campus, but you get identity from groups of varying sizes: From your college or university—"He's a Yale-ie." From your class and dormitory—"She's a Grant Tower sophomore." From your political affiliations—"He's president of the Young Republicans." From religious ties—"She's Jewish." And so forth. From Ellul's perspective, propaganda works because American society, á la John Dewey, strives for individualism while technology and other forces create *mass* audiences, *mass* media, *mass* movements, and other masses in which individualism is submerged.

4. The purpose of modern propaganda is not to agitate the masses to action but to integrate them into society. This is done through peer pressure, social norms, and collective standards—usually expressed by a leader. For example, if you are a good American, you will urge Congress to cut the budget to stop inflation. Or if you believe in a free public education, you will approve this school referendum. Or, if you believe in the standards of fair play, you will see that American auto manufacturers cannot compete with foreign automakers unless we have trade quotas.

5. Most present-day propaganda comes from three "propaganda blocs": the United States and its allies, the U.S.S.R. and its allies, and China.

6. Propaganda in a highly technological society is *totalitarian*: Everything is infused with some element of a propagandistic message designed to promote uniformity of action and behavior, rather than uniformity of belief or *dogma*. For example, the words "In God We Trust" on our money tell us and others that we picture our nation as righteous and religious. The eagle frequently seen on our money depicts our society as saying "hands off" while remaining ready to fight. The great heroes of our history are pictured on our money. Other propaganda sources use similar devices. Totalitarian propaganda would also infuse our social interactions. And, indeed, we do find flags in church, pledges of allegiance at the Lions club, patriotic songs sung at school and church, and mealtime prayers in many homes. If you search further, you will find many traces of Ellul's *totalitarian propaganda*.

7. Among the effects of contemporary propaganda are isolation of the individual, stereotyping of public opinion, and simplistic answers to social questions. For example, American propaganda offers insecure people clear-cut solutions to complex problems (e.g., "make the people on welfare go get a job"). It might also provide surrogate heroes or friends to the lonely or weak.

8. Once we consider the mass media, propaganda in Ellul's terms is everywhere. The entertainment shows on TV promote the values of our society. They teach our young how to grow up and how to behave as adults. News programs report the accomplishments of our society and identify its weaknesses and its enemies—criminals, other countries, or our own shortcomings. Our art and music—even anti-patriotic and nonpolitical art and music—identify our cultural values and beliefs. These things are expressed even when producers of the message do not intentionally engage in propaganda. In fact, this book, which asks you to be a conscientious receiver of persuasion, would be but another example of propaganda if seen through Ellul's eyes.

Of course, Ellul's claims or central ideas are controversial. Certainly we can see many examples of propaganda infusing itself into our daily lives. Few would deny that organizational efficiency is an unquestioned premise of our times. Nor would many deny the power of modern technology to make us behave in ways that could destroy personal freedom. But on the other hand, "propaganda is everything" is not a very useful definition. It doesn't allow for categories of communication; it doesn't allow for degrees of persuasion. If everything is propaganda, Ellul's theories and books are propaganda, too. They employ *la technique* just as much as *W.K.R.P. in Cincinnati*, N.F.L. football, the evening newspapers, our music and art, or our textbooks. Moreover, if everything is propaganda, why be concerned about it? There isn't much that you or I can do.

This is where Ellul most comes under fire. Nonetheless, even if Ellul overstates his case, his work is useful. It jars us. It forces us to look deeper—to take a second and even a third look at many of the things that are happening around us. In those second or third looks, we often can identify persuasion that we might otherwise have overlooked.

A Review and Conclusion

Our interest in propaganda and its uses usually comes to the fore during times of war or national crisis. It is then that we see the one-sided, monolithic, blatant use of propaganda. When we are not faced with war or national crisis, our interest in propaganda diminishes. We become more concerned with the events of the day and with our personal problems. Yet, as we have seen, the absence of war does not necessarily mean the absence of propaganda. It can still occur, it can still affect us. A major difficulty arises in identifying just what propaganda is, in determining its sources and intent, and in determining how and why it affects us. Nonetheless it is useful to stop and observe the communications going on around us with the concept of propaganda in mind. Do these messages try to indoctrinate us? Are ideological issues being pressed on us? Who is the source? What is the source's intent or goal? Is there another side to the story that is being concealed? Are techniques such as subliminal messages being employed without our knowledge? If we follow the advice sent to us, what will happen? All these questions and others can help us to responsibly receive the persuasion aimed at us.

Questions for Further Thought

1. Where in your world is the value of efficiency being espoused? Look at advertisements, editorials, etc.

2. Look back at the cultural values discussed in Chapter 6. Are any of these values being urged on you? If so, can you identify the source of the urging?

3. Are you being persuaded through a "technique" of which you are only dimly aware?

4. In what ways do you agree and disagree with Jacques Ellul?

5. What is the "plain folks" device? Identify it being used in the persuasion you encounter.

6. What is the "glittering generalities" device? Identify uses of it.

7. What is the "transfer" device? Identify uses of it.

8. What is "card-stacking"? Identify uses of it.

9. Where have you seen "testimonial" being used? Explain how it works.

10. Where have you seen "bandwagon" being used? Explain.

11. Do you think propaganda is good or bad? Explain.

12. Have you ever engaged in the production of propaganda (review the definition given here)? Explain.

Experiences in Persuasion

1. Get copies of newsletters, leaflets, or newspapers from ideological or political groups. See if they are using any of the devices of propaganda described in this chapter. Share your findings with your class.

2. Develop your own definition of propaganda. See if your definition can help you distinguish between propaganda and other forms of persuasion.

3. Make a propaganda scrapbook using newspaper clippings, advertisements, and so on. Label the uses of propaganda and explain them in a paragraph or two.

4. Film is a medium that naturally lends itself to propagandistic uses. Try to obtain some obvious propaganda film (e.g., *Triumph of the Will* or many of the commercial movies produced during World War II). Compare these with contemporary films and share the differences with your class. This will be especially useful if there is some relevant contemporary film that many or most of the class has seen.

5. Listen to the lyrics of popular hit music. Are the lyrics intended to promote an ideology or set of values? Analyze the lyrics for their propagandistic potential. Then compare these lyrics with those of songs written during wartime or with songs written to promote some movement (e.g., antiwar or protest songs, union songs, civil rights songs, Women's Movement songs). Develop a tape with dubs of these lyrics and share it with the class. See if you can determine whether songs carry contemporary "propaganda" messages.

11

Perspectives on Ethics in Persuasion

Richard L. Johannesen, Northern Illinois University

Some Ethical Perspectives
    Religious Perspectives
    Human Nature Perspectives
    Political Perspectives
    Situational Perspectives
    Legal Perspectives
    Dialogical Perspectives
Some Fundamental Ethical Issues
Ethics, Propaganda, and the Demagogue
Ethical Standards for Political Persuasion
Ethical Standards for Commercial Advertising
Ethics for Nonverbal Communication
Ethical Responsibilities of Receivers

I magine that you are an audience member listening to a speaker, call him Mr. Bronson. His aim is to persuade you to contribute money to the cancer research program of a major medical research center. Suppose that, with one exception, all the evidence, reasoning, and motivational appeals he employs are valid and above ethical suspicion. However, at one point in his speech, Mr. Bronson *consciously* chooses to use a *false* set of statistics to scare you into believing that, during your lifetime, there is a much greater probability of your getting some form of cancer than there actually is.

To promote analysis of the ethics of this hypothetical persuasive situation, consider these issues: If you, or the society at large, view Mr. Bronson's persuasive end or goal as worthwhile, does the worth of his end justify his use of false statistics as one means to achieve that end? Does the fact that he consciously chose to use false statistics make a difference in your evaluation? If he used the false statistics out of ignorance, or out of failure to check his sources, how might your ethical judgment be altered? Should he be condemned as an unethical person, as an unethical speaker, or in this instance for use of a specific unethical technique?

Carefully consider the standards, and the reasons behind those standards, that you would employ to make your ethical judgment of Mr. Bronson. Are the standards purely pragmatic? In other words, should he avoid the false statistics because he might get caught? Are they societal in origin? If he gets caught, his credibility as a representative would be weakened with this and future audiences. Or his getting caught might weaken the credibility of other cancer society representatives. Should he be ethically criticized for violating an implied agreement between you and him? You might not expect a representative of a famous research institute to use questionable techniques and thus you would be especially vulnerable. Finally, should his conscious use of false statistics be considered unethical because you are denied accurate, relevant information you need to make an intelligent decision on a public issue?

As receivers and senders of persuasion, we have the responsibility to uphold appropriate ethical standards for persuasion, to encourage freedom of inquiry and

Figure 11.1. Woody Allen on American ethics. (© King Features Syndicate, Inc. 1977.)

expression, and to promote the health of public debate as crucial to democratic decision making.[1] To achieve these goals, we must understand their complexity and recognize the difficulty of achieving them.

In this chapter I do not intend to argue my own case for the merit of any one particular ethical perspective or set of criteria as *the best one*. Rather, I view my role in this chapter, as I do in the classroom, as one of providing information, examples, and insights and of raising questions for discussion. The purpose is to stimulate you to make reasoned choices among ethical options in developing your own position or judgment.

The process of persuasion involves your presenting good reasons to people for a specific choice among probable alternatives. Whether you are a candidate seeking votes, an elected official urging citizen adoption of a governmental policy, a protestor demanding reform by the Establishment, an advertiser appealing to consumers to purchase a product, a citizen urging others to accept your belief as sound, or a student advocating a change in your school's educational programs, alternatives are present, and you marshal logical and psychological supports for the choice of specific alternatives.

Receivers of persuasive messages evaluate them according to standards they perceive as relevant. For example: Is the message interesting and directly related to my concerns? Am I clearly understanding the message as intended by the persuader? What is the persuader's purpose? Do I perceive the persuader as a credible source on this subject (expert, competent, trustworthy, experienced, sincere, honest, concerned)? Has the persuader presented sufficient evidence and reasoning for me to accept the message as reasonable (workable, practical, efficient, and so forth)?

As a receiver do I see a legitimate connection between the persuader's message and my related needs, motives, and goals? Is the persuader's message consistent with my related beliefs and attitudes? Is the message consistent with my relevant values, my conceptions of the good or desirable? As a receiver do I feel that the nonverbal elements of the persuader's message reinforce or conflict with

---

1. For a much more extensive exploration of the perspectives, standards, and issues discussed in this chapter and identification of relevant resource materials, see Richard L. Johannesen, *Ethics in Human Communication*, 2nd ed. (Prospect Heights, Illinois: Waveland Press, 1983). The present chapter, in whole or in part, may not be reproduced without written permission from the publisher and from the author.

the verbal aspects? How do I perceive the persuader's view of my personal worth and abilities? What role does the persuader's message play in some larger, continuous campaign of persuasion? To what degree are the persuader's techniques, appeals, arguments, and purpose ethical?

Ethical issues focus on value judgments concerning right and wrong, goodness and badness, in human conduct. Persuasion, as one type of human behavior, always contains *potential* ethical issues because:

1. It involves one person, or a group of persons, attempting to influence other people by altering their beliefs, attitudes, values, and overt actions.

2. It involves conscious choices among ends sought and rhetorical means used to achieve the ends.

3. It necessarily involves a potential judge (any or all of the receivers, the persuader, or an independent observer).

How, as receivers and senders of persuasion, you evaluate the ethics of a persuasive instance will differ, depending upon the ethical standards you are using. You may even choose to ignore ethical judgment entirely. One of several justifications often is used to avoid direct analysis and resolution of ethical issues in persuasion:

1. Everyone knows this appeal or tactic obviously is unethical, so there is nothing to talk about.

2. Since only success matters, ethics are irrelevant to persuasion.

3. After all, ethical judgments are only matters of our individual personal opinion anyway so there are no final answers.

Nevertheless, potential ethical questions are there, regardless of how they are answered. Whether you wish it or not, consumers of persuasion generally will judge, formally or informally, your effort in part by their relevant ethical criteria. If for none other than the pragmatic reason of enhancing chances of success, you would do well to consider ethical standards held by the audience.

In making judgments of the ethics of our own communication and of the communication to which we are exposed, our aim should be specific rather than vague assessments and carefully considered rather than "gut-level" reactions. The quality of judgment of ethics of persuasion usually would be improved by:

1. *Specifying exactly* what ethical criteria, standards, or perspectives we are applying.

2. Justifying the *reasonableness and relevancy* of these standards.

3. Indicating in what respects the persuasion evaluated *fails to measure up* to the standards.

Some Ethical Perspectives

We shall briefly explain six major ethical perspectives as potential viewpoints for analyzing ethical issues in persuasion. As categories, these perspectives are not exhaustive, mutually exclusive of one another, or given in any order of precedence.

As receivers of persuasion, we can employ one or a combination of such perspectives to evaluate the ethical level of a persuader's use of language (such as metaphors, ambiguity, and what Richard M. Weaver labels God terms and Devil terms) or of evidence and reasoning (such as what Stephen Toulmin calls data, warrant, backing, reservation, qualifier, and claim). We also can utilize them to assess the ethics of psychological techniques, such as appeals to needs and values, the stimulation and resolution of dissonance and imbalance, or the appeal to widely held cutural images and myths. The persuasive tactics of campaigns and social movements also can (indeed must) be subjected to ethical scrutiny.

Religious Perspectives

Religious perspectives stem from the moral guidelines and the "thou-shalt-nots" embodied in the ideology and sacred literature of various religions. For instance, the Bible warns against use of lies, slander, and bearing false witness. Taoist religion stresses empathy and insight, rather than reason and logic, as roads to truth. Citing facts and demonstrating logical conclusions are minimized in Taoism in favor of feeling and intuition. These and other religiously derived criteria could be used to assess the ethics of persuasion.

Human Nature Perspectives

These perspectives probe the *essence* of human nature by asking what makes a human fundamentally human. Unique characteristics of human nature that set us apart from "lower" forms of life are identified. Such characteristics then can be used as standards for judging the ethics of persuasion. Among some of the characteristics that have been suggested are capacity to reason, capacity to create and utilize symbols, cappaciy for mutual appreciative understanding, and capacity to make value judgments. The assumption is that uniquely human attributes should be promoted, thereby promoting fulfillment of maximum individual potential. A determination could be made of the degree to which a persuader's appeals and techniques either foster or undermine the development of a fundamental human characteristic. A technique that *de*humanizes, that makes a person less than human, would be unethical. Whatever the political, religious, or cultural context, a person would be assumed to possess certain uniquely human attributes worthy of promotion through communication.

Political Perspectives

The implicit or explicit values and procedures accepted as crucial to the health and growth of a particular political-governmental system are the focus of political perspectives. Once these essential values are identified for that political system, they can be used for evaluating the ethics of persuasive means and ends within that system. The assumption is that public communication should foster achievement of these values; persuasive techniques that retard, subvert, or circumvent these basic political values would be condemned as unethical. Different political systems usually embody differing values leading to differing ethical judgments. Within the context of American representative democracy, for example, various analysts pinpoint values and procedures they deem fundamental to healthy functioning of our political system, and, thus, values that can guide ethical scrutiny of persuasion therein. Such values and procedures might include enhancement of citizen capacity to reach rational decisions, access to channels of public communication, access to relevant and accurate information on public issues, maximization of freedom of choice, toleration of dissent, honesty in presenting motivations and consequences, and thoroughness and accuracy in presenting evidence and alternatives.

Situational Perspectives

To make ethical judgments, situational perspectives focus *regularly* and *primarily* on the elements of the specific persuasive situation at hand. Virtually all perspectives (those mentioned here and others) make some allowances, on occasion, for the modified application of ethical criteria due to special circumstances. However, an extreme situational perspective *routinely* makes judgments *only* in light of *each different context.* Criteria from broad political, human nature, religious, or other perspectives are minimized; absolute and universal standards are avoided. Among the concrete contextual factors that may be relevant to making a purely situational ethical evaluation are:

1. The role or function of the persuader for the audience.

2. Expectations held by receivers concerning such matters as appropriateness and reasonableness.

3. Degree of receiver awareness of the persuader's techniques.

4. Goals and values held by the receivers.

5. Degree of urgency for implementation of the persuader's proposal.

6. Ethical standards for communication held by receivers.

From an extreme situational perspective, it might be argued that an acknowledged leader in a time of clear crisis has a responsibility to rally support and thus could employ so-called emotional appeals that circumvent human processes of rational, reflective decision making. Or it might be argued that a persuader may ethically employ techniques such as innuendo, guilt by association, and unfounded name-calling as long as the receivers both recognize and approve of those methods.

Legal Perspectives

Legal perspectives would take the general position that illegal communication behavior also is unethical. That which is not specifically illegal is viewed as ethical.

Such an approach certainly has the advantage of allowing simple ethical decisions. We would need only to measure persuasive techniques against current laws and regulations to determine whether a technique is ethical. We might, for example, turn for ethical guidance to the regulations governing advertising set forth by the Federal Trade Commission or the Federal Communications Commission. However, we also must consider to what degree legal perspectives lead to oversimplified, superficial judgments of complex persuasive situations.

Dialogical Perspectives

Dialogical perspectives emerge from current scholarship on the nature of communication as dialogue rather than as monologue.[2] Such perspectives contend that the attitudes toward each other among participants in a communication situation are an index of the ethical level of that communication. Some attitudes are held to be more fully human, humane, and facilitative of personal self-fulfillment than are other attitudes.

Communication as dialogue is characterized by such attitudes as honesty, concern for the welfare and improvement of others, trust, genuineness, open-mindedness, equality, mutual respect, empathy, humility, directness, lack of pretense, nonmanipulative intent, sincerity, encouragement of free expression, and acceptance of others as individuals with intrinsic worth regardless of difference over belief or behavior. Communication as monologue, in contrast, is marked by such qualities as deception, superiority, exploitation, dogmatism, domination, insincerity, pretense, personal self-display, self-aggrandizement, judgmentalism that stifles free expression, coercion, possessiveness, condescension, self-defensiveness, and viewing others as objects to be manipulated. In the case of persuasion, then, the techniques and presentation of the persuader would be scrutinized to determine the degree to which they reveal an ethical dialogical attitude or an unethical monological attitude toward receivers.

Some Fundamental Ethical Issues

With the above six ethical perspectives (religious, human nature, political, situational, legal, dialogical), we can confront a variety of questions that underscore difficult issues relevant to ethical problems in persuasion. As receivers constantly bombarded with a variety of verbal and nonverbal persuasive messages, we continually face resolution of one or another of these fundamental issues.

To what degree should ethical criteria for assessing persuasion be either absolute, universal, and inflexible or relative, context-bound, and flexible? Surely the more absolute our criteria are, the easier it is to render simple, clear-cut judgments. However, in matters of human behavior and public decision making, the ethics of persuasive ends and means are seldom simple. In making ethical

---

2. For a general analysis of communication as dialogue and monologue, see Richard L. Johannesen, "The Emerging Concept of Communication as Dialogue," *Quarterly Journal of Speech*, Vol. 57 (December 1971), pp. 373–382.

evaluations of persuasion, we probably should avoid snap judgments, carefully examine the relevant circumstances, determine the perspectives most appropriate to the instance, and consider the welfare of all involved.

Do the ends justify the means? Does the necessity of achieving a goal widely acknowledged as worthwhile justify the use of ethically questionable techniques? To say that the end does not *always* justify the means is different from saying that ends *never* justify means. The persuasive goal is probably best considered as one of a number of potentially applicable criteria, from among which the most appropriate standards (perspectives) are selected. Under some circumstances, such as threat to physical survival, the goal of personal security—temporarily—may take precedence over other criteria. In general, however, we can best make mature ethical assessments by evaluating the ethics of persuasive techniques apart from the worth of the persuasive goal. We can strive to judge the ethics of techniques and ends separately. In some cases we may find ethical persuasive devices employed to achieve an unethical goal. In other cases unethical techniques may be aimed at an entirely ethical goal.

Are all so-called "emotional appeals" inherently unethical? Although a countertrend seems to be emerging, as reflected by encounter groups and sensitivity training, our culture traditionally has viewed with suspicion the expression of or capitalization on emotion. The Aristotelian heritage in rhetorical theory has perpetuated the primacy of logic over emotion in selecting ethical persuasive strategies. However, one point that has emerged from behavioral science research on persuasion is that receivers of persuasive messages find it difficult to categorize appeals or supporting materials as either emotional or logical in exactly the same manner as the persuader intends them. Differing audiences may view the same appeal differently. A given technique, such as a set of statistics indicating the high probability of falling victim to cancer during one's lifetime, may be perceived as possessing both logical and emotional components.

Since neither logical nor emotional appeals are inherently unethical, but depend largely on manner and circumstance of usage, the need to dichotomize persuasive appeals into logical and emotional categories is not very great. If you do wish to evaluate the ethics of a persuasive technique that you perceive as emotional appeal, the following guideline is suggested. Assuming that the appeal is ethical in light of other relevant perspectives, the emotional device is ethical if it is undergirded by a substructure of sound evidence and reasoning to support it. Presentation of this substructure could accompany the appeal in the persuasive message or the substructure could exist apart from the message and should be produced upon the request of a critic. The emotional appeal is ethical if you are asked to view it not as proof for justification but as the expression of the persuader's internal emotional state. Generally, the emotional appeal is unethical when it functions as pseudoproof giving the appearance of evidence or if it functions to short-circuit your capacity for free, informed, responsible choice.

Does sincerity of intent release a persuader from ethical responsibility relative to means and effects? Could we say that if Adolf Hitler's fellow Germans judged him to be sincere, his fellow citizens could not assess the ethics of his persuasion?

In such cases, evaluations probably are best carried out if we appraise sincerity and ethics separately. Thus, for example, a persuader sincere in his or her intent may be found to utilize an unethical strategy.

Is intentional use of ambiguity ethical? Clear communication of intended meaning usually is one major aim of an ethical communicator, whether that person seeks to enhance receiver understanding or seeks to influence belief, attitude, or action. Textbooks on oral and written communication typically warn against ambiguity and vagueness; often they directly or indirectly take the position that intentional ambiguity is an unethical communication tactic. In some situations, however, persuaders may feel that the intentional creation of ambiguity or vagueness is necessary, accepted, expected as normal, and even ethically justified.

Such might be the case at times, for example, in religious discourse, in some advertising, in international diplomatic negotiations, or in labor-management bargaining. A persuader might feel that ambiguity is justified ethically in order to heighten receiver attention through puzzlement, to promote maximum psychological participation of receivers by letting them create relevant meanings, to satisfy receiver expectation of ambiguity as a norm for a certain type of communication, or to promote maximum latitude for revision of position in later dealings with opponents or constituents (avoidance of being locked-in to a single position). In some advertising, for instance, intentional ambiguity seems to be understood as such by consumers and even accepted by them. Consider possible ethical implications of the advertisement for Noxema Shaving Cream which urged (accompanied by a beautiful woman watching a man shave in rhythm with strip-tease music): "Take it off. Take it *all* off." Or what about the "sexy" woman in the after-shave cologne advertisement who says, "All my men wear English Leather, or they wear *nothing at all.*" Consider whether intentional ambiguity should uniformly and always be condemned as unethical.

To what degree is use of racist/sexist language unethical? At the least, racist/sexist terms place people in artificial and irrelevant categories. At worst, such terms intentionally demean and "put down" other people through embodying unfair negative value judgments concerning traits, capacities, and accomplishments. What are the ethical implications, for example, of calling a Jewish person a "kike," a black person a "nigger" or "boy," an Italian person a "wop," an Asiatic person a "gook" or "slant-eye," or a thirty-year-old woman a "girl" or "chick"?

Within a particular political perspective we might value access to relevant and accurate information needed to make reasonable decisions on public issues. But racist/sexist language, by reinforcing stereotypes, conveys inaccurate depictions of people, dismisses taking serious account of people, or even makes them invisible for purposes of the decision. Such language denies us access to necessary information and thus is ethically suspect. From human nature perspectives, such language is ethically suspect because it dehumanizes by undermining and circumventing the essentially human capacity for rational thought or for symbol use. From a dialogical perspective, racist/sexist language is ethically suspect because it reflects a superior, manipulative, exploitative, inhumane attitude of one person toward others, thus hindering equal opportunity for self-fulfillment for some people relevant to the communication situation. Consider what the ethicality of racist/sexist language might be in light of other ethical perspectives or criteria.

The foregoing questions highlight only some of the complex issues involved in determining the ethics of persuasion. Several additional areas of concern—such as propaganda and the demagogue, political persuasion, commercial advertising, and nonverbal communication—will be discussed at greater length.

Ethics, Propaganda, and the Demagogue

Is propaganda unethical? The answer to this question in part depends on how propaganda is defined. Numerous, often widely divergent, definitions abound. Originally the term "propaganda" was associated with the efforts of the Roman Catholic Church to persuade people to accept the Church's doctrine. Such efforts were institutionalized in 1622 by Pope Gregory XV when he created the Sacred Congregation for Propagating the Faith. The word "propaganda" soon came to designate not only institutions seeking to propagate a doctrine but also the doctrine itself and the communication techniques employed.

Today one cluster of definitions of propaganda presents a *neutral* position toward the ethical nature of propaganda. A definition combining the key elements of such neutral views might be: Propaganda is a *campaign* of *mass* persuasion. According to this view, propaganda represents an organized, continuous effort to persuade a mass audience, primarily using the mass media.[3] Propaganda thus would include advertising and public relations efforts; national political election campaigns; the persuasive campaigns of some social reform movements; and the organized efforts of national governments to win friends abroad, maintain domestic morale, and undermine an opponent's morale both in hot and cold war. Such a view stresses communication channels and audiences and categorizes propaganda as one species of persuasion. Just as persuasion may be sound or unsound, ethical or unethical, so too may propaganda.

Another cluster of definitions of propaganda takes a *negative* stance toward the ethical nature of propaganda. Definitions in this cluster probably typify the view held by many average American citizens. A definition combining the key elements of such negative views might be: Propaganda is the intentional use of suggestion, irrelevant emotional appeals, and pseudoproof to circumvent human rational decision-making processes.[4] Such a view stresses communication techniques and sees propaganda as *inherently* unethical.

---

3. For example see Terrence H. Qualter, *Propaganda and Psychological Warfare* (New York: Random House, 1962), Chapter 1; Paul Kecskemeti, "Propaganda," in Ithiel de Sola Pool, Wilbur Schramm, Frederick W. Frey, Nathan Maccoby, and Edwin B. Parker, eds., *Handbook of Communication* (Chicago: Rand McNally, 1973), pp. 844–870.

4. For example, see W. H. Werkmeister, *An Introduction to Critical Thinking*, rev. ed. (Lincoln, Neb.: Johnson, 1957), Chapter 4; Stuart Chase, *Guides to Straight Thinking* (New York: Harper & Row, 1956), Chapters 20 and 21.

Are the traditional propaganda devices always to be viewed as unethical? Textbooks in such fields as journalism, speech communication, and social psychology often discuss the traditional list: name-calling, glittering generality, transfer, testimonial, plain folks, card-stacking, and bandwagon. Such a list does not constitute a sure-fire guide, a "handy-dandy" checklist, for exposure of unethical persuasion. The ethics of at least some of these techniques depends on how they are employed in a given context.

The *plain folks* technique stresses humble origins and modest backgrounds shared by the communicator and audience. The persuader emphasizes to the audience, although usually not in these words, that "we're all just plain folks." In his whistle-stop speeches to predominantly rural, Republican audiences during the 1948 presidential campaign, Democrat Harry Truman typically used the plain folks appeal to establish common ground in introductions of his speeches. He used the device to accomplish one of the purposes of the introductory segment of most speeches—namely, establishment of rapport; he did not rely on it for proof in the main body of his speeches. If a politician relied primarily on the plain folks appeal as pseudoproof in *justifying* the policy he or she advocated, such usage could be condemned as unethical. Furthermore, Truman really was the kind of person who could legitimately capitalize on his actual plain folks background. A politician of more privileged and patrician background, such as Edward Kennedy, could be condemned for using an unethical technique *if* he were to appeal to farmers and factory workers by saying "you and I are just plain folks."

Today the label "demagogue" frequently is used to render a negative ethical judgment of a communicator. Too often the label is left only vaguely defined; the criteria we are to use to evaluate a person as a demagogue are unspecified. In ancient Greece, a demagogue simply was a leader or orator who championed the cause of the common people.

In the following journalistic description of a former Southern governor, what characteristics are suggested as marks of a demagogue? To what extent should we agree with them as appropriate criteria for judging a demagogue?

> He is the quintessential demagogue, combining the missionary zeal of a Barry Goldwater, the raw pursuit of power of a Kennedy, the expansive populism of a Huey Long, the chameleon-like adaptability of a Nixon, and the disarmingly blunt, or somewhat crude, appeal of an Archie Bunker.[5]

You now are invited to consider the following five characteristics collectively as possible appropriate guides for determining to what degree a persuader merits the label "demagogue."[6]

---

5. Stephen Lesher, "The New Image of George Wallace," *Chicago Tribune*, January 2, 1972, Sec. 1A, p. 1.

6. The basic formulation from which these guidelines have been adapted first was suggested to me by Professor William Conboy of the University of Kansas. These five characteristics generally are compatible with the standard scholarly attempts to define a demagogue. For instance, Reinhard Luthin, *American Demagogues*, reprinted ed. (Gloucester, Mass.: Peter Smith, 1959), pp. ix, 3, 302–319; Barnet Baskerville, "Joseph McCarthy: Briefcase Demagogue," reprinted in Haig A. Bosmajian, ed., *The Rhetoric of the Speaker* (New York: D.C. Heath, 1967), p. 64.

1. A demagogue wields popular or mass leadership over an extensive number of people.

2. A demagogue exerts primary influence through the medium of the spoken word—through public speaking, whether directly to an audience or by means of radio or television.

3. A demagogue relies heavily on propaganda defined in the negative sense of intentional use of suggestion, irrelevant emotional appeals, and pseudoproof to circumvent human rational decision-making processes.

4. A demagogue capitalizes on the availability of a major contemporary social issue or problem.

5. A demagogue is hypocritical; the social cause serves as a front or persuasive leverage point while the actual primary motive is selfish interest and personal gain.

Several cautions are in order in applying these guidelines. A persuader may reflect each of these characteristics to a greater or lesser degree and only in certain instances. A persuader might fulfill only several of these criteria (such as items 1, 2, and 4) and yet not be called a demagogue; characteristics of 3 and 5 seem to be central to a conception of a demagogue. How easily and accurately can we usually determine a persuader's *actual* motivations? Should we limit the notion of a demagogue solely to the political arena?

Ethical Standards for Political Persuasion

Directly or indirectly, we daily are exposed to political and governmental persuasion in varied forms. The President appeals on national television for public support of a diplomatic treaty. A senator argues in Congress against ratification of a treaty. A government bureaucrat announces a new regulation and presents reasons to justify it. A federal official contends that information requested by a citizen-action group cannot be revealed for national security reasons. At any given moment, somewhere a national, state, or local politician is campaigning for election. At a city council meeting, a citizen protests a proposed property tax rate increase. What ethical criteria should we apply to judge the many kinds of political-governmental persuasion? We shall consider a number of potential sets of criteria in the hope that among them you will find ones especially useful in your own life.

Traditional American textbook discussions of the ethics of persuasion, rhetoric, and argument often include lists of standards suggested for evaluating the ethicality of an instance of persuasion. Such criteria often are rooted, implicitly if not explicitly, in what we earlier in this chapter described as a political perspective for judging the ethics of persuasion. The criteria usually stem from a commitment to values and procedures deemed essential to the health and growth of the American political-governmental system of representative democracy. Obviously other cultures and other governmental systems may embrace basic values that lead to quite different ethical standards for persuasion.

What follows is my synthesis and adaptation of a number of such typical traditional lists of ethical criteria for persuasion.[7] Within the context of our own society, the following criteria are not necessarily the only or best ones possible; they are suggested as general guidelines rather than inflexible rules, and they may stimulate discussion on the complexity of judging the ethics of persuasion. Consider, for example, under what circumstances there may be justifiable exceptions to some of these criteria. Also bear in mind that one difficulty in applying these criteria in concrete situations stems from differing standards and meanings people may have for such key terms as: distort, falsify, rational, reasonable, conceal, misrepresent, irrelevant, and deceive.

1. Do not use false, fabricated, misrepresented, distorted, or irrelevant evidence to support arguments or claims.

2. Do not intentionally use specious, unsupported, or illogical reasoning.

3. Do not represent yourself as informed or as an "expert" on a subject when you are not.

4. Do not use irrelevant appeals to divert attention or scrutiny from the issue at hand. Among the appeals that commonly serve such a purpose are: "smear" attacks on an opponent's character, appeals to hatred and bigotry, innuendo, and God terms or Devil terms that cause intense but unreflective positive or negative reactions.

5. Do not ask your audience to link your idea or proposal to emotion-laden values, motives, or goals to which it actually is not related.

6. Do not deceive your audience by concealing your real purpose, by concealing self-interest, by concealing the group you represent, or by concealing your position as an advocate of a viewpoint.

7. Do not distort, hide, or misrepresent the number, scope, intensity, or undesirable features of consequences or effects.

8. Do not use "emotional appeals" that lack a supporting basis of evidence or reasoning, or that would not be accepted if the audience had time and opportunity to examine the subject themselves.

9. Do not oversimplify complex, gradation-laden situations into simplistic two-valued, either/or, polar views or choices.

---

7. For example, see the following sources: E. Christian Buehler and Wil A. Linkugel, *Speech Communication for the Contemporary Student*, 3rd ed. (New York: Harper & Row, 1975), pp. 30–36; Robert T. Oliver, *The Psychology of Persuasive Speech*, 2nd ed. (New York: Longmans, Green, 1957), pp. 20–34; Wayne Minnick, *The Art of Persuasion*, 2nd ed. (Boston: Houghton Mifflin, 1968), pp. 278–287; Henry Ewbank and J. Jeffery Auer, *Discussion and Debate*, 2nd ed. (New York: Appleton-Century-Crofts, 1951), pp. 255–258; Wayne Thompson, *The Process of Persuasion* (New York: Harper & Row, 1975), Chap. 12; Bert E. Bradley, *Fundamentals of Speech Communication*, 3rd ed. (Dubuque, Ia.: William C. Brown Co., 1981), pp. 23–31; Thomas R. Nilsen, *Ethics of Speech Communication*, 2nd ed. (Indianapolis: Bobbs-Merrill, 1974); Karl R. Wallace, "An Ethical Basis of Communication," *Speech Teacher*, 4 (January 1955), pp. 1–9.

10. Do not pretend certainty where tentativeness and degrees of probability would be more accurate.

11. Do not advocate something in which you do not believe yourself.

Some guidelines for evaluating the ethical responsibility of governmental communication have been developed by Dennis Gouran.

1. The deliberate falsification of information released to the public, especially under circumstances involving the general welfare, is inappropriate and irresponsible.

2. The classification of government documents for the purpose of deceiving or otherwise keeping the public uninformed on matters affecting private citizens' well-being is inappropriate and irresponsible.

3. The deliberate use of official news sources for the purpose of obscuring embarrassing and deceitful governmental acts is inappropriate and irresponsible.

4. Criticism of the press for the purpose of assuring that governmental acts are viewed only in favorable terms is inappropriate and irresponsible.

5. Deliberate attempts by governmental agents to suppress or otherwise interfere with an individual's legitimate exercise of free expression within the limits defined by our courts are inappropriate and irresponsible.

6. Overt and covert governmental acts designed to misrepresent a political candidate's, or any other citizen's, character or position or to violate said individual's rights are inappropriate and irresponsible.

7. Language employed by governmental figures for the purpose of deliberately obscuring the activity or idea it represents is inappropriate and irresponsible.[8]

For the 1976 presidential campaign, Common Cause, a national citizens' lobbying group, proposed a set of standards that, even today, easily might aid in assessing the ethics of any political candidate's campaign. According to their criteria, an ethical candidate exhibits the following behavior:

1. Engages in unrehearsed communication with voters, including participation in open hearings and forums with other candidates on the same platform, where the public is given opportunities to express their concerns, ask questions, and follow up on their questions.

2. Holds press conferences at least monthly throughout the campaign, and in every state where contesting a primary, at which reporters and broadcasters are freely permitted to ask questions and follow-up questions.

---

8. For a detailed discussion of the guidelines, see Dennis Gouran, "Guidelines for the Analysis of Responsibility in Governmental Communication," in Daniel Dieterich, ed., *Teaching About Doublespeak* (Urbana, Ill.: National Council of Teachers of English, 1976), pp. 20–31.

3. Discusses issues which are high on the list of the people's concerns, as evidenced, for example, by national public opinion polls; clarifies alternatives and tradeoffs in a way that sets forth the real choices involved for the nation; and makes clear to the American people what choices he or she would make if elected to office.

4. Makes public all information relating to a given poll if releasing or leaking any part of a campaign poll (including when and where the poll was conducted, by whom, a description of the sample of the population polled, as well as all questions and responses).

5. Allows interviews by a broad spectrum of TV, radio and newspaper reporters, including single interviewer formats which provide maximum opportunity for in-depth questions.

6. Takes full public responsibility for all aspects of his or her campaign, including responsibility for campaign finance activities, campaign practices of staff, and campaign statements of principal spokespersons.

7. Makes public a statement of personal financial holdings, including assets and debts, sources of income, honoraria, gifts, and other financial transactions over $1,000, covering candidate, spouse and dependent children.

8. Does not use taxpayer-supported services of any public office now held—such as staff, transportation or free mailing privileges—for campaign purposes, except as required for personal security reasons.

9. Uses only advertising which stresses the record and viewpoint on issues of the candidates.

The Fair Campaign Practices Committee, a national nonpartisan watch-dog organization that monitors campaigns, urges political candidates to sign the following code of Fair Campaign Practices:

1. I shall conduct my campaign in the best American tradition, discussing the issues as I see them, presenting my record and policies with sincerity and frankness, and criticizing without fear or favor the record and policies of my opponent and his party which merit such criticism.

2. I shall defend and uphold the right of every qualified American voter to full and equal participation in the electoral process.

3. I shall condemn the use of personal vilification, character defamation, whispering campaigns, libel, slander, or scurrilous attacks on any candidate or his personal or family life.

4. I shall condemn the use of campaign material of any sort which misrepresents, distorts, or otherwise falsifies the facts regarding any candidate, as well as the use of malicious or unfounded accusations against any candidate which aim at creating or exploiting doubts, without justification, as to his loyalty.

5. I shall condemn any appeal to prejudice based on race, sex, creed, or national origin.

6. I shall condemn any dishonest or unethical practice which tends to corrupt or undermine our American system of free elections or which hampers or prevents the full and free expression of the will of the voters.

7. I shall immediately and publicly repudiate support from any individual or group which resorts, on behalf of my candidacy or in opposition to that of my opponent, to the methods and tactics which I condemn.

Frequently, political candidates are condemned for stressing "image" over "issues" in their campaigns. Traditionally, so-called image-oriented campaigns are viewed as ethically suspect. However a contrasting view should be considered.[9] Some scholars argue that issues and stands on issues are too transitory and too complex for voters to make dependable judgments. For example, an issue vital today often fades quickly, to be replaced by one unforeseen during the campaign. Or issues may have to be created if none loom large in the public mind at the inflexible time when the campaign occurs. Instead, suggest some scholars, voters should assess the basic dimensions of the candidate's image (personal qualities) as a better basis for evaluations. In the long run, the key questions would be: Does the candidate's past record demonstrate strength of character, decisiveness of action, openness to relevant information and alternative viewpoints, thoroughness in studying a problem, respect for intelligence of others, and the ability to lead through public and private communication?

Ethical Standards for Commercial Advertising

Consumers, academic experts, and advertisers themselves clearly do not agree on any one set of ethical standards as appropriate for assessing commercial advertising. Here we will simply survey some of the widely varied criteria that have been suggested. Among them you may find guidelines that you feel will aid your own assessments.

Using a kind of religious perspective, John McMillan contends that the first responsibility of an advertiser is not to either business or society but rather to God and to principles higher than self, society, or business.[10] Thus, advertisers are responsible to multiple neighbors—to owners, employees, clients, customers, and the general public. Second, they have a responsibility for objective truth. Third, they are responsible for preparing advertising messages with a sense of respect for their audience. Finally, argues McMillan, advertisers are responsible for seeking product improvements.

---

9. See for example, Dan F. Hahn and Ruth M. Gonchar, "Political Myth: The Image and the Issue," *Today's Speech*, Vol. 20 (Summer 1972), pp. 57–65; James David Barber, *The Presidential Character: Predicting Performance in the White House* (Englewood Cliffs, New Jersey: Prentice-Hall, 1972), Chapter 1.

10. John E. McMillan, "Ethics and Advertising," in John S. Wright and Daniel S. Warner, eds., *Speaking of Advertising* (New York: McGraw-Hill, 1963), pp. 453–458.

Several writers on the ethics of advertising suggest the applicability of perspectives rooted in the essence of human nature. Thomas Garrett contends that a person becomes more truly human in proportion as his or her behavior becomes more conscious and reflective.[11] Because of the human capacity for reason and because of the equally distinctive fact of human dependence on other people for development of potential, Garrett suggests there are several ethical obligations. As humans we are obliged, among other things, to behave rationally ourselves, to help others behave rationally, and to provide truthful information. Suggestive advertising, in Garrett's view, is that which seeks to bypass human powers of reason or to some degree render them inoperative. Such advertising is unethical not just because it uses emotional appeal, Garrett feels, but because it demeans a fundamental human attribute and makes people less than human.

Clarence Walton observes that some critics employ a philosophical model that identifies three components of human nature as vital elements to be considered in evaluating the ethics of marketing practices: (1) human capability for rational judgment, (2) human capacity for exercising free options among defined alternatives, and (3) human motivation to serve primarily selfish interests or to serve the welfare of others.[12] By extending the implications of such a framework, advertising and marketing tactics could be judged by the degree to which they undermine the human capacity for rational decision, constrict free choice among alternatives, and foster largely selfish interests.

Theodore Levitt uses a human nature position to *defend* advertising techniques often viewed by others as ethically suspect. While admitting that the line between distortion and falsehood is difficult to establish, his central argument is that "embellishment and distortion are among advertising's legitimate and socially desirable purposes; and that illegitimacy in advertising consists only of falsification with larcenous intent." Levitt grounds his defense in a "pervasive, . . . *universal*, characteristic of human nature—the human audience *demands* symbolic interpretation of everything it sees and knows. If it doesn't get it, it will return a verdict of 'no interest.' " Because Levitt sees humans essentially as symbolizers, as converters of raw sensory experience through symbolic interpretation to satisfy needs, he can justify "legitimate" embellishment and distortion. He contends:

> Many of the so-called distortions of advertising, product design, and packaging may be viewed as a paradigm of the many responses that man makes to the conditions of survival in the environment. Without distortion, embellishment, and elaboration, life would be drab, dull, anguished, and at its existential worst.[13]

---

11. Thomas M. Garrett, S.J., *An Introduction to Some Ethical Problems of Modern American Advertising* (Rome: Gregorian University Press, 1961), pp. 39–47.

12. Clarence C. Walton, "Ethical Theory, Societal Expectations and Marketing Practices," in John S. Wright and Daniel S. Warner, eds., *Speaking of Advertising* (New York: McGraw-Hill, 1963), pp. 359–373.

13. Theodore Levitt, "The Morality (?) of Advertising," reprinted in John S. Wright and John E. Mertes, eds., *Advertising's Role in Society* (St. Paul, Minnesota: West Publishing Co., 1974), pp. 278–289.

Sometimes advertisers adopt what we earlier in the chapter called legal perspectives in which ethicality is equated with legality. However, Harold Williams observes, concerning the ethics of advertising:

> What is legal and what is ethical are not synonymous, and neither are what is legal and what is honest. We tend to resort to legality often as our guideline. This is in effect what happens often when we turn to the lawyers for confirmation that a course of action is an appropriate one.
>
> We must recognize that we are getting a legal opinion, but not necessarily an ethical or moral one. The public, the public advocates, and many of the legislative and administrative authorities recognize it even if we do not.[14]

Typically, commercial advertising has been viewed as persuasion that argues a case or demonstrates a claim concerning the actual nature or merits of a product. To such attempts at arguing the quality of a product, many of the traditional ethical standards for "truthfulness" and "rationality" have been applied. For instance, are the evidence and the reasoning supporting the claim clear, accurate, relevant, and sufficient in quantity? Are the emotional and motivational appeals directly relevant to the product?

The American Association of Advertising Agencies, in a code of ethics revised in 1962, went beyond simple obedience to the laws and regulations governing advertising to broaden and extend "the ethical application of high ethical standards." As you read the following standards, consider their degree of adequacy, the degree to which they still are relevant and appropriate today, and the extent to which they presently are followed by advertisers. Association members agree to avoid intentionally producing advertising that contains:

1. False or misleading statements or exaggerations, visual or verbal.

2. Testimonials that do not reflect the real choice of a competent witness.

3. Price claims that are misleading.

4. Comparisons that unfairly disparage a competitive product or service.

5. Claims insufficiently supported or that distort the true meaning or practicable application of statements made by professional or scientific authority.

6. Statements, suggestions, or pictures offensive to public decency.

What if ethical standards of truthfulness and rationality are *irrelevant* to most commercial advertising? What if the primary purpose of most ads is *not* to prove a claim? Then what ethical standards we apply may stem from whatever alternative view of the nature and purpose of advertising we do hold. Some advertisements function primarily to capture and sustain consumer attention, to announce a

---

14. Harold M. Williams, "What Do We Do Now, Boss? Marketing and Advertising," *Vital Speeches of the Day,* Vol. 40 (February 15, 1974), pp. 285–288.

product, to create consumer awareness of the name of a product.[15] What ethical criteria are most appropriate for such attention-getting ads?

Lawrence W. Rosenfield views commercial advertising as a type of poetic game.[16] Here techniques of making the commonplace significant, of esthetically pleasing structure, of connotation, and of ambiguity all combine to invite consumers to participate in a recreational, emotionally satisfying experience. If there is such a thing as commercial "advertising-as-poetic," what ethical standards should we use to judge this kind of poetry?

Finally, consider again Tony Schwartz's resonance theory of electronic media persuasion discussed earlier.[17] As part of his view he argues that because our conceptions of truth, honesty, and clarity are a product of our print-oriented culture, these conceptions are appropriate in judging the content of printed messages. In contrast, he contends that the "question of truth is largely irrelevant when dealing with electronic media content." In assessing the ethics of advertising by means of electronic media, Schwartz feels that the Federal Trade Commission should focus not on truth and clarity of content but on effects of the advertisement on receivers. He laments, however, that at present "we have no generally agreed-upon social values and/or rules that can be readily applied in judging whether the effects of electronic communication are beneficial, acceptable, or harmful." Schwartz summarizes his argument by concluding that

> truth is a print ethic, not a standard for ethical behavior in electronic communication. In addition, the influence of electronic media on print advertising (particularly the substitution of photographic techniques for copy to achieve an effect) raises the question of whether truth is any longer an issue in magazine or newspaper ads.[18]

Ethics for Nonverbal Communication

Nonverbal factors play an important role in the persuasion process. In a magazine advertisement, for example, the use of certain colors, pictures, layout patterns, and typefaces all influence how the words in the advertisement are received. In *The Importance of Lying*, Arnold Ludwig underscores the ethical implications of some dimensions of nonverbal communication:

> Lies are not only found in verbal statements. When a person nods affirmatively in response to something he does not believe or when he feigns attention

15. See, for example, Lawrence W. Rosenfield, Laurie Schultz Hayes, and Thomas S. Frentz, *The Communicative Experience* (Boston: Allyn and Bacon, 1976), pp. 310–312, 324.

16. Rosenfield et al., pp. 254–283.

17. Tony Schwartz, *The Responsive Chord* (Garden City, N.Y.: Anchor Books, 1974), pp. 1–18, 23–25, 92–97. See also Rosenfield et al., pp. 313–323.

18. Schwartz, pp. 18–22.

to a conversation he finds boring, he is equally guilty of lying. . . . A false shrug of the shoulders, the seductive batting of eyelashes, an eyewink, or a smile may all be employed as nonverbal forms of deception.[19]

Silence, too, may carry ethical implications. If to be responsible in fulfillment of our role or position demands that we speak out on a subject, to remain silent may be judged unethical. On the other hand, if the only way that we successfully can persuade others on a subject is to employ unethical communication techniques or appeals, the ethical decision probably would be to remain silent.

Spiro T. Agnew, when Vice-President of the United States, catalogued numerous nonverbal elements of television news broadcasts that he felt carried ethical implications: facial expressions, sarcastic tone of voice, raised eyebrow, and vocal inflection.[20] In the context of contemporary American political campaigns, Dan Nimmo questions the ethicality of electronically induced voice compression in radio or television advertisements for candidates. "A slow talking, drawling Southerner can be made to speak at the rate of a clipped-worded New Englander. A hesitant, shy-sounding speaker becomes decisive and assured."[21]

In *Harper's* magazine, Earl Shorris condemns as unethical the nonverbal tactics of the *New York Times* in opposing Mrs. Bella Abzug as a candidate for the mayor of New York City.[22]

> The *Times*, having announced its preference for almost anyone but Mrs. Abzug in the mayoral election, published a vicious photograph of her taken the night of her winning the endorsement of the New Democratic Coalition. In the photograph, printed on page 1, Mrs. Abzug sits alone on a stage under the New Democratic Coalition banner. There are three empty chairs to her right and five empty chairs to her left. In this forlorn scene the camera literally looks up Mrs. Abzug's dress to show the heavy calves and thighs of an overweight woman in her middle years.
>
> While the editorial judgment may be right, in that Bella Abzug is probably not the best choice or even a good choice for mayor of New York, the photograph is an example of journalism at its lowest. . . .

Do the ethical standards commonly applied to verbal persuasion apply equally as appropriately to nonverbal elements in persuasion? Should there be a special ethic for nonverbal persuasion in place of, or in addition to, the ethical criteria for assessing human use of language to persuade? For instance, what ethical standards should govern eye contact, facial expression, tone of voice, or gestures? How should the ethics of silence be judged? In television news coverage or political

19. Arnold M. Ludwig, *The Importance of Lying* (Springfield, Illinois: Charles C Thomas, 1965), p. 5.

20. Spiro T. Agnew, "Television News Coverage," *Vital Speeches of the Day*, December 1, 1969, pp. 98–101.

21. Dan Nimmo, "Ethical Issues in Political Campaign Communication," *Communication*, Vol. 6, No. 2 (1981), pp. 187–206.

22. Earl Shorris, "The Fourth Estate," *Harper's*, October 1977, p. 106.

advertisements, what ethical standards should govern editing out of material, camera angles, or lighting of a person's face as they stimulate accurate or inaccurate meanings and impressions in the viewer?

As elements in the human communication process, many nonverbal signals seem unintentional or semiconscious. To the extent that a nonverbal element reflects lack of conscious choice or intent, to that degree should we consider that element as outside the realm of ethical scrutiny? On the other hand, because some nonverbal cues often are less consciously controlled by the communicator than words and because they usually are assumed by receivers to be more believable than words as keys to real sender intent and meaning, should we view nonverbal elements as *better* indexes than words of the ethical level of communication?

Ethical Responsibilities of Receivers

What are your ethical responsibilities as a receiver or respondent in persuasion? An answer to this question may stem in part from the image we hold of the persuasion process. Receivers would seem to bear little if any responsibility if audience members are viewed as inert, passive, defenseless receptacles, as mindless blotters uncritically accepting ideas and arguments. In contrast, persuasion can be viewed as a transaction where both persuaders and persuadees bear mutual responsibility to participate actively in the process. This image of persuadees as active participants may suggest several responsibilities, perhaps captured by two phrases: **reasoned skepticism** and **appropriate feedback.**

Reasoned skepticism includes a number of elements. It represents a balanced position between the undesirable extremes of being too open-minded, too gullible, on the one hand and being too closed-minded, too dogmatic, on the other. You are not simply an unthinking blotter "soaking up" ideas and arguments. Rather you exercise your capacities actively to search for meaning, to analyze and synthesize, and to judge soundness and worth. You do something to and with the information you receive; you process, interpret, and evaluate it. Also, you inform yourself about issues being discussed and you tolerate, even seek out, divergent and controversial viewpoints, the better to assess what is being presented.

As receivers of persuasion, we must realize that accurate understanding of a persuader's message may be hindered by our attempt to impose our own ethical standards on him or her. Our immediate "gut-level" ethical judgments may cause us to distort the intended meaning. Only after reaching an accurate understanding of the persuader's ideas can we reasonably evaluate the ethics of his or her persuasive strategies or purposes.

In this era of public distrust of truthfulness of public communication, reasoned skepticism also requires that we combat the automatic assumption that most public communication always is untrustworthy. Just because a communication is of a certain type or comes from a certain source (government, candidate, news media, advertiser), it must not automatically, without evaluation, be rejected as tainted or untruthful. Clearly, we must always exercise caution in acceptance and care in evaluation, as emphasized throughout this book. Using the best evidence available to us, we may arrive at our best judgment. However, to condemn a message as untruthful or unethical solely because it stems from a suspect source and before directly assessing it is to exhibit decision-making behavior detrimental to our political, social, and economic system. Rejection of the message, if such be the judgment, must come after, not before, our evaluation of it. As with a defendant in the courtroom, public communication must be presumed ethically innocent until we, or experts we acknowledge, have proved it guilty. However, when techniques of persuasion do weaken or undermine the confidence and trust necessary for intelligent public decision making, they can be condemned as unethical.

As an active participant in the persuasion process, the feedback you provide to persuaders needs to be appropriate in a number of senses. Your response, in most situations, should be an honest and accurate reflection of your true comprehension, belief, feeling, or judgment. Otherwise persuaders are denied the relevant and accurate information they need to make decisions. Your response might be verbal or nonverbal, oral or written, immediate or delayed. A response of understanding, puzzlement, agreement, or disagreement could be reflected through your facial expression, gestures, posture, inquiries, statements during a question-and-answer period, and letters to editors or advertisers. In some cases, because of your special expertise on a subject, you even may have the obligation to respond, to provide feedback, while other receivers remain silent. You need to decide whether the degree and type of your feedback is appropriate for the subject, audience, and occasion of the persuasion. For instance, to interrupt with questions, or even to heckle, might be appropriate in a few situations but irresponsible for many others.

A Review and Conclusion

The process of persuasion demands that you make choices about the methods and content you will use in influencing receivers to accept the alternative you advocate. These choices involve issues of desirability and of personal and societal good. What ethical standards are you to use in making or judging these choices among techniques, contents, and purposes? What should be the ethical responsibility of a persuader in contemporary American society?

Obviously, answers to these questions have not been clearly or universally established. However, the questions are ones we must face squarely. In this chapter, we have explored some perspectives, issues, and examples useful in evaluating the ethics of persuasion. Our interest in the nature and effectiveness of persuasive techniques must not overshadow our concern for the ethical use of such techniques. We must examine not only *how* to, but also *whether* to, use persuasive techniques. The issue of "whether to" is both one of audience adaptation and one of ethics. We should formulate meaningful ethical guidelines, not inflexible rules, for our own persuasive behavior and for use in evaluating the persuasion to which we are exposed. It is hoped that we will share the sincere concern for ethical communication expressed by the late Secretary General of the United Nations, Dag Hammarskjöld, in his book *Markings:*

Respect for the Word—to employ it with scrupulous care and an incorruptible heartfelt love of truth—is essential if there is to be any growth in a society or in the human race.

To misuse the word is to show contempt for man. It undermines the bridges and poisons the wells. It causes Man to regress down the long path of his evolution.[23]

Questions for Further Thought

1. Why are potential ethical issues inherent in every persuasive situation?

2. Can you briefly and clearly explain the nature of the six perspectives suggested for possible application in judging the ethics of persuasion?

3. Should criteria for assessing ethics of persuasion be absolute or relative?

4. To what degree can a worthy end justify use of unethical persuasive techniques?

5. When might intentional use of ambiguity be ethically justified?

6. In what ways may some of the traditional propaganda devices not be inherently unethical?

7. To what degree are all emotional appeals unethical?

8. To what degree does sincerity of intent free a persuader from ethical responsibilities toward receivers?

9. What standards do *you* believe are most appropriate for judging the ethics of political-governmental persuasion?

10. What ethical criteria do *you* feel should be used to evaluate commercial advertising?

11. To what degree is use of racist/sexist language unethical?

12. What standards should be used to assess the ethicality of nonverbal elements of persuasion?

13. What are some ethical responsibilities of persuadees? Of receivers of persuasion?

Experiences in Persuasion

1. Read a chapter in *The Duping of the American Voter*, by Robert Spero,[24] and explain points at which you agree or disagree with Spero's judgment of the

---

23. Dag Hammarskjöld, *Markings* (New York: Alfred A. Knopf, 1964), p. 112.

24. Robert Spero, *The Duping of the American Voter: Dishonesty and Deception in Presidential Television Advertising* (New York: Lippincott and Crowell, 1980).

ethicality of specific Presidential television advertisements. As an alternative, read Chapter 10 and determine how sound and appropriate you personally feel is the new code of political campaign ethics he proposes.

2. With the most recent national presidential campaign as your focus, hold a small-group discussion with four to six people in which you assess the persuasive ethics of the major candidates. Be sure to clearly identify the ethical standards and perspectives you employ.

3. In Saul Alinsky's *Rules for Radicals*,[25] read pages 24 to 47 and then present your assessment of the soundness of his suggested ethical guidelines. As an alternative, read pages 125 to 164 and present your evaluation of the ethics of the tactics he discusses.

4. Read *one* of the chapters on use of racist-sexist language in Haig Bosmajian, *The Language of Oppression*, Chapters 2, 3, 4, or 5.[26] For the chapter you select, develop your own judgment, including appropriate standards, as to why the examples of language usage described should be considered ethical or unethical.

5. Select a chapter on a twentieth-century politician in Reinhard Luthin's *American Demagogues*.[27] Based on your reading of that chapter, present your evaluation of the persuasive ethics of that politician.

6. Read Chapter 4 on propaganda devices in W. H. Werkmeister's *An Introduction to Critical Thinking* (rev. ed., 1957).[28] Select three propaganda devices and describe how they might be unethical *or ethical* in two different situations or from two different ethical perspectives.

7. Read one of the following journal articles and determine how adequately the author (a) specifies precisely what ethical standards or perspectives are being applied, (b) justifies the reasonableness and relevance of those standards, and (c) clearly indicates in what respects the persuasion being evaluated fails to measure up to those standards. Dan Hahn, "Corrupt Rhetoric: President Ford and the Mayaguez Affair," *Communication Quarterly*, 28 (Spring 1980), 38–43; Karen Rasmussen, "Nixon and the Strategy of Avoidance," *Central States Speech Journal*, 24 (Fall 1973), 193–202; Wayne Flynt, "The Ethics of Democratic Persuasion and the Birmingham Crisis," *Southern Speech Journal*, 35 (Fall 1969), 40–53; Patricia Lynn Freeman, "An Ethical Evaluation of the Persuasive Strategies of Glenn W. Turner of Turner Enterprises," *Southern Speech Communication Journal*, 38 (Summer 1973), 347–361.

---

25. Saul Alinsky, *Rules for Radicals* (New York: Random House, 1971).

26. Haig Bosmajian, *The Language of Oppression* (Washington: Public Affairs Press, 1974).

27. Reinhard Luthin, *American Demagogues* (Boston: Beacon Press, 1954; reprinted Russell and Russell, 1968).

28. W. H. Werkmeister, *An Introduction to Critical Thinking*, rev. ed. (Lincoln, Nebraska: Johnson, 1957).

Epilogue

$\mathbf{I}$n his best-selling book *The Third Wave*, Alvin Toffler observes that the future we face is likely to be one of immense change. As he says:

> A powerful tide is surging across much of the world today, creating a new, often bizarre, environment in which to work, play, marry, raise children, or retire. In this bewildering context, businessmen swim against highly erratic economic currents; politicians see their ratings bob wildly up and down; universities, hospitals, and other institutions battle desperately against inflation. Value systems splinter and crash, while the lifeboats of family, church, and state are hurled madly about.... Many of today's changes are not independent of one another. Nor are they random.... They are, in fact, parts of a much larger phenomenon: the death of industrialism and the rise of a new civilization.[1]

This new civilization is, according to Toffler, filled with promise as well as peril. It is a civilization in which technology will be the dominant feature of human life. The old industrial world grew out of the invention of factories and machines that could do the work of many and could thus make items that had once been luxuries available to the masses. It was based on a certain kind of lifestyle and on certain kinds of values. For example, workers needed to be able to bear the monotony of doing the same thing over and over all day long without complaining. They needed to return to their homes and families to recharge for another day's work on the morrow. They were supposed to be stable, family-oriented, churchgoing, hardworking, for those were the virtues that the industrial age needed to prosper and advance. But, says Toffler, the new age of technology—the third wave of innovation—presents us with entirely different options. Whereas the machine freed human muscles so that more work could be produced more quickly and more cheaply, electronic technology will free our *minds* to do more

---

1. Alvin Toffler, *The Third Wave* (New York: William Morrow, 1980), pp. 17 and 18.

thinking, more cheaply and efficiently. Think what the computer has done to your and my lifestyle. We are billed by it, we vote through it, our weather is predicted using it, we are educated with it, and we are governed by it in many ways. And that is just one kind of electronic technology. Think about the ways in which television, videotape, and videodiscs shape our lives. Or try to imagine what our world would be like if there were no telephones. In short, we are potentially on the leading edge of a new Renaissance. While it is comforting to imagine that things in the next twenty years will be the same as they have been for the last twenty years, realistically, we know that they will not.

In the world of *The Third Wave*, with the many new technologies dominating our lives and with new values emerging while old ones fade, persuasion will be central to our existence. Between now and the year 2000, the new technology, the growing average age of our population, the problems likely to be faced by countries of the Third World, the world's economic future, and many other factors will combine to face us as persuadees with more options than ever before. Questions we are just beginning to face will become more and more urgent. Should we have mandatory retirement? Is it ethical to lie to the computer when it is investigating our backgrounds? How far should advertisers be allowed to go in order to appeal to the subconscious mind? Should governments "give in" to the demands of terrorists? How much further can we afford to go with "image politics"? Are we really getting the full story of our government's foreign policy through the press? Should you "cheat" on your income tax? Other questions arising from new situations are certain to emerge.

Persuaders will be vying for our support and belief for all of the sides of every issue, and we will have to sift out and choose from among them. Perhaps some of the work you have done for this course and some of the material you have discovered in this text can be of aid to you as consumers of persuasion. As has been reiterated a number of times throughout the text, the worst thing we, as persuadees, can do is blindly to follow the advice of the many persuaders around us. Recent trends are discouraging in this regard. For example, a survey by *Psychology Today* indicates that in a number of areas, Americans are becoming less and less optimistic about the world around them.[2] Fewer than in any previous survey expected that the lives of their children would be as good as or better than their own. Less than 5 percent of respondents expressed concern over religious and ethical issues—down from nearly 20 percent in 1974. This suggests a perilous aspect of the Third Wave future. Toffler speaks to its promise:

> . . . machine synchronization shackled the human to the machine's capabilities and imprisoned all of social life in a common frame. It did so in capitalist and socialist societies alike. Now, as machine synchronization grows more precise, humans, instead of being imprisoned, are progressively freed.[3]

---

2. William Watts, "Americans' Hopes and Fears: The Future Can Fend for Itself," *Psychology Today,* Vol. 15, No. 9 (September 1981), pp. 36–48.

3. Toffler, p. 270.

But a responsibility is attached to this new freedom, and it is undeniably tied to critical consumers of persuasion. Toffler addresses the issue in the closing pages of *The Third Wave:*

> The responsibility for change, therefore, lies with us. We must begin with ourselves, teaching ourselves not to close our minds prematurely to the novel, the surprising, the seemingly radical. This means fighting off the idea assassins. . . . It means fighting for the freedom of expression—the right of people to voice their ideas even if heretical.
>
> Above all, it means starting the process of reconstruction now. . . . If we begin now, we and our children can take part in the exciting reconstruction not merely of our obsolete political structures but of civilization itself.
>
> Like the generation of the revolutionary dead, we have a destiny to create.[4]

That future depends on the responsible reception of persuasion—on the kind of critical consumer of persuasion that you have started to become.

---

4. Toffler, p. 459.

Index